Governance, Human Rights, and Political Transformation in Africa

Michael Addaney · Michael Gyan Nyarko ·
Elsabé Boshoff
Editors

Governance, Human Rights, and Political Transformation in Africa

palgrave
macmillan

Editors
Michael Addaney
Research Institute of
Environmental Law
Wuhan University
Wuhan, China

Michael Gyan Nyarko
Centre for Human Rights
University of Pretoria
Pretoria, South Africa

Elsabé Boshoff
African Commission on Human
and Peoples' Rights
Banjul, The Gambia

ISBN 978-3-030-27051-3   ISBN 978-3-030-27049-0   (eBook)
https://doi.org/10.1007/978-3-030-27049-0

This Palgrave Macmillan imprint is published by the registered company Springer Nature
Switzerland AG
The registered company address is: Gewerbestrasse 11, 6330 Cham, Switzerland

FOREWORD

Good governance underpinned by the rule of law and respect for human rights is one of the imperatives for building sustainable societies. Good governance manifesting itself through participatory democracy and respect for fundamental rights is a central mechanism for sustainable human development in Africa. It creates an environment conducive for a multiparty democracy where everyone freely participates in the political, social and economic affairs of their country, and thereby contributes to building inclusive societies.

While governance is getting better in Africa, key challenges remain. Most of the authors in this book appear to agree with this assertion. The general observation is that, although there are improvements in governance and human rights protection across the continent, progress remains fragile. In many African countries, law enforcement and other security agencies violate the rights of people with impunity. This volume of essays chronicles the current developments in governance, human rights protection and democratisation processes in Africa. It underscores the significance of good governance and the respect for fundamental rights in building a more inclusive and sustainable Africa.

In unpacking challenges to the continent's democratisation efforts, the authors provide theoretical and practical insights based on country studies and from comparative analysis across African states. The authors examine developments in the regulatory framework governing the democratisation efforts of selected countries. This is preceded by insights on how the African human rights system responds to the challenges confronting human rights and democratisation in Africa and how regional institutions can turn values and rights into reality. This volume offers a thorough examination of contemporary developments in Africa in the spheres of governance, rule of law, human rights and the environment. The 15 chapters of this book interrogate the history, strengths, weaknesses and prospects of good governance and human rights as instruments of social transformation and question whether or not the governance aspirations and practices of the African Union and its member states enables the sustenance of a democratic culture and respect for human rights.

The contributing authors have drawn from their research experiences across the fields of governance, human rights, law and political science in Africa and beyond. In an era where multiparty democracy and constitutionalism are in crisis across the world, including in Africa, and calls for good governance and democracy, based on strong democratic institutions, rule of law and respect for human rights are rife, this books gives scholarly and practical insights into the history, economic and political conditions that gave rise to some of our current predicament, and offers possible solutions.

It is not only a book *on* Africa, but also one *by* Africans. The editors and contributors are all emerging African scholars. Many of them have studied human rights and democratisation at the Centre for Human Rights, University of Pretoria. Both the focus of the book and the voices emerging from the various essays make this a very timely publication.

Frans Viljoen
Professor of International Human
Rights Law and Director
Centre for Human Rights
University of Pretoria
Pretoria, South Africa

PREFACE

Governance, Human Rights, and Political Transformation in Africa provides a wide-ranging assessment of the effectiveness, breakthroughs and challenges in the protection of human rights and advancement of good governance at the regional and national level in Africa. The chapters are written by emerging African and internationally recognised scholars, and provide a contemporary overview of a wide variety of topics, ranging from criminal law reform, to the right to peaceful assembly and the impacts of climate change on the enjoyment of human rights in Africa. The book can either be read as a whole in order to gain an overview of some of the most pertinent legal and political questions on the continent today, or the chapters can be read as stand-alone theses addressing questions related to country- or theme-specific challenges. However, even the chapters dealing with issues in specific African States also carry lessons and recommendations with application to the rest of the continent and beyond. The chapters in the book have undergone rigorous peer review process, and can thus be consulted with confidence by scholars, students, activists and practitioners of national law, international law, human rights, political science, social sciences and diplomacy in Africa. The editors of this book hope that this project will inspire other thinkers to engage with the challenges facing our continent and address them head-on. We would also to acknowledge the hard work and dedication of the authors, peer reviewers and others who have contributed to making this book a success.

Wuhan, China   Michael Addaney
Banjul, The Gambia   Elsabé Boshoff
Pretoria, South Africa   Michael Gyan Nyarko

Acknowledgements

The editors would like to thank the contributing authors for their time, knowledge and resources towards completing this book project. The success of this book is attributable to their strong contributions and commitment. The editorial team at Palgrave Macmillan, Alina Yurova (editor) and Mary Fata (editorial assistant) of Regional Politics and Development Studies were very supportive along the way, as were the copyeditors and the anonymous reviewers. They assisted in shaping the concept of the book and refined the final output to ensure that the publication was on schedule. Our sincere appreciation goes to all who assisted and supported this vision to completion, especially to our colleagues who assisted in reviewing some of the chapters. We are grateful for the time you committed to support this project.

Contents

Notes on Contributors

Michael Addaney is a Scholar at the Research Institute of Environmental Law, School of Law, Wuhan University, Wuhan, China; and senior research assistant at the University of Energy and Natural Resources, Sunyani, Ghana. He is also a member of the PhD Academy of the Cross-Cultural Human Rights Centre at the Vrije University in Amsterdam, The Netherlands. The Centre operates as a think tank, which draws the attention, mainly of Northern audiences, to Southern ideas, concepts and accomplishments in the area of human rights. Michael's research interests broadly focus on the role of international human rights law in framing and implementing responses to sustainability challenges in sub-Saharan Africa.

Elsabé Boshoff is a technical assistant at the African Commission on Human and Peoples' Rights Secretariat in Banjul, The Gambia. She supports the Working Group on Extractive Industries, Environment and Human Rights, as well as the focal point for the Studies on Human Rights and Conflict in Africa and Transitional Justice in Africa, respectively, together with the responsible legal officer. Elsabé's research interests include international human rights law, environmental and climate change law, and business and human rights.

Ashwanee Budoo (Ph.D.) is the project manager for the Master's programme in Human Rights and Democratisation in Africa offered by the Centre for Human Rights, University of Pretoria (South Africa), in partnership with 13 other universities across Africa. She holds an LL.B. from the University of Mauritius and the degrees LL.M. (Human Rights and

Democratisation in Africa) and LL.D. from the University of Pretoria, Pretoria, South Africa. Her research area is the African human rights system, with particular focus on the rights of women in Africa, state reporting, budgeting for human rights, and gender budgeting.

Godwin E. K. Dzah is a doctoral candidate at the Allard School of Law, University of British Columbia (UBC). He holds a Bachelor of Arts degree and a Bachelor of Laws degree from the University of Ghana, and a Master of Laws degree from Harvard Law School. He holds a Qualifying Certificate in Law from the Ghana School of Law, and is admitted to law practice in Ghana. He was a United Nations Visiting Research Scholar at the Schulich School of Law, Dalhousie University, and a Visiting Fellow at the Division of Ocean Affairs and Law of the Sea, Office of Legal Affairs at the United Nations Secretariat in New York. Godwin's principal research interests are third world approaches to the interface between national legal regimes and international obligations, constitutional law, environmental law and policy, and natural resource governance.

Ademola Oluborode Jegede (Ph.D.) is a Professor in the Department of Public Law, University of Venda, Thohoyandou, South Africa. He holds degrees from Obafemi Awolowo University Ile-Ife, University of Ibadan and the Centre for Human Rights, Faculty of Law, University of Pretoria. He has been a research visitor to the Centre for International Environmental Law, USA, Human Rights Institute at Abo Akademi, Finland, and a fellow of Salzburg Global Seminar, Austria. His research focuses on the interface of climate change with human rights of vulnerable groups and general international human rights law.

Charlotte Kabaseke obtained an LL.B. from Uganda Christian University and Postgraduate Diploma in Legal Practice from the Law Development Centre, Kampala, following which she obtained a LL.M. from Makerere University, Kampala, Uganda. Charlotte worked as a Legal Assistant at the Justice Centres Uganda, a legal aid service provider. She was appointed Lecturer of Laws at Bishop Stuart University and later became an acting Dean of the Faculty of Law in the same institution. Charlotte is currently a Ph.D. candidate at the Research Institute of Environmental Law at the School of Law, Wuhan University, Wuhan, China. Charlotte's research is focused on the intersectionality between gender and climate change adaptation in East Africa.

Mariam Kamunyu (Ph.D.) is an advocate of the High Court of Kenya, a human rights practitioner and an academic in Kenya and South Africa. She obtained her LL.D. and LL.M. in Human Rights and Democratisation from the Centre for Human Rights, University of Pretoria.

Kennedy Kariseb is currently a doctoral candidate at the Centre for Human Rights, University of Pretoria, where he is also an academic associate and tutor. He holds a LL.M. in Human Rights and Democratisation (with distinction) from the same institution. His areas of research are broadly blended between (international) human rights law, gender law and family law.

Emma Charlene Lubaale (Ph.D.) is a senior lecturer in the Department of Jurisprudence at the School of Law of the University of Venda, Thohoyandou, South Africa. Prior to teaching at the University of Venda, she taught and researched law in the capacity of a post-doctoral research fellow at the Institute of International and Comparative Law in Africa, University of Pretoria, South Africa. She holds an LL.M. and doctorate in law from the University of Pretoria and an LL.B. from Makerere University, Uganda and a postgraduate diploma in legal practice from the Law Development Center, Kampala, Uganda. Emma's current areas of research interest are international human rights law, international criminal law, constitutional law and criminal law in the domestic perspective. She is widely published in these fields.

Roopanand Amar Mahadew is a senior lecturer and heads the Department of Law, University of Mauritius, Moka, Mauritius. His research areas are human rights law, public international law and environmental law. He holds an LL.B. (Hons) degree from the University of Mauritius and an LL.M. in Human Rights and Democratisation in Africa from the Centre for Human Rights (Class 2011) University of Pretoria. He is in the final year of his doctoral studies at the University of Western Cape, South Africa investigating the human rights impact of large-scale land investments amounting to land grabbing.

Edward Kahuthia Murimi is an Advocate of the High Court of Kenya and is currently a Technical Advisor in the Good Governance Programme at GIZ-Kenya. He holds an LL.B. from the University of Nairobi, Diploma in Human Rights and Gender Equality from Uppsala University and LL.M. (Cum Laude) from the University of Pretoria.

Michael Gyan Nyarko is a doctoral candidate at the Centre for Human Rights, University of Pretoria, where he is also the editor of the Centre's blog, AfricLaw and Coordinator of the Litigation and Implementation Unit. He holds an LL.M. in Human Rights and Democratisation in African (with distinction) from the University of Pretoria and Bachelor of Laws degree from the Kwame Nkrumah University of Science and Technology, Kumasi—Ghana. Michael was called to the Ghana bar in 2011 and was part of a flourishing pan-African commercial law practice headquartered in Accra, Ghana before joining the Centre for Human Rights as a master's student in 2014. His research interests include law of international organisations, international human rights law, African human rights system, socio-economic rights, business and human rights, women's rights, children's rights, implementation of international human rights law in national systems, and democratic governance.

Chairman Okoloise is a Doctor of Laws (LL.D.) candidate and academic tutor at the Centre for Human Rights, University of Pretoria, South Africa. He obtained a Master of Laws (LL.M.) degree in Human Rights and Democratisation in Africa *cum laude* at the University of Pretoria in 2015. He is also an alumnus the Global Campus Alumni based at the European Inter-University Centre for Human Rights and Democratisation (EIUC), Lido-Venice, Italy. Before his postgraduate studies, he obtained his Bachelor of Laws (LL.B.) degree in 2010 at the Ambrose Alli University in Nigeria and attended the Nigerian Law School in Lagos before his admission to the Nigerian Bar in 2012. Chairman is a two-time DAAD Scholar—an award he currently holds and a former postgraduate intern at the Department of Political Affairs of the African Union Commission Headquarters in Addis Ababa, Ethiopia. His specialties are human rights and democratic governance in Africa. He is currently working on the role of regional organizations in the regulation of abusive corporate businesses in Africa.

Bamisaye Olutola is an LL.D. Candidate at the Centre for human rights, University of Pretoria, South Africa and a Lecturer at the Faculty of Law, University of Lagos, Nigeria. His writings cover International human rights law, with particular preference for Youth, Women, Children and Socio-economic rights; Environmental Law, Comparative Constitutional Law, Good Governance and Democratization. He is a graduate of the University of Lagos (LL.B.), subsequently called to the Nigerian Bar, and also had his LL.M. (Human Rights and

Democratization in Africa) from the Centre for human rights, University of Pretoria. He has several published and unpublished works to his credits.

Bright Sefah is a political officer at the African Union Commission (AUC) in Addis Ababa, Ethiopia. He works with the Governance Cluster within the African Governance Architecture (AGA) Platform of the Department of Political Affairs (DPA), African Union Commission. Bright holds an M.Phil. in Human Rights and Democratisation in Africa from the Centre for Human Rights, University of Pretoria, Pretoria, South Africa and a B.A. in Sociology and Social Work from the Kwame Nkrumah University of Science and Technology, Kumasi, Ghana. Bright has a vested interest of research in areas such as international human rights law, rights of prisoners, peace and security in Africa, elections and governance. Bright has in the past researched on the above interests.

Sidogi Tendani holds an LL.B. from the University of Venda, South Africa. He is presently serving his article of clerkship. Sidogi researches on governance and human rights in South Africa and Africa.

Tilahun Adamu Zewudie holds LL.M. from the University of Pretoria, South Africa; LL.B. from Debre Markos University and PDip in Diplomacy and International Relations from Civil Service University, Ethiopia. He has served in different diplomatic functions at the Ministry of Foreign Affairs, Permanent Mission of Ethiopia to the African Union as well as the Embassy of Ethiopia in Mogadishu (Somalia). Currently he is a political officer at the Embassy of Ethiopia in Washington DC.

Abbreviations and Acronyms

ACHPR	African Commission on Human and Peoples' Rights
ACRWC	African Charter on the Rights and Welfare of the Child
AHRLR	African Human Rights Law Report
ANC	African National Congress
ANPP	All Nigerian Peoples' Party
AU	African Union
AUC	African Union Commission
AUEOM	African Union Election Observation Mission
BPfA	Beijing Platform for Action
BVR	Biometric Verification Register
CBO	Community-Based Organisations
CCCC	Children in a Changing Climate Coalition
CEDAW	Convention on the Elimination of all forms of Discrimination Against Women
CESCR	International Covenant on Economic, and Social Cultural Rights
CFRN	Constitution of the Federal Republic of Nigeria
CI	Constitutional Instruments
CODEO	Coalition of Domestic Election Observers
CODESA	Convention for a Democratic South Africa
COFEK	Consumer Federation of Kenya
CRC	Convention on the Rights of the Child
CRPWD	Committee on the Rights of Persons with Disabilities
CSO	Civil Society Organisations
DEAU	Democracy and Electoral Assistance Unit
DPSPs	Directive Principles of State Policy
EC	Electoral Commission (of Ghana)

ECOSOCC   Economic, Social and Cultural Council of the African Union
ECOWAS   Economic Community of West African States
EMBs   Electoral Management Bodies
EOMs   Election Observation Missions
FAWU   Food and Allied Workers Union
FBO   Faith Based Organisations
GaP   Governance and Peace Polls
GC14   General Comment 14 on the right of the child to have his or her
           best interests taken as a primary consideration
GHG   Greenhouse Gas
HRC   Human Rights Committee
ICC   International Criminal Court
ICCPR   International Covenant on Civil and Political Rights
ICESCR   International Covenant on Economic, Social and Cultural Rights
ICJ   International Court of Justice
ID   Independent Democrats
IG   Inspector General
IHRDA   Institute for Human Rights and Development in Africa
ILM   International Legal Materials
INEC   Interim National Electoral Commission
IPAC   Inter-Party Advisory Committee
LGBTI   Lesbian, Gay, Bisexual, Transgender and Intersex
NCC   Nigerian Criminal Code
NCCE   National Commission for Civil Education
NCCRP   National Climate Change Response Policy White Paper
NGOs   Non-Governmental Organisations
NPA   Nigerian Police Act
NPF   Nigerian Police Force
NPP   New Patriotic Party
OAU   Organisation of African Unity
ODIHR   Office for Democratic Institutions and Human Rights
OSCE   Organization for Security and Co-operation in Europe
PAP   Pan African Parliament
PCC   Police Code of Conduct
PDS   Public Distribution System
POA   Public Order Act
PRC   Permanent Representatives Committee of the African Union
RTC   Right to Food Campaign
SAFRU   South African Rugby Federation Union
SAPS   South African Police Services
SCA   Supreme Court of Appeal
TAC   Treatment Action Campaign

TUT	Tshwane University of Technology
TWAIL	Third World Approaches to International Law
UK	United Kingdom
UN	United Nations
UNDP	United Nations Development Programme
UNHCR	United Nations High Commissioner for Refugees
UNICEF	United Nations International Children's Emergency Fund
UNTS	United Nations Treaty Series
US	United States
VCLT	Vienna Convention on the Law of Treaties
WHO	World Health Organisation

LIST OF FIGURES

Chapter 3

CHAPTER 1

Historical Context of Governance and Human Rights in Africa

Michael Gyan Nyarko, Michael Addaney and Elsabé Boshoff

1   INTRODUCTION

Discussions on the struggle for democratic governance and human rights in Africa are like the proverbial old wine in new bottle. Indeed the post-World War II independence struggles in Africa were largely premised on a desire for self-governance (self-determination) and human rights. Particularly, the language of human rights provided "a powerful mobilizing rhetoric" for the anti-colonial movement.[1] The leaders of the

---

[1] Henry K. Prempeh, "Africa's 'Constitutional Revival': Fake Start or New Dawn?" *International Journal of Constitutional Law* 5, no. 3 (2007): 469–473; see, also, Michael Addaney and Michael G. Nyarko, "Governance and Human Rights in Twenty-First Century Africa: An Introductory Appraisal," in *Ghana @ 60: Governance and Human Rights in Twenty-First Century Africa*, ed. Michael Addaney and Michael G. Nyarko (Pretoria:

M. G. Nyarko (✉)
Centre for Human Rights, University of Pretoria, Pretoria, South Africa

M. Addaney
Research Institute of Environmental Law, Wuhan University, Wuhan, China

E. Boshoff
Technical Assistant, African Commission on Human and Peoples' Rights, Banjul, The Gambia

© The Author(s) 2020
M. Addaney et al. (eds.), *Governance, Human Rights, and Political Transformation in Africa,*
https://doi.org/10.1007/978-3-030-27049-0_1

1

independence movements "freely invoked affirmations of human rights in international as well as national thinking".[2] This was partly influenced by the adoption of the United Nations (UN) Charter in 1945, which contained provisions on the respect for human rights; the adoption of the Universal Declaration of Human Rights (UDHR) in 1948, which provided an elaborate yardstick for human rights and was "a powerful source of inspiration for the founding pattern of African nations"; and the adoption of the European Convention of Human Rights in 1950, which for the first time in the international system "translated human rights into precise [binding] legal rights".[3] These were further reinforced by the political and constitutional ideas of the colonial powers,[4] who in their bid to seek a "dignified retreat from the empire", ensured that the independence constitutions they negotiated with the nationalist movements made provision for the "protection [of] opposition parties, individual rights, independent courts and some measure regional or local autonomy".[5]

Additionally, indigenous African processes were not alien to the concept of human rights. Gluckman asserts that indigenous African systems had well-developed notions of natural justice and legality.[6] For instance, the concept of due process of law was well respected in indigenous African systems; arbitrary deprivation of liberty or property was treated cautiously; the security of person protected; and meticulous decision-making procedures were followed when the liberty of the individual

---

Pretoria University Law Press, 2017), 2; Lucian W. Pye, *Aspects of Political Development: An Analytical Study* (Boston, MA: Little, Brown and Company, 1966), 71; El-Obaid A. El-Obaid and Kwadwo Appiagyei-Attua, "Human Rights in Africa: A New Perspective on Linking the Past to the Present," *McGill Law Journal* 41 (1996): 819; and Walter Rodney, *How Europe Underdeveloped Africa* (Washington, DC: Howard University Press, 1974).

[2] S.K.B. Asante, "Nation Building and Human Rights in Emergent African Nations," *Cornell International Law Journal* 2, no. 1 (1969): 72.

[3] Ibid.

[4] Ibid.

[5] Prempeh, "Africa's Constitutional Revival," 469; see also Addaney and Nyarko, *Ghana @ 60.*

[6] See, generally, Max Gluckman, "Natural Justice in Africa," *Natural Law Forum* 81 (1964).

was at stake.[7] Asante notes further that the "African conception of human rights was an essential aspect of African humanism sustained by religious doctrine and the principle of accountability to the ancestral spirits".[8] Indigenous African governance usually revolved around the family or clan, which served as limitation on the sovereign power of the chief, who could be deposed for violating community norms, including human rights.[9]

These circumstances therefore, made it "virtually automatic" that the constitutions of the newly independent African nations would contain entrenched human rights. Human rights principles were thus, in varying degrees included in the constitutions of almost all the newly independent African states.[10] In most parts of Africa today, most people enjoy human rights and democratic freedoms more than ever before but these did not come as a natural progression of the governance and human rights ideals touted by anti-colonial struggle leaders just before independence. As history bears witness, most African states soon after independence abandoned the democracy and human rights ideals they espoused in opposition to colonialism in favor of one party autocratic systems that were abhorrent of political dissent and largely disapproving of human rights, deeming such institutions to be the antithesis to progress.[11]

It was around this time of increasing negation of the ideals of democracy and human rights by the postindependence African leaders that the Organisation of African Unity (OAU) was formed. It therefore came as no surprise that the Charter of the OAU did not pay much attention to the issue of human rights, save for brief references to the UDHR in the preamble and article 2(1)(e), which required member states to have "due

---

[7] Ibid.

[8] Asante, "Nation Building," 73.

[9] Ibid., 73–74.

[10] See, generally, Morris Kiwinda Mbondenyi, *International Human Rights and Their Enforcement in Africa* (Nairobi: LawAfrica Publishing, 2010), 89–90; Morris Kiwinda Mbondenyi and Tom Ojienda "Introduction to and Overview of Constitutionalism and Democratic Governance in Africa," in *Constitutionalism and Democratic Governance in Africa: Contemporary Perspectives from Sub-Saharan Africa*, ed. Morris Kiwinda Mbondenyi and Tom Ojienda (Pretoria: Pretoria University Law Press, 2013), 4.

[11] Prempeh, "Africa's Constitutional Revival," 469; Addaney and Nyarko, *Ghana @ 60*, 3.

regard" to the human rights provided in the UDHR.[12] The only human right that seemed important to the OAU was the right to self-determination, which was an important tool in its continued struggle against colonialism.[13] This fixation with the right to self-determination bolstered by its policy on "noninterference" (perhaps as a consequence of its opposition to the interference of the colonial powers), led the OAU to ignore allegations of human rights violations reported in its member states.[14] The only other human rights issue that the OAU appeared to be concerned about, mainly out of the necessity of the increasing number of refugees following the numerous conflicts that arose at the time, was the right of refugees, leading to the adoption of the OAU Convention Governing the Specific Aspects of Refugee Problems in Africa.[15]

This period of despotic one party regimes were associated with various rights violations which were not taken kindly by the citizens of most African states. In many states, this led to military takeovers, usually premised on the need to curb the abuses, but which themselves soon became very characteristic of the very abuses they claimed to want to stop and in many instances even worse.[16] In other instances, the closing political space occasioned by the despotic one party system and military dictatorships forced opposition elements to resort to violence and civil wars to seek a restoration of governance and human rights that would ensure the equal participation of everyone in the economic, social and political affairs of the state.[17]

---

[12] Frans Viljoen, *International Human Rights Law in Africa* (Oxford: Oxford University Press, 2012), 156; El-Obaid and Appiegyei-Attua, "Human Rights in Africa," 826–827; see, also, Keba M'Baye and B. Ndiaye, "The Organisation of African Unity," in *The International Dimensions of Human Rights*, ed. Karel Vasak (Westport, CT: Greenwood Press, 1982), 583.

[13] Viljoen, *Human Rights Law in Africa*, 157.

[14] Ibid., 156.

[15] Ibid., 158.

[16] Mbonyeni and Ojienda, "Constitutionalism and Democratic Governance in Africa," 4; see, also, Oji Umozurike, *The African Charter on Human and Peoples' Rights* (Zuidpoolsingel: Brill/Noijhoff, 1997), 23; Bahane T. Nyanduga, "Conference Paper: Perspectives on the African Commission on Human and Peoples' Rights on the Occasion of the 20th Anniversary of the Entry into Force of the African Charter on Human and Peoples' Rights," *African Human Rights Law Journal* 6, no. 2 (2006): 255.

[17] Makau Mutua, *Human Rights: A Political and Cultural Critique* (Philadelphia: University of Pennsylvania Press, 2002), 74–82.

In the midst of this political turmoil and gross human rights violations, the OAU had to review its policy of noninterference. Viljoen notes that most commentators ascribe the adoption of the African Charter on Human and Peoples' Rights (African Charter) in 1981 as the OAU's response to the human rights abuses that occurred in the period immediately preceding its adoption.[18] The drafting and adoption of the African Charter was by no means a swift process, as some states while not prepared to openly show their opposition to the African Charter, tried to silently stifle the process through nonparticipation in governmental expert meetings that were convened to draft the Charter.[19] The adoption of the African Charter did not only mark a first of its kind in Africa, but also the first time in international human rights law that a legally binding human rights treaty combined civil and political and economic, social and cultural rights, including the right to development, in the same document. The African Charter also established a supervisory body, the African Commission on Human and Peoples' Rights (African Commission), which was established in 1987, one year after the Charter came into force. However, the African Commission only became operation in 1989.[20] The Commission's mandate was to promote and protect human rights, including through the instrument of state reporting and receiving complaints from member states, individuals and nongovernmental organizations.

The establishment of the African Commission came at an opportune time—in the midst of the third wave of democratization that swept through Africa in the late 1980s and early 1990s.[21] This wave

[18] Gino Naldi, *The Organisation of African Unity: An Analysis of Its Role* (London: Mansell, 1989) 108–109; Uji Umozurike, *Five Years of the African Commission on Human and Peoples' Rights* (Ile-Ife: Obafemi Awolowo University, 1992). On the postcolonial history of Africa, see also, Martin Meredith, *The State of Africa: A History of the Continent Since Independence* (London: Jonathan Ball Publisher, 2005); Guy Arnold, *Africa: A Modern History* (London: Atlantic Books, 2005); and Richard J. Reid, *A History of Modern Africa: 1800 to the Present* (Oxford: Wiley, 2012).

[19] Viljoen, *Human Rights Law in Africa*, 160; see also Keba M'Baye, *Les droits de l'homme en Afrique* (Paris: Pedone, 1992), 153.

[20] Viljoen, *Human Rights Law in Africa*, 161.

[21] Samuel Huntington, *The Third Wave: Democratization in the Late Twentieth Century* (Norman: University of Oklahoma Press, 1991); Gabrielle Lynch and Gordon Crawford, "Democratization in Africa 1990–2010: An Assessment," *Democratization* 18, no. 2 (2011): 275.

of democratization was occasioned by increasing political pressure from within the African populace due to economic hardships coupled with the pressure from the Bretton Woods institutions, which coerced African governments to adopt "good governance" in exchange for financial assistance.[22] Within this period, multi-party elections were organized all over the continent including in South Africa, marking the end of apartheid.[23] This wave of democratization brought with it new constitutions that provided generous stipulations of mostly civil and political rights and some economic, social and cultural rights, with South Africa standing out as the only country that included a broad range of enforceable socioeconomic rights in its constitution at the time. Within this period of renewed interest in democratization and human rights "the OAU adopted two of its most progressive human rights instruments".[24] The first was African Charter on the Rights and Welfare of the Child (African Children's Charter) an instrument dedicated to the protection of children's rights issues that were peculiar to Africa and were thus not sufficiently covered by the United Nations Convention on the Rights of the Child.[25] The African Children's Charter was accompanied by a supervisory body, which was mandated to monitor state compliance through periodic state reports and individual complaints. The second instrument adopted in 1998 was the Protocol to the African Charter on the Establishment of the African Court on Human and Peoples' Rights, which established the African Court on Human and Peoples' Rights (African Court) mandated to provide binding judicial decisions on human rights violations.

The momentum flowing from this wave of democratization also brought about new governance dynamic within African states that provided an impetus for the rebirth of Africa's continental body, the OAU into a new organization, the African Union (AU). The Constitutive Act of the AU, which was adopted in 2000 and came into force in 2001, culminated in the official inauguration of the AU in 2002. The AU set

---

[22] Prempeh, "Africa's Constitutional Revival," 469.

[23] Viljoen, *Human Rights Law in Africa*, 161.

[24] Ibid., 162.

[25] Ibid., 392; Michael G. Nyarko and Henrietta M. Ekefre, "Recent Advances in Children's Rights in the African Human Rights System: A Review of the Decision of the African Committee of Experts on the Rights and Welfare of the Child in the Talibé's Case," *Law and Practice of International Courts and Tribunals* 15 (2016): 385.

out for itself new ideals more focused on good governance, human rights and the rule of law. The Constitutive Act of the AU explicitly indicates, as one of its objectives, the protection of human rights in accordance with the African Charter and other relevant instruments.[26] In addition to this, six out of the 16 guiding principles of the AU make either explicit or implicit reference to human rights.[27] Even more far-reaching is the power granted to the AU to intervene in member states in cases of war crimes, crimes against humanity and genocide.[28] The Constitutive Act also makes references to "gender equality, respect for democratic principles, human rights, the rule of law, and good governance; the promotion of social justice [...] and the rejection of unconstitutional changes of government".[29] While the AU Constitutive Act is far from perfect in terms of its commitment to democratic governance and human rights, it marks a great departure from the noninterventionist approach of the OAU, and places at its core the prosperity of the African peoples.

The last two decades of the AU has been characterized by a proliferation of normative standards as well as institutional arrangements on governance and human rights. Some of the notable normative standards that have been adopted under the AU include the Protocol on the Rights of Women in Africa (Maputo Protocol); African Union Convention for the Protection and Assistance of Internally Displaced Persons in Africa (Kampala Convention); African Charter on Democracy, Elections and Governance (ACDEG); African Charter on the Values and Principles of Decentralisation, Local Governance and Local Development; African Youth Charter; African Union Convention on Preventing and Combating Corruption; Protocol on the Rights of Older Persons; and the Protocol on Rights on the Rights of Persons with Disabilities in Africa. In order to strengthen governance on the continent, 2012 saw the entry into force of the ACDEG, with the aim to enhance rule of law, prohibit unconstitutional change of government, promote regular free and fair elections and a gender balance in governance, among other laudable aims. In terms of institutional arrangements, the African Court on Human and Peoples' Rights came into force and has been operational since 2006.

---

[26] Article 2(h); Viljoen, *Human Rights Law in Africa*, 165.

[27] Viljoen, *Human Rights Law in Africa*, 165.

[28] Article 4(h); Viljoen, *Human Rights Law in Africa*, 165.

[29] Viljoen, *Human Rights Law in Africa*, 165.

Other institutions which have mandates related to governance and human rights include the New Partnership for Africa's Development (NEPAD); African Peer Review Mechanism (APRM); African Governance Architecture; African Peace and Security Council (APSC); Pan African Parliament and the AU Advisory Board on Corruption (AU-ABC).

Beyond the AU, democracy and human rights have increasingly become important issues within the regional economic communities (RECs), which were initially established to champion economic integration. Notably, the Economic Community of West African States (ECOWAS) and the East African Community (EAC) have established the ECOWAS Community Court of Justice (ECCJ) and the East African Court of Justice (EACJ) respectively, with mandates to adjudicate on human rights issues. The now suspended human rights mandate of the Southern African Development Community (SADC) Tribunal was occasioned by strong human rights decisions given by the Tribunal against Zimbabwe. These institutions established within the RECs have thus become important avenues for the vindication of human rights, complementing the AU institutions.

Africa in the twenty-first century is what may be termed a "mixed bag". While the continent continues to face many challenges, including under development, lack of accountability and good governance, as well as access to basic amenities and security challenges, much progress has also been made in the last two decades which means that the continent is a very different place from what it was at the beginning of the century. In the last decade, the continent has seen the removal from power of Laurent Gbagbo of Cote d'Ivoire, Blaise Compoaré of Burkina Faso, Yahya Jammeh of The Gambia and Robert Mugabe of Zimbabwe, all presidents who had outstayed their welcome, either through hanging on to power for decades or refusing to accept defeat following elections. Others, like Mohamed Ghannouchi, who was Prime Minister of Tunisia from 1999 to 2011 and a long-standing figure in the government under President Zine El Abidine Ben Ali, Hosni Mubarak of Egypt and Muammar Gaddafi of Libya were removed through popular uprisings which became known as the Arab Spring. Economies, particularly, of Ghana, Ethiopia and Cote d'Ivoire have seen growth as high as 7 or 8% in recent years. In addition, South Sudan became independent in 2011, bringing the total number of African countries to 55, and Morocco rejoined the AU in 2017, despite its continued struggle with the Saharawi Arab Democratic Republic, a State recognized by the AU. March 2018 saw the historic signing of the African Continental Free Trade Area agreement by 44 African States. All African States on April 22, 2016 also became signatories to the Paris Agreement on Climate Change.

In 2013, after a comprehensive consultation with all relevant stakeholders including women and the youth, the AU heads of states and government devoted themselves to transform Africa's social, economic and political arena through a 50 year plan commonly referred to as "the Agenda 2063". Among others, the Agenda is underpinned by the AU's strategic vision of building "an integrated, prosperous and peaceful Africa, driven by its own citizens and representing a dynamic force in the international arena".[30] The agenda is structured around seven key aspirations. Aspiration one seeks to build a prosperous Africa based on inclusive growth and sustainable development.[31] Through this, the AU and its member states are determined to eradicate poverty in this generation and build shared prosperity through social and economic transformation of the continent. In aspiration three, the AU envisions an "Africa of good governance, democracy, and respect for human rights, justice and the rule of law".[32] It specifically provides that "Africa shall have a universal culture of good governance, democratic values, gender equality, and respect for human rights, justice and the rule of law".[33]

In aspiration six, the AU commits itself to building "an Africa, whose development is people-driven, relying on the potential of African people, especially its women and youth, and caring for children".[34] Furthermore, aspiration seven also focuses on building an Africa that is strong, united, resilient and influential global player and partner. It specifically indicates Africa shall be an inclusive continent where no child, woman or man will be left behind or excluded, on the basis of gender, political affiliation, religion, ethnic affiliation, locality or age.[35] Despite being touted

---

[30] The African Union Commission, "Agenda 2063: The Africa We Want, a Shared Strategic Framework for Inclusive Growth and Sustainable Development," in *First Ten-Year Implementation Plan 2014–2023* (2015a), 33.

[31] Ibid.

[32] Ibid.

[33] Ibid.

[34] Ibid., 12.

[35] Ibid.

as an ambitious and comprehensive blueprint for Africa,[36] the Agenda 2063 faces major challenges such as lack of resources for its effective and efficient execution as well as lack of commitment from African leaders and the AU itself.[37] The AU and African leaders are known for publicly agreeing on issues that they do not actually believe in or fully support and commit to. There are records of similarly failed continental agenda and blueprints that were adopted by the OAU (currently AU) thought to drive inclusive economic growth and sustainable development by advancing political, economic, social, and technological transformation similar to the new Agenda.[38]

While the progress made should be celebrated, it is also worthy to note that the twenty-first-century Africa has also been plagued by its own challenges, ranging from the rise in terrorism, including most prominently in the Sahel region, the Lake Chad region and Somalia, as well as political violence, which have led to an increase in the number of refugees and internally displaced persons across the continent. Other threats such as environmental degradation and climate change present challenges. Within the AU's institutional arrangements, recent attempts by the African Commission to protect the rights of lesbian, gay, bisexual, transgender and intersex (LGBTI) people by granting observer status to the Coalition of African Lesbians, was not treated kindly by the Executive Council, which requested the Commission to review its guidelines on granting observer status. This has raised issues among human rights activists and academics as to the institutional independence of the AU's human rights institutions vis-à-vis the political organs. These and the other issues discussed in this book highlight the need for a continuous assessment of the human rights and governance situation within the continent. Consequently, in this book, we seek to take stock of some of the progress that has been made, highlight some of the challenges

---

[36] African Union Commission, *Agenda 2063: The Critical Factors for Success* (Addis Ababa: African Union, 2015b), accessed August 26, 2018, http://agenda2063.au.int/en/sites/default/files/05%20Critical%20Factors%20For%20Success_pdf.

[37] Sahra El Fassi and Faten Aggad, *Implementing African Development Initiatives: Opportunities and Challenges to Securing Alternative Financing for the Agenda 2063* (Maastricht: European Centre for Development Policy Management, 2014), 8.

[38] Michael Addaney, "The African Union's Agenda 2063: Education and Its Realization," in *Education Law, Strategic Policy and Sustainable Development in Africa*, ed. Onuora-Oguno Azubike, Egbewole Wahab, and Thomas E. Kleven (Cham: Palgrave Macmillan, 2018), 182.

and suggest solutions to some of these pertinent issues confronting the realization of good governance, democratization and human rights both within the African Union and selected African states.

2 AFRICAN PERSPECTIVES ON GOOD GOVERNANCE, DEMOCRATIZATION AND HUMAN RIGHTS: OVERVIEW OF THE BOOK

Any attempt to cover the whole range of challenges and promises of contemporary Africa is ambitious to say the least, even if it narrowed to focus only on governance and human rights. Therefore, this book aims to provide a particular selection of issues which scholars from across Africa are grappling with as we approach the third decade of the twenty-first century. Contributions cover the continent as a whole, as well as perspectives from West, East and Southern Africa.

Part I focuses on the developments within the African Union (AU) such as the relationship between the AU policy organs and human rights bodies (discussed by Zewudie in Chapter 2) and the implications of the African Governance Architecture for continental governance and human rights (discussed by Kariseb and Okoloise in Chapter 3).

Contributions in Part II tackle selected issues on constitutional and judicial protection of human rights in various countries. In Chapter 4, Jegede and Tendai reflect on the interdependence between the three arms of government of South Africa and in particular, how the South African Constitutional Court serves as an important check on the powers of the executive and legislative arms of government, while Budoo and Mahadew articulate in Chapter 5, the need for constitutional review in Mauritius 50 years after its first and only post-independence constitution. Dzah addresses Ghana's dualist approach to treaty incorporation in Chapter 6, arguing that 60 years after independence Ghana needs to reevaluate its strict adherence to dualism with regard to all treaties. He advocates that "Ghana should consider distinguishing between indirect incorporation of human rights treaties on the basis of legitimate expectation and transjudicial communication, and other treaties requiring explicit legislative expression; thus, creating a self-executing and non-self-executing treaty categorisation as exists elsewhere". On her part, Lubaale in Chapter 7 analyzes the continued criminalization of certain offences inherited through colonial criminal codes, namely, the crime of attempted suicide and sodomy in many African countries despite the adoption of constitutions that contain various human rights provisions and ratifying several international and regional human rights treaties. She argues that African states need to hasten the pace of decriminalizing these offences which are remnants of colonization and not in conformity with their human rights obligations.

Part III turns to the consideration of civil engagement in governance and human rights. Kamunyu and Murimi make a case for the adoption of a "negotiated management" model as a suitable alternative for policing protests in Kenya to enhance the enjoyment of the right to assembly in Chapter 8. Relatedly, Olutola discusses the protection of the right to life during public protests in Nigeria in Chapter 9, highlighting that article 33(2) of the Constitution of Nigeria poses a significant threat to the protection of the right to life during protests in so far as it permits the use of lethal force for the protection of property, unlawful violence and quelling insurrection, contrary to the internationally accepted best practice of the 'protect life' principle, which only allows the use of lethal force to protect life. He recommends, among others, the revisions of the Nigerian constitution to remove provisions that are 'anti protect life principle'. Nyarko, in Chapter 10, addresses the role of the judiciary in protecting the right to assembly and public protest in Ghana, highlighting that [l]iberal legal frameworks and strong courts are necessary for the protection of these right and to challenge arbitrary executive action where necessary. He, however, cautions that "liberal interpretation by courts alone is not sufficient to protect the right peaceful assembly from illiberal policing tactics" and urges that civil society and other stakeholders "need to constantly be on the lookout for … police maneuvering to ensure that judicial and legislative gains are not circumvented". In the last contribution for this part, Sefah assesses in Chapter 11 the role of electoral management bodies in enhancing democracy in Africa, using the Electoral Commission of Ghana as a case study.

Part IV considers some of the emerging challenges in governance and human rights in Africa, commencing in Chapter 12 with Okoloise, who discusses balancing national security and human rights in the fight against Boko Haram in Nigeria—highlighting that while Nigeria is at liberty to pursue counter-terrorism measures best suited for its context, these measures cannot be devoid of consideration for and adherence to its international human rights obligations. In Chapter 13, Addaney addresses the legal challenges relating to the protection of climate refugees in Africa, highlighting that the Kampala Convention and OAU Refugee Convention provide sufficient normative bases for the protection of climate refugees in Africa. The best interest of the child and climate adaption is discussed by Boshoff in Chapter 14, where she argues, among others, that adaption policies will benefit from a child-centered approach which "will ensure that interventions are less focused on the short term thereby taking account of the needs of future generations and will provide the long-term view necessary to prevent short-term maladaptation". Finally, in Chapter 15, Addaney, Olutola and Kabaseke reflect on the protection of environmental rights in the context of oil extraction in Africa.

REFERENCES

Addaney, Michael. "The African Union's Agenda 2063: Education and Its Realization." In *Education Law, Strategic Policy and Sustainable Development in Africa*, edited by Onuora-Oguno Azubike, Egbewole Wahab, and Thomas E. Kleven, 182. Cham: Palgrave Macmillan, 2018.

Addaney, Michael, and Michael Gyan Nyarko. "Governance and Human Rights in Twenty-First Century Africa: An Introductory Appraisal." In *Ghana @ 60: Governance and Human Rights in Twenty-First Century Africa*, edited by Michael Addaney and Michael Gyan Nyarko, 2. Pretoria: Pretoria University Law Press, 2017.

African Union Commission. "Agenda 2063: The Africa We Want, a Shared Strategic Framework for Inclusive Growth and Sustainable Development." In *First Ten-Year Implementation Plan 2014–2023*. Addis Ababa: African Union, 2015a.

———. *Agenda 2063: The Critical Factors for Success*. Addis Ababa: African Union, 2015b.

Arnold, Guy. *Africa: A Modern History*. London: Atlantic Books, 2005.

Asante, S.K.B. "Nation Building and Human Rights in Emergent African Nations." *Cornell International Law Journal* 2, no. 1 (1969): 72.

El Fassi, Sahra, and Faten Aggad. *Implementing African Development Initiatives: Opportunities and Challenges to Securing Alternative Financing for the Agenda 2063*. Maastricht: European Centre for Development Policy Management, 2014.

El-Obaid, El-Obaid A., and Kwadwo Appiagyei-Attua. "Human Rights in Africa: A New Perspective on Linking the Past to the Present." *McGill Law Journal* 41 (1996): 819.

Gluckman, Max. "Natural Justice in Africa." *Natural Law Forum* 81 (1964).

Huntington, Samuel. *The Third Wave: Democratization in the Late Twentieth Century*. Norman: University of Oklahoma Press, 1991.

Lynch, Gabrielle, and Gordon Crawford. "Democratization in Africa 1990–2010: An Assessment." *Democratization* 18, no. 2 (2011): 275.

M'Baye, Keba. *Les droits de l'homme en Afrique.* Paris: Pedone, 1992.

M'Baye, Keba, and Birame Ndiaye. "The Organisation of African Unity." In *The International Dimensions of Human Rights,* edited by Karel Vasak, 583. Westport, CT: Greenwood Press, 1982.

Mbondenyi, Morris Kiwinda. *International Human Rights and Their Enforcement in Africa.* Nairobi: LawAfrica Publishing, 2010.

Mbondenyi, Morris Kiwinda, and Tom Ojienda. "Introduction to and Overview of Constitutionalism and Democratic Governance in Africa." In *Constitutionalism and Democratic Governance in Africa: Contemporary Perspectives from Sub-Saharan Africa,* edited by Morris Kiwinda Mbondenyi and Tom Ojienda, 4. Pretoria: Pretoria University Law Press, 2013.

Meredith, Martin. *The State of Africa: A History of the Continent Since Independence.* London: Jonathan Ball Publisher, 2005.

Mutua, Makau. *Human Rights: A Political and Cultural Critique.* Philadelphia: University of Pennsylvania Press, 2002.

Naldi, Gino. *The Organisation of African Unity: An Analysis of Its Role.* London: Mansell, 1989.

Nyanduga, Bahane T. "Conference Paper: Perspectives on the African Commission on Human and Peoples' Rights on the Occasion of the 20th Anniversary of the Entry into Force of the African Charter on Human and Peoples' Rights." *African Human Rights Law Journal* 6, no. 2 (2006): 255.

Nyarko, Michael Gyan, and Henrietta M. Ekefre. "Recent Advances in Children's Rights in the African Human Rights System: A Review of the Decision of the African Committee of Experts on the Rights and Welfare of the Child in the Talibé's Case." *Law and Practice of International Courts and Tribunals* 15 (2016): 385.

Prempeh, Henry Kwesi. "Africa's 'Constitutional Revival': Fake Start or New Dawn?" *International Journal of Constitutional Law* 5, no. 3 (2007): 469–473.

Pye, Lucian W. *Aspects of Political Development: An Analytical Study.* Boston, MA: Little, Brown and Company, 1966.

Richard J. Reid, *A History of Modern Africa: 1800 to the Present.* Oxford: Wiley, 2012.

Rodney, Walter. *How Europe Underdeveloped Africa.* Washington, DC: Howard University Press, 1974.

Viljoen, Frans. *International Human Rights Law in Africa.* Oxford: Oxford University Press, 2012.

Umozurike, Uji. *Five Years of the African Commission on Human and Peoples' Rights.* Ile-Ife: Obafemi Awolowo University, 1992.

———. *The African Charter on Human and Peoples' Rights.* Zuidpoolsingel: Brill/Noijhoff, 1997.

Governance and Human Rights in the African Union

CHAPTER 2

Toward an Effective African Human Rights System: The Nature and Implications of the Relationship Between the African Union Policy Organs and Human Rights Bodies

Tilahun Adamu Zewudie

1 INTRODUCTION

The realization of the human rights objectives of the AU requires collaboration between all of its organs and alignment of their activities. This is so primarily because, as Udombana correctly observed, an organization that is divided against itself cannot stand or achieve its objectives.[1] A good working relationship between the AU Policy organs (the Assembly, the Executive Council and the Permanent Representatives' Committee of the African Union) and the key human rights bodies is a prerequisite for an effective African human rights system.[2] There are

---

[1] Nsongurua Udombana, "The Institutional Structure of the African Union: A Legal Analysis," *California Western International Law Journal* 33, no. 1 (2002): 133.

[2] Morris Mbondenyi, *International Human Rights and Their Enforcement in Africa* (Nairobi: LawAfrica Publishing, 2011), 131.

T. A. Zewudie (✉)
Embassy of Ethiopia, Washington, D.C., USA

© The Author(s) 2020
M. Addaney et al. (eds.), *Governance, Human Rights, and Political Transformation in Africa,*
https://doi.org/10.1007/978-3-030-27049-0_2

17

a number of factors which impact the relationship between the AU and the human rights organs. First, while there was initially hope that the AU decision-making process would be flexible, open, participatory and consensual to avoid discord and division and to create harmony among AU organs,[3] the recent AU decision-making practice has revealed several discrepancies between the decisions of the policy organs and human rights bodies.[4] A consensual decision-making process on the AU human rights agenda would require constructive engagement between these bodies. Second, the discretion of the Assembly to delegate any of its powers to 'any' organ of the AU was criticized as having significant potential problems since it was not the intention of the drafters of the Constitutive Act of the AU (Constitutive Act) to have a lesser organ decide on 'fundamental issues'.[5] It was then recommended that the Assembly takes 'the necessary care and utmost caution' while exercising its discretion to delegate its powers.[6] Nevertheless, the Assembly has delegated a great deal of its human rights functions to the Executive Council, hence broadening the discretion of the Executive Council beyond its powers and functions as explicitly provided for in the Constitutive Act.[7] Concentration of power in few political organs increases the likelihood of human rights violations as it leads to 'extension of the political decision-making process to the legal decision-making processes.[8] Following this delegation to the Executive Council there is a rising controversy and criticism that policy organs are

---

[3] Udombana, "The Institutional Structure of the African Union," 133.

[4] African Union, Executive Council, *Decision on the Thirty-Seventh Activity Report of the African Commission on Human and Peoples' Rights—Doc.EX.CL/887(XXVI), EX.CL/Dec.864(XXVI)* (January 2015), para. 7; *Decision on the Thirty-Eighth Activity Report of the African Commission on Human and Peoples' Rights—Doc.EX.CL/921(XXVII), EX.CL/Dec.887(XXVII)* (June 2015), paras. 7, 12, accessed October 16, 2016, https://au.int/en/decisions/council).

[5] Konstantinos Magliveras and Gino Naldi, "The African Union—A New Dawn for Africa?" *International and Comparative Law Quarterly* 51, no. 2 (2002): 419–420.

[6] Ibid., 420.

[7] Constitutive Act of the African Union (Constitutive Act), July 11, 2000, art 13, accessed March 9, 2018, https://au.int/en/constitutive-act.

[8] Ben Chigara, "Tentative Reflection on the African Charter on Human and Peoples' Rights," in *The African Regional Human Rights System: 30 Years After the African Charter on Human and Peoples' Rights*, ed. Manisuli Ssenyonjo (The Hague: Martinus Nijhoff Publishers, 2012), 404.

heavily intruding in the functional autonomy and institutional independence of human rights bodies.[9]

The discretion of the policy organs and the way they interpret and apply this discretion has serious implications for the effectiveness of the African human rights system, and thus requires critical analysis. Furthermore, the potential of the existing AU platforms to encourage productive dialogue on human and people's rights requires further consideration. Against this backdrop, this Chapter analyzes the relationship between the AU policy organs and the AU human rights bodies with a focus on the Court and the Commission, and its impact on the African human rights system. To provide a clear context, the Chapter starts by briefly discussing the relevant powers and functions of policy organs and human rights bodies.

2   THE POWERS AND FUNCTIONS OF THE AFRICAN UNION POLICY ORGANS AND HUMAN RIGHTS BODIES

The AU policy organs and human rights bodies derive their powers and functions mainly from the AU Constitutive Act,[10] their respective establishment instruments and Rules of Procedures as well as from subsequent decisions and resolutions. Before getting to analyze the specific powers and functions of these bodies, it is important to give a brief account of the guiding ideals provided for in the Constitutive Act.

The Constitutive Act, by including protection and promotion of human and peoples' rights, both in the principles and objectives of the AU,[11] aspires 'to concretize the relationship between the regional human rights system and its political affiliates'.[12] It also provides the AU's right to intervention during grave violations of human rights—genocide, war crimes and crimes against humanity.[13] Furthermore, these human

---

[9] Centre for Human Rights, Statement at the 57th session of the African Commission on Human and Peoples Rights (2015), accessed November 30, 2016, http://www.chr.up.ac.za/index.php/centre-news-a-events-2015/1551-statement-by-the-centre-for-human-rights-at-the-57th-session-of-the-african-commission-on-human-and-peoples-rights-.html.

[10] Constitutive Act, arts 9, 13, 21.

[11] Ibid., arts 3(h), 4(m).

[12] Mbondenyi, *International Human Rights and Their Enforcement in Africa*, 131.

[13] Constitutive Act, art 4(h).

rights aspirations are backed by sanction in case of noncompliance.[14] In addition, it establishes organs whose mandate have significant implication for human and peoples' rights, including policy organs, the African Court of Justice, Pan African Parliament (PAP) and Economic, Social and Cultural Council (ECOSOCC).[15] In the Constitutive Act, all the AU organs are equal in hierarchy except for the Assembly.[16] The establishment of the AU with parliamentary, judicial and executive bodies implies the legal doctrine of separation of powers.[17] The Constitutive Act also underscores the need to strengthen these institutions and improve their effectiveness by providing 'the necessary power and resources'.[18]

2.1   Functions and Powers of Policy Organs

The Assembly

Established as the highest policy organ of the AU by the Constitutive Act[19] the Assembly has the power to make common policies of the AU, to consider reports of other organs of the AU and monitor and ensure their implementation, and to consider and adopt the budget of the AU and its organs.[20] Some of the functions and powers of the Assembly are derived from instruments other than the Constitutive Act. These include election of members of the Commission[21] as well as election, supervision or removal of judges of the Court.[22] It also has the power to restructure organs of the AU.[23] Furthermore, the Assembly decides on intervention

---

[14] Ibid., art 23.

[15] Ibid., art 5.

[16] Udombana, "The Institutional Structure of the African Union," 86.

[17] Ibid.

[18] Constitutive Act, Preamble, para. 10.

[19] Ibid., arts 5(1)(a), 6(1).

[20] Ibid., art 9(1).

[21] African Charter on Human and People's Rights (African Charter), June 27, 1981, art 23, accessed March 6, 2018, http://www.achpr.org/files/instruments/achpr/banjul_charter.pdf.

[22] Protocol to the African Charter on Human and Peoples' Rights on the Establishment of the African Court on Human and Peoples' Rights (African Court Protocol), June 10, 1998, arts 14, 19, accessed March 5, 2018, https://au.int/en/treaties.

[23] Constitutive Act, art 14(2).

of the AU in member states, determines sanctions and interprets and may amend the Constitutive Act.[24]

The Assembly has both legislative and executive functions. It is the highest legislative organ of the AU as far as the PAP is not yet conferred with full legislative power.[25] The executive function of the Assembly could be inferred from its monitoring power, as well as its duty to ensure implementation of decisions of other organs of the AU.[26] The above mandates put the Assembly at the highest position in making the AU human rights policies and monitoring their implementation. The Assembly could use these powers to buttress the effectiveness of the African human rights system.[27]

The recent AU decision-making process shows that only few matters are considered by the Assembly.[28] This is so particularly following the decision of the Assembly to streamline the works of the AU by limiting itself to consider only 'key strategic policy issues' such as peace and security, integration, finance and governance issues.[29] This decision transfers a number of human rights issues that were under the Assembly's domain to the Executive Council. Furthermore, the Assembly has stopped its earlier practice of considering matters on which the Executive Council made decision thereby reaffirming the final decision-making power of the Executive Council.[30]

[24] Rules of Procedure of the Assembly of the African Union (Assembly Rules of Procedure), July 10 2002), r 4, accessed March 6, 2018, https://www3.nd.edu/~g-goertz/rei/rei040/rei040.13tt1.pdf.

[25] Protocol to the Treaty Establishing the African Economic Community Relating to the Pan-African Parliament, March 2, 2001, art 2, accessed March 6, 2018, https://au.int/en/treaties.

[26] Constitutive Act, art 9.

[27] Mbondenyi, *International Human Rights and Their Enforcement in Africa*, 282.

[28] African Union, "Decisions and Declarations of the Assembly," accessed March 6, 2018, https://au.int/en/decisions/assembly.

[29] African Union, Assembly, *Decision on Streamlining of the AU Summits and the Working Methods of the African Union—Doc. Assembly/AU/4(XXV), Assembly/AU/Dec.582 (XXV)* (June 2015), accessed March 6, 2018, https://au.int/en/decisions/assembly.

[30] Ibid.

The Executive Council

Established in terms of article 5(1)(b) of the Constitutive Act and answerable to the Assembly,[31] the Executive Council has the power to coordinate and make decisions on matters of common interest to member states of the AU.[32] It considers issues that are submitted to it by the PRC and follows up on the implementation of decisions taken by the Assembly.[33] Furthermore, its functions include electing members of AU organs for subsequent appointment by the Assembly and considering the structure and functions of organs of the AU.[34] In the context of human rights, these functions signify that the Executive Council has a great deal of power in determining the structure and composition of human rights bodies and giving them policy directions that can help strengthen the African human rights system.

The Executive Council has been delegated by the Assembly to 'consider' activity reports of the Commission since 2003.[35] It has also been considering the activity reports of the Court. Moreover, as mentioned above, since June 2015 the Executive Council has been further authorized to make final decisions on all matters other than 'key strategic policy issues' of the AU.[36] This elevates the Executive Council to a final policy-making body on human and people's rights.

The Permanent Representatives Committee

The Permanent Representatives Committee is an organ of the AU established by the Constitutive Act.[37] It is composed of Permanent Representatives (Ambassadors) of member states to the AU.[38] Its mandates include organizing the activities of the Executive Council and

---

[31] Ibid., art 13(2).

[32] Ibid., art 13(1).

[33] Ibid., art 13(2).

[34] Rules of Procedure of the Executive Council of the African Union, r 5(1)(f).

[35] African Union Assembly, *Decision on the 16th Annual Activity Report of the African Commission on Human and Peoples' Rights, Assembly/AU/Dec.11 (II)* (2003), accessed March 22, 2018, https://au.int/en/decisions/assembly-african-union-second-ordinary-session.

[36] Executive Council, *EX.CL/Dec.864 (XXVI)*, para. 7.

[37] Constitutive Act, art 5(f).

[38] Ibid., art 21(1).

undertaking tasks that might be given to it by the Executive Council.[39] It is the most active political body in the AU and meets at least once a month.[40] Set to serve as the principal advisory body of the Executive Council on the AU affairs,[41] the PRC provides recommendations to the Executive Council on a number of issues including on the budget and activity reports of organs of the AU and on the implementation of decisions of the Executive Council.[42] This encompasses consideration of the activity reports of human rights bodies.

Since its establishment, the PRC has never made a standalone policy outcome document in the form of final decision during the AU summits as its decisions are set to remain 'recommendations until adopted by the Executive Council'.[43] However, permanently situated at the headquarters of the AU following up on the day-to-day activities of the AU and its organs, the PRC makes decisions on a number of issues, including on human rights, before and after the deliberations of the Assembly and the Executive Council. The established practice of the AU shows the critical role of the PRC in the preparation of draft decisions during AU summits.[44] As a result, it has been taken as a body that 'shifts technical drafting into policymaking' hence a de facto policymaking body.[45]

The PRC links the AU with member states.[46] This is particularly relevant for human rights as States take the primary responsible to 'respect,

[39] Ibid., art 21(2).

[40] Rules of Procedure of the Permanent Representatives Committee (PRC Rules of Procedure), July 10, 2002, r 5(1), accessed March 6, 2018, https://issuu.com/85991/docs/perm-reps-ctte.

[41] Ibid., r 1(1).

[42] Ibid., r 4.

[43] Ibid., r 26.

[44] African Union, *Draft Report of the Twenty-Ninth Ordinary Session Permanent Representatives Committee PRC/Rpt (XXIX)*, January 2015; *Draft Report of the Thirty-First Ordinary Session Permanent Representatives Committee PRC/Draft/Rpt (XXXI)*, January 2016, accessed March 5, 2018, https://portal.africa-union.org/DVD/Documents/DOC-AU-WD/PRC%20Rpt%20(XXIX)%20_E.pdf; http://archive.au.int/collect/oaucounc/import/English/PRC%20Rpt%20(XXXI)%20_E.pdf.

[45] Jacob Lisakafu, "Exploring the Role and Place of the Permanent Representative Committee within the African Union," *South African Journal of International Affairs* 23 (2016): 225.

[46] PRC Rules of Procedure, r 4(e).

protect, promote and fulfill' human rights. Furthermore, since members of the PRC are by law the highest-ranking full representatives of their respective countries to the AU,[47] their pronouncement concerning human rights in itself reflects the position of their respective countries. Moreover, although PRC's primary function is to advise the Executive Council, its members are in practice key advisors of their respective Heads of State or Government during the AU summits. Concerning human rights, the PRC has been the most active political organ in the AU policymaking process as relevant sector ministers responsible for human rights do not usually participate in the AU Ordinary Sessions.[48]

2.2   Powers and Functions of Human Rights Bodies

The African Commission on Human and Peoples' Rights

An autonomous quasi-judicial human rights body, the Commission is the only enforcement mechanism established by the African Charter.[49] The Commission's mandate can be summarized into three broad categories: protection mandates, promotional mandates and interpretative mandates.[50] Its protection mandate includes consideration of communications, issuing provisional measures and letters of urgent appeals, examining states' reports and providing observations and comments, issuing public statements and reports and undertaking protective missions.[51] The Commission's promotional mandate includes undertaking missions, organizing sensitization programs and conferences, issuing reports and statements, and providing supports to national authorities.[52] Some of its mandates such as examination of state reports, adoption of resolutions

---

[47] Vienna Convention on Diplomatic Relations, April 18, 1961, arts 3(1), 5(3). https://treaties.un.org/pages/ViewDetails.aspx?src=TREATY&mtdsg_no=III-3&article=3.

[48] Lisakafu, "Exploring the Role and Place of the Permanent Representative Committee within the African Union," 225.

[49] African Charter, art 30.

[50] African Charter, arts 30, 45.

[51] Udeme Essien, "The African Commission on Human and Peoples' Rights: Eleven Years After," *Buffalo Human Rights Law Review* 97, no. 6 (2000): 95–102.

[52] Ibid.

and statements are crosscutting—they fall within the domain of both its protection and promotional mandates.[53]

Not all the mandates of the Commission are explicitly provided for in the African Charter. As the Commission observed in its subsequent decisions, its mandate extends to receiving individual communications,[54] granting specific compensations for victims of human rights violations,[55] and protecting and promoting rights that are not explicitly provided for in the Charter such as the right to privacy, right to food, right to water and right to adequate housing as implied rights.[56] These tasks denote the expanding jurisdiction of the Commission beyond what is explicitly provided for in the African Charter.

The Commission faces several challenges and limitations that emanate from its establishment as well as its subsequent practices. While it has its own internal limitations external factors that are beyond its control have been heartrending its effectiveness. The major challenges include lack of sufficient guarantee for its independence and impartiality, lack of professionalism due to the appointment politicians and diplomats as members (this has now been improved), lack of capacity to handle cases promptly due to the part-time nature of its members, lack of sufficient human and financial resource and sometimes lack of flexibility in its engagement with politicians and diplomats on issues involving human rights violations.

The African Court on Human and Peoples' Rights
Established within the AU framework, the Court is the only operational permanent judicial body that makes binding decisions within the AU system.[57] Perhaps the most depressing feature of the Court is that its jurisdiction to receive cases directly from individuals and NGOs is dependent on state parties' acceptance through a special declaration.[58] Only the Commission, state parties and African intergovernmental organizations

---

[53] Badawi Ibrahim, "The African Commission on Human and People's Rights: Prospects and Problems," *Netherlands Quarterly of Human Rights* 7, no. 3 (1989): 280, 279.

[54] *Jawara v The Gambia* (2000) AHRLR 107 (ACHPR 2000) 42.

[55] *Communication 341/2007, Equality Now and Ethiopian Women Lawyers Association (EWLA) v Ethiopia*, Thirty Ninth Activity Report (ACHPR) 160(c) & (e).

[56] *Social and Economic Rights Action Centre (SERAC) and Another v Nigeria* (2001) AHRLR 60 (ACHPR 2001) 47, 116, 229.

[57] African Court Protocol, arts 1, 27.

[58] Ibid., arts 5(3), 34(6).

can access the Court without waiting for a declaration of acceptance.[59] The Court's jurisdiction includes receiving cases concerning the interpretation of all relevant human rights instruments to which the state concerned is a party.[60]

Since January 2016 the Court has been explicitly empowered to receive complaints from individuals on the implementation of decisions of the policy organs provided that the state concerned accepted its competence to receive cases from individuals.[61] This is an explicit endorsement of the rising area of the Court's jurisdiction in using the legal instruments and decisions of policy organs as primary sources of its interpretative and adjudicatory functions.

The other key development in the African regional human rights landscape is the establishment of the merged African Court of Justice on Human and People's Rights (ACJHPR), a court which is set to have three sections and jurisdiction on international criminal issues, human and peoples' rights issues and general legal issues.[62] The establishment of the ACJHPR was largely motivated by the desire to respond the alleged bias of the International Criminal Court (ICC) against Africa by establishing an African criminal court. Having participated as a state representative during the consideration of the draft Protocol of the ACJHPR by the AU Specialized Technical Committee on Justice and Legal Affairs as well as the policy organs of the AU, the author has observed that the establishment of the ACJHPR was driven more by emotion than by a proper examination and understanding of substantive mattes and the potential challenges and implications of the Court. Most of the statements of state delegates were focused on issues involving the immunities of senior officials and unconstitutional change of government. Speaking in favor of the establishment of the ACJHPR with provisions that accord immunity to Heads of State and Government and senior officials was literally considered by state representatives as an expression of solidarity to the African leaders who were indicted by ICC and an act of preservation

---

[59] Ibid., art 5.

[60] Ibid., art 3.

[61] African Union, Assembly, *Decision on Streamlining of the African Union Summits and the Working Methods of the African Union Assembly/AU/Dec.597(XXVI)* (January 2016), para. 2, accessed March 5, 2018, https://au.int/en/decisions/assembly.

[62] Protocol on Amendments to the Protocol on the Statute of the African Court of Justice and Human Rights, accessed September 19, 2016, http://www.au.int/en/treaties.

of the sovereignty of African states. Member states saw it as an exemplary achievement toward 'African solution to African problems'. The adoption was taken as a victory against ICC which was perceived to have targeted Africans.

The establishment of the ACJHPR has several legal and institutional implications. The ACJHPR is expected to replace the existing African Court.[63] As a result, its establishment has the potential to delay or prevent new ratification of the protocol of the (African) Court as states may desist from ratifying it with the understanding that the Court will be replaced. Furthermore, the establishment of a court with jurisdictions on the three broad international legal issues has the likelihood to reduce the 'focus on and prominence of human rights' in Africa.[64] Moreover, such a complex and broad court will require huge resource for it to effectively and efficiently deliver on its mandates. From the experience of the existing AU legal and human rights bodies, it is anticipated that the AU will not be able to allocate sufficient resources and create enabling condition for the Court to effectively deliver on its mandates. Viljoen observed that the ACJHPR is doomed to be ineffective for it provides 'an all or-nothing option' for states whereby a state has to accept all of its three jurisdictions or avoid it entirely.[65] The immunity clause will also affect its legitimacy hence discouraging partners from funding it. In general, although the decision to establish an African criminal court is a welcome endeavor, the expanded jurisdiction of the ACJHPR that encompasses human rights, justice and criminal matters makes the project pragmatically unfeasible.

3   The Relationship Between the Policy Organs and Human Rights Bodies and Its Implication(s)

3.1 The Assembly and Human Rights Bodies

As highlighted in the previous sections, the Assembly has transferred most of its functions concerning human rights to the Executive Council

---

[63] As above.

[64] F. Viljoen, "AU Assembly Should Consider Human Rights Implications Before Adopting the Amending Merged African Court Protocol," accessed September 19, 2016, https://africlaw.com/2012/05/23/au-assembly-should-consider-human-rights-implications-before-adopting-the-amending-merged-african-court-protocol/.

[65] As above.

through delegation. This has significantly reduced the level of engagement between human rights bodies and the Assembly. But, it does not result in a complete detachment between human rights bodies and the Assembly. There are still several avenues of interface. For example, since the Executive Council has to report to the Assembly about the consideration of activity reports of human rights bodies,[66] the latter can proactively engage with human rights bodies on issues that are not settled by the Executive Council. The Assembly can also engage with human rights bodies using its inherent discretion to reconsider any matter decided by the Executive Council and to take additional measures or give any other task to human rights bodies by its own initiative.[67] Besides, as part of its mandate to request the Commission to undertake studies during 'series of serious and massive violation' of human rights,[68] the Assembly can dialogue with the Commission.

Nonetheless, all these avenues of engagement are subject to the discretion of the Assembly. There is neither institutionalized regular engagement nor a concrete strategy on their relationship. Furthermore, the aforementioned avenues have not been effectively utilized, mainly due to the Assembly's reluctance. For instance, the Assembly has never responded to the Commission's requests for authorization to undertake in-depth studies on serious violations of human rights.[69] Let alone requesting the Commission to undertake in-depth study and provide recommendations during 'series of serious or massive human rights violations' as required by the law,[70] the Assembly has repeatedly ignored the Commission's requests and failed to act on the findings of the Commission on such violations.[71] This led the Commission to desist from making requests to the Assembly and to avoid determining serious

---

[66] Assembly, Assembly/AU/Dec.11 (II).

[67] Makua Mutua, "The African Human Rights System: A Critical Evaluation," DOCPA-2000-15, *United Nations Development Program*, 30, accessed October 8, 2016, http://hdr.undp.org.sites/default.files.mutua.pdf.

[68] African Charter, art 58(2).

[69] Rachel Murray, *The African Commission on Human and Peoples' Rights and International Law* (Oxford and Portland, OR: Hart Publishing, 2000), 20.

[70] African Charter, art 58.

[71] Mbondenyi, *International Human Rights and Their Enforcement in Africa*, 132.

and massive violations in its decisions unlike its previous practice.[72] As a result, this has been an area where the Assembly's relations with the Commission exists only on paper. Moreover, the Assembly has been proven reluctant to act when a deadlock occurred between the human rights bodies and the Executive Council over decisions that the latter made on the basis of the power delegated to it by the Assembly.[73]

The Assembly, being the only organ of the AU that determines sanction(s) on disobedient member states, could be the most effective body to monitor and enforce decisions of human rights bodies.[74] However, it has not been effectively exercising its power to ensure the enforcement of decisions of human rights bodies during noncompliance by state parties and during violations of human rights.[75] The low level of implementation of decisions of human rights bodies is therefore partly attributed to the Assembly's reluctance to effectively use its power to ensure implementation of the decisions. This is indicative of the insufficient importance the Assembly attaches to the work of the human rights bodies. For instance, although the Court requested the Assembly to make decision requiring Libya to comply with its judgment in the case of *African Commission on Human and Peoples' Rights v Libya*,[76] it failed to use its discretion to enforce the decision of the Court.[77]

---

[72]Frans Viljoen, *International Human Rights Law in Africa* (Oxford: Oxford University Press, 2012), 183.

[73]Executive Council, *EX.CL/Dec.887 (XXVII)*, para. 7.

[74]Constitutive Act, art 23.

[75]Bience Gawanas, "The African Union: Concepts and Implementation Mechanisms Relating to Human Rights," in *Human Rights in Africa: Legal Perspectives on Their Protection and Promotion*, ed. Anton Bösl and Joseph Diescho (Windhoek: Macmillan Education Namibia 2009), 140.

[76]Interim report of the African Court on Human and Peoples' Rights notifying the Assembly of the noncompliance of Libya, accessed September 19, 2016, http://en.African-court.org/images/Other%20Reports/AFCHPR_Interim_Report__Non_compliance_by_a_State__-_Libya.pdf.

[77]A. Ibrahim, "Evaluating a Decade of the African Union's Protection of Human Rights and Democracy: A Post-Tahrir Assessment," *African Human Rights Law Journal* 57 (2012): 1.

3.2   The Executive Council and Human Rights Bodies

The Executive Council and the Commission: Nature and Avenues of Engagement

Although the Assembly's transfer of its human rights functions to the Executive Council has brought increment in the time allocated for discussions on human rights issues including on activity reports of human rights bodies,[78] the adequacy and substance of engagements between human rights bodies and the Executive Council has been disputed. Currently, ordinary sessions of the Executive Council are the sole legally established regular avenues of engagement between human rights bodies and the Executive Council.[79] Accordingly, a major gap in the Commission's relationship with policy organs has been lack of institutional engagement that could facilitate robust interaction on the AU human rights agenda and on issues that affect their relationship.[80] This is a common challenge for all human rights bodies.

The human rights challenges in Africa require political as well as legal solutions through institutionalized engagement between policy organs and human rights bodies. The current setting of engagement between these bodies, being limited to AU ordinary sessions, is inadequate and thus hinders the desired speedy and coherent response to human rights violations. Furthermore, the dialogues conducted between policy organs and human rights bodies, particularly with the Commission, have been largely unconstructive, hence resulting in undesirable decisions.[81] The approach followed during meetings between policy organs and human rights bodies has been predominantly 'formal and rigid rather than substantive and flexible'.[82] Furthermore, existing engagements between these bodies lack adequate focus on the policy implications of the works of human rights bodies, thereby preventing the necessary policy directions from policy organs.[83]

[78] Viljoen, *International Human Rights Law in Africa*, 182.

[79] African Charter, art 59; African Court Protocol, art 57.

[80] Solomon Dersso, email message to author, September 29, 2016. Dersso is a member of the African Commission.

[81] Executive Council, *EX.CL/Dec.887(XXVII)*.

[82] Ibid.

[83] Ibid.

Often dialogues between the Commission and the Executive Council lead to erosion of the guarantees provided for in the African Charter and the established practices.[84] This happens mainly because of Executive Council's recurrent excessive use of its discretion which has been manifested, for example, through its decisions requesting amendment to the Commission's reports and recommendations, refusing the authorization of the publication of activity reports and allowing censorship of the Commission's decisions by states before their inclusion in the activity reports.[85]

The past five years have witnessed serious acts of *ultra vires* and a dangerous tendency by the Executive Council to perceive that its power includes reversing the Commission's decisions on substantive human rights matters and recurrently curtailed authorization of publication of findings on communications.[86] In June 2018 the Executive Council decided that the Commission's autonomy is only 'functional in its nature' and not independent from policy organs.[87] This is not only a narrow interpretation of the Commission's autonomy enshrined in the African Charter but also a manifest deviance from the principle of separation of power among the AU organs implied in the Constitutive Act.

The Executive Council's interference in the substantive activities of the Commission is blatantly manifested in its June 2015 decision requesting the Commission to withdraw the observer status it had granted to an NGO called Coalition of African Lesbians (CAL) saying that the objectives of CAL, as an NGO working on the rights of lesbians, is inconsistent with 'African values and traditions' and hence the African Charter.[88] The Commission refused to implement the decision contending that the granting of observer status to CAL was appropriate and falls within its competence[89] whereas the Executive Council in its subsequent decisions reiterated its position for the withdrawal of the observed status of

---

[84] Viljoen, *International Human Rights Law in Africa*, 187.

[85] Ibid.

[86] Executive Council, *EX.CL/Dec.887(XXVII)*, paras. 7, 11, 12.

[87] AU Executive Council, "Decision on the African Commission on Human and Peoples' Rights—Doc. EX.CL/1058(XXXII)," *EX.CL/995(XXXII)*, para. 5.

[88] Executive Council, *EX.CL/Dec.887(XXVII)*, para. 7.

[89] African Commission, 43rd Activity Report, para. 53. http://www.achpr.org/activity-reports/43/ (accessed March 8, 2018).

CAL.[90] After over three years of stalemate, the Commission was forced to withdraw CAL's observer status on 08 August 2018.[91] Beyond its devastating impact on the rights of 'sexual minorities', the decision indicates the hostile political environment in which human rights bodies are functioning.

A suitable way to examine the relationship between the Commission and the Executive Council is by considering the changes and continuities in the submission and consideration of the Commission's activity reports. In the absence of clarity as to whether its activity report should incorporate specific findings of communications the Commission in earlier years have had a practice of incorporating, in its reports, a broad list of issues including resolutions, agendas of its sessions, recommendations on states' periodic reports and summary of findings of communications.[92] Nevertheless, as member states threatened to curtail the publication of findings by requesting prior discussion to amend the activity reports and findings on communications, the Commission stopped this practice and opted to present a general report without including findings on communications.[93] After the Executive Council was delegated by the Assembly to consider the Commission's activity reports, it refused to authorize publication of reports and communications more frequently than the Assembly used to do,[94] blocking the Commission from utilizing its 'most powerful tool' to deliver on its mandates.[95] In January 2015, the Executive Council requested the Commission 'to provide the states concerned with certain paragraphs of the report and the communications therein for such amendments as are deemed necessary and justified'.[96]

---

[90] African Union, Executive Council, Decision on the African Commission on Human and Peoples' Rights—Doc. *EX.CL/1058(XXXII)*, para. 3, accessed March 8, 2018, https://au.int/sites/default/files/decisions/33909-ex_cl_decisions_986-1007_e.pdf.

[91] International Justice Resource Centre, "African Commission Bows to Political Pressure, Withdraws NGOs Observer Status," accessed December 19, 2018, https://ijrcenter.org/2018/08/28/achpr-strips-the-coalition-of-african-lesbians-of-its-observer-status/.

[92] See particularly, the 7th Activity Report of the Commission, Annex I–XI, accessed March 8, 2018, http://www.achpr.org/activity-reports/43/.

[93] Viljoen, *International Human Rights Law in Africa*, 188.

[94] Ibid., 187.

[95] Christof Heyns, "The African Regional Human Rights System: In Need of Reform?" *African Human Rights Law Journal* 155, no. 2 (2002): 164.

[96] Executive Council, *EX.CL/Dec.864 (XXVI)*, para. 7.

This allows censorship of the findings on communications by member states. Furthermore, in a significant departure from its previous practice, the Commission has, since its 37th activity report, avoided addressing the recommendations contained in its activity reports to the Executive Council and opted to address it to the Assembly while it is well aware that the Assembly will not consider its reports because it has already transferred this mandate to the Executive Council.[97] This is indicative of the unfriendly relationship between the Commission and the Executive Council.

The other contentious issue concerning the relationship between the Executive Council and the Commission has been the growing role and participation of NGOs. In June 2015, the Executive Council passed a decision requesting the Commission to 'avoid undue interference' of non-African NGOs/INGOs in its functions.[98] The decision seems harmless on the face of it, but is inspired by the deep mistrust and suspicion that States have against NGOs and was intended to weaken the Commission's relation with NGOs. Given the invaluable role NGOs have been playing to strengthen the Commission's effectiveness,[99] this decision has counterproductive effects on the protection and promotion of human rights. The decision disregards two major facts: the fact that NGOs have been the main force behind the growing achievement of the Commission[100] and the fact that the Commission's reliance on NGOs grew as a result of the lack of adequate support from policy organs, which is identified as a 'disconnect between Addis Ababa and Banjul'.[101] The decision contrasts the pressing need to increase the role of NGOs to strengthen the African human rights system.[102]

The effectiveness of the human rights bodies requires, at the minimum, autonomy to exercise their functions independently.[103] The role of the Assembly and the Executive Council is political, and not legal, hence they should abstain from giving 'prescription' on the substantive

---

[97] See generally, 37th–40th Activity Reports of the African Commission.

[98] Executive Council, *EX.CL/Dec.887(XXVII)*, paras. 9–12.

[99] Viljoen, *International Human Rights Law in Africa*, 384.

[100] Solomon Dersso, email message to author, September 29, 2016.

[101] Ibid.

[102] Mbondenyi, *International Human Rights and Their Enforcement in Africa*, 430.

[103] Ibrahim, "The African Commission on Human and Peoples' Rights," 275.

activities of the Commission.[104] Interpretation of the African Charter is the exclusive mandate of the Commission and the Court.[105] Thus, decisions of the Executive Council that intend to alter the substantive activities of the Commission[106] amount to changing the Commission's status from an autonomous professional body to a de facto representative of policy organs. Furthermore, the independence of the Commission is not just from policy organs—it also implies independence from other 'third parties' including NGOs.[107] It has been known that NGOs often twist the Commission toward their own 'political economy' hence encouraging bias toward certain issues.[108] Thus, the Commission should control its own agenda.

The Executive Council and the Court

The Court has been experiencing several challenges that could be addressed through collaboration with and support from policy organs. Perhaps, the top three infamous issues with respect to the Court's relation with the policy organs are lack of direct access to the Court, implementation of its decisions and low level of ratification of the Protocol of the Court. Policy organs have shown little disposition to solve these challenges.[109]

The Court has been relentlessly seeking Executive Council's willpower to request member states of the AU to ratify its Protocol and make the declaration to enable individuals and NGOs to get direct access to it. The reaction of the Executive Council to this request has been positive on paper as demonstrated on its decisions urging member states to ratify the Protocol and make the declaration.[110] However, its response to the question of direct access to individuals is unenthusiastic.

---

[104] Mbondenyi, *International Human Rights and Their Enforcement in Africa*, 126.

[105] Chigara, "Tentative Reflection on the African Charter on Human and Peoples' Rights," 404.

[106] Executive Council, *EX.CL/Dec.864(XXVI)*, para. 7; *EX.CL/Dec.887(XXVII)*, para. 12.

[107] Solomon Dersso, email message to author, September 29, 2016.

[108] Ibid.

[109] African Union, accessed October 20, 2016, http://www.au.int/en/treaties.

[110] African Union, Executive Council, decisions on the Activity Reports of the Court from January 2013–2016, accessed October 2, 2016, http://www.au.int/en/decisions/council.

Although the Court submitted a recommendation for the policy organs to repeal article 34(6) of the Protocol, so that states would automatically accept individuals' direct access to it upon ratification of the Protocol,[111] the Executive Council by-passed the proposal and to its despair, member states, in January 2015, barefacedly notified the Court to not bring the proposal to the attention of policy organs again, stating that it is 'inappropriate to reintroduce an issue that has already been rejected by the Executive Council'.[112]

The effectiveness of the Court relies on the universal ratification of its Protocol and individuals' direct access to it. As of today, the Court does not have jurisdiction on 24 AU member states and it cannot receive cases from individuals and NGOs against 46 member states.[113] The cumulative result of these decisions is sustaining the crippled state of the Court, thereby limiting the effectiveness of the African human rights system.

3.3   The Permanent Representatives Committee and Human Rights Bodies

The relationship between the PRC and human rights bodies is an area that is not well researched mainly due to the misunderstanding that the PRC has a secondary role in the decision-making process of the AU.[114] This misconception on the status and role of the PRC has been a major but overlooked factor that affected policy organs' relations with other AU organs including human rights bodies.[115]

Like other policy organs, there is no institutionalized engagement between the PRC and human rights bodies. Unlike other policy organs, there is no explicit provision in the AU legal instruments that guides the relationship between the PRC and human rights bodies. The founding instruments of human rights bodies and their Rules of Procedures are silent about the modus operandi of these bodies with the PRC.

---

[111] Activity Report of the African Court, June 2014, para. 77(ii).

[112] Permanent Representatives Committee, *PRC/Rpt (XXIX)*, para. 124(iv).

[113] Ratification Table: African Court Protocol, accessed December 19, 2018, http://www.achpr.org/instruments/court-establishment/ratification/.

[114] Lisakafu, "Exploring the Role and Place of the Permanent Representative Committee Within the African Union," 225–226.

[115] Ibid.

Apart from the meetings during ordinary summits of the AU, the PRC rarely meets with human rights bodies on a one-on-one basis. Following the establishment of the African Governance Architecture (AGA), the PRC undertook few 'one-on-one meetings' with human rights bodies during the meetings organized by the AGA Secretariat.[116] On June 2018 a joint retreat between the PRC and the Commission that was aimed at resolving concerns about the relationship between the Commission and the Policy Organs was held.

These consultations suggested the need to a regularized and more frequent engagement where the human rights bodies could regularly brief the PRC on the state of human rights in Africa.[117] The AGA consultations projected regularizing 'one-on-one meetings' between the PRC and the Commission and regular participation of the Chairperson of the PRC in the ordinary sessions of the Commission.[118] However, no Chairperson of the PRC has ever attended the sessions of the Commission. Nor has the idea on regularizing meetings become effective. Likewise, although the Court and the PRC have had similar consultations, it was not taken further.[119]

Furthermore, the dialogues between the PRC and the Commission and the Court during reporting periods have been predominantly antagonistic. Almost all the decisions of the Executive Council that have been detrimental to its relationship with the Commission were recommended by the PRC after awkward dialogues on the Commission's activity reports.[120] Furthermore, the proposal of the Court to repeal article 34(6) of the Protocol was rejected by the PRC before it reached the Executive Council.[121]

---

[116] African Union, "Permanent Representative Committee Consultation on the African Governance Architecture and the State Reporting Processes Under the African Charter on Democracy, Elections and Governance," Arusha, September 2–4, 2015. (On file with the author.)

[117] Ibid., 3.

[118] Ibid., 7.

[119] Ibid., 8.

[120] Executive Council, *EX.CL/Dec.864 (XXVI)*; *EX.CL/Dec.887 (XXVII)*, para. 7.

[121] Permanent Representatives Committee, *PRC/Draft/Rpt (XXXI)*, para. 98.

3.4   *The Diminishing Mutual Trust and Confidence*

The recent state of the relationship between policy organs and human rights bodies casts a doubt on the existence of mutual trust and confidence between these bodies. As Dersso, a member of the Commission observed, there is visible 'mutual misperception' between policy organs and the Commission.[122] While there is a perception in the Commission that states are generally unsupportive to its work and that they usually neglect their duties enshrined in the African Charter, member states, on the other hand, perceive the Commission as an institution that lacks 'Africanness' and works against states rather than supporting them.[123] According to Dersso states' perception toward the Commission is negative and misguided.[124]

Policy organs' diminished trust and confidence in the work of the Commission can also be noted from the Executive Council's decision allowing states to approach the Commission to discuss its findings on communications made against them and make amendments on activity reports of the Commission before its submission for authorization.[125] Furthermore, subjecting the Commission's findings to the authorization of political bodies in itself is indicative of policy organs' lack of trust in the Commission. Hence, there is 'a rift and disconnect, years of misperception' and suspicion between policy organs and the Commission which is distorting the necessary synergy between these organs and leaving human rights in a limbo.[126]

4   Conclusion and Recommendations

This Chapter discussed a number of factors affecting the relationship between policy organs and human rights bodies, and analyzed their implications to the African human rights system. It identified that the current relationship between human rights bodies and policy organs is generally poor. In the main, there is no institutionalized engagement that could facilitate robust interaction and hence a productive approach

---

[122] Solomon Dersso, email message to author, September 29, 2016.

[123] Ibid.

[124] Ibid.

[125] Executive Council, *EX.CL/Dec.864 (XXVI)*, para. 7.

[126] Solomon Dersso, email message to author, September 29, 2016.

to the human rights agenda within the AU policymaking process. There is routine and inadequate engagement limited to reporting periods and budget presentation. Furthermore, mutual misperceptions and mistrust between policy organs and human rights bodies have resulted in unconstructive dialogues impeding the effective functioning of human rights bodies. Due to the rising extension of the political decision-making process into the legal decision-making process, the AU decision-making process threatens the autonomy of human rights bodies thereby weakening their potential to deliver into the African human rights system.

There is a need to bring about a paradigm shift in the nature and frequency of engagement between policy organs and human rights bodies. This should include a shift from a routine engagement limited to reporting periods to a substantive formal and institutionalized engagement in between the reporting periods. More avenues of engagement should be created for policy organs and human rights bodies to interact on a one-on-one basis. One possible way to commence this process is through the AGA platform. A clear guideline that details the nature of the engagement between policy organs and human rights bodies as well as their particular tasks should be developed.

The need to reform the African human rights system has been recommended for a long time now. But proposals have predominately been concentrated on the establishment instruments of human rights bodies. Since ensuring the protection and promotion of human rights in Africa is the joint responsibility of human rights bodies and policy organs, mere amendment of the establishment instruments of human rights bodies is not enough. Hence, it is submitted that the reform should encompass a comprehensive review of the founding instruments of policy organs, essentially the Constitutive Act and their Rules of Procedures. At present, there is a good opportunity in the AU to undertake such amendments as part of the ongoing 'AU Institutional Reforms' initiative.[127] Policy organs should put human rights at the center of this reform process. As part of the reforms, there is a need to explicitly embrace human rights bodies as organs of the AU in the Constitutive Act and specify their key powers and functions. It would also be important to clearly define the nature of decisions of policy organs in their Rules

---

[127] African Union, "AU Reforms," accessed December 25, 2018, https://au.int/en/AUReforms.

of Procedures to the effect that their decisions be exclusively aimed at giving policy directions and not reversing or altering the substantive activities, decisions or recommendations of human rights bodies. It is also essential to specify in the Rules of Procedure of the Assembly and the Executive Council the modalities in which the Executive Council exercises powers transferred to it from the Assembly.

An effective African human rights system could not be viable without mutual trust and confidence between policy organs and human rights bodies. There is a need to bring a change of attitude by human rights bodies, policy organs and States. Policy organs and states should shift from viewing human rights bodies as naming and shaming institutions to a collaborative and critically constructive relationship that recognizes the purpose of human rights bodies in supporting, encouraging and mobilizing states to respect and promote human and peoples' rights. Likewise, human rights bodies should bring a change of attitude toward policy organs and states. One way in which the human rights bodies can change this conduct is through a stronger diplomatic approach toward policy organs and states in order to win back their trust and confidence, as opposed to the current 'informal' and predominately inflexible approach.

It is alarming that more than any other time the African human rights system has recently suffered from the recurrent interference of policy organs in the substantive activities of human rights bodies. Policy organs should lift existing decisions that threaten the independence of human rights bodies and refrain from taking any measure that compromises their autonomy. Additional guarantees should be entrenched in the Constitutive Act and the African Charter. While providing the autonomy of human rights bodies in their establishment instruments is a positive legal measure, their independence should also be explicitly provided for in the Constitutive Act as it gives them the maximum legal guarantee.

REFERENCES

Books and Articles in Books

Chigara, Ben. "Tentative Reflection on the African Charter on Human and Peoples' Rights." In *The African Regional Human Rights System: 30 Years After the African Charter on Human and Peoples' Rights*, edited by Manisuli Ssenyonjo, 401–420. The Hague: Martinus Nijhoff Publishers, 2012.
Gawanas, Bience. "The African Union: Concepts and Implementation Mechanisms Relating to Human Rights." In *Human Rights in Africa: Legal Perspectives*

on *Their Protection and Promotion*, edited by Anton Bösl and Joseph Diescho, 135–163. Windhoek: Macmillan Education Namibia, 2000.

Mbondenyi, Morris. *International Human Rights and Their Enforcement in Africa*. Nairobi: LawAfrica Publishing Ltd, 2011.

Murray, Rachel. *The African Commission on Human and Peoples' Rights and International Law*. Oxford: Hart Publishing, 2000.

Viljoen, Frans. *International Human Rights Law in Africa*. Oxford: Oxford University Press, 2012.

Journal Articles

Essien, Udeme. "The African Commission on Human and Peoples' Rights: Eleven Years After." *Buffalo Human Rights Law Review* 97, no. 6 (2000): 93–111.

Heyns, Christof. "The African Regional Human Rights System: In Need of Reform?" *African Human Rights Law Journal* 1, no. 2 (2002): 155–174.

Ibrahim, Badawi. "The African Commission on Human and Peoples' Rights: Prospects and Problems." *Right* 7, no. 3 (1989): 272–283.

Lisakafu, Jacob. "Exploring the Role and Place of the Permanent Representative Committee Within the African Union." *South African Journal of International Affairs* 23, no. 2 (2016): 225–241.

Udombana, Nsongurua. "The Institutional Structure of the African Union: A Legal Analysis." *California Western International Law Journal* 33, no. 1 (2002): 133.

Websites

"Activity Reports." African Commission on Human and People's Rights. Last modified, March 9, 2018. http://www.achpr.org/activity-reports/.

"Advisory Proceedings." African Court on Human and Peoples Rights. March 9, 2018. http://www.african-court.org/en/index.php/cases/2016-10-17-16-19-35.

"Decisions and Declarations." African Union. Last modified, March 9, 2018. https://au.int/en/decisions/decisions-declarations-and-resolution-assembly-union-twenty-seven-ordinary-session.

Reflections on the African Governance Architecture: Trends, Challenges and Opportunities

Kennedy Kariseb and Chairman Okoloise

1 Introduction

The African Governance Architecture (AGA) was developed in 2010 as a mechanism for dialogue between various African Union (AU) stakeholders and sub-regional organs and institutions to promote good democratic governance in Africa.[1] Following the adoption of the theme of the 2011

[1] "Strategic Plan 2009–2012," African Union Commission, May 19, 2009, para. 97. NB: The Strategic Plan was recommended for adoption by AU Executive Council decision EX.CL/Dec.499(XV) Rev.1 "Decision on the African Union Commission Strategic

The authors are grateful to the Centre for Human Rights, University of Pretoria and the Department of Political Affairs of the African Union for granting them a fellowship that informs this chapter contribution. All errors and omissions, if any, are however solely our responsibility.

K. Kariseb (✉)
University of Namibia, Windhoek, Namibia

C. Okoloise
University of Pretoria, Pretoria, South Africa

© The Author(s) 2020
M. Addaney et al. (eds.), *Governance, Human Rights, and Political Transformation in Africa,*
https://doi.org/10.1007/978-3-030-27049-0_3

41

Ordinary Summit dedicated to the Shared Values of the AU, the Assembly endorsed the Executive Council's decision EX.CL/Dec.525(XVI) that called on the AU Commission to identify obstacles and measures aimed at facilitating regional integration premised on such values, and devise a Pan-African architecture on governance. Consequently, the AGA was established primarily to promote the shared values of AU Member States as reflected in AU instruments and coordinate initiatives that advance human rights and democratic governance in Africa.[2] The AGA Framework is an outcome document of the AU Commission Strategic Plan 2009–2012 (Strategic Plan), originally conceptualised as part of the AUC's strategic objective for moving forward the continent's integration and development agenda. The framework charts the immediate and long-term direction of the Commission towards entrenching good governance on the continent under its third pillar on African shared values.[3] AGA was formally adopted in 2011 as a working mechanism within the superstructure of the AU,[4] and came in operation in 2012.

Although a relatively new initiative, the AGA Framework draws its substantive basis from existing AU instruments as exemplified in the objectives and principles of the AU Constitutive Act 2000, as well as substantive provisions of the African Charter on Human and Peoples' Rights 1981 (African Charter), the African Charter on Democracy, Elections and Governance 2007 (African Democracy Charter), and other AU norms and instruments. These instruments detail the shared values of AU Member

Plan 2009–2012 doc. ex.cl/501(xv)," Fifteenth Ordinary Session Executive Council Sirte, Libya, July 1, 2009, and endorsed by the AU Assembly Assembly/AU/Dec.247(XIII) "Decision on the African Union Commission Strategic Plan 2009–2012," Thirteenth Ordinary Session of the Assembly Sirte, Libya, July 3, 2009; "Framework of the African Governance Architecture (AGA)," para. 3, accessed January 7, 2019, https://www.iag-agi.org/IMG/pdf/aga-framework9183.pdf.

[2] "Declaration on the Theme of the Summit: 'Towards Greater Unity and Integration Through Shared Values,'" AU Doc Assembly/AU/Decl.1(XVI), para. 2, Sixteenth Ordinary Session, 30–31 January 2011, Addis Ababa, Ethiopia, accessed December 28, 2018, https://au.int/sites/default/files/decisions/9645-assembly_en_30_31_january_2011_auc_assembly_africa.pdf.

[3] "Strategic Plan 2009–2012," paras. 88–96; "African Governance Architecture Framework," para. 1.

[4] "Decision on the Theme, Date and Venue of the Sixteenth Ordinary Session of the Assembly of the African Union," AU Doc Assembly/AU/Dec.304(XV), Fifteenth Ordinary Session, Kampala, Uganda, July 27, 2010; "Decision on the Theme of the January 2011 Summit," AU Doc EX.CL/Dec.525(XVI), Sixteenth Ordinary Session of the Executive Council, Addis Ababa, Ethiopia, February 1, 2010, para. 2.

States to promote and respect democratic principles and institutions, human rights, popular participation, the rule of law, and good governance, as fundamental values of the Union. To implement its key objectives, the AGA Framework establishes the African Governance Platform (AGP) as 'a basis for facilitating harmonisation of instruments and coordination of initiatives in governance and democracy'.[5] The Platform acts as the concentric circle for dialogue and engagement between AU organs, institutions and Regional Economic Communities (RECs), on the one hand, and other national and external stakeholders, on the other.

Since the transformation of the Organisation of African Unity (OAU) into the AU in 2000, there has been a growing realisation that much of Africa's success will heavily depend on its human rights and good governance profile. Accordingly, the AU's 'Agenda 2063' development strategy has been premised on the promotion and realisation of democracy, respect for human rights, and the rule of law and the preservation of peace and security in Africa as clearly indicated in its aspiration 3.[6] The AU Constitutive Act, the African Charter, and the African Democracy Charter are some of the notable normative instruments that speak to the growing shift to a culture of good governance that is predicated on the respect for the rule of law and human rights on the continent. However, while the AGA clearly has a meaningful role in spearheading this paradigm shift in AU's political circles, the overtly vague nature of its mandate, coupled with its seemingly uncoordinated Addis Ababa-based secretariat undermines its potential.

This chapter is a reflection of the AGA and the AGP (and to a lesser extent its secretariat), highlighting the trends, challenges and feasibility of the architecture in the human rights and governance agenda of the AU. The chapter is divided into four parts, this first section being an overview of the AGA and the circumstances of its establishment. The second section examines the rationale for the AGA, including its historical and

---

[5] "Declaration on the Theme of the Summit," para. 11.

[6] "Agenda 2063: The Africa We Want," accessed January 7, 2018, http://archive.au.int/assets/images/agenda2063.pdf. Agenda 2063 outlines the African Shared Values programme of the AU. Generally, the AU Shared Values are ideal norms and standards deducible from the various policy and legal instruments of the AU, particularly those forming part of its human rights system, envisaged as commonly applicable, if not, binding on all AU member States. The AGA framework and its enforcement arm; the African Governance Platform are envisaged to play a pertinent role in the materialisation and implementation of both 'Agenda 2063' and the 'African Shared Values'. For a historical exposition on Africa's shared values see generally, Shadrack Gutto, ed., *Shared Values, Constitutionalism and Democracy in Africa* (Johannesburg: Fortune Africa Publishing, 2011), 1–102.

political underpinnings. The third section takes a cursory look at the normative and institutional foundations of the AGA and its platform, including the latter's mandate, structural composition and operational as well as thematic activities. The aim of this section is to analyse the embedded substantive and functional challenges of the Framework. The fourth section outlines possible incremental reforms and structural modifications that can be explored to address some of the major challenges facing the AGA Secretariat and the fifth section concludes the chapter.

2   RATIONALE FOR THE AGA FRAMEWORK

The conceptualisation, formation and operationalisation of the AGA framework was heavily influenced by the ideological and political transformations that took place with the founding of the AU.[7] Ideologically, the AU has adopted a policy of 'non-indifference' as set out in Article 4(h) of its Constitutive Act, in contrast to the pre-2000 African human rights system that gave much emphasis to the 'sanctity of national sovereignty and non-interference in [the] domestic affairs' of states.[8] The primary impact of Article 4(h) of the AU Constitutive Act has been that it empowers the AU an unprecedented right of (military) intervention in a member State in cases of war crimes, genocide and crimes against humanity. An acute problem however with this provision is the question whether prior UN Security Council authorisation is required.[9] The answer is not a settled one, however, the 2003 amendments to the AU Constitutive Act may serve as a hint on the possible interpretation that should be given. In terms of these amendments, the AU extended the right of intervention to what it termed '...a serious threat to a legitimate order to restore peace and stability to the member state of the Union upon the recommendation of the Peace and Security Council',[10] clearly

[7] Frans Viljoen, *International Human Rights Law in Africa*, 2nd ed. (Oxford: Oxford University Press, 2012), 156–170.

[8] Nicolla Tissi and Faten Aggad-Clerx, "The Road Ahead for the African Governance Architecture: An Overview of Current challenges and Possible Solutions," *South Africa Institute for International Affairs Policy Brief* 174, no. 1 (2014): 5; see generally AU Constitutive Act, art 4(h).

[9] See generally, Gabriel Amvane, "Intervention Pursuant to Article 4(h) of the Constitutive Act of the African Union without United Nations Security Council Authorization," *African Human Rights Law Journal* 15, no. 2 (2005): 282–298.

[10] African Union, "Protocol on Amendments to the Constitutive Act of the African Union," July 11, 2003, para. 4(h).

ousting UN Security Council authorisation. The African Democracy Charter further cemented the ideological shift within the AU brought about by provisions such as Article 4(h) of the AU Constitutive Act by incorporating in its framework the principle that unconstitutional changes of government, which was previously a common practice in many parts of Africa, is a violation of international law.[11]

As much as the AGA framework forms part of this new ideological and normative paradigm shift within the AU, it has not been given a concrete institutional status, thereby leading to confusion as to its place and scope. If the thematic and operational design of the Framework were merely fraught with subtle ambiguity, that would have been the least of its challenges. Not only are its founding documents not readily obtainable, the available delineations from the AGA framework give little, if any, insight into its nature and scope. Under the Rules of Procedure of the African Governance Platform, for instance, the AGA is defined as 'a platform for dialogue between the various stakeholders with the mandate to promote good governance and strengthen democracy in Africa', while the AGP is crafted as 'the institutional mechanism of AGA comprising African Union organs, RECs and institutions with a mandate to promote governance, democracy and human rights'.[12] A cursory reading of these definitions depicts the inherent limitations, conflations and shortcomings surrounding the AGA framework. It is logically inappropriate to refer to the AGA as a platform. What should instead be referred to as the 'platform' is the AGP, as its title clearly indicates. The AGA, which is a portmanteau of the terms 'African', 'Governance' and 'Architecture', it is submitted, should be viewed literally as an 'architecture'. In other words, it is a mere framework, collectively referring to the various AU legal instruments, norms and standards relating to governance, human rights and democracy broadly. Given that its mandate focuses on continental

---

[11] Stacy-Ann Elvy, "Towards a New Democratic Africa: The African Charter on Democracy, Elections and Governance," *Emory International Law Review* 27, no. 1 (2013): 43–113; Patrick Glen "Institutionalising Democracy in Africa: A Comment on the African Charter on Democracy, Elections and Governance," *Africa Journal of Legal Studies* 5 (14 June 2012): 149–175; Ibrahima Kane, "The Implementation of the African Charter on Democracy, Elections and Governance," *Africa Security Review* 17, no. 4 (2008): 43–63.

[12] "Rules of Procedure of the African Governance Platform," rule 1, accessed January 7, 2019, http://aga-platform.org/sites/default/files/2018-10/Rules%20Of%20Procedure%20 FINAL.pdf.

governance in its broadest sense, it should be understood in this context as embracing democracy, human rights, peace and security, the rule of law, and humanitarian affairs.

The rationale for the AGA lies in the AU's effort to better organise its scattered policy and institutional frameworks relating to good governance and democracy. It has often been said, and perhaps rightly so, that the AU's approach has been uncoordinated and inept.[13] This has resulted in 'inefficiency, ineffectiveness, and duplication of efforts and resources'.[14] It is unsustainable for the AU to continue an unsystematised approach given its limited financial and human resources. This explains why the AGA and its Platform were formed—to rationalise and coordinate its overarching institutions, policies and initiatives, mandated in some form on matters relating to good governance and democracy. The aim, it seems, is to cement efforts directed at these mandates, and to do away with unnecessary and unwarranted institutional and policy duplication. The underlying objective is to materialise, or, at the very least, make a meaningful contribution towards the realisation of good democratic governance in Africa.

3   SUBSTANTIVE AND INSTITUTIONAL STRUCTURE

3.1   Mandate and Objectives

The mandates of the AGP and the AGA Secretariat are articulated in its 2013 Framework document and the AGP Rules of Procedure 2016. Generally, the objectives of the AGA are anchored on two parallels. One is on the legal domain and the other on the political front. On the political front, it draws its legitimacy and inspiration from the AU Shared Values, which derives its substance from the deliberations and outputs

---

[13] George Wachira, "Consolidating the African Governance Architecture," *Southern African Institute of International Affairs (SAIIA) Policy Briefing* 1, no. 96 (2014): 1; Solomon Ebobrah, "Human Rights Realisation in the African Sub-Regional Institutions," in *The African Regional Human Rights System: 30 Years After the African Charter on Human and Peoples' Rights*, ed. Martinus Ssenyonjo (Boston: Martinus Nijhoff Publishers, 2011), 283–300.

[14] Wachira, "African Governance Architecture," 1; Morris Mbondenyi, "Institutional Mainstreaming and Rationalisation," in *The African Regional Human Rights System: 30 Years After the African Charter on Human and Peoples' Rights*, ed. Martinus Ssenyonjo (Boston: Martinus Nijhoff Publishers, 2011), 421–453.

of the 16th Ordinary Session of the Assembly of Heads of State and Government of the AU that took place in January 2011.[15] As far as the legal basis is concerned, the objectives of the AGA draw inspiration from the legal instruments of the AU, particularly the Constitutive Act 2000 and the African Democracy Charter. The primary objective of the AGA, therefore, is to serve as the 'overall political and institutional framework for the promotion, protection and sustenance of democracy, governance, human rights and humanitarian assistance on the continent'.[16] According to the Framework document,[17] the objectives of the AGA are to:

a. deepen synergy, coordination, cooperation and harmonisation of shared values instruments among AU organs, institutions and RECs on democracy, governance, human rights and humanitarian affairs;

b. foster effective implementation and cooperation among AU organs decisions and norms on democracy, good governance, human rights and humanitarian assistance;

c. Deepen popular participation and citizen engagement in attainment of democracy, governance and respect for human and peoples' rights;

d. Promote African Shared Values (AU norms and standards on democracy, governance and human rights);

e. Enhance the capacity of AU organs, institutions and RECs to support Member States to strengthen governance and consolidate democracy;

f. Coordinate evaluation and report on implementation and compliance with AU norms on governance and democracy as envisaged by articles 44, 45 and 49 of the African Democracy Charter;

g. Foster dialogue and share comparable lessons on trends, challenges, opportunities and prospects for improving governance and democracy among Member States;

---

[15] "Decisions, Declarations and Resolution' Assembly/AU/Dec.332–361(XVI)," Assembly/AU/Decl.1–3(XVI), Assembly/AU/Res.1(XVI) 16th Ordinary Session of the Assembly of Heads of State and Government, January 30–31, 2011, Addis Ababa, Ethiopia, accessed February 27, 2018, https://au.int/sites/default/files/decisions/9645-assembly_en_30_31_january_2011_auc_assembly_africa.pdf.

[16] "African Governance Architecture Framework," 5.

[17] Ibid., 1–31.

h. Generate, manage and disseminate knowledge on good governance and democracy in Africa; and

i. Facilitate joint engagement in strategic interventions: preventive
diplomacy, conflict prevention and post-conflict, reconstruction and
development in Africa.

Read neatly, these objectives colour two notable impressions about
the nature of the Framework as a governance vision for Africa. First, it
reveals that the AGA's role is one of coordination between AU organs,
regional groupings, Member States and other external stakeholders
dealing with democracy, good governance, and human rights matters.
Second, the AGA only has a promotional role to play. Nowhere in these
objectives can it be inferred that the AGA has any protective mandate.
It cannot make binding decisions, nor compel enforcement, regarding
States obligations for democracy and governance, although this position may change if the AGP starts exercising its powers as a state report
monitoring body as envisaged under the African Democracy Charter.[18]
Viewed based on the current practice and developments orienting the
AGA Secretariat, AGA's role can be and is better felt through technical assistance and support to States in their own domestic approaches to
entrench good governance.

Taken as a whole, one can only hold that these functions are rational
and materially well-founded. A problem has however arisen in the
mechanism that the AGP, including the AGA Secretariat, seeks to use
in achieving its mandates. To date, there has not been (and if there has
been, it is only minimally), a clear formulation of the mechanisms and
approaches envisaged to carry out the AGA and AGP functions and
mandates. Put differently, under the AU framework, more particularly
that of the AGA Secretariat, the role of the AGA and the AGP in seeking to realise human rights has either not been defined or not adequately
determined.

This setback is further eroded by ancillary problems. First, the AGA
and the AGP, are relatively new initiatives of the AUC, still finding

---

[18]Articles 44 and 45 of the African Democracy Charter empowers the AU Commission
to develop benchmarks for the Charter's implementation, and to be the central coordinating structure for its implementation. In essence, the AGP is understood as the AU
Commission's apparatus for executing its mandate under those provisions of the African
Democracy Charter.

their place and space in the midst of pre-existing initiatives with related mandates. The New Partnership for Africa's Development (NEPAD), the African Peace and Security Architecture (APSA) and the African Peer Review Mechanism (APRM) are some notable examples of these pre-existing initiatives. Second, the AGA, unlike for instance the APSA—which is more concrete and specific—is an overly opaque initiative. Third, and perhaps more importantly, the current mechanisms, such as the non-binding, often informal High Level Panel Dialogues carried out under the auspices of the AGP generally, are not sustainably impactful. These realities, to a large extent, can be viewed as clouding the AGP's capabilities in fulfilling its mandates, particularly as it relates to the realisation of human rights and good governance on the continent.

As alluded to earlier, the AGA's objectives have their roots in a vague construction, namely the so-called 'African shared values'. According to rule 1 of the Rules of Procedure of the African Governance Platform, African shared values are defined as 'the norms, principles and practices adopted by the African Union Member States, which provide the basis for collective actions and solutions in addressing the political, economic and social challenges that impede Africa's integration and development'.[19] Similarly, Matlosa defines AU Shared Values as 'those values, norms, and standards as enshrined in the Union's various instruments such as freedom, human rights and the rule of law, tolerance, respect, community spirit, gender equality, youth empowerment, unity in diversity, constitutionalism, democratic governance, peace, security, stability, development, environmental protection, popular participation, accountability and transparency, strong democratic institutions, anti-corruption, improved service delivery, equality, credible and democratic elections, durable solutions to humanitarian crises and free movement of African citizens across borders of AU member States'.[20]

The concept of African shared values remains unclear and can mislead. This is because perspectives relating to issues such as human rights, democracy and good governance on the African continent are diverse.

---

[19] Rules of Procedure of the African Governance Platform, Rule 1.

[20] Khabele Matlosa, "The African Union's African Governance Architecture Linkages with the African Peace and Security Architecture," *Great Insight Magazine* 4, no. 1 (2014): 14.

According to Viljoen, there are obvious nuances amongst African states on a variety of social, cultural, legal and political issue[21]:

> African States differ in obvious ways.... Socio-economic conditions and levels of development vary greatly across the continent. Political systems and levels of democratisation differ. Even in countries where elections have been held since the 1990s, the levels of liberty and democratic participation differ significantly. Cultures differ. In some instances cultural practices, which are widely condemned in human rights circles, such as female circumcision are rife.

He further argues that[22]:

> The impact of colonial control is another cause for variance, being still reflected in different legal systems and language policies... Ethnic diversity is another factor that creates diversity, not only within but also between States.

Based on this diverse legal and sociopolitical context, as Viljoen aptly portrays, the question may legitimately therefore be posed, whether we can truly speak of 'African shared values' in Africa. Put somewhat differently, does Africa have a commonly shared value system? Assuming that it does, what is the nature of that value system, and what are its normative elements? Some scholars, notably Smith, state that Africans have no codified or clearly defined value system. Rather, they are ingrained in customs, traditions and settled practices.[23] Gluckman, however, argues that 'the denial of an African conception and system of law is a mistaken position arising from a tradition imbued with ignorance about how law

[21] Frans Viljoen, "The Realisation of Human Rights in Africa Through Inter-Governmental Institutions" (LLD Thesis, University of Pretoria, South Africa, 1997), 19–20, accessed September 12, 2016, http://repository.up.ac.za/dspace/handle/2263/27810?show=full.

[22] As above.

[23] Michael Smith, "The Sociological Framework of Law," in *African Law: Adaptation and Development*, ed. Hilda Kuper and Leo Kuper (Berkeley: University of California Press, 1965), 32; Keba M'Baye, "The African Conception of Law," in *The Legal Systems of the World and Their Common Comparison and Unification*, ed. René David (London: Stevens and Sons, 1975), 56.

works among Africans'.[24] Another prominent scholar, Mapaure, in agreement with Gluckman, reaffirms that[25]:

> [T]he non-existence of an African philosophy of law is premised on the non-existence of written records about law. Is this position tenable? In all societies, the people's philosophy constitutes their system of thought and has always served as the basis for their attitudes on life. In this light, to deny the existence of African law is to deny the premise of African life and the values that underpin it.

It is true, as Mapaure captures above, that Africans always had a philosophy about identity, life and governance that were peculiar to them. However, what remains to be clearly established is the common denominator of that philosophy, and whether it was widespread, settled and accepted by all Africans as a value system they identify with. This scepticism about the existence of such a common philosophy beclouds the value construction of the so-called 'African shared values' advanced by the AU.

3.2   Institutional Structure

The AGA framework is structured under three interrelated components. The first is the norms and standards component, comprising AU legal instruments relating to governance, human rights, democracy and humanitarian affairs.[26] The second leg of the AGA is its institutional

---

[24] Max Gluckman, *The Allocation of Responsibility* (Manchester: Manchester University Press, 1986), 173.

[25] Clever Mapaure, "Reinvigorating African Values for SADC: The Relevance of Traditional African Philosophy of Law in a Globalising World of Competing Perspectives," *SADC Law Journal* 1, no. 1 (2011): 152.

[26] These instruments include (but are not limited to): The AU Constitutive Act, African Charter on Democracy, Elections and Governance, African Charter on Human and Peoples' Rights; OAU Convention Governing the Specific Aspects of Refugee Problems in Africa; African Charter on the Rights and Welfare of the Child; Protocol to the African Charter establishing the African Court on Human and Peoples' Rights; Protocol to the African Charter on Human and Peoples' Rights on the Rights of Women in Africa; African Charter on Values and Principles of Public Service and administration; AU Convention for the Protection and Assistance of Internally Displaced Persons in Africa; Protocol on the Statute of the African Court of Justice and Human Rights; Protocol Relating to the Establishment of the Peace and Security Council of the African Union; AU Convention on Preventing and Combating Corruption; African Youth Charter; Algiers Declaration

framework consisting of AU organs and institutions (including RECs) with a formal mandate to promote democracy, human rights, governance and humanitarian programmes.[27] The AGP operates as a forum for interaction among the representatives of the AU Peace and Security Council (PSC), AU Commission, RECs, African Commission on Human and Peoples' Rights, African Court on Human and Peoples' Rights, Pan-African Parliament, APRM, Economic, Social and Cultural Council, AU Advisory Board on Corruption, African Committee of Experts on the Rights and Welfare of the Child, African Commission on International Law; and the NEPAD Planning and Coordination Agency. The third leg of the framework is the African Governance Facility, which is the instrument for mobilisation resources for the AGA Platform and its Secretariat's day-to-day operations.

The AGP's Activities

The AGP is the enforcement mechanism of the AGA framework. Representatives from various AU institutions and organs highlighted above collectively make up the AGP. Since its operationalisation in 2013, the AGA Secretariat and the AGP have been undertaking several activities and programmatic initiatives in order to fulfil their mandates and strategic objectives. These activities can broadly be divided into three main categories: activities administered and executed by the AGA Secretariat, activities carried out by the AGP, and activities individually spearheaded by AGP member organs and institutions. The first two categories are relevant for the purposes of this chapter and will be considered together because the Secretariat is really more of the vehicle by which the AGP functions. The third category, which should ideally fall within the ambit of the AGA but generally does not, is barely relevant to the present chapter and therefore will not be considered.

on Unconstitutional Changes of Governments; Lome Declaration on Unconstitutional Changes of Government; Conference on Stability, Security, Development and Democracy (CSSDCA) Memorandum of Understanding; OAU/AU Declaration on Principles Governing Democratic Elections' AU Post-conflict and Reconstruction Policy Framework; New Partnership for Africa's Development (NEPAD) Declaration on Democracy, Political, Economic and Corporate Governance; Memorandum of Understanding on the African Peer Review Mechanism (APRM); and the Kigali Declaration on Gender Equality in Africa.

[27] "African Governance Architecture Framework," para. 9.

Four notable activities of the AGA Secretariat are briefly discussed below. These are: (a) the High Level Dialogues on governance, democracy and human rights; (b) AGP's supervisory role over the African Democracy Charter; (c) the youth engagement strategy; and (d) knowledge management.

High Level Dialogue on Governance, Democracy and Human Rights
The High Level Dialogue, which is regarded as the 'flagship' initiative of the AGA framework, has been annually hosted by the AGP since 2012. The dialogues are usually presided over by African personalities of the highest calibre, with a political, legal, diplomatic or international relations background. The purpose of these dialogues is to provide the much-needed environment conducive to candid, open and comprehensive conversations on the status of democracy, human rights and good governance on the continent. It is a platform that teases out comparative experiences and encounters by platform members for structural, legal and political reforms that can improve the state of governance on the continent. It is often preceded by pre-youth forums, in order to facilitate the inclusion of this specific interest group's insight in the proceedings. This is done in addition to an AU Commission-led comprehensive background paper that outlines the framework, content and scope of the dialogue, addressing pertinent questions and issues that will be covered at the dialogue.

Although non-binding, the overall outcomes deduced from the High Level Dialogues are submitted to the policy organs of the AU through the AUC Chairpersons Office for further deliberations, consideration and possible implementation.[28] To date, seven such High Level Dialogues have been hosted. The inaugural dialogue, which was hosted in Dakar, Senegal in 2012 focused on the state of democratic governance in Africa. The 2013 and 2014 dialogues, too, were hosted in Dakar and focused on the enhancement of constitutionalism and the rule of law in Africa, and the strengthening of governance in the resolution of conflicts in Africa, respectively. The 2015 dialogue, held in Kigali, Rwanda, dealt with the state of women's equal participation and leadership in political parties in Africa. The 2016 High Level Dialogue was hosted in Arusha, Tanzania. In implementation of Executive Council decision EX.CL/Dec.842(XXV) that declared 2016 as the 'African Year of Human Rights

---

[28] Rule 27 of the AGP Rules of Procedure.

with a particular focus on the Rights of Women', the fifth High Level Dialogue session gave particular attention to AU Member States efforts aimed at enhancing the status of women and girls on the continent.

South Africa hosted the sixth High Level Dialogue from the 6–8 December 2017 with a particular focus on enhancing participation and representation in governance in Africa. In line with its promotional role over the Democracy Charter, the sixth High Level Dialogue session was preceded by an expert seminar aimed at commemorating the 10th anniversary of the Democracy Charter. More recently, the seventh Dialogue was hosted in Gaborone, Botswana from 26 to 27 November 2018 christened 'Winning the fight against corruption: A sustainable path to Africa's transformation'. The meeting was preceded by a Gender pre-forum to strengthen stakeholders' appreciation of the gendered aspects of corruption and discuss innovative ways to enhance the position of women in the fight against corruption.[29]

Monitoring Mechanism of the African Democracy Charter

The AGP, under the coordination of the Department of Political Affairs (DPA), serves as the supervisory mechanism for the implementation of the African Democracy Charter.[30] To date, however, even though the Charter has received the required fifteen ratifications to come into force,[31] the Commission has received only one state party report from Togo on the implementation of the Democracy Charter.[32] Thus, the AGP's supervisory role remains dormant until such time as State reports are periodically received under the Democracy Charter. To improve on substantive outcomes, the AGP must make effective use of its role as an oversight body for the Democracy Charter. In practice, however, the APRM is more likely to spearhead this process of analysing state party reports primarily

---

[29] "Press Statement—2018 High Level Dialogue," November 25, 2018, accessed January 5, 2019, http://aga-platform.org/8HLDPress.

[30] Rule 4(a) of the AGP Rules of Procedure; articles 44, 45 and 49 of the African Democracy Charter.

[31] Article 48 of the Charter. Only 32 state parties had ratified the African Democracy Charter of January 7, 2019.

[32] "Togo, First AU Member State to Submit State Report on African Charter on Democracy, Elections and Governance," African Union, March 27, 2017, accessed February 27, 2018, https://au.int/en/pressreleases/20170327/togo-first-au-member-state-submit-state-report-african-charter-democracy.

because it has a longstanding record and experience in handling State party reports relating to democracy and governance.

Once States start submitting their reports to the Commission, the AGP is better suited to use this monitoring process to mobilise States to implement the provisions of the Democracy Charter. The AGP may also initiate a popularisation programme solely focused on convincing States to ratify the Democracy Charter. Such an initiative would ideally aim at having regular consultations with States that have ratified the Democracy Charter based on their periodic reports and the AU Commission's concluding observations. In order to be more meaningful and yield more substantive outcomes, the AGP must be more creative with its mandate of being an oversight body over the Democracy Charter.

Youth Engagement Strategy (AGA-YES)

The African Youth Engagement Strategy (YES) is a strategy introduced by the AGA Secretariat to engage the African youth on the developments (policy, institutional or administrative) taking place under the AU governance framework. The YES seeks to aggregate youth voices in the programmes and projects as well as the policymaking processes and organs of the AU. The YES initiative is imperative, given the reality that the African youth population is rapidly growing. By 2015, the African youth population was estimated at 226 million, aged 15–24 years (excluding the youth in the Diaspora), accounting for 19% of the global youth population.[33] The AGA Secretariat's methodology of youth engagement is premised on periodic youth consultations and pre-youth forums. For example, in 2018, the regional youth consultation took place in Casablanca, Morocco (North Africa) from 19–21 September 2018, Dakar, Senegal (Central and West Africa) from 5–7 September 2018, and Gaborone, Botswana (East and Southern Africa) from 15–17 September 2018.[34] The consultations focused on 'Leveraging youth capacities for the fight against corruption', framed after the AU's theme for 2018, dubbed 'Winning the fight against corruption: A sustainable path for

[33] "Factsheet: Youth Population Trends and Sustainable Development," United Nations (2015): 1–2, accessed October 12, 2016, http://www.un.org/en/development/desa/population/publications/pdf/popfacts/PopFacts_2015-1.pdf.

[34] "Leveraging Youth Capacities for the Fight Against Corruption: Report of 2018 Regional Youth Consultations," Published December 2018, accessed January 6, 2019, http://aga-platform.org/sites/default/files/2018-12/AGA2018RegionalReport_Webnew.pdf.

Africa's transformation'. Since 2014, the High Level Dialogue has been preceded by a pre-youth forum, and the issues covered at that consultation ranged from youth participation in peace building processes, to the role of youth in fostering accountability, responsive and effective governance in Africa, as well as youth involvement in political processes for sustainable peace in Africa.[35] Similar pre-youth forums were held in 2016 and 2017, premised on the AU theme of the year.[36]

Knowledge Management

The AGA Secretariat also spearheads an information production and dissemination system essential to its mandate. Through its ongoing knowledge management system, the Secretariat strives to facilitate 'dialogue and share comparable lessons as well as generate and contribute to knowledge on trends, challenges, opportunities and prospects for improving governance and democracy in Africa'.[37] However, there is hardly any indication that this important administrative mechanism is effectively utilised nor is it serving its purpose. For the institutional memory of the AGA secretariat to survive, it cannot afford to manage the interactions and knowledge production between its various stakeholders on a provisional basis. To do so will be to leave room for many of the AGP's works to slip through the cracks. To be impactful, it must be overhauled, resourced and well-financed to meet the larger aspirations of the AGA framework.

Composition of the AGA Secretariat

The AGA Secretariat is superintended by the DPA and operates within the superstructure of the AU Commission, the overall secretariat of all the organs and institutions of the African Union.[38] As such, the DPA

---

[35] The event was held under the theme: "Silencing the Guns: Youth Building a Culture of Democracy and Peace in Africa."

[36] Consultations for the Southern African region held in Windhoek, Namibia, September 8–9, 2016; West Africa region consultations held in Accra, Ghana, August 23–24, 2016; Central and Eastern Africa regional consultations held in Kampala, Uganda, September 2016; North Africa region consultations held in Tunis, Tunisia, September 28–29, 2016.

[37] "What We Do—AGA Areas of Focus," accessed January 5, 2019, http://aga-platform.org/what-we-do.

[38] Articles 5(1)(e) and 20 of the Constitutive Act (establishes the Commission is an organ and as the secretariat of the Union); Statute of the African Union Commission on International Law article 3 for the broader functions of the Commission.

hosts the Secretariat of the AGA, including its clusters. The AGP and its secretariat collectively are compartmentalised into thematic clusters aimed at enforcing the overall objectives of the AGA. In terms of Rule 5 of the Rules of Procedure of the AGP, five clusters have been identified, namely: Democracy and Elections cluster,[39] Human Rights and Transitional Justice cluster,[40] Constitutionalism and Rule of Law cluster,[41] Socio-economic, Service Delivery and Urbanisation cluster (formerly Governance cluster),[42] and Humanitarian Affairs cluster[43] (see Fig. 1 for the original structure of the AGA Secretariat).

As a result of this structural orientation, the DPA gives direction to the AGP's operational and financial functioning. Although the AGA Secretariat operates within the DPA, it is not clear whether the Secretariat is equal to a division of the DPA, and there is still some considerable uncertainty as to the status and place of the AGA Secretariat. This confusion is further exacerbated by the fact that its clusters simultaneously serve as the units within the two main divisions of the DPA. The

---

[39] Rule 5(1)(a) of the Rules of Procedure of the AGP. The cluster serves as the overall coordinating mechanism for all democracy and elections processes that falls within the ambit of the AUC. The work of the cluster is largely supported and carried out by the Democracy and Electoral Assistance Unit (DEAU) within the DPA. It carries out democracy assessments of AU member States as well as undertakes electoral observation missions, including providing electoral support and training to AU member States.

[40] Rule 5(1)(b) of the Rules of Procedure of the AGP. The cluster bears the primary responsibility to interact and engage with AU organs and institutions, AU member States and regional economic communities in the promotion and protection of human (and peoples') rights on the continent. Its mandate also includes work relating to transitional and post-conflict reconstruction processes.

[41] Rule 5(1)(c) of the Rules of Procedure of the AGP. The Constitutionalism and Rule of law cluster aims at promoting constitutionalism and rule of law principles and processes amongst AU member States. It also seeks to provide support to AU member States in constitutional reform and State building processes.

[42] Rule 5(1)(d) of the Rules of Procedure of the AGP. Previously referred to as the governance cluster, this cluster is aimed at addressing issues that have a direct impact on member States governance. These issues include but are not limited to; public service delivery, globalization, urbanisation, political processes, urban development, political accountability and resource management.

[43] Rule 5(1)(e) of the Rules of Procedure of the AGP. The humanitarian affairs cluster is responsible for coordinating responses to emergency situations relating to AU member States. It engages AU organs and institutions in developing responses to conflict, disaster and humanitarian crisis situations. Its scope also includes work relating to refugees, migration, as well as internally displaced persons.

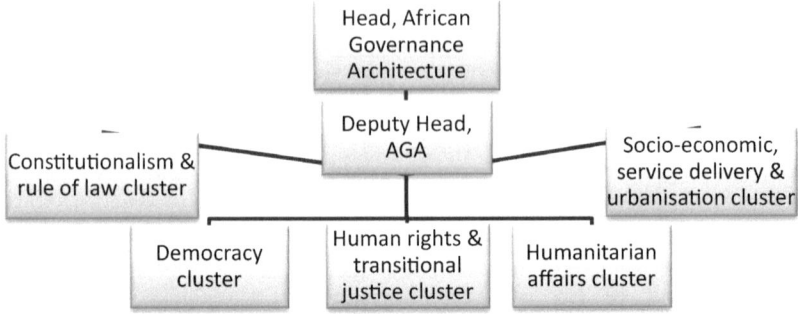

Fig. 1 Previous internal structure of the AGA Secretariat

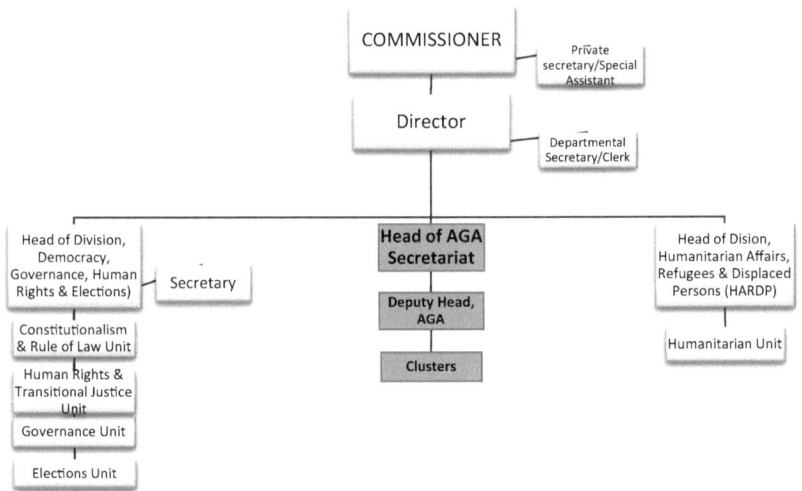

Fig. 2 Current location and structure of the DPA and the AGA Secretariat

impression is given that the Secretariat does not fall within the formal structural setting of the DPA and that its seat is merely to render administrative support to the divisional units of the DPA and the activities and projects of the AGA. This situation leads to an overlap and duplication of work and efforts between the DPA and the AGA Secretariat (see Fig. 2 for the current structure of the AGA Secretariat as of January 2019).

The African Governance Facility

To support the initiatives and programmes of the AGP, an African Governance Facility ('Facility') was established as a strategic component of the AGA framework 'towards the promotion of and consolidation of democratic governance on the continent'.[44] The Facility was established as one of the resource mobilisation strategies of the AGP. It is jointly owned and resourced by AGP members and AU Member States as a way to sustain the AGP's initiatives. Presently, the Facility is managed by the Commission and therefore administered under the rules and regulations on AU finances.

4 Challenges and Opportunities

Both the OAU and its successor organisation, the AU, have birthed important instruments, organs, institutions and initiatives that are relevant for good governance in Africa, and the AGA Framework should be counted among these. However, despite these commendable developments over the past 50 years, the realisation of good governance in Africa remains a major challenge.[45] The challenge lies in the lack of consolidation and integration of AU organs. Institutions and initiatives like the AGA and the AGP are well-placed to fill this gap. What this Framework has done to date to harmonise AU organs and instruments with a human rights, democracy, and governance mandate is commendable given the limited time within which it has been operational—2019 being its eighth year of existence. Yet the challenges and, perhaps, opportunities underlying it are formidable, and need to be interrogated, explored, and reform measures put in place, if the AGA is to yield more substantive outcomes.

Like most of the initiatives under the African human rights system, the AGA and the AGP face tremendous challenges. While the political will to advance the mandates of the AGP seems to be in place, funding has largely limited the operational capacity of the Platform and its Secretariat. The Secretariat, as is the case with most AU organs and

---

[44] "African Governance Architecture Framework," para. 13.

[45] Anton Bösl and Joseph Diescho, eds., *Human Rights in Africa: Legal Perspectives on Their Protection and Promotion* (Windhoek: Macmillan Education Namibia, 2009), 1–210; John Akokpari and Daniel Zimbler, *Africa's Human Rights Architecture* (Cape Town: Centre for Conflict Resolution, 2008), 1–126.

institutions, relies heavily on external funding. This potentially limits its direction and operational focus, and colours a worrisome picture of the structural, financial and institutional independence of the Platform. As it stands, an ad hoc system of funding does not augur well for the sustainability of the Secretariat, and there is a need for strategies to be put in place to secure financial resources in order to ensure its effective, independent and semi-autonomous functioning.

The question however remains, how best can the Framework become financially independent? The response to this question is complex. The AGA and the AGP operate within the Commission and thus depend on the Commission for financial support. Any attempt to make the AGA Secretariat and the AGP financially sustainable will therefore have to begin with the Commission. One avenue to resolve this problem is for the AGA Secretariat and the AGP to establish a Democracy and Governance Fund (DGF) to support their activities. Ideally, such a fund should be directed at consolidating all the financial schemes administered under the AGA framework, such as the Facility and the Democracy and Electoral Assistance Fund (DEAF) in order to do away with the current trend of disjointed financial mobilisation.[46] The AGA and the AGP can use the framework of the DGF to engage States (and external stakeholders where appropriate) to financially support the work of the fund and partly subsidise its activities and programmes by offering to host the activities and functions of the AGP, or alternatively by way of direct financial contributions to the DGF. Another possibility is the sourcing of financial contributions internally by requesting or obligating AU organs and agencies to make periodic and/or annual financial contributions. Alternatively, another feasible possibility is that a Sub-Committee on Democracy and Governance may be established within the AU Permanent Representative Committee (PRC) so as to get more support politically and financially from Member States.

Also worthy of note is that the Platform's overarching mandate of being the 'overall political and institutional framework for the promotion, protection and sustenance of democracy, governance, human rights and humanitarian assistance on the continent',[47] is a burdensome responsibility. This requires tremendous coordination and interaction

[46]Articles 18(1) and 44(2) of the African Democracy Charter.
[47]"African Governance Architecture Framework," 5.

between Platform members and AU organs mandated with governance, human rights, democracy and humanitarian affairs. The continental nature of the respective mandates of the Platform's members, with offices across Africa, coupled with the budgetary challenges enumerated above, account for weak ties between AGP members and AU Member States, and the AGA Framework has been heavily criticised on this score.[48] This is particularly true of the weak synergies between the APSA (and principally its enforcement mechanism, the PSC) and the APRM, on the one hand, and the AGA and the AGP on the other.

In terms of workflow, the AGA and the PSC have launched and undertaken several discussions on how best to strengthen the linkages between the APSA and the AGA. So far, discussions and engagements on mutual cooperation have taken place through periodic informal and formal meetings. An interdepartmental task force has already been formed to deepen the synergies between and among Platform members on the development of the AGA-APSA Roadmap. This is a commendable step that must further be cemented.

Equally of note is the use of the concept 'governance' in the portmanteau 'African Governance Architecture', which cannot be equated to the concept of 'good governance' as envisaged in the Constitutive Act.[49] It is only logical that since the Constitutive Act makes reference to 'good governance' as opposed to mere 'governance', the framing of the AGA should have followed a similar trend of wording.

Also, the AGP's direct engagement with States, as compared to citizens and the youth, has been marginal. This is a major shortcoming on the part of the AGP. States are central to the implementation of regional treaties, declarations and resolutions. It is States that spearhead domestic resource, budgeting and decision-making processes. States bear the primary responsibility to respect, promote, defend and fulfil

---

[48] Khabele Matlosa, "The African Union's African Governance Architecture Linkages with the African Peace and Security Architecture," *GREAT Insight Magazine* 4, no. 1 (2014): 26–32; Tissi and Aggad-Clerx, "The Road Ahead," 13–16; George Wachira, "Consolidating the African Governance Architecture," *Southern African Institute of International Affairs (SAIIA) Policy Briefing* 1, 96 (2014): 3–4 and 43.

[49] See also similar arguments by Sabelo Gumedze, "The Challenges Facing Africa's Emerging Governance Architecture," Institute for Security Studies Blog, September 22, 2011: 1–12, accessed March 22, 2018, https://issafrica.org/iss-today/the-challenges-facing-africas-emerging-governance-architecture.

human rights,[50] especially the rights of the most marginalised and disenfranchised in society. Thus, State engagement needs to be vigorously pursued by the AGP. In fact, direct State engagement needs to permeate its operations. The current fluid relationship with States has immensely contributed to the minimal impact that the architecture has had on universal State ratification and implementation of AU instruments and policies on the continent. In the context of human rights, to date, only the African Charter on Human and Peoples' Rights (1981) has received near universal State ratification. More State engagement and mobilisation can assist in improving the status quo of low ratifications of AU legal instruments, particularly those pertaining to human rights and good governance.

The appendage of the AGA to the DPA tends to dash any hope of independence that a supposed treaty-monitoring mechanism should possess. As the primary AU mechanism responsible for monitoring the implementation of the African Democracy Charter, its authority to monitor state party compliance in an independent and fair manner must be impeccable. At present, the lack of any objective criteria for the appointment of AGP representatives or the AGA staff suggests that it is not immune to the vagaries of external influence. Also, the AGA Secretariat's functioning within the DPA, as illustrated in Fig. 2, apart from being an overlap and duplication of work and efforts, means that it is under constant monitoring by top echelon AUC leadership and politically exposed personnel. One only envisages that in the near future, the AGA Secretariat will be detached from the DPA and serve as an autonomous or semi-autonomous organ, more along the semblance of the African Commission on Human and Peoples' Rights, or the PSC.

Perhaps, the biggest criticism one can level against the Platform and its Secretariat is the informal nature of its internal workings and the misfortune of understaffing. For over half a decade of its existence, its processes were carried out in a casual manner without clearly defined bureaucracy. Such a mode of operation could be problematic. While a working atmosphere that is simple and less process bound has its obvious advantages, it can also conversely mean that the expected outputs will most likely not draw the much-needed attention and urgency from strategic bodies and individuals that have enforcement authority. Since the deliberations emanating from the AGP and its Secretariat are

---

[50]Dugard John, *International Law: A South African Perspective*, 4th ed. (Cape Town: Juta and Company, 2014), 2–5.

non-binding, this weakens the operational impact that they can have on the AU's policy and decision-making processes.

Despite these challenges, the AGA framework remains incredibly relevant. Its impact, particularly in the context of promoting human rights and democratic values on the continent remains relevant to achieving the AU Agenda 2063. The AGA Secretariat and AGP remain committed to the long-term strategic plans of the AU. The annual High Level Dialogues and youth consultations are strategies targeted at directly engaging citizens across the continent, by registering their concerns and suggestions on the policymaking and formulation processes of the AU. Another notable prospect of the AGP is its central role in promoting and pushing for State ratification of the African Democracy Charter. As of January 2019, thirty-two States have ratified the Charter.[51] One of the crucial functions of the AGP will be its monitoring and evaluation of State reports made in terms of article 49 of the Democracy Charter. In this regard, the knowledge management system of the Secretariat will prove even more relevant to create a coherent and unified approach in information gathering and dissemination on the activities, programmes and initiatives of all AGP members. Although progress is slow, largely due to the deficit of skilled personnel in this area, it remains a promising component of the AGA framework.

That the Platform, since its inception has been focused on process-bound initiatives such as dialogues and consultations, overlooks the importance of State engagement measures and processes. Its working operations have been non-confrontational, primarily orienting around advocacy and outreach. It seems to have also not clearly understood or embraced its oversight mandate, as it is lacking in its ability to strengthen synergies and relations between AU organs and institutions with a human rights, democracy and governance mandate. With much emphasis on democracy and governance themes, its human rights work is ancillary and barely visible. For the AGA Secretariat and the AGP to be viewed as avenues for realising human rights and good governance on the continent, including the AU's Agenda 2063 project, certain structural and substantive reforms must be introduced:

---

[51] "Ratification Status of the African Charter on Democracy, Elections and Governance," last modified September 29, 2018, accessed January 5, 2019, https://au.int/sites/default/files/treaties/7790-sl-african_charter_on_democracy_elections_and_governance.pdf; See also article 48 of the African Democracy Charter.

a. *Financial sustainability*

The Commission needs to revamp the current disjointed approach of mobilising resources on an ad hoc basis by establishing a consolidated fund that focuses on State, donors and development partners for funding. Ideally, such a fund should be directed at consolidating all the financial schemes administered under the AGA framework, such as the Facility and the DGF into one scheme and make use of its framework to engage States to financially support the work of the fund. To lessen the costs from its depleting funds, the Secretariat of the AGP can, if the option of direct State financial mobility fails, negotiate with States to subsidise the costs of any of its activities hosted in their territories as an indirect form of financial contribution to the funding scheme.

b. *Strengthening synergies between AGP members*

Despite most AGP members not being stationed together, the Secretariat and the AGP can still work on an integrated and inclusive approach in its operations. The establishment of inter-departmental taskforce or teams (as is the case between the DPA and the Department of Peace and Security) is commendable and should be explored by other AGP members. Since the AGP consists of a Secretariat that acts as the highest decision-making body, the Secretariat can give directive to all AGP members to take up at least one joint initiative or activity with another platform member annually. This can be a small but noble step towards joint effort and cooperation between AGP members. The Secretariat and the AGP should also make use of existing processes to carry out joint tasks. For example, the monitoring or implementing role under the African Democracy Charter can be done jointly by AGP members such as the African Commission on Human and Peoples' Rights, and the African Court on Human and Peoples' Rights, with technical support from the Secretariat.

c. *Conceptual clarifications*

The technical misuses in the definitions of AGA and AGP, as discussed above, should be reconsidered. It is recommended that rule 1 of the Rules of Procedure of the AGP be amended to reflect the primary intentions of the AGA framework documents. In particular, 'platform' as used in the definition of the AGA should be amended. The following definitions are proposed: 'African Governance Architecture' means the oversight and monitoring mechanism of all the African Union organs, RECs and institutions mandated to promote good governance, democracy, human rights and humanitarian affairs in Africa. 'African Governance Platform' means the institutional [or operational] mechanism and platform for dialogue between the various AU stakeholders on human rights and democratic governance.

d. *Strengthen AGA processes and organs*

Clearly, the Secretariat and the AGP can be more impactful if given more authority. More authority means that boosting the institutional capacity of the AGP to make recommendations and produce work outcomes. Considering the monitoring responsibility imposed by the Democracy Charter, it is hard to see how the AGP will be able to perform its monitoring role for all fifty-five states, if it is not adequately empowered to do so. The AU Assembly should consider giving more explicit decision-making powers to the AGP for stronger monitoring of state compliance with the Democracy Charter.

e. *Staff capacity and structural reforms of the AGA Secretariat*

Depending on its financial status, the Secretariat needs to increase its staff capacity to at least two additional personnel annually. Due to the nature of its work, such personnel should be primarily schooled (both academically and practically) in the social sciences, particularly, political science, sociology, human rights, international law, international relations, development studies and ICT since the Secretariat encounters a lack of skilled personnel in these fields. As argued in this chapter, the current stationing of the Secretariat within the DPA is controversial bearing in mind that the structural and institutional independence of the AGA Secretariat is at stake. The Secretariat should be given institutional autonomy such as the case with the African Commission on Human and Peoples' Rights. This is to enable the Secretariat and the AGP to serve as semi-autonomous bodies, independent and free from any actual or perceived interference.

5   Conclusion

In the final analysis, for good governance practices to take root and be widespread in Africa, as contemplated by the Constitutive Act, the African Democracy Charter and aspiration 3 of Agenda 2063, deeper engagement and synergies among AU institutions and Member States must take place for integration to happen. The establishment of a continental architecture on democratic governance in Africa is plausible in that respect. However, the realisation of its ultimate strategic objectives rests on the efficiency of its institutional processes. As much as the AGP provides an avenue for AU institutions and Member States to align their governance objectives in ways that best reflect the fundamental objectives and principles of the AU, its Platform and Secretariat's current operational methods and strategies raise pressing questions about the sustainability of the architecture, the authoritativeness of its treaty-monitoring mandate, and the quality of its impact. More than half a decade after its inauguration, there is still an urge to 'define its operational priorities and the role that existing governance instruments and actors can play to support its agenda'.[52] If the AGA framework is to function effectively as a policy response mechanism targeted at normative and institutional convergence on human rights, democracy and governance issues, its Platform and administrative processes, including its Secretariat will need to be overhauled and empowered to effectively steer a result-oriented dialogue on issues and their implementation. The major problem which is faced is the lack of ownership not only by Member States but also by Platform forums such as the RECs and the other AU organs. This analysis therefore identifies the trends and challenges that the AGP and its Secretariat must confront, and the opportunities presented by such a valuable undertaking.

---

[52]Tissi and Aggad-Clerx, "The Road Ahead," 8.

REFERENCES

Books and Edited Volumes

Akokpari, John, and Daniel Zimbler. *Africa's Human Rights Architecture*. Cape Town: Centre for Conflict Resolution, 2008.

Bösl, Anton, and Joseph Diescho, eds. *Human Rights in Africa: Legal Perspectives on Their Protection and Promotion*. Windhoek: Macmillan Education Namibia, 2009.

Dugard, John. *International Law: A South African Perspective*, 4th ed. Cape Town: Juta and Company, 2014.

Gluckman, Max. *The Allocation of Responsibility*. Manchester: Manchester University Press, 1986.

Gutto, Shadrack, ed. *Shared Values, Constitutionalism and Democracy in Africa*. Johannesburg: Fortune Africa Publishing, 2011.

Viljoen, Frans. *International Human Rights Law in Africa*, 2nd ed. Oxford: Oxford University Press, 2012.

Book Chapters

Ebobrah, Solomon. "Human Rights Realisation in the African Sub-Regional Institutions." In *The African Regional Human Rights System: 30 Years After the African Charter on Human and Peoples' Rights*, edited by Martinus Ssenyonjo, 283–300. Boston: Martinus Nijhoff Publishers, 2011.

M'Baye, Keba. "The African Conception of Law." In *The Legal Systems of the World and Their Common Comparison and Unification*, edited by René David, 42–64. London: Stevens and Sons, 1975.

Smith, Michael. "The Sociological Framework of Law." In *African Law: Adaptation and Development*, edited by Hilda Kuper and Leo Kuper, 24–50. Berkeley: University of California Press, 1965.

Journal Articles

Amvane, Gabriel. "Intervention Pursuant to Article 4(h) of the Constitutive Act of the African Union Without United Nations Security Council Authorization." *African Human Rights Law Journal* 15, no. 2 (2005): 282–298.

Elvy, Stacy-Ann. "Towards a New Democratic Africa: The African Charter on Democracy, Elections and Governance." *Emory International Law Review* 27, no. 1 (2013): 43–113.

Glen, Patrick. "Institutionalising Democracy in Africa: A Comment on the African Charter on Democracy, Elections and Governance." *Africa Journal of Legal Studies* 5, no. 1 (2012): 149–175.

Kane, Ibrahima. "The Implementation of the African Charter on Democracy, Elections and Governance." *Africa Security Review* 17, no. 4 (2008): 43–63.

Mapaure, Clever. "Reinvigorating African Values for SADC: The Relevance of Traditional African Philosophy of Law in a Globalising World of Competing Perspectives." *SADC Law Journal* 1, no. 1 (2011): 149–173.

Matlosa, Khabelo. "The African Union's African Governance Architecture Linkages with the African Peace and Security Architecture." *GREAT Insight Magazine* 4, no. 1 (2014): 8–11.

Tissi, Nicolla, and Faten Aggad-Clerx. "The Road Ahead for the African Governance Architecture: An Overview of Current Challenge and Possible Solutions." *South Africa Institute for International Affairs Policy Brief* 174, no. 1 (2014): 1–22.

Wachira, George. "Consolidating the African Governance Architecture." *Southern African Institute of International Affairs Policy Briefing* 1, 96 (2014): 1–4.

Web Sources

Gumedze, Sabelo. "The Challenges Facing Africa's Emerging Governance Architecture." Institute for Security Studies Blog, September 22, 2011: 1–12. Accessed March 22, 2018, https://issafrica.org/iss-today/the-challenges-facing-africas-emerging-governance-architecture.

Viljoen, Frans. "The Realisation of Human Rights in Africa Through Inter-Governmental Institutions." LLD Thesis, University of Pretoria, South Africa, 1997, 1–743. Accessed September 12, 2016, http://repository.up.ac.za/dspace/handle/2263/27810?show=full.

PART II

Constitutional and Judicial Protection of Human Rights

CHAPTER 4

Interdependence Versus Checks and Balances of Power: A Reflection on the Role of Constitutional Court in South Africa

Ademola Oluborode Jegede and Sidogi Tendani

1 INTRODUCTION

Due to the colonial link of South Africa to Britain for several decades, South Africa adopted for a long time the Westminster model of governance that allowed for parliamentary sovereignty, a concept which signifies that the law-making function of the Parliament is not subjected to review by courts.[1] Another distinguishing feature of the model is that there is no clear separation between the executive and legislative branches of government in that members of the Executive also served as members of the Legislature.[2] What is indeed clear about the era is that a number

---

[1] Danie Brand et al., eds., *South African Constitutional Law in Context* (Cape Town: Oxford University Press Southern (Pty) Limited, 2014).

[2] Ibid., 43.

A. O. Jegede (✉) · S. Tendani
School of Law, University of Venda, Thohoyandou, South Africa

© The Author(s) 2020   71
M. Addaney et al. (eds.), *Governance, Human Rights,
and Political Transformation in Africa*,
https://doi.org/10.1007/978-3-030-27049-0_4

of legislation passed to legitimize racial discrimination and dispossess peoples of their lands was beyond judicial scrutiny in South Africa.[3] However, as part of the negotiation process to end apartheid and birth a democratic dispensation, it was proposed and agreed at the Convention for a Democratic South Africa (CODESA), that the final Constitution should embrace the system of checks and balances.[4] Consequently the constitutional principle VI of the resultant Interim Constitution provided that "the final Constitution shall provide for separation of powers between the Legislature, Executive and the Judiciary with appropriate checks and balances to ensure accountability, responsiveness and openness."[5] Similarly, although the final Constitution, that is, the 1996 Constitution does not expressly mention checks and balances, it establishes not only the division of state power between the legislative, judicial and executive branches.[6] In particular, the Constitution establishes the Constitutional Court as the final voice on all constitutional and human rights-related matters among the government and the governed, and more importantly, it vests the courts with the power to review parliamentary actions.[7] Also in terms of the 1996 Constitution, the Executive is not spared from judicial scrutiny, in particular, in relation to the realization of socio-economic rights. However, the involvement of the judiciary in reviewing the activities of these organs has not occurred without criticisms. For instance, it has been argued that judges lack both the constitutional mandate, the institutional expertise and the democratic legitimacy to hand down orders impacting on government's social and economic priorities.[8] Regarding legislative action, the criticisms are premised on the position that judicial review is inherently undemocratic

[3] Examples of such legislation include Native Land Act 27 of 1913, Prohibition of Mixed Marriages Act of 1949, Suppression of Communism Act 44 of 1950 and Bantu Education Act 47 of 1953

[4] Pieter Labuschagne, "The Doctrine of Separation of Powers and Its Application in South Africa," *Politeia* 23, no. 3 (2004): 53.

[5] Interim Constitution of South Africa Act 200 of 1993 (Interim Constitution 1993).

[6] Constitution of the Republic of South Africa, 1996 (South African Constitution 1996); This chapter, and Chapters 5 and 8 dealing respectively with powers of the Parliament, Executive and the Judiciary in South Africa

[7] Ibid., section 165.

[8] Anashri Pillay, "Toward Effective Social and Economic Rights Adjudication: The Role of Meaningful Engagement," *International Journal of Constitutional Law* 10, no. 3 (2012): 733

and therefore ill-suited to resolving disputes on complex political issues which fall within the domain of legislators.[9]

Nonetheless, as has been argued, the main objective of the above arrangement is to ensure separation of power and allow for checks and balances whereby the branches of government regulate each other and prevent the abuse of power.[10] Whether or not the objective is in fact to support the interdependence of the executive, legislature and judiciary and not simply rigid adherence to separation of powers merits an examination. If construed as a means of ensuring an interdependence that meets checks and balances purpose, whether or not the interventions of courts in relation to the works of the branches of government aid similar reasoning equally deserves some reflection. This contribution demonstrates that although there is textual division of state power between the Legislature, Judiciary and Executive in the Constitution, in practice, the main end of this division is to achieve interdependence of the executive, legislature and judiciary that allows the branches of government to be complementary as well as serve as checks and balances on one another. This argument is further reinforced by the analysis of judicial interventions by the Constitutional Court in South Africa.

2   Interdependence of Arms of Government Versus Checks and Balances

As evident in this chapter and Chapters 5 and 8 of the Constitution dealing respectively with powers of the Parliament, Executive and the Judiciary in South Africa, the Legislature, Executive and Judiciary are distinct institutions. Their functioning is not, however, totally independent of one another as shall be made manifest. The Constitution, in terms of its provisions and application allows for an overlap in the interactions among different arms of government signifying an interdependent relationship which does not foreclose the application of checks and balances among these branches. Literally, the strict understanding of the idea of interdependence of arms of government appears inconsistent with checks

---

[9] Annabelle Lever, "Is Judicial Review Democratic?" *Public Law* (2007): 285; Jeremy Waldron, "The Core of the Case Against Judicial Review," *Yale Law Journal* 115, no. 6, (2006): 1346

[10] Phineas Mojapelo, "The Doctrine of Separation of Powers: A South African Perspective," *Advocate* (2013): 39.

and balances which is largely in contemporary constitutional development traceable to the application of separation of powers in the United States system. Under that system, there is distinct and notable separation of personnel and functions between the branches of government. For example, the President and the cabinet are clearly not members of the Parliament.[11] In South Africa, however, interdependence of relationship allows for members of the Executive to serve as partial members of the Legislature.[12] This dual or interdependent membership by Executive members and the Parliament is the result of the influence of the Westminster system which was in operation before 1994.[13] This signifies that despite the institutional separation between the Executive, the Legislature and the Judiciary, there can be an overlap of personnel and functions in the constitutional role of these three branches.

For instance, the main function of the Legislature as set out in the Constitution is to "amend the Constitution, to pass legislation, to assign any of its legislative powers, except the power to amend the Constitution to other legislative bodies in another sphere of government,"[14] while the Executive power is allocated to the President and his cabinet.[15] Yet the Executive is involved in the law-making process, for instance, the Constitution provides that Executive members must initiate and introduce legislation to the Parliament.[16] Also, the President as the head of the Executive is involved in the legislative function since he is required to either assent to and sign passed bills into law.[17] Far from only performing law-making role, the legislature has other constitutional function which requires it to oversee the activities of all cabinet members in line with the provision of the Constitution that they must be held accountable individually and collectively to the Parliament and must regularly provide reports concerning the execution of their duties.[18]

---

[11] Pieter (n. 4), 34.

[12] South African Constitution 1996 (n. 6), Chapter 4.

[13] Sherilyn Naidoo, "Does the Lack of Sufficient Formulation and Articulation of the Principles Guiding Limits of the Constitutional Court Undermine Its Legitimacy?" (LLM dissertation, University of Cape Town, South Africa 2014), 9.

[14] South African Constitution 1996 (n. 6), section 44(1).

[15] Ibid., section 85(1).

[16] Ibid., section 85(2)(d).

[17] Ibid., section 79(1).

[18] Ibid., section 92(1).

Although, functions of the branches are overlapping, the above arrangement does not foreclose the application of checks and balances in that the main aim of this interaction is to make these branches accountable to each other and ensure smooth running of the government.[19] In the *First Certification* case some negotiators of CODESA argued that the overlap of powers between the Executive and the Parliament is incompatible with the separation of power envisaged under the Interim Constitution and will undermine checks and balances in the fulfillment of constitutional role. Accordingly, they submitted that the 1996 Constitution should adopt separation of powers which complies with the principle of separation of personnel and functions.[20] The Constitutional Court held that separation of powers is not a fixed constitutional doctrine and can be subjected to different modification.[21] Arguably, for the Court to decide otherwise would have undermined the idea of interdependence which underlies the interaction of the different arms of government. In fact as De Waal and Currie argue, checks and balances set out in section 92 of the Constitution which requires Ministers to account to the Parliament will not work effectively if the ministers are not members of the Legislature.[22]

The concern regarding the lack of separation of personnel and functions appears misplaced in that it does not foreclose the application of checks and balances among the branches of government as envisaged in the doctrine of separation of power. In practice, the Legislature checks and balances the powers possessed by the Executive by electing and removing the state President.[23] It also checks the Executive by requiring both the state President and Ministers to appear before the National Assembly to answer questions from parliament members concerning the exercise of their powers.[24] The Executive, on the other hand, checks the Legislature by taking part in the law-making process while the President

---

[19] Brand et al. (n. 1), 91.

[20] Interim Constitution 1993 (n. 5), schedule 4.

[21] *Certification of the Constitution of the Republic of South Africa* 1996 (4) SA 744 (CC), paras. 108–112.

[22] Iain Currie and Johan de Waal, *The New Constitutional & Administrative Law* (Cape Town: Juta, 2001), 97.

[23] South African Constitution 1996 (n. 6), section 89.

[24] Ibid., section 55(2)(b).

should assent to and sign national Bills before they come into force.[25] The President or the Premier, as the case may be, may also refer a Bill to the Constitutional Court if the President or the Premier has objections about its constitutionality. The President or the premier has the power to decide when the legislation will come into force.[26] This provision allows the President or Premier to act as checks on the power of the Parliament to legislate as it makes it likely that neither the President nor the Premier will approve for implementation a legislation of doubtful constitutional status.

Similarly, evidence of interdependence among the arms of government is as feasible in the interaction of the Legislature and Executive with the Judiciary as the application of checks and balances. For instance, the Constitution confers judicial powers on courts which are said to be independent and only subject to the constitution,[27] but, this does not mean that the Executive and Parliament are not involved in the functioning of the Court. Members of the Executive and Parliament take part in the appointment of judges.[28] In terms of section 177(1) of the Constitution, members of the Legislature together with the members of the Executive, indeed, form part of the Judicial Service Commission which is responsible for appointment of judges. The Executive also balances the powers possessed by courts by executing orders of courts. The Constitution generally provides in section 171 that courts must exercise their powers in terms of the national legislation which is passed by the Legislature. As Currie and De Waal argue, the Legislature checks the Judiciary by passing legislation that regulates the exercise of powers by courts.[29] Hence, in the context of the interaction of the Legislature and Executive with the Judiciary, it is safe to assert that the notion of interdependence only means that neither the Executive nor the Parliament can interfere in the performance of the role of the Judiciary. While one can argue that interference of the Judiciary into the activities of other branches is also precluded, there should be no difficulty in accepting that intervention by the Judiciary is a given. The core business of the Judiciary as set out by the Constitution is, through its decisions, to

---

[25] Ibid., section 79.

[26] Mojapelo (n. 10), 56.

[27] South African Constitution 1996 (n. 6), section 165.

[28] Currie and De Waal (n. 22), 113.

[29] Ibid., 117.

intervene and not to be interfered with in its interventions. In terms of section 165 of the Constitution, courts are independent and subject only to the Constitution and the law, and no person or organ of state may interfere with the functioning of courts. However, the courts, and for that matter, the Constitutional Court can review and overturn legislation as well as executive acts or inaction, and as shall be made manifest in the next section, it has in fact done so on a number of occasions.

The next section addresses how courts have intervened in the tensions arising from the interaction among different arms of government by focusing on case law concerning the relationship between these branches. In doing so, emphasis is placed on the Constitutional Court because in addition to being the highest court in South Africa and the final voice on any legal question, the Court is established to protect the Constitution and to guard against any violation of rights contained therein.[30] As De Vos argues, the establishment of the Constitutional Court was a significant move to ensure progressive democracy in South Africa.[31] As evident in the ensuing discussion, it has played a pivotal role in the application of checks and balances in the democratic development of South Africa.

3   THE CONSTITUTIONAL COURT AS A CHECK OF TENSIONS RELATED TO INTERDEPENDENT ROLE

This argument that the relationship between the branches of government can be complementary does not deny that tensions do arise from the interdependence among the various arms of government. This is well evident by the analysis of judicial interventions by the Constitutional Court in tensions that feature in the interaction between the Legislature and the Executive, between the Judiciary and Legislature, and between the Judiciary and the Executive in South Africa.

3.1   *Legislature and Executive*

In the majority of cases where the legislative and executive branches were in dispute the Constitutional Court held that the intrusions of one into the functioning of the other are justifiable as checks and balances.

---

[30] South African Constitution 1996 (n. 6), section 167(3)

[31] Brand et al. (n. 1), 209.

In *Executive Council Western Cape Legislature v President of Republic of South Africa*,[32] the Constitutional Court was faced with the question as to whether the national parliament may delegate law-making power to the Executive. The Constitutional Court held that the Legislature may not delegate complete law-making powers to the Executive. However, it may delegate subsidiary law-making powers. In the case, the Western Cape provincial government approached the Court for an order declaring section 16 of the Local Government Transition Act[33] to be invalid and unconstitutional in so far as it empowers the President to amend the Local Government Transition Act by publishing a Proclamation in the Gazette. Majority of judges agreed that the Parliament must have powers to delegate law-making powers. According to the Court:

> The legislative authority vested in Parliament under s 37 of the Constitution is expressed in wide terms - 'to make laws for the Republic in accordance with this Constitution'. In a modern State detailed provisions are often required for the purpose of implementing and regulating laws and Parliament cannot be expected to deal with all such matters itself. There is nothing in the Constitution which prohibits Parliament from delegating subordinate regulatory authority to other bodies. The power to do so is necessary for effective law-making. It is implicit in the power to make laws for the country and I have no doubt that under our Constitution parliament can pass legislation delegating such legislative functions to other bodies.[34]

The above decision connotes that the Constitution does not prohibit the delegation of law-making powers to the Executive and that such procedure is not necessarily in violation of the principle of checks and balances.

3.2   Judiciary and Legislature

The Judiciary is vested with judicial review powers, connoting that courts can inevitably interfere with the Parliament processes.[35]

---

[32] *Executive Council Western Cape Legislature v President of Republic of South Africa* (10) BCLR 1289 (B).

[33] Local Government Transition Act 209 of 1993.

[34] *Executive Council, Western Cape Legislature v President of the Republic of South Africa*, para. 57.

[35] South African Constitution 1996 (n. 6), section 165.

This is well evident as courts are often called upon to adjudicate over disputes arising from legislative processes. In *Speaker of the National Assembly v De Lille (Speaker v De Lille)*,[36] as a result of statement made by one of opposition parties member in the National Assembly, Ms Patricia De Lille the then leader of Independent Democrats (ID) alleged that she was in possession of evidence that some members of the ruling party the (ANC), had been spies for the apartheid government. The Speaker of the Parliament ruled that it was unparliamentary to call some members of the Parliament "spies" and ordered her to withdraw her comments which she did. The speaker later appointed a committee to deal with the De Lille issue, which subsequently recommended her punishment. Ms De Lille then approached the Court to challenge the decision to suspend her taken by the National Assembly. The Cape High Court ruled in her favor and set aside the resolution. On the appeal by the Speaker of the Assembly to the Supreme Court of Appeal (SCA), the Court held that "the question that had to be considered was whether Parliament had any lawful authority to take any steps to suspend one of its members in these circumstances." The Speaker argued that section 57 of the Constitution which allows the National Assembly to determine and control its internal activities was the basis of its power. Mahomed CJ stated that the possibility that a member of the Parliament may be suspended for something said in the assembly impedes freedom of expression in parliament.[37]

The other case which dealt with the relationship between the Judiciary and the Parliament is the case of *Pharmaceutical Manufacturers Association of SA and Others.*[38] In this case, the Court was confronted with the question relating to the extent of the power of the President in legislative process, in particular, whether the exercise of such power amounts to law-making by the Executive. In examining the powers of the President in law-making processes, Chaskalson CJ reasoned as follows:

---

[36] *Speaker of the National Assembly v De Lille (Speaker v De Lille)*, 1998 (3) SA 430 (C).

[37] Ibid., para. 20.

[38] *Pharmaceutical Manufacturers Association of SA and Others: in re: Ex parte Application of the President of the RSA and Others* 2000 (2) SA 674.

The power is derived from legislation and is close to the administrative process. In my view, however, the decisions to bring the law into operation did not constitute administrative action. When he purported to exercise the power, the President was neither making the law, nor administering it. Parliament had made the law, and the Executive would administer it once it had been brought into force. The power vested in the President thus lies between the law-making process and the administrative process. The exercise of that power requires a political judgment as to when the legislation should be brought into force, a decision that is necessarily antecedent to the implementation of the legislation which comes into force only when the power is exercised. In substance the exercise of the power is closer to the legislative process than the administrative process.[39]

The Court then held that the President's power is subject to judicial review to check its constitutionality, and ordered to have the Executive proclamation by the President set aside.[40]

In *Doctors for Life International v Speaker of the National Assembly and Others*,[41] the main issue was whether the Constitutional Court may interfere with the processes of the Parliament in order to ensure public involvement in the law-making processes. The applicant challenged the Parliament for failing to comply with the constitutional provision which requires public involvement when the Parliament is passing laws. The Parliament had passed four statutes without engaging the public. The applicant approached the Constitutional Court to determine whether or not the Parliament failure to comply with constitutional provision was constitutional. The applicant based its application on section 167 of the Constitution which provides that only the Constitutional Court may decide that the Parliament has failed to achieve a constitutional duty. Upon hearing the matter, the Constitutional Court acknowledged that the Parliament is the major law-making branch of the state, which has the power to regulate its own proceedings, hence, should not be disturbed while carrying out its functions.[42] According to the further view of the Constitutional Court, if the Parliament were always to explain its

---

[39] *Speaker v De Lille* (n. 36), para. 34.

[40] Ibid., para. 36.

[41] *Doctors for Life International v Speaker of the National Assembly and Others* 2006 (6) SA 416 (CC) (*Doctors for Life*).

[42] Ibid., para. 36.

conduct in courts it would negatively affect government processes.[43] The Court, however, held that in so far as the legitimate procedure of the Parliament on public participation was not followed, the statutes should be set aside. The Constitutional Court justified encroaching into the legislative functions in this case by asserting its constitutional obligation to ensure that all organs of state act in line with the Constitution.[44] It then stated that it could only intrude in exceptional circumstances where rights of citizens are at risk of being grossly violated.[45]

The Constitutional Court also scrutinized the domain of the Legislature in the case of *United Democratic Movement v Speaker of the National Assembly (UDM v speaker)*.[46] In that case, the applicant applied to the Constitutional Court for an order compelling the Speaker of the National Assembly to prescribe that voting in the "motion of no confidence" against President Zuma should be conducted through secret ballot. In addressing this issue, the Constitutional Court held that the Executive must be subjected to extensive checks and balances to ensure accountability,[47] and that the Parliament has a duty to guard against abuse of power by the president and his cabinet. The Constitutional Court emphasized that when regular checks and balances are failing to hold the Executive accountable, it can intervene to hold the Executive accountable for breach of their Constitutional obligation.

In *Glenister v President of RSA and Others*,[48] the cabinet initiated legislation that will see the crime investigative institution known as the Scorpions merged with the South African Police Services (SAPS). The bill was already before the Parliament when the applicant applied for interdict in the Pretoria High Court. The application was rejected at the High Court on the basis that such an intervention will undermine the law-making powers of the Parliament. At the Constitutional Court, the applicant argued that court intervention will not amount to breach of the doctrine of separation of powers since South African model of separation of powers is flexible. Applicant further argued that courts

---

[43] Ibid., para. 37.

[44] Ibid., para. 38.

[45] Ibid., para. 39

[46] *United Democratic Movement v Speaker of the National Assembly (UDM v Speaker)* 2017 ZA (CC) 21

[47] Ibid., para. 7.

[48] *Glenister v President of RSA and Others 2009* (1) SA 287 (CC) (*Glenister* case)

are ultimate guardians of the Constitution and are given power to review conducts of other branches.[49] The respondents in this case (the President and the Minister of Justice and Constitutional Development) contended that intervention will amount to serious breach of the constitutional principle of separation of powers.[50] The Constitutional Court conceded that courts being the guardian of the Constitution are more likely to intrude into the domain of other branches when securing the Constitution. The Court further stated that it is an important component of separation of powers that courts oversee the exercise of state power by other branches of government.[51] In the circumstance, although the Court refused to intervene to stop the proposed bill, it clearly asserted it is within its purview to review the constitutionality of parliamentary functions.

Few of the cases which went to the Constitutional Court concern the invasion of the Judiciary by other branches, in particular, the Parliament. In *S v Dodo*,[52] however, the Constitutional Court had to deal with the tension between the Legislature and the Judiciary caused by the Legislature expanding its powers to the sphere of the Judiciary. In this case, the applicant challenged section 51(1) of the Criminal Law Amendment Act[53] which obliged judges in the High Court to sentence an accused to life imprisonment if the accused is found guilty of committing some particular offences stated in the Act. The section was initially declared invalid in the Eastern Cape High Court because it was found to be infringing the Constitution and the doctrine of separation of powers. The High Court stated that sentencing is primarily the duty of courts and that section 51 of the Criminal Law Amendment Act constitutes an invasion of the area of the Judiciary by the Legislature since it limits the discretion of judges in sentencing.

The Constitutional Court stated that the process of punishing offenders requires all branches to play part. The Executive must provide efficient resources to support the criminal justice system, while the Legislature determines which conduct should be criminalized and punished.[54]

---

[49] Ibid., para. 22.

[50] Ibid.

[51] Ibid., para. 33.

[52] *S v Dodo* 2001 (5) BCLR 423 (CC).

[53] Criminal Law Amendment Act 105 of 1997.

[54] *S v Dodo* (n. 52), para. 22.

The Court in support of its findings stated that checks and balances establish a significant aspect of separation of powers' principle. They prevent each branch of the state from becoming excessively powerful while performing functions allocated to it. The Court, however, dismissed the decision of the High Court and held that section 51 of the Criminal Law Amendment Act does not infringe separation of powers; it merely acts as checks and balances. This case indicates that although sentencing is primarily a Judiciary duty, parliaments remained active in the criminal justice system by passing laws regulating minimum sentence. In fact, the Court would have reached a similar and arguably a more coherent conclusion if it had based its analysis on the need for different arms of government to be inter-reliant, a reasoning which could have signified that the passing of such legislation by the Legislature is supportive of the role of the Judiciary.

3.3   Judiciary and Executive

The Constitutional Court is established by the Constitution as an independent entity vested with the power to review the constitutionality of all law and conduct of the Executive.[55] In *President of the Republic of South Africa v SARFU*, the President power to appoint a commission of inquiry was reviewed by the Constitutional Court. In this case, the then South African President Mr. Nelson Mandela appointed a commission of inquiry to investigate the state of affairs of the South African Rugby Federation Union which were alleged to be misusing its funds and discriminating black rugby players (SAFRU). The Constitutional Court held that it was ill-advised for the President to intrude into the daily running of SAFRU. The Constitutional Court emphasized that courts have powers to review any conduct by the President.

Arguably, the involvement of courts in the sphere of the Executive has become even more prominent as a result of the inclusion of socio-economic rights in the Constitution.[56] Socio-economic rights are those rights which entitle the citizens to resources of the state. These rights include the right to proper health care, right to housing, right to free

---

[55] South African Constitution 1996 (n. 6), section 164(4); see also, Sebastian Seedorf and Sanele Sibanda, "Seperation of Powers," in *Constitutional Law of South Africa*, ed. Stu Woolman et al. (Cape Town: Juta, 2013), 12–26.

[56] Patrick Lenta, "Democracy, Rights, Disagreements and Judicial Review," *South African Journal on Human Rights* 20, no. 1 (2004): 39.

basic education and etc.[57] The extent of the involvement of the Judiciary in ensuring the implementation of these rights is often a source of tension between the Executive who makes policy consideration on how resources of the State are to be utilized and courts' duty as interpreter of human rights. This category of rights causes a lot of tension between courts and Executive because the realization of these rights depends highly on availability of resources. However, the enforcement of socio-economic rights has given courts a lot of freedom to intervene in the functions of the Executive. In many occasions, courts are approached by civilians for relief in cases where the Executive is failing to provide required services.[58] In *Soobramoney v Minister of Health KwaZulu-Natal* (Soobramoney case)[59] which was later followed by the case of *Government of the Republic of South Africa v Grootboom (Grootboom)*,[60] the focus was on the enforcement of socio-economic rights by the Judiciary. In both cases it was argued that the enforcement of these rights result in courts expanding their powers to the preeminent domain of the Executive, but, courts reached different decisions.

In *Soobramoney* case, the applicant had a chronic heart disease which was in a worse stage requiring regular dialysis to keep him alive. The Addington hospital had only 20 dialysis machines and could not accommodate him for regular dialysis. Due to shortage of dialysis machines the Addington hospital had developed criteria to determine who qualify for dialysis, but, the applicant did not qualify since he was chronically ill and would require daily dialysis. While urging the Court to set aside the decision of the hospital not to admit him for treatment, the applicant contended that failure to admit him to renal dialysis violates his constitutional right to life and right to health care. It was the hospital's response that it could not provide the service required by the applicant as there were not enough machines and there were a number of other patients requiring dialysis. The hospital had requested funds to buy the machines

---

[57] Sandra Liedenberg and Konesh Pillay, *Socio-economic Rights in South Africa: A Resource Book* (Cape Town: Community Law Center University of the Western Cape, 2012), 56.

[58] Ibid., 12.

[59] *Soobramoney v Minister of Health KwaZulu-Natal* 1998 (1) SA 765 (CC) (*Soobramoney* case).

[60] *Government of the Republic of South Africa v Grootboom and others* 2001 (1) SA 46 (CC) (*Grootboom* case).

from the provincial department of health but they were told that there is no budget available. The Constitutional Court held that it is not its responsibility to regulate state budget in a particular manner or question decisions taken in good faith by the political structures and medical authorities who acts within the scope of their duties.[61]

In *Grootboom case*, however, the Constitutional Court held that the Executive should take reasonable steps to ensure realization of socio-economic rights. In this case, the applicants were forcibly removed from private land which they occupied unlawfully. The applicants went to court to compel the municipal government to provide them with better houses on the basis of section 26(1) of the Constitution which provides that everyone has the right to have access to adequate housing. Although the Executive argued that there is lack of resources to realize the applicant's rights, the Court ordered the Executive to take necessary steps to ensure that applicants receive adequate housing. The Constitutional Court in this case crossed its line to enforce socio-economic rights reasoning that socio-economic rights are also fundamental rights in the Bill of rights which must be enforced like civil-political rights.

In *Treatment Action Campaign*[62] *(the Treatment Action Campaign case)*, an appeal was lodged against the decision of the High Court which ordered the state to expand its program to provide Nevarapine drugs for preventing the transmission of HIV & AIDS from mother to child. The state had implemented such a program in few selected areas which was to run as experimental program for two years. The applicants in the High Court challenged the state for not providing Nevarapine drugs nationally arguing that the failure by the state to provide the Nevarapine drugs nationally violates the right to health care services guaranteed by the Constitution. The High Court accordingly ordered the state to extend the program of providing Nevapine drugs, a decision which the State appealed to the Constitutional Court. On appeal, the Minister of health argued that the order of the High Court was inconsistent with the doctrine of separation of powers. The state contended that formulation of policy was an Executive role which should not be exercised by any other branch or interfered with. However, the Constitutional Court overruled this argument and held that there is no constitutional matter

---

[61] *Soobramoney* case (n. 59), para. 54.

[62] *Treatment Action Campaign v Minister of Health* 2002 (4) BCLR 356 (T) 132 (*Treatment Action Campaign*).

which is beyond its adjudicatory competence.[63] While there can be specific matters that are predominantly within the province of one branch, courts have the role to ensure lawful exercise of power.[64] In particular, where state policy is challenged, according to the Constitutional Court, examining whether due regard is accorded by the State to its constitutional responsibilities in formulating and implementing such policy is in order.[65] Hence, the intervention by courts to review the functions of the Executive is constitutional.[66] Accordingly, the Constitutional Court upheld the High Court decision and ordered the Government to expand its program and make Nevirapine drugs instantly available.[67]

All said, having closely observed the decisions of courts regarding socio-economic rights it is evident that arms of government can be symbiotic while serving as checks and balances. The enforcement of socio-economic rights inevitably requires the intrusion by courts into the domain of the Executive.[68] The problem, however, is that the Constitutional Court has not been consistent with its decisions regarding socio-economic rights. For example in *Soobramoney* case, it was reasoned that courts could not interfere with the functions of the Executive as such an intervention will violate the doctrine of separation of powers. However, in *Grootboom* and *Treatment Action Campaign* cases, the Constitutional Court was more firm in enforcing socio-economic rights even where doing so could intrude in Executive policy-making role.

Besides the foregoing, the Executive and the Judiciary work together in the law enforcement processes. The Executive investigates the crime and commits offenders to courts. Ultimately both the branches play a complementary role in the law enforcement.[69] However, tension often arises even in the fulfillment of that role. For instance, in *Kaunda v*

---

[63] Ibid., para. 98.

[64] Ibid., para. 99.

[65] Ibid., para. 114.

[66] Ibid.

[67] Oscar Sang, "The Separation of Powers and New Judicial Power: How the South African Constitutional Court Plotted Its Course," *ELSA Malta Review*, no. 3 (2013): 117.

[68] Ibid., 118.

[69] Kate O'Regan, "Checks and Balances Reflections on the Development of the Doctrine of Separation of Powers Under the South African Constitution," *Potchefstroom Electronic Law Journal* 8, no. 1 (2008): 187.

President of the Republic of South Africa,[70] the Court reviewed the power of the Executive to deal with foreign affairs affecting 69 soldiers who were South African Citizens captured in Zimbabwe and allegedly heading to Equatorial Guinea to overthrow government. The Court needed to review the Executive's powers to make diplomatic arrangements under international law with other states in the interest of those nationals. Powers to deal with foreign affairs is vested in the Executive particularly the Minister of International Relations. The soldiers applied to the Pretoria High Court for an order declaring that South Africa is obliged to extradite them to South Africa so that they could stand trial in South Africa. The applicants also sought for an order compelling South Africa to prevent the applicants to be extradited to Guinea since they would be subjected to injustices.

The Court asserted that section 3 of the Constitution qualifies residents for diplomatic protection, but, cautioned on the extent of court's involvement in the process. According to Chaskalson CJ:

> If citizens have a right to request government to provide them with diplomatic protection, then government must have a corresponding obligation to consider the request and deal with it consistently with the constitution there may even be a duty in extreme cases for the government to act on its own initiative. This, however, is a terrain in which courts must exercise discretion and recognise that government is better placed than they are to deal with such matters.[71]

The Court then observed that while "it is unlikely that such a request would ever be refused by government, but if it were, the decision would be justiciable and a court could order the government to take appropriate action".[72] All the judges in the Kaunda case recognized that the Executive is the only one with special competence to deal with diplomatic representations and that court should avoid dictating to the Executive how they should exercise the powers. However, all of them likewise perceived that the power was to some degree, justiciable in spite of that competence. The Constitutional Court in Kaunda case deviated

---

[70] *Kaunda v President of the Republic of South Africa* 2004 (10) BCLR 1009 (CC); 2005 (4) SA 235 (CC) (*Kaunda* case)

[71] Ibid., para. 67.

[72] Ibid., para. 69.

from the previous judgment in case of *Mohamed v President of Republic of South Africa*[73] which challenged the constitutionality of the South African government extraditing a foreigner wanted by the United States for terrorism. The applicant in this case sought an order compelling the Executive to intervene urgently to protect him against the US authorities. The State argued that such an order would infringe the doctrine of separation of powers'. In the view of the Court, the Executive had a duty to protect the applicant since failure to do so would violate the Bill of Rights.[74] Although the Constitutional Court reached two different decisions in similar facts, one can conclude that the Constitutional Court is willing to intrude in appropriate circumstances to the sphere of other branches.

As evident in the case of South Africa, courts process and approaches are well suited to play the abovementioned role. This is also generally true of Africa, a continent where democratic structure is largely fragile, corruption remains a challenge, awareness and the pressure for fulfillment of human rights is ever-increasing, yet, politicians rarely live up to their electoral promises. In the spirit of interdependence, the mandate of courts to take up legislation and government decisions using the ground of constitutionality must remain intact. There is merit and good sense in empowering the judiciary to declare laws and actions unconstitutional in order to serve as a check against excesses by other branches of government.[75] The court remains the last bastion of hope for the rich and the poor in crisis situations. They cannot only check excesses of government, courts' decisions in certain matters help decision-makers to prioritize resources in a manner that ensures progressive realization of rights and fulfill the general aspirations of the Constitution. Not only true of South Africa, the judiciary can help the state break with its authoritarian past and develop a constitutional culture that inspires state actors in Africa that only public good should be the end of governance, not mere partisan gains.

---

[73] *Mohamed and another v President of the Republic of South Africa and Others* 2001 (3) SA 893 (CC).

[74] *Kaunda* case (n. 70), para. 123.

[75] Erik S. Herron and Kirk A. Randazzo, "The Relationship Between Independence and Judicial Review in Post-Communist Courts," *The Journal of Politics* 65, no. 2 (2003): 422; Christopher M. Larkins, "Judicial Independence and Democratization: A Theoretical and Conceptual Analysis," *American Journal of Comparative Law* 44 (1996): 605.

4 CONCLUSION

This paper sets out to argue that despite the textual distinction in the 1996 Constitution of the powers of the legislative, executive and judicial arms of government, their role is in a number of ways dependent on one another. Yet, such interdependence does not compromise checks and balances. The pattern of interaction, as has been shown, indicates that in terms of their functioning, branches of government are complementary to one another. This relationship, as made manifest in the paper, offers unique opportunities for branches to serve as checks and balances on one another. The Legislature is involved in the work of the Executive through its provision of oversight while the Executive shapes the Parliament role in the sense that apart from initiating bills, the President or the Premier as the case may be, determines the coming into effect of legislation. The Judiciary, as has been demonstrated, is shaped by both the Executive and Parliament in terms of appointment and legislation governing some aspects of its functioning. In turn, through its decisions, as the analysis of decisions of Constitutional Court has shown, the Judiciary shapes the realization, for instance, of socio-economic rights which do not only fall within the province of the Executive but also the Parliament. In all, these possibilities reinforce the conclusion that there exists interdependence in the functioning of different arms of government that allows the branches of government to be complementary as well as serve as checks and balances on one another in South Africa.

REFERENCES

Erik, Herron S., and Randazzo A. Kirk. "The Relationship Between Independence and Judicial Review in Post-Communist Courts." *The Journal of Politics* 65, no. 2 (2003): 422–438.

Labuschagne, Pieter. "The Doctrine of Separation of Powers and Its Application in South Africa." *Politeia* 23, no. 3 (2004): 84–102.

Larkins, Christopher M. "Judicial Independence and Democratization: A Theoretical and Conceptual Analysis." *American Journal of Comparative Law* 44 (1996): 605–626.

Lenta, Patrick. "Democracy, Rights, Disagreements and Judicial Review." *South African Journal on Human Rights* 20, no. 1 (2004): 1–31.

Lever, Annabelle. "Is Judicial Review Democratic?" *Public Law* (2007): 280–298.

Liedenberg, Sandra, and Konesh Pillay. *Socio-economic Rights in South Africa: A Resource Book.* Cape Town: Community Law Center, University of the Western Cape, 2012.

Mojapelo, Phineas. "The Doctrine of Separation of Powers: A South African Perspective." *Advocate* 26, no. 1 (2013): 37–46.

Naidoo, Sherilyn. *Does the Lack of Sufficient Formulation and Articulation of the Principles Guiding Limits of the Constitutional Court Undermine Its Legitimacy?* LLM dissertation, University of Cape Town, South Africa, 2014.

O'Regan, Kate. "Checks and Balances Reflections on the Development of the Doctrine of Separation of Powers Under the South African Constitution." *Potchefstroom Electronic Law Journal* 8, no. 1 (2008): 120–150.

Pierre, De Vos, Warren Freedman, and Danie Brand, eds. *South African Constitutional Law in Context.* Cape Town: Oxford University Press Southern (Pty) Limited, 2014.

Pieterse, Maurius. "Coming to Terms with Judicial Enforcement of Socio-economic Rights." *South African Journal of Human Rights* 20 (2004): 383–417.

Pillay, Anashri. "Toward Effective Social and Economic Rights Adjudication: The Role of Meaningful Engagement." *International Journal of Constitutional Law* 10, no. 3 (2012): 732–755.

Sang, Oscar. "The Separation of Powers and New Judicial Power: How the South African Constitutional Court Plotted Its Course." *ELSA Malta Review* no. 3 (2013): 96–123.

Seedorf, Sebastein, and Sanele Sibanda. "Separation of Powers." In *Constitutional Law of South Africa*, edited by Stu Woolman and Michael Bishop, 12–26. Cape Town: Juta, 2013.

Waldron, Jeremy. "The Core of the Case Against Judicial Review." *Yale Law Journal* 115, no. 6 (2006): 1346–1406.

The Golden Jubilee of the Mauritian Bill of Rights: A Milestone to Celebrate or Time for Reflections?

Ashwanee Budoo and Roopanand Amar Mahadew

1 Introduction

Mauritius, the inspiration for the creation of heaven,[1] celebrated the golden jubilee of its independence on 12 March 2018.[2] The Republic of Mauritius obtained its independence from the British in 1968 and it became a Republic in 1992. Situated in the Indian Ocean with

---

[1] Mark Twain, *Following the Equator: A Journey Around the World* (Hartford, CT: The American Publishing Company, 1897), Chapter 62: "Mauritius Was Made First and Then Heaven; and Heaven Was Copied After Mauritius."

[2] "National Day 2018," Republic of Mauritius, accessed April 11, 2018, http://www.govmu.org/English/Pages/default.aspx.

A. Budoo (✉)
University of Pretoria, Pretoria, South Africa
e-mail: ashwanee.budoo@up.ac.za

R. A. Mahadew
University of Mauritius, Moka, Mauritius
e-mail: r.mahadew@uom.ac.mu

© The Author(s) 2020
M. Addaney et al. (eds.), *Governance, Human Rights,
and Political Transformation in Africa*,
https://doi.org/10.1007/978-3-030-27049-0_5

a population of about 1.3 million, it consists of the main island of Mauritius and other smaller islands with Rodrigues being the second largest. The legal system of Mauritius is a hybrid one which includes both French civil law and English common law. This is so because when the British took over the island from the French in 1814, by virtue of the Treaty of Capitulation, they 'guaranteed that they would respect the language, the customs, the laws and the traditions of the inhabitants'.[3]

The Constitution of the Republic also turned 50 this year since it was adopted on the same day as the country was freed from colonial rule.[4] Recognising that respect for human rights is the pillar of a country, the Constitution was adopted with a Bill of Rights. For 50 years, this Bill of Rights has been ensuring the protection of the fundamental human rights and freedoms of the Mauritian citizen, so much so that the Mo Ibrahim Index has ranked it as the leading country in Governance in Africa in 2017.[5] The index takes into account four indicators that are safety and rule of law, participation and human rights, sustainable economic opportunity, and human development.[6] Participation and human rights is further broken down into participation, rights and gender.

Additionally, the United Nations (UN) Human Development Report of 2016 ranked the country 64 out of 188, and first in Africa.[7] This report takes into account factors such as human development, inequality, gender development, gender inequality and multidimensional poverty. Since Mauritius has been ranked first in Africa in these two rankings that focus heavily on issues that concern human rights, it could imply that the country is one that assures optimum human rights protection. The Bill of Rights is the supreme law[8] concerning human rights protection in the country and this chapter assesses whether the Bill of Rights' provisions enable human rights realisation and ensure that the country has good human rights records.

---

[3] "History," Republic of Mauritius, accessed April 18, 2018, http://www.govmu.org/English/ExploreMauritius/Pages/History.aspx.

[4] GN 54/1968, *The Constitution of the Republic of Mauritius* (1968).

[5] Mo Ibrahim Foundation, *2017 Ibrahim Index of African Governance: Index Report* (2017), 58.

[6] Mo Ibrahim Foundation, *Index Report*, 9.

[7] United Nations Development Programme, *Human Development Report 2016: Human Development for Everyone* (Ottawa, ON: Lowe-Martin Group, 2016), 271.

[8] Section 2 of the Constitution: "This Constitution is the Supreme Law of Mauritius…".

It first gives a brief history of the Constitution of Mauritius and tries to elaborate on the origin of the Bill of rights. Second, the provisions of the Bill of Rights are studied and this section provides instances when the courts of Mauritius have made reference to the Bill of Rights. Third, there is a critical analysis of the Bill of Rights with the view of ascertaining whether the document offers maximum human rights protection or whether there is a need to reform. Finally, there is a conclusion with the way forward.

2 HISTORY OF THE CONSTITUTION OF MAURITIUS[9]

Smith expands on the constitutional and political development of Mauritius till 1967,[10] just before independence. According to him, it was the British and the French who dealt with the public affairs of the country before 1948 until James Pope-Hennessy came forward with the proposition of a 'Mauritius for Mauritians'.[11] This concept led to the birth of the first Mauritian Constitution in 1885 that established a new form of Government that consisted of 'the Governor, eight *ex-oficio* members, nine nominated members (of whom at least three were to be non-officials), and ten other members elected on a narrow franchise'.[12] Despite the fact that the Governor still had 'wide executive powers', it was considered as a 'liberal' Constitution for the colony.[13] This Constitution prevailed in Mauritius for more than half a century except for an amendment in 1933 when the number of non-official nominated members increased to six.

The major constitutional reform came after World War II in 1947 where provisions were made for the Legislature to be consisted by an elected majority and for an extension in the group of electorate.

---

[9]For detailed information about the history of the Constitution of Mauritius, please see Ashwanee Budoo and Nora Ho Tu Nam, "The Republic of Mauritius," in *Oxford Constitutions of the World*, ed. Institute for International and Comparative Law in Africa (Oxford: Oxford University Press, 2016).

[10]Stanley A de Smith, "Mauritius: Constitutionalism in a Plural Society," *The Modern Law Review* 31, no. 6 (1968): 603–611.

[11]James Pope-Hennessy, *Verandah: Some Episodes in the Crown Colonies (1867–1889)* (London: Allen and Unwin, 1964), 231–302.

[12]De Smith, "Mauritius: Constitutionalism in a Plural Society," 604.

[13]As above.

This brought a drastic change in the political landscape in Mauritius where Indo-Mauritians were elected in mass (eleven out of nineteen seats). Nevertheless, this did not change much at the Executive Council and Legislative Council level and hence there were calls for a constitutional reform. Since then till 1968, several documents were adopted to adapt to the evolving situation including the 1958 Constitution that provided for universal suffrage, and the creation of the office of a Chief Minister following the Constitutional Review Conference held in 1961. The Bill of Rights was also part of these reforms and was first introduced in 1964.

The Constitutional Conference on Mauritius that took place in 1965 is considered as a milestone for the document since this event established the Banwell Commission that would investigate the situation on the ground and make recommendations for the electoral system of independent Mauritius.[14] The Banwell Commission made several propositions to ensure the rights of minority groups but they were rejected since they did not take into account the Muslim Committee of Action. Mr. Stonehouse, the Parliamentary Under-Secretary for the Colonies was then sent to Mauritius and he proposed an amended version of the Banwell Commission recommendations that put forward the best loser system.[15] The elections were finally held on 7 August 1967[16] and 12 March 1968 was set as the independence date of Mauritius.[17]

The current Constitution was adopted at independence and although it went through amendments, with the latest one being in 2016, the current provisions are mostly the same as when they had been inherited. Chapter II of the 1968 Constitution made provisions for a Bill of Rights.[18] As can be noted from the history of the Constitution, little emphasis was placed on the Bill of Rights and the focus was on the electoral system. This is rightly so since at the time it was being framed, the electoral system and safeguard of minority groups were pressing issues

---

[14] De Smith, "Mauritius: Constitutionalism in a Plural Society," 608.

[15] For more information about the best loser system in Mauritius, please see: Roopanand Mahadew, "The Best Loser System in Mauritius: An Essential Tool for Representing Political Minorities," in *Constitution-Building in Africa*, ed. Jaap de Visser, Nico Steytler, Derek Powell, and Ebenezer Durojaye (Baden-Baden: Nomos Verlagsgesellschaft, 2015).

[16] De Smith, "Mauritius: Constitutionalism in a Plural Society," 610.

[17] De Smith, "Mauritius: Constitutionalism in a Plural Society," 611.

[18] Sections 3–16 of the Constitution.

that needed attention. Hence, the Bill of Rights contents were merely inherited from the Colonial Master and there was no scope for the population to discuss its provisions.

3 THE BILL OF RIGHTS

The Bill of Rights of the Constitution has played a critical role in the protection and promotion of civil and political rights in Mauritius. The more so since it is the only legal instrument that is enforceable before the Supreme Court of Mauritius. Despite having ratified a plethora of legal instruments pertaining to human rights such as the International Covenant on Civil and Political Rights (ICCPR),[19] the International Covenant on Economic, Social and Cultural Rights (ICESCR),[20] the African Charter on Human and Peoples' Rights (African Charter),[21] and the Protocol to the African Charter on the Rights of Women in Africa (Maputo Protocol),[22] none of these instruments have been domesticated. Being a dualist country[23] where international law only finds domestic application after transposition of norms through an act of parliament, provisions of international law cannot be enforced by local courts in Mauritius. Domestic courts have therefore been reluctant to make reference to international law that have not been incorporated into domestic laws while deciding cases. It follows that since independence, Mauritians have solely relied on the Bill of Rights and certain acts of parliament[24] to enforce their fundamental rights and freedoms.

The following section analyses how the Bill of Rights have fared so far in protecting civil and political rights of Mauritians. It focuses on sections that provides for the right to life, the right to personal liberty, the right to protection from torture and the right to freedom of expression. The reason is based on the fact that these are the categories of rights

---

[19] Date of accession: 12 December 1973.

[20] Date of accession: 12 December 1973.

[21] Date of ratification: 19 June 2002.

[22] Date of ratification: July 2017 with reservations.

[23] *Matadeen v Pointu* Privy Council Appeal No. 14 of 1997, paragraph 24; *Jordan v Jordan* 2000 SCJ 226; *Pulluck v Ramphul* 2005 SCJ 196; and *Ex Parte Hurnam Devendranath, a Barrister-at-Law* 2007 SCJ 289.

[24] For instance Protection of Human Rights Act; Employment Rights Act; Employment Relations Act; Equal Opportunities Act; Protection from Domestic Violence Act.

that are most debated in the Supreme Court and that perhaps require redrafting as would be discussed later in this section. Other rights such as property,[25] conscience,[26] assembly and association,[27] movement,[28] securing the protection of the law[29] or discrimination[30] have been very positively interpreted and applied by local courts and can no doubt be the focus of another piece of research.[31] Since the purview of this article is to look at sections of the Bill of Rights from a critical angle, a selected group of rights as mentioned above would be the focus.

3.1   The Probative Force of Section 3

Section 3 introduces the Bill of Rights in the Mauritian Constitution declaring that 'in Mauritius there have existed and shall continue to exist' a series of civil and political rights which are the subject of discussion of this section. The Supreme Court of Mauritius has confirmed in the case of *Peerbocus v R*[32] that human rights in Mauritius have existed since the French colonisation period through the 1794 Colonial Assembly Declaration based on the Declaration of Rights which was proclaimed in France. It is a judicial practice for both the Supreme Court and the Privy Council to refer to the said declaration when dealing with cases of human rights.[33] It is also relevant to note that way before the adoption

---

[25] Section 8 of the Constitution.

[26] Section 11 of the Constitution.

[27] Section 13 of the Constitution.

[28] Section 15 of the Constitution.

[29] Section 10 of the Constitution.

[30] Section 16 of the Constitution.

[31] *The Society United Docks and Others v Government of Mauritius* 1985 UKPC 42 for compulsory acquisition of property; *Darmalingum v The State* 2000 MR 210 for fair trial within a reasonable time; *Bhewa and Alladeen v Government of Mauritius & DPP* 1990 MR 79 for freedom of conscience; *The Union of Campement Sites Owners and Lessees v The Government of Mauritius* 1984 MR 100 for the concept of equality of the law and non discrimination.

[32] 1991 MR 90.

[33] Milan Meetarbhan, *Constitutional Law of Mauritius: Constitution of Mauritius with Commentaries* (2016), 23.

of the Mauritian Constitution in 1968, the Mauritian Civil Code already provided for human rights and fundamental liberties in article 11.[34]

This implies that the applicability of human rights in Mauritius does not find its source solely from the Constitution. It exists in other forms as mentioned above. In the event that the Constitution is repealed in Mauritius, there is other legal basis on which human rights can advocated for. However, these forms of law are to be found in rules that are easily amended by a simple majority in Parliament whereas constitutionally entranced provisions enjoy higher status and enforceability.

The purpose of section 3 of the Mauritian Constitution has also been long debated before the Supreme Court and the Privy Council. At some point, section 3 was regarded as a preamble to the Bill of Rights and therefore not enforceable as stated in *Jaulim v DPP*.[35] In this case, the Supreme Court was of the view that 'the guarantee in section 3 has no separate existence'. However, this stand was reversed in the case of *Matadeen v Pointu*[36] whereby the Court declared that section 3 is not a mere preamble but an enforceable section with substantive content. It implies that a complainant can enter a case before the Supreme Court solely on the basis of section 3 and it does not have to be coupled with another section. Section 3 has its own substance and content and can be enforced independently as it is not a preamble to the Bill of Rights.

3.2   Limitation of Rights Enshrined in the Bill of Rights

Meetarbhan argues that the Mauritian Constitution has a general construct which can be qualified as follows: (a) the right or freedom is set out as the general rule; (b) there may be exceptions to the rule in specified circumstances or for specified purposes; and (c) these exceptions are set out in the Constitution or they must be provided under a law and that the law must be reasonably justifiable in a democratic society.[37] The exercise of limitation of rights provided by the Bill of Rights is based on jurisprudence from the European Court of Human Rights.

---

[34] Article 11 of the Mauritian Civil Code (authors' translation): "One Cannot Renounce the Enjoyment of His Civil Rights and Fundamental Freedoms."

[35] 1976 MR 96.

[36] 1998 MR 172.

[37] Meetarbhan 31.

The Supreme Court guides itself by cases such as *S and Marper v the United Kingdom*[38] and *Sahin v Turkey*.[39] For instance, in the case of *Madhewoo v the State*,[40] the Supreme Court cited the case of *S and Marper v the United Kingdom* in the following terms—An interference will be considered necessary in a democratic society for a legitimate aim if it answers a pressing social need and, in particular, if it is proportionate to the legitimate aim pursued and if the reason adduced by the national authorities to justify it are relevant and sufficient. In the case of *DPP v Boodhoo*,[41] the Supreme Court, referring to section 12 on freedom of expression, held that:

> ...section 12 which sets out the specific aims of those limitations but which subject those limitations themselves to the governing norms of what is reasonably justifiable in a democratic society. The necessity of any constitutionally permissible limitations must, like all derogations, be narrowly construed and must respond to what has generally been understood to be a pressing social need. Thus, the application in practice of limitations which are permissible in principle must be closely monitored so as to ensure that they stay, in any particular case, within the limits proportionate to the legitimate aim pursued.

At this point, it is relevant to point out that the Supreme Court has always carried out the essential task of limitation of rights based on international standards and guided by relevant jurisprudence. The interest of the society and the need of the government have been carefully balanced as evidenced by several cases mentioned above. So far, the stand taken by the Supreme Court has been one which will only limit rights when it is necessary and proportionate and that limitations provided by the law will only be interpreted and construed in their narrow sense. This is more in line with protection of rights rather than protection of limitations.

---

[38] 2008 European Court of Human Rights 1581.
[39] 2005, 41 European Human Rights Reports 8.
[40] 2015 SCJ 177.
[41] 1992 MR 284.

3.3   The Content of the Bill of Rights

The rights protected from sections 3–17 in the Mauritian Constitution can be summarised as follows—section 3 Fundamental rights and freedoms of individual, section 4 Protection of right to life, section 5 Protection of right to personal liberty, section 6 Protection from slavery and forced labour, section 7 Protection from inhuman treatment, section 8 Protection from deprivation of property, section 9 Protection for privacy of home and other property, section 10 Provisions to secure protection of law, section 11 Protection of freedom of conscience, section 12 Protection of freedom of expression, section 13 Protection of freedom of assembly and association, section 14 Protection of freedom to establish schools, section 15 Protection of freedom of movement, section 16 Protection from discrimination and section 17 Enforcement of protective provisions.

The provisions cited above are largely inspired by the European Convention on Human Rights and they correspond to a significant degree to the articles from the ICCPR. However, while the substance of the Bill of Rights may be similar to the ICCPR, it has to be noted that the provisions of the latter instrument cannot be directly enforced before Mauritian courts. Mauritius is a dualist state which requires domestication of international laws for them to have effect and to be enforceable in domestic courts. The ICCPR has not yet been domesticated despite their provisions often cited by the Supreme Court for their persuasive value as indicated in the case of *Matadeen v Pointu*.[42] The United Nations Human Rights Committee has recommended that citizens of Mauritius be enabled to enforce the ICCPR provisions directly before domestic courts.[43] But so far, the state has not given an indication of bringing such changes to the legal framework on civil and political rights in Mauritius.

---

[42] 1998 MR 112.

[43] Paragraph 6 of the Human Rights Committee's Concluding observations on the fifth periodic report of Mauritius adopted on 11 December 2017 CCPR/C/MUS/CO/5: "The State party should give full effect to the Covenant in its domestic legal order and should also raise awareness of the rights in the Covenant among judges, lawyers and prosecutors so that its national laws are interpreted and applied in line with the Covenant."

Section 4—Protection of Right to Life
Section 4(1) of the Mauritian Constitution provides for the right to life in the following terms—'No person shall be deprived of his life intentionally save in the execution of the sentence of a court in respect of a criminal offence of which he has been convicted'. This right is eventually limited in section 4(2) by four specific circumstances namely (a) for the defence of any person from violence or for the defence of property (b) in order to effect a lawful arrest or to prevent the escape of a person lawfully detained (c) for the purpose of suppressing a riot, insurrection or mutiny and (d) in order to prevent the commission by that person of a criminal offence, or if he dies as the result of a lawful act of war.

The corresponding article from the African Charter provides that 'Human beings are inviolable. Every human being shall be entitled to respect for his life and the integrity of his person. No one maybe arbitrarily deprived of this right' (article 4). It has to be noted that section 4 of the Mauritian Constitution has been negatively drafted in the sense that more emphasis seems to be laid on the exceptions or limitations to the right rather than the right itself. In comparison with article 4 of the African Charter where the essence and meaning of human life have been given much importance, the corresponding Mauritian provision only guarantees that no person shall be deprived of his life.

It required judicial interpretation from the Supreme Court to reiterate that section 4 adequately protects the right to life. In the case of *Madhewoo v The State*, the Supreme Court held that:

> ...the wording go section 4 of our Constitution makes it clear that the constitutional protection afforded is in respect of life in contradistinction from death. It is significant that all four circumstances set out under the section 4(2) as those where a person shall not be regarded as having been deprived of his life in breach of the section relate to the person's death as a result of force that is reasonably justifiable for certain purposes.

In relation to the debate on death penalty in Mauritius, it has to be highlighted that the Mauritian Parliament only suspended death penalty through the Abolition of Death Penalty Act. In the case of *Roger F.P. de Boucherville v the State of Mauritius*,[44] the Judicial Committee provided for a summary of the Abolition of Death Penalty Act as follows:

[44] 2008 United Kingdom Privy Council 37.

...Section 2 of the Act amended the law in three significant ways. First, it abolished the death penalty (section 2(1)). Secondly, it provided that where under any enactment a court was empowered to impose a sentence of death it should instead of the death sentence impose sentence of penal servitude for life (section 2(2)). Thirdly, if provided that where any person had been sentenced to death, and the sentence had not, at the commencement of the Act, been executed, that person should be deemed to have been sentenced to penal servitude for life and should undergo that sentence (section 2(3)).

Despite the wording of the Abolition of Death Penalty Act which gives the impression that death penalty has been abolished, section 4 of the Constitution has not yet been changed. It should also be noted that the above Act can easily be amended by a simple majority to restore death penalty in the criminal justice system of Mauritius. It implies that the matter on the abolition of death penalty has not been concluded yet and for now it has only been suspended.

Section 5—Protection of the Right to Personal Liberty
Section 5(1) of the Constitution stipulates that no person shall be deprived of his personal liberty except as is provided by the law. A list of limitations is then provided in the same section. Subsection 2 and 3 focus more on the loss of liberty pursuant to an arrest or a detention following a criminal offence. One major interrogation on section 5 has been the interpretation of the concept of liberty. Very often, the question that arises is whether liberty is only physical or much broader than that. In the case of *Madhewoo v The State*, the Supreme Court took the view that liberty should only be construed in the physical sense. According to the Court, 'there is close similarity between section 5 of the Constitution and article 5 of the European Convention', hence the propriety of referring to the jurisprudence on the European Convention. An overview of local jurisprudence, as well as that of the European Court of Human Rights in relation to section 5 of the Constitution and article 5 of the European Convention, reveals that the right to liberty being conferred is the right not to be detained physically either arbitrarily or unlawfully.

Section 5 also seems to be focused significantly on the powers of arrest. There area number of other legislation that has been drafted based on section 5 namely the Police Act and section 22 of the District and Intermediate Courts (Criminal Jurisdiction) Act. For instance, this section provides that 'an officer may arrest a party without warrant, in all cases where a private person may so arrest, and also on a reasonable charge made of a crime committed or of dangerous wounds inflicted by the party arrested'. In *Dahoo v State of Mauritius*,[45] the Supreme Court emphasised that section 5 provides that no person shall be deprived of his liberty except if same is justified by the law in certain specified circumstances. The Court further added that it is the obligation of the person who has effected an arrest to show the applicability of one of the provided derogations from the right to liberty.

The existence of the concept of provisional information or provisional charge in the criminal justice system of Mauritius also gives rise to the debate of whether a person held on remand on a provisional charge still should be enjoying his right to liberty under section 5. The question of provisional charge was addressed by the Supreme Court in the case of *Jugnauth P K v The Secretary to the Cabinet and Head of the Civil Service Affairs &Ors.*[46] According to the Court:

> When a provisional charge is lodged against an accused party at the stage of the investigation, this does not mean that he is brought to trial on that charge. the provisional charge is merely a preliminary stage when the prosecution is still carrying its investigation and has not made any decision whether to lodge a criminal charge or not. The provisional charge does not lead to a determination of issues of guilt or otherwise and an accused party does not run any risk of being convicted or of being sentenced at this stage. A provisional charge may culminate into a criminal charge or it may be purely and simply struck out without any further charge.

It is argued that the prosecution has a duty to complete its investigation in the shortest possible delay before deciding on whether a case would be formally lodged or not. In the meantime, while a warning or an objection to departure, for instance can logically and legitimately be imposed on the person, it does not seem to be in line with section 5 of the Constitution to arrest and detain that person. This holds true especially in cases when investigation would be very long and unsuccessful. Detention affects the reputation and also economic rights such as employment of a person. The concept of provisional

---

[45] 2007 SCJ 156.
[46] 2013 SCJ 132.

charge seems to infringe the liberty and associated rights that a person is constitutionally entitled to enjoy.

Section 5 is equally associated with the notion of bail applicable in criminal cases. Bail is regulated by the Bail Act 2000 in Mauritius. According to the Act, the rule is that a person is entitled to be released on bail and the exception to this rule is provided by section 4 of the Act. In deciding bail matters, courts are supposed to weigh the interest of society in releasing the accused party and the rights of the latter as provided by the Constitution. In *Hurnam v The State*,[47] the Privy Council synthesised the law of bail in the following words:

> In Mauritius, as elsewhere, the courts are routinely called upon to consider whether an unconvicted suspect or defendant should be released on bail, subject to conditions, pending his trial. Such decisions very often raise questions of importance both to the individual suspect or defendant and to the community as a whole. The interest of the individual is of course to remain at liberty, unless or until he is convicted of a crime sufficiently serious to justify depriving him of his liberty. Any loss of liberty before that time, particularly if he is acquitted or never tried, will inevitably prejudice him and, in many cases, his livelihood and family. But the community has a countervailing interest, in seeking to ensure that the course of justice is not thwarted by the flight of the suspect or defendant or perverted by his interference with witnesses or evidence, and that he does not take advantage of the inevitable delay before trial to commit further offences.

Section 5 of the Constitution has so far been rightly but rather restrictively been interpreted along the lines of bail, provisional charge and detention. It is important to highlight that liberty can also be interpreted as mental liberty or physical liberty itself but outside the purview of detention and criminal offences. For instance, collection of data by the state or the use of biometric features of the individual for National Identity Cards (as was the case in *Madhewoo v The State*) can also sometimes infringe the right to liberty. The Supreme Court must therefore adopt a more constructive and purposive approach to the interpretation of section 5. In addition, the possibility of amending section 5 for it to be applicable in the larger sense and not only in limited instances can also be envisaged.

---

[47] 2005 United Kingdom Privy Council 49.

Section 7—Protection from Inhuman Treatment
Section 7 provides that 'no person shall be subjected to torture or to inhuman or degrading punishment or other such treatment'. In the case of *Virahsawmy and Anor v The Commissioner of Police*,[48] the Supreme Court qualified inhuman as 'brutal, unfeeling and barbarous'. Expanding on whether solitary confinement amounted to torture the Court held that:

> ...solitary confinement and the physical and mental discomfort caused by such confinement cannot, in the circumstances of this case, be said to constitute torture or inhuman treatment within the meaning of section 7(1) of the Constitution. Mental or physical discomfort is not necessarily caused by torture or inhuman treatment.

In several cases (*Philibert v The State*[49] and *Bhinkah v The State*[50]) the Supreme Court has been called upon to adjudicate whether mandatory criminal sentences or other criminal punishments are in conformity with section 7. In *Philibert v The State* the Court of Criminal Appeal held that section 41(3) of the Dangerous Drugs Act which provides for mandatory sentence of 45 years' penal servitude in all drug offences infringed section 7(1) of the Constitution as it is against the principle of proportionality and amounts to inhumane and degrading punishment. In *Bhinkah v The State*, the Supreme Court held that even a minimum penalty could be considered as being disproportionate if '*the imposition of a mandatory minimum sentence would be startlingly or disturbingly inappropriate with respect to hypothetical cases which could be foreseen as likely to arise commonly*'.[51]

However, one very important aspect that should also be considered under section 7 is the unfortunate and popular subject of police brutality in the form of physical violence utilised by police officers on accused. In the case of *DPP v Jagdawoo*,[52] the Supreme Court reiterated that 'the peremptory nature of the right to freedom from torture and other cruel, inhuman and degrading treatment cannot be derogated from

---

[48] 1972 SCJ 169.
[49] 2007 SCJ 274.
[50] 2009 SCJ 102.
[51] See Meetarbhan 56–57.
[52] 2016 SCJ 100.

even in the gravest of crises'. The critical issue of police brutality had prompted the state to come up with the Police Complaint Act and to amend the Protection of Human Rights Act to include under the aegis of the National Human Rights Commission a Police Complaint Division. Under the Police Complaint Acts 2012, the Police Complaint Division has the power to investigate any complaint made by any person, or on his behalf, against any act, conduct or omission of a police officer in the performance of his duty, other than a complaint made in relation to an act of corruption or a money laundering offence; to investigate the death of any person which occurred when the person was in police custody or as a result of police action; to advise on ways in which any police misconduct may be addressed and eliminated and to perform such other function as may promote better relations between the public and the police and as may be conferred upon it by any other enactment.[53] Upon completion of investigation, the matter can be referred to either the Director of Public Prosecutions or the Disciplined Forces Service Commission or the Attorney General depending on the ensuing course of action.[54] However the major criticism remains the fact that it does not seem to be independent since police officers themselves investigate cases of police brutality perpetrated by their fellow colleagues from the police force.

Section 12—Protection of Freedom of Expression
Freedom of expression is protected by section 12 which provides for the freedom to (a) hold opinions (b) to receive ideas and information without interference (c) impart ideas and information without interference and (d) enjoy freedom from interference with one's correspondence. One major debate surrounding section 12 has been the fact that it does not explicitly mention freedom of the press. The question has often been raised as to whether freedom of the media should be entrenched in the Constitution or should the protection of the freedom of expression of every individual be interpreted as inclusive of journalists and the media.

Although not specifically mentioned in section 12, freedom of the press and media has been the subject of various decisions of the Supreme

---

[53] Section 4 of the Police Complaint Act 2012.
[54] Section 14 of the Police Complaint Act 2012.

Court and the Judicial Committee. In the case of *Ohsan-Bellepeau v La Sentinelle*,[55] the Judicial Committee noted that:

> ...responsible journalism is the point at which a fair balance is held between freedom of expression on matters of public concern and the reputations of individuals. Maintenance of this standard is in the public interest and in the interests of those whose reputations are involved. It can be regarded as the price journalists pay in return for the privilege.

The Supreme Court of Mauritius admonishes journalists about the critical role that they play in the democratic society of Mauritius in the case of *Bunwaree V K v La Sentinelle*.[56] The following passage is noteworthy:

> No doubt the media has a very important role to play in a democratic society, one of which is to impart reliable information to the public at large and to act as a fearless watchdog. This is rightly so by scrutinising and denouncing, without fear or favour not only the acts and doings of public figures and that of public administration, but also those of the private sector. However, this must de done in a responsible manner, not speculating or going into sensationalism and on unchecked materials gathered from various sources, reliable or not. Good practice would require the author before publishing the article to seek the view and comment of the person concerned by the article. It is also the role of the responsible officer of the publication to censor those reporters whose article does not reflect accurately the facts. It has a duty before publishing any matter which might be harmful to others to scrutinise and ascertain its source and the reliability of the information. It is insufficient for any journalist to come up with stereotyped blanket formula to buttress his comments. So long as the message is clear, having the hallmark of accuracy and truth, freedom of expression will always prevail in this country.

The Supreme Court and the Judicial Committee have both played a critical role in upholding freedom of the press and media and also protecting the reputations of individuals whenever required by the law. However, since freedom of the press and media is an inevitable pillar of any democracy, it is a dangerous proposition to allow it to be guaranteed only by case law. It is mandatory that such freedom be enshrined

[55] 2009 SCJ 114.
[56] 2012 SCJ 84.

in the Constitution in clear words as is the case for the Constitution of Switzerland,[57] that of the Cape Verde[58] or the Canadian Charter of Rights and Freedoms.[59] There has been much debate in Mauritius for the inception of a Media Commission to regulate the role of journalists in Mauritius. The functions and powers of the Commission seem to be grounds on which no consensus has been reached among stakeholders.

The current Bill of Rights and the selected section have stood the test of time for 50 years since independence. It has to be borne in mind that the European Convention on Human Rights was the instrument from which inspiration was drawn to draft Mauritian Bill of Rights. Fifty years down the line, with a much-evolved Mauritian society, it is now time to revisit it and to tune it to the existing social, political and economic contexts of Mauritius. The next section initiates a debate along the line of amendments and changes required within the Bill of Rights as well as outside it with the introduction of other legal and judicial tools necessary for the promotion and protection of human rights of Mauritians.

4 Critical Assessment of the Bill of Rights

It has to be noted that the Constitution of Mauritius did not emanate from its people as has been the case with the South African one where a Constituent Assembly consisting of, among others, the peoples and their representatives, contributed to its drafting. Our Constitution was granted by our colonial master through a UK legal instrument. A compromised Bill of Rights was, arguably logically, bestowed on Mauritians though the Constitution, taking into account the prevailing social, political and economic situations at that time. Fifty years after independence, it is now time for each and every Mauritian to model his/her own Bill of

---

[57] Article 17: (1) Freedom of the press, radio and television and of other forms of dissemination of features and information by means of public telecommunications is guaranteed. (2) Censorship is prohibited.

[58] Article 46: (1) The freedom of the press shall be guaranteed... (3) The freedom and the independence of the media in relation to the political and economic power and its non-subjection to censorship of any type shall be guaranteed. (4) The expression and confrontation of ideas of different currents of opinion in the media owned by the public sector shall be guaranteed.

[59] Section 2(b): Everyone has the following fundamental freedoms: ... freedom of thought, belief, opinion and expression, including freedom of the press and other media of communication.

Rights. A general amendment is mandatorily required and this should be carried out in an inclusive, participatory and consultative manner where everyone can bring his/her own building block. This section examines the different aspects of the Bill of Rights that need to be revisited.

4.1   Civil and Political Rights

The change should start with what we already have in our Constitution—that is civil and political rights. Though inspired from the European Convention on Human Rights,[60] our civil and political rights are drafted in a limitative manner which can be restrictive from a judicial interpretation viewpoint. As a matter of illustration, our Constitution provides in its section 4 that 'no person shall be deprived of his life intentionally...' whereas the European Convention on Human Rights says 'everyone's right to life shall be protected by law'.[61] The ICCPR provides that 'every human being has the inherent right to life'[62] while the African Charter stipulates that 'every human being shall be entitled to respect for his life and the integrity of his person'.[63] In addition, most of the rights are followed by heavy claw-back clauses which limit the rights. While such clauses are essential in any democracy, it certainly creates problems of interpretation. There is no doubt a need to redraft the existing rights in a more positive manner that put the human being forward.

In line with the above argument, the substance of some of the rights in the Constitution has to be reviewed. For example, in the case of *Madhewoo v The State*, the Supreme Court indicated that the right to privacy encompasses only privacy of the home, property and protection from bodily search of a person. Other essential components of the right to privacy such as protection of the private life, family life and correspondence arguably do not find any constitutional guarantee under the Constitution unless, based on facts, a connection can be established with home, property and body of a person.

It is therefore essential that civil and political rights in our Constitution be reviewed based on the United Nations' ICCPR and the

---

[60] *Darmalingum v The State* 2000 United Kingdom Privy Council 30.

[61] Article 2.

[62] Article 6.

[63] Article 4.

African Union's African Charter. With all due respect to the European Convention on Human Rights which can certainly serve as inspiration while interpreting those rights, Mauritius is a state party to the United Nations and the African Union. It is all but logical and relevant to base our civil and political rights on instruments under the aegis of the latter organisations.

4.2   Economic, Social and Cultural Rights[64]

Economic, social and cultural rights, also known as second-generation rights, and third-generation rights such as the right to development and the right to environment are absent from the Mauritian Constitution.[65] There is no mention of right to health, housing, education, culture, work, leisure, development, environment and others. This position has created a legal vacuum when it comes to cases based on socio-economic rights or the right to development and environment. For instance, the policy decision of nine-year schooling, the Metro Express project, the stock out ARVs for children in 2017 or the changes made to the methadone programme cannot be challenged before the Supreme Court and allowing the latter to review the obligations of the government because of the absence of the right to education, right to development and right to health respectively. It is therefore primordial that these rights be enshrined in the Constitution. The reason for this is not necessarily to harass the government with court cases. Instead, it provides for the possibility for more social justice. As Albie Sachs once stated, 'the notion of a bill of rights can sometimes be a narrow one, presupposing that the function of a bill of rights was simply to limit the power of government, yet there was no reason why the bill of rights should not also be an instrument for advancing the claims of the dispossessed'.[66]

---

[64]An unrevised version of this part on economic, social and cultural Rights has been published in Business Magazine for the 50th Anniversary of the Independence of Mauritius.

[65]Law Reform Commission, *Constitution Protection of Human Rights* (Mauritius, October 2010), http://lrc.govmu.org/English/Documents/Reports%20and%20Papers/32%20humrightpro.pdf.

[66]Albie Sachs, *The Strange Alchemy of Life and the Law* (Oxford: Oxford University Press, 2009), 166.

The United Nations Committee on Economic, Social and Cultural Rights has prompted the State of Mauritius on the inclusion of socio-economic rights in the Constitution. The position of Mauritius has been based on the argument that socio-economic rights are already catered for through the Welfare State system in Mauritius.[67] While it is true that Mauritians do enjoy free education, free transport for students, old age pensions and so on, these are only political privileges, often granted on the even of elections, which can be taken back any time. It is therefore fundamentally different to provide for free education as a political decision and to constitutionally guarantee the right to education based on which many policies can be challenged.

4.3   Inclusion of Actio Popularis

Section 17 of the Bill of Rights provides for enforcement of the rights in the document. Section 2 of the Supreme Court (Constitutional Relief Rules)[68] provides for the procedure for an application under section 17 of the Constitution. These rules clearly establish that only an aggrieved person can initiate an action for violation of the rights in the Bill of Rights. The landmark case in this area is that of *Noordally versus the Attorney General and the Director of Public Prosecutions*[69] where the Supreme Court held that only the applicant must make an application under section 17 of the Constitution. The Court further held that only when the applicant is physically unable to enter such action will the Supreme Court allow someone else to represent him/her but this would be in exceptional cases.

Moreover, in the case of *Tengur versus Minister of Education and Scientific Research and Another*,[70] the applicant was contending that his right to be protected from discrimination is being infringed since the state was using taxpayers money to fund catholic schools which practice discrimination on the basis of religion in admitting pupils. His argument was that being a taxpayer, he had sufficient interest in the matter since his money was being used for such discrimination. The Court held that

---

[67] UN Committee on Economic, Social and Cultural Rights Concluding Observation UN Doc. E/C.12/MUS/CO/4, 3–21 May 2010, para. 7.

[68] Adopted in 2000.

[69] 1986 MR 220/SCJ 339.

[70] 2002 MR 166/SCJ 48.

the mere fact that the applicant pays tax does not demonstrate that he has sufficient interest and that the applicant failed to prove that the state discriminated against him.

The above cases demonstrate that the Supreme Court of Mauritius has been very cautious in entertaining plaints where the applicant did not have sufficient *locus standi*. Indeed as rightly pointed out by Astley, such strict requirements limit aggrieved persons' access to remedy.[71] In the current situation, a person cannot bring a class complaint that concerns a category of persons since the court would require all of them to be complainants in the case. Hence, *actio popularis* is not an option provided by the Mauritian Constitution and there is a need to provide for such types of complaints, specially in cases where plaintiffs cannot be individually identified.

4.4   Shift from Dualist to Monist State

It is equally critical that the government reviews its political and legal commitment to the international normative framework on human rights. Mauritius is a state party to several treaties and conventions drafted by the United Nations or the African Union. Some treaties and conventions have been signed only and others signed and ratified. The problem is with the level of domestication. As a dualist state, laws ratified at the international level only become applicable in the domestic jurisdiction after domestication by Parliament. In simple terms, a Mauritian cannot invoke the violation of an article from the African Charter before the Supreme Court because the Charter has not been domesticated. The situation is similar for the ICCPR and the ICESCR. Many conventions related to women's rights, children's rights, corruption, environment or disability rights cannot be used before the Supreme Court because of lack of domestication. There is therefore a pressing need to domesticate all these laws to ensure that Mauritians have a better protection of all their human rights over and above what the Constitution would confer.

---

[71] Matthew Astley, "Attaining *Locus standi* as a Private Party in Judicial Review Proceedings in European Community Law: A Virtually Impossible Task?" *Diffusion: The UCLan Journal of Undergraduate Research* 2, no. 2 (2009): 1.

5   CONCLUSION

Mauritius is positively viewed on the African as well as global level when it comes to human rights in the country. While it would be too fatalistic to say that there exists a different reality within the country, it is fair to mention that there is still much room for improvement. As stated earlier, the Bill of Rights has served its purpose well during the last 50 years. It is now begging for crucial amendments and changes which have been discussed above. However, all these would not succeed until and unless every Mauritian, not only legal practitioners or academic, understand the importance and the relevance of the Constitution and its Bill of Rights. Education and sensitisation campaigns are critical and the Constitution must be introduced in one way or another in primary and secondary schools and tertiary institutions. Every Mauritian should know that the Constitution, through its Bill of Rights and other provisions, determines our lives socially, politically, culturally and economically. At the same time, drawing inspiration from the Supreme Court's words, it acts as a citadel which guards the people against despotism and the government against anarchy.[72]

At this stage, it is also worth mentioning that human rights institutions such as the National Human Rights Commissions (through its various divisions), the Equal Opportunities Commission and the Ombudsperson for Children office, to name a few, have a critical role to play in the advancement of human rights 50 years post-independence. It is mandatory that they take a more visible and active role in the defence of human rights in Mauritius. They must strengthen and rethink their collaboration with other actors such as civil society organisations, educational institutions and research think tanks.

While celebrating the golden jubilee of the Mauritian Bill of Rights, the citizens, the state and its institutions need to come together to review the Constitution with the objective of ensuring maximum human rights protection. Despite being ranked first in different indexes, this chapter has pointed out to the loopholes of the Bill of Rights that need to be addressed in order to ensure that Mauritius keeps leading in these rankings. If a status quo is maintained, Mauritians will have no constitutional safeguards against many potential human rights violations.

---

[72] *Mahboob v The Government of Mauritius* 1982 MR 135.

How can the courts relying on other jurisdictions and jurisprudence try to engage in judicial activism? Has there been any attempt by lawyers to seek justice of ESR? How did it fare in court?

REFERENCES

Books

Meetarbhan, Milan. *Constitutional Law of Mauritius: Constitution of Mauritius with Commentaries.* Mauritius: Milan JN Meetarbhan, 2016.

Pope-Hennessy, James. *Verandah: Some Episodes in the Crown Colonies (1867–1889).* London: Allen and Unwin, 1964.

Sachs, Albie. *The Strange Alchemy of Life and the Law.* Oxford: Oxford University Press, 2009.

Twain, Mark. *Following the Equator: A Journey Around the World.* Hartford, CT: The American Publishing Company, 1897.

Chapters in Books

Budoo, Ashwanee, and Nora Ho Tu Nam. "The Republic of Mauritius." In *Oxford Constitutions of the World*, edited by Institute for International and Comparative Law in Africa. Oxford: Oxford University Press, 2016.

Mahadew, Roopanand. "The Best Loser System in Mauritius: An Essential Tool for Representing Political Minorities." In *Constitution-Building in Africa*, edited by Jaap de Visser, Nico Steytler, Derek Powell, and Ebenezer Durojaye. Baden-Baden, Germany: Nomos Verlagsgesellschaft, 2015.

Journal articles

Astley, Matthew. "Attaining *Locus standi* as a Private Party in Judicial Review Proceedings in European Community Law: A Virtually Impossible Task?" *Diffusion: The UCLan Journal of Undergraduate Research* 2, no. 2 (2009): 1–20.

de Smith, Stanley A. "Mauritius: Constitutionalism in a Plural Society." *The Modern Law Review* 31, no. 6 (1968): 601–622.

Reports

Law Reform Commission. *Constitution Protection of Human Rights.* Mauritius, October 2010.

Mo Ibrahim Foundation. *2017 Ibrahim Index of African Governance: Index Report.* 2017.

United Nations Development Programme. *Human Development Report 2016: Human Development for Everyone.* Ottawa, ON: Lowe-Martin Group, 2016.

Cases

European Court of Human Rights

S and Marper v the United Kingdom 2008 European Court of Human Rights 1581

Sahin v Turkey 2005 41 European Human Rights Reports 8

Privy Council

Matadeen v Pointu Privy Council Appeal No 14 of 1997

The Society United Docks and Others v Government of Mauritius 1985 UKPC 42

Darmalingum v The State 2000 United Kingdom Privy Council 30

Roger F.P. de Boucherville v the State of Mauritius 2008 United Kingdom Privy Council 37

Hurnam v The State 2005 United Kingdom Privy Council 49

Mauritius

Bhewa and Alladeen v Government of Mauritius & DPP 1990 MR 79

Bhinkah v The State 2009 SCJ 102

Bunwaree V K v La Sentinelle

Dahoo v State of Mauritius 2007 SCJ 156

DPP v Boodhoo 1992 MR 284

DPP v Jagdawoo 2016 SCJ 100

Ex Parte Hurnam Devendranath, a Barrister-at-Law 2007 SCJ 289

Jaulim v DPP 1976 MR 96

Jordan v Jordan 2000 SCJ 226

Jugnauth P K v The Secretary to the Cabinet and Head of the Civil Service Affairs &Ors 2013 SCJ 132

Madhewoo v The State 2015 SCJ 177

Mahboob v The Government of Mauritius 1982 MR 135

Matadeen v Pointu 1998 MR 172

Noordally v The Attorney General and the Director of Public Prosecutions 1986 MR 220/SCJ 339

Ohsan-Bellepeau v La Sentinelle 2009 SCJ 114

Peerbocus v R 1991 MR 90

Philibert v The State 2007 SCJ 274

Pulluck v Ramphul 2005 SCJ 196

Tengur v Minister of Education and Scientific Research and Another 2002 MR 166/SCJ 48

The Union of Campement Sites Owners and Lessees v The Government of Mauritius 1984 MR 100

Virahsawmy and Anor v The Commissioner of Police 1972 SCJ 169

Concluding Observations

Human Rights Committee's Concluding Observations on the Fifth Periodic Report of Mauritius Adopted on 11 December 2017 CCPR/C/MUS/CO/5.

UN Committee on Economic, Social and Cultural Rights Concluding Observation UN Doc. E/C.12/MUS/CO/4, 3–21 May 2010.

CHAPTER 6

Transcending Dualism: Deconstructing Colonial Vestiges in Ghana's Treaty Law and Practice

Godwin E. K. Dzah

1   INTRODUCTION

Ghana identifies as a dualist state. Upon ratification, Ghana must domesticate a treaty; otherwise the treaty is inapplicable under its law. Ghana's slow or almost non-existent practice of domesticating treaties entered into renders several ratified treaties unenforceable, or at least has left their status within Ghana's legal system uncertain. In this chapter, I argue that strict adherence to dualism in a context where no consistent commitment to domestication exists defeats the object and purposes of ratified treaties and assumed international commitments.

G. E. K. Dzah (✉)
University of British Columbia, Vancouver, BC, Canada
e-mail: elidzah1@mail.ubc.ca

© The Author(s) 2020
M. Addaney et al. (eds.), *Governance, Human Rights,
and Political Transformation in Africa*,
https://doi.org/10.1007/978-3-030-27049-0_6

Thus, this inconsistency poses a significant challenge for actualising rights-conferring treaties, particularly the 1981 African Charter on Human and Peoples' Rights.[1]

Today, the distinction between international law and municipal law is blurred and the two realms are increasingly influencing each other in a mutually iterative manner.[2] Drawing on Third World Approaches to International Law (TWAIL), I argue that dualism as "practised" in Ghana is an uncritical continuation of an inherited colonial legacy; that in a postcolonial context frustrates the domestic applicability of treaties and impedes local efforts aimed at realising the treaty intent of rights-conferring treaties. I contend that the continual observance of dualism inhibits the implementation of rights-conferring treaties that have been entered into by Ghana. Specifically, I argue that, if the object of the African Charter is to be realised, it is important that Ghana acknowledges and pursues, through the complementary force of proactive judicial action and the collective efforts of the Executive and Legislature, a path that transcends the monist–dualist divide.

This chapter is organised into five sections. The first is this introduction. This is followed by a historical overview of the monist–dualist divide and its contemporary manifestation. The next section analyses treaty reception in Africa, focusing on Ghana's attitude towards dualism. Drawing on TWAIL-oriented insights, the fourth section proffers suggestions on how to make unincorporated treaties applicable in Ghana law. The fifth section concludes this contribution.

2   Monist–Dualist Divide: Navigating Imposed "Rules"

The monist–dualist divide revolves around whether international law and municipal law are independent of each other, or are part of the same legal order. The quintessence of the monist–dualist divide is "the role of the legislative branch in incorporating and implementing treaties domestically."[3] Thus, it is important that a discussion of monism and dualism precedes further analysis.

---

[1] 21 I.L.M. 58 (1982) [Hereinafter the African Charter or the Charter]; Ghana deposited its instrument of ratification on March 1, 1989.

[2] Melissa Walters, "Creeping Monism: The Judicial Trend Toward Interpretive Incorporation of Human Rights Treaties," *Columbia Law Review* 107 (2007): 643.

[3] David Sloss, "Domestic Application of Treaties," in *The Oxford Guide to Treaties*, ed. Duncan Hollis (Oxford: Oxford University Press, 2012), 367.

2.1   Monism: A Unitary View of Law

Under monism, a treaty is incorporated into municipal law once the state executes the treaty without the need for subsequent action; namely, the passage of an enabling legislation.[4] Once entered into, the treaty becomes effective within the state's jurisdiction.[5] Monism underlies the relationship between international law and domestic law where the consensus is the "unity of the international and municipal legal orders."[6] Also that where international law and municipal law are in conflict, the conflict must be resolved in favour of international law[7] because the former supersedes the latter.[8] On the strength of this premise, monists argue international law predominates municipal law in the hierarchy of legal norms.[9] Formulated differently, for monists, international law is the foundation of municipal law.[10]

2.2   Dualism: Infrequent Convergence of Parallel Realms

For dualists, international law and municipal law exist separately and cannot purport to have an effect on, or take precedence over each other. This distinction derives from the political doctrine of separation of powers.[11] Jan Klabbers credits Henirich Triepel with the theoretical origins of dualism.[12] In Klabbers' view, Triepel argued that international law

[4] Ibid., 373.

[5] P.F. Gonidec, "Relationship Between International Law and National Law in Africa," *African Journal of International and Comparative Law* 10 (1998): 245.

[6] Boleslaw Boczek, *International Law: A Dictionary*, vol. 2 (Lanham, MD: Scarecrow Press, 2005), 6; Martin Dixon, *Textbook on International Law*, 3rd ed. (London: Blackstone Press, 1996), 65.

[7] Edwin Borchard, "The Relationship Between International Law and Municipal Law," *Virginia Law Review* 27, no. 2 (1940): 137.

[8] Ibid., 139.

[9] W.B. Stern, "Kelsen's Theory of International Law," *American Political Science Review* 30, no. 4 (1936): 737.

[10] Jordan Paust, "Basic Forms of International Law and Monist, Dualist, and Realist Perspectives," in *Basic Concepts of International Law: Monism and Dualism*, ed. Marko Novakovic (Belgrade: University of Belgrade, 2013), 246.

[11] Malcolm Shaw, *International Law*, 5th ed. (Cambridge: Cambridge University Press, 2003), 135–136.

[12] Heinrich Triepel, "Les Rapports entre Le Droit Interne et Le Droit International," *Recueil des Cours* 1 (1923): 77.

regulates state-to-state relations, while municipal law regulates state–individual relations and that international law can only be brought into the municipal domain only through a legislative act.[13] Dualism, from the foregoing, emerges as inordinately focused on the authority of a legislative body to enact domestic law, without taking into account the normative fluidity of what is broadly classified as international or local.[14] Thus, in keeping with its connection to the doctrine of separation of powers, dualism tends to be exceedingly rigid over the distinct legal structure of international law and municipal law; hence, glossing over how power interactions at both national and international levels increasingly defy strict categorisation.[15]

Originating from the common law system, dualism distinguishes international law from municipal law. In the United Kingdom (UK), one of the remaining prerogative powers of the Crown is the capacity to enter into, i.e., sign and ratify, treaties in the performance of its international obligations.[16] In the UK, "no rule of law requires that a treaty be approved by Parliament prior to ratification."[17] Thus, treaty-making, including ratification, is an exclusive Executive function.[18] Upon ratification, the treaty binds the UK and any other party to the treaty as it relates to its *international application*, and no parliamentary process is required for the assumption of such obligations.[19] However, despite ratification, a treaty does not operate to alter a legal

---

[13] Jan Klabbers, *International Law* (Cambridge: Cambridge University Press, 2013), 289.

[14] Paust, "Basic Forms," 247–248.

[15] Ibid.

[16] Robert Stewart, "Treaty-Making Procedure in the United Kingdom," *American Political Science Review* 32, no. 4 (1938): 655.

[17] Ibid., 659.

[18] Jill Barrett, "The United Kingdom and Parliamentary Scrutiny of Treaties: Recent Reforms," *International Comparative Law Quarterly* 60, no. 1 (2011): 228; Arabella Lang, "Parliament's Role in Ratifying Treaties," *House of Commons Briefing Paper* 5855 (2017): 3–4. The UK's Constitutional Reform and Governance Act, 2010 (CRGA) affirmed the Executive's treaty-making powers by clarifying the Ponsonby Rule. Under the Ponsonby Rule, the Executive laid treaties before Parliament for 21 "sitting days" prior to ratification. Parliament could debate the treaty, but neither the debate nor its outcome was binding on the Executive. Today, the CRGA gives statutory backing to this rule which, previously, was merely a convention.

[19] Stewart, "Treaty-Making Procedure," 666.

rule or a right under UK law even though the UK is bound at the international level.[20] It is Parliament's duty to pass an enabling legislation to *transform* (or domesticate) the treaty.[21] Thus, it is only when the treaty is domesticated that it can alter UK's municipal law.[22]

During colonial overrule, the UK conducted the external affairs of its colonies in similar form and substance as its own. In a far-reaching judicial decision relating to the conduct of external relations, the UK's Privy Council unilaterally enhanced the scope of this dualist doctrine beyond the UK to cover all of its colonies.[23] Subsequently, Parliament extended an incorporated treaty's domain from the *metropole* to the colony. This politico-legal doctrine thus became a permanent, inherited, and almost intractable feature of colonial legal governance that was carried over into the postcolonial existence of newly independent states even where legislative and constitutional modifications have occurred.[24]

2.3   *The Fuzzy Middle Between*

As explained above, the reception and application of treaties within a state follows either mode: monism or dualism. However, recent evidence shows the monist–dualist divide is beginning to pale into insignificance as courts in some common law jurisdictions are increasingly enforcing obligations arising from unincorporated treaties.[25] However, this trend is yet to translate into a regular, accepted practice because courts in some dualist states still adhere, in principle, to dualism.[26] Yet, while there is some judicial resistance to this emerging practice, it is unlikely this will

---

[20] Ibid., 666.

[21] John Jackson, "Status of Treaties in Domestic Legal Systems," *American Journal of International Law* 86, no. 2 (1992): 315; Joseph Chitty, *A Treatise on the Law of the of the Prerogatives of the Crown: And the Relative Duties and Rights of the Subject* (London: J. Butterworth and Son, 1820), 3–4.

[22] Stewart, "Treaty-Making Procedure," 666.

[23] *Attorney-General for Canada v. Attorney-General for Ontario*, A.C. 326 (1937).

[24] Kenneth Twitchett, "Colonialism: An Attempt at Understanding Imperial, Colonial and Neo-colonial Relationships," *Political Studies* 13, no. 3 (1965): 319.

[25] Emmanuel Quansah, "An Examination of the Use of International Law as an Interpretative Tool in Human Rights Litigation in Ghana and Botswana," in *International Law and Human Rights Litigation in Africa*, ed. Magnus Killander (Pretoria: Pretoria University Law Press, 2010), 37–38.

[26] Sloss, "Domestic Application of Treaties," 373.

translate into a frequent pattern of political hostility towards this trend as courts are showing greater willingness to overcome this hurdle.[27] Today, the prevailing argument is that a court's overreliance on the "pedigree of norms" to the neglect of the law's normative substance risks glossing over the import of law.[28] Consequently, there is progress towards a convergence of monism and dualism.[29]

3   AFRICA: TREATY RATIFICATION AND DOMESTICATION

The reception of international law in Africa follows whether a state identifies as monist or dualist, and whether the law is treaty-based or devolves from customary international law.[30] Regarding treaty incorporation, African countries with civil law systems ply the monist route while common law states are dualist.[31] As an exception, customary international law is considered to be domestically applicable irrespective of whether the state is monist or dualist.[32] While contestable, the "distinguishing feature of customary international law is that it binds all members of the

---

[27] Walters, "Creeping Monism", 652; Lang, "Parliament's Role," 20.

[28] Richard Oppong, "Re-imagining International Law: An Examination of Recent Trends in the Reception of International Law into National Legal Systems in Africa," *Fordham International Law Journal* 30, no. 2 (2006): 298.

[29] Ibid.

[30] David Kennedy, "Sources of International Law," *American University Law Review* 2, no. 1 (1987): 8–10.

[31] Mirna Adjami, "African Courts, International Law, and Comparative Case Law: Chimera or Emerging Human Rights Jurisprudence," *Michigan International Law Journal* 24 (2002–2003): 109; Ernest Yaw Ako and Richard Frimpong Oppong, "Foreign Relations Law in the Constitutions and Courts of Commonwealth African Countries," in *The Oxford Handbook of Comparative Foreign Relations Law*, ed. Curtis A. Bradley (Oxford: Oxford University Press, 2019), 586–591, argue that there are variations within Africa as some common law states have altered their dualist heritage to take the form of a monist-like approach, either by judicial practice, statutory change or constitutional intervention.

[32] Christian Okeke, "The Use of International Law in the Domestic Courts of Ghana and Nigeria," *Arizona Journal of International and Comparative Law* 32, no. 2 (2015): 395; Gib van Ert, "The Domestic Applicability of International Law in Canada," in *The Oxford Handbook of Comparative Foreign Relations Law*, ed. Curtis A. Bradley (Oxford: Oxford University Press, 2019), 510, argues that the reception of customary international law in dualist states "is a significantly monist element in a system too often depicted as dualist."

international community, or of a regional group, in the case of a regional custom."[33]

3.1 Treaty Incorporation: A Brief Continental Perspective

A treaty concluded within the remit of the Organisation of African Unity (OAU) and its successor organisation, the African Union (AU), expressly requires state parties to indicate their consent to be bound when they sign the treaty.[34] In this regard, Article 1 of the African Charter provides that "... parties to the present Charter shall recognise the rights, duties and freedoms enshrined in this Charter and shall undertake to adopt legislative or other measures to give effect to them."[35] State parties are, therefore, required to realign their domestic legal regimes to accord with the object of the treaty pending ratification. Once ratified, the treaty becomes binding on the state.[36]

The African Charter also requires state parties to provide biennial reports on "legislative or other measures" that they have undertaken in compliance with the Charter.[37] Reading the Charter, one gets the sense that the OAU/AU may have contemplated the dualist challenge and sought to overcome that obstacle by providing that the Charter is binding once a state has ratified it,[38] even to the extent that the Charter places on states an "obligation of domestic incorporation of the Charter."[39] From the foregoing, it appears state parties are obliged to implement the African Charter irrespective of the limitations of domestic law[40]; a state may not invoke its internal law (including dualism) as justification for non-compliance with its treaty obligations.[41]

---

[33] Andre Ferreira et al., "Formation and Evidence of Customary International Law," *UFRGS Model United Nations Journal* 1 (2013): 185.

[34] Tijanyawa Maluwa, "Ratification of African Union Treaties by Member States: Law, Policy and Practice," *Melbourne Journal of International Law* 13, no. 2 (2012): 7.

[35] African Charter, art. 1.

[36] Maluwa, "Ratification of African Union Treaties," 8.

[37] African Charter, art. 62.

[38] Adjami, "African Courts," 111; African Charter, arts. 1 and 62.

[39] Ibid., 110.

[40] African Charter, art. 1.

[41] Vienna Convention on the Law of Treaties 1155 U.N.T.S. 331 [hereinafter VCLT], art. 27.

Thus, non-incorporation could be construed as a Charter violation[42] since under international law, even where a state has only signed a treaty and is yet to ratify it, that state is still required not to act in contravention of the treaty's overall purpose.[43]

3.2   Treaty Ratification in Ghana

As a successor state to the UK's Gold Coast colony,[44] Ghana's legal system is closely modelled after the UK's common law system.[45] Prior to independence, the UK, through the Secretary of State for the Colonies, was responsible for the Gold Coast's external affairs.[46] At independence, Ghana and the UK entered into an Exchange of Letters Constituting an Agreement which established an inheritance agreement of treaties entered into or on behalf of Ghana—this agreement became the basis for Ghana's treaty practice.[47] Consequently, Ghana parenthetically absorbed the British politico-legal doctrine of dualism as part of its colonial heritage.[48] Thus, Ghana's adherence to dualism mirrors its historical connection to the British colonial project,[49] and without scrutiny, this doctrine has become embedded in how postcolonial Ghana structures its interaction with international law.[50]

Following this dualist practice, it has been argued that a treaty ratified by Ghana does not ordinarily confer rights until it is domesticated.[51]

---

[42] Adjami, "African Courts," 110.

[43] VCLT, art. 18.

[44] William Thompson, *Ghana's Foreign Policy, 1957–1966: Diplomacy Ideology, and the New State* (Princeton: Princeton University Press, 1969), xvii.

[45] Francis Bennion, *Constitutional Law of Ghana* (London: Butterworths, 1962), 259.

[46] Stanley de Smith, "The Independence of Ghana," *Modern Law Review* 20 (1957): 351–352.

[47] Victor Essien, "Ghana," in *Sources of State Practice in International Law*, ed. Ralph Gaebler and Alison Shea, 2nd revised ed. (Leiden: Brill, 2014), 254.

[48] Kwadwo Appiagyei-Atua, "Ghana at 50: The Place of International Human Rights Norms in Ghana's Courts," in *Ghana Law Since Independence: History, Development and Prospects*, ed. Henrietta Mensa-Bonsu et al. (Accra: Black Mask, 2007), 184.

[49] Emmanuel Benneh, "The Sources of Public International Law and Their Applicability to the Domestic Law in Ghana," *University of Ghana Law Journal* 26 (2013): 91.

[50] *Armon v. Katz* 2 G.L.R. 115 (1976), 123.

[51] A.K.P. Kludze, "Constitutional Rights and Their Relationship with International Human Rights in Ghana," *Israel Law Review* 41, no. 3 (2008): 679.

Little wonder, then, that is has been noted "[t]his follows the old British practice ... inherited from our colonial past."[52] To clarify, Kludze draws a distinction between Ghana and the United States (US) and argues that whereas both countries were colonised by the UK, the US does not follow the UK practice; opting for a monist-like approach.[53] In the US, a treaty becomes part of the domestic law after ratification, "in fact a part of the supreme law, of the United States."[54] However, there are some exceptions to this general position based on the concept of non-self-executing treaties.[55] Non-self-executing treaties relate to the structure of the political branches of government; therefore, are only enforceable upon express incorporation by legislation.[56] This observation is profound guidance for Ghana's postcolonial reality—that, a state is not bound to continue its colonial legacy; it may depart from that history and chart a new course by pursuing its own national interests.

As noted earlier, a large number of treaties ratified by Ghana, especially those relating to human rights, are yet to be domesticated.[57] Yet, the 1992 Constitution, through the directive principles of state policy (DPSPs), directs the government to be guided by international human rights treaties in the conduct of its international affairs.[58] Specifically, the Constitution enjoins Ghana to adhere to the principles of the OAU Charter (now the Constitutive Act of the AU).[59] Despite these constitutional imperatives, in a recent critique, "Ghana's notoriety for

[52] Ibid., 681.

[53] Ibid.

[54] Ibid., 680.

[55] Ibid.; Carlos Vazquez, "The Four Doctrines of Self-Executing Treaties," *American Journal of International Law* 89 (1995): 695; Duncan B. Hollis and Carlos M. Vasquez, "Treaty Self-Execution as "Foreign" Foreign Relations Law," in *The Oxford Handbook of Comparative Foreign Relations Law*, ed. Curtis A. Bradley (Oxford: Oxford University Press, 2019), 468.

[56] Kludze, "Constitutional Rights," 680.

[57] Essien, "Ghana," 256.

[58] 1992 Constitution of the Republic of Ghana, art. 37(3) and art. 73 [hereinafter 1992 Constitution or the Constitution]. Office of Attorney General and Ministry of Justice, Republic of Ghana: Treaty Manual (2009).

[59] 1992 Constitution of the Republic of Ghana, art. 40. By extension, the reference to the OAU/AU foundational texts contemplates treaties made under the authority of this continental organisation.

non-domestication of international human rights instruments" was, once again, highlighted.[60]

While the DPSPs may come across as aspirational, they have a unique history in Ghana's jurisprudence with significant implications for international obligations. To begin, the DPSPs were previously considered non-justiciable.[61] However, in 2008, the Supreme Court in the *Ghana Lotto Operators Association v. National Lottery Authority*, held that as a legal document, the Constitution in its entirety is presumably justiciable.[62] On the strength of the *Lotto Case*, the DPSPs was adjudged *prima facie* justiciable unless there is contrary evidence requiring an alternative construction. In addition to this imaginative interpretation, the Constitution also fosters "virtual incorporation of human rights instruments; even those treaties which have not been legislated into municipal law may be relevant in the adjudication of certain rights."[63] In this respect, the tenor of Article 37(3) suggests that Ghana's (domestic) law is presumed to be consistent with the state's assumed international human rights obligations.[64] Consequently, the African Charter can be construed as incorporated under Ghana law.[65]

3.3   Domesticating Ghana's International Obligations

I now turn to Ghana's constitutional framework and how it interacts with the state's international obligations. To begin, Ghana's 1957 Independence Constitution did not expressly provide for how to bring international law into the domain of municipal law.[66] The subsequent 1960 Constitution did not also provide for the reception of international

---

[60] Michael Nyarko, "The Impact of the African Charter and Maputo Protocol in Ghana," in *The Impact of the African Charter and Maputo Protocol in Selected African States*, ed. Victor Ayeni (Pretoria: Pretoria University Law Press, 2016), 99.

[61] Tarunabh Khaitan, "Directive Principles and the Expressive Accommodation of Ideological Dissenters," *International Journal of Constitutional Law* 16 (2018): 396.

[62] *Ghana Lotto Operators Association v. National Lottery Authority*, S.C.G.L.R. 1088 (2007–2008) (hereinafter *Lotto Case*).

[63] Kludze, "Constitutional Rights," 682; 1992 Constitution, art. 37(3).

[64] Ibid., 683.

[65] Ibid., 679.

[66] Essien, "Ghana," 254.

law.[67] It would seem the inherited common law practice prevailed until succeeding constitutions which provided for the execution and incorporation of treaties. This begun with the 1969 Constitution which tasked the President (or her lawful representative) with entering into treaties on behalf of Ghana.[68] Since then, the reception of treaties has become a two-step process: the President executes treaties, and the treaties became domestically applicable only upon parliamentary ratification, either by way of an Act or a resolution.[69] The 1979 Constitution repeated *verbatim* the 1969 constitutional provisions relating to treaty execution and incorporation.[70] Finally, the current 1992 Constitution continued this practice by vesting the President with the power to enter into treaties,[71] and entrusting Parliament with the authority to ratify treaties either by an Act[72] or a parliamentary resolution.[73]

The constitutional changes introduced by the 1969 Constitution, and continued till date, fundamentally modified Ghana's common law heritage. The 1969 Constitution did continue the common law practice which vested the Executive with the power to enter into treaties; however, it also departed considerably from that practice by vesting Parliament with authority to ratify treaties. This is markedly different from the UK practice where Parliament does not ratify treaties in the same way as is done in Ghana.[74] Therefore, it is quite logical that before a ratified treaty becomes part of UK law, its Parliament should have the opportunity to assess the treaty's implications on existing law, whereas Ghana's Parliament is given the authority to scrutinise an executed treaty's compatibility with existing law during the ratification process.

Accordingly, unless incorporated, a treaty is deemed domestically unenforceable.[75] That treaty may not be invoked in court even if it

---

[67] Oppong, "Re-imagining International Law," 255.

[68] 1969 Constitution, art. 59(1).

[69] 1969 Constitution, art. 59(2).

[70] 1979 Constitution, art. 62.

[71] 1992 Constitution, art. 75(1).

[72] 1992 Constitution, art. 75(2)(a).

[73] 1992 Constitution, art. 75(2)(b); Richard Oppong, "The High Court of Ghana Declines to Enforce an ECOWAS Judgment," *African Journal of International and Comparative Law* 25, no. 1 (2017): 129.

[74] Lang, "Parliament's Role," 3–4.

[75] Oppong, "The High Court of Ghana," 129.

confers a right.[76] Going strictly by this argument, the African Charter rights would be construed as excluded from Ghana's legal domain due to the Charter's non-incorporation. Nonetheless, it is understood that the list of rights provided under the 1992 Constitution are not exhaustive: all rights considered to be part of a democratic society can be inferred as present in Ghana's jurisprudence by virtue of referential incorporation.[77] Therefore, there is little risk in assuming that Ghana is bound to give effect to rights contained in supposedly unincorporated human rights treaties, including the African Charter. But then, how do the courts receive and apply unincorporated treaties?

3.4   Ghana's Courts and the Reception of International Law

Ghana's jurisprudence on the reception and application of unincorporated treaties has a chequered past. Concerning this history, I will briefly outline three Supreme Court decisions of varied significance to dualism.

In the first case, the late Chief Justice Archer had held that non-incorporation of the African Charter into Ghana law does not preclude the courts from enforcing the Charter.[78] He held, thus:

> The African Charter and members of the OAU and parties to the Charter are expected to recognise the rights, duties and freedoms enshrined in the Charter and to undertake to adopt legislative and other measures to give effect to the rights and duties. I do not think the fact Ghana has not passed specific legislation to give effect to the Charter means the Charter cannot be relied upon.[79]

In the second case, there were two competing views on the domestic applicability of unincorporated treaties.[80] Justice Atuguba held that international legal instruments relating to fundamental human rights

---

[76] Shazia Qureshi and Ernest Owusu-Dapaa, "The International Human Right to Health: What Does It Mean for Ghana and Pakistan?" *Journal of Political Studies* 21, no. 1 (2014): 322.

[77] Ibid., 323; 1992 Constitution, art. 33(5).

[78] *New Patriotic Party v. Inspector-General of Police* 2 G.L.R. 459 (1993–1994) [*IGP* Case].

[79] *IGP* Case, 466.

[80] *New Patriotic Party v. Attorney-General* 1 G.L.R. 378 (1997–1998) [*CIBA* Case].

are enforceable under Ghana law by virtue of Article 33(5).[81] Justice Ampiah held a contrary view, noting that "[I]nternational laws, including inter-African enactments, are not binding on Ghana until such laws have been adopted or ratified by the municipal laws."[82]

In the third instance, the court adopted a position similar to Justice Ampiah's decision in the *CIBA* Case.[83] In a unanimous decision, Justice Date-Bah, held that, "... even when treaties have been ratified by Parliament, they do not alter municipal law until they are incorporated into Ghana law by appropriate legislation."[84] Additionally, he held that treaties ratified by an Act must be incorporated "by appropriate language."[85]

Much of my subsequent critique is founded on this third decision as I find Justice Date-Bah's interpretation of Article 75 in the *ARA Libertad* Case to be problematic. First, by restricting ratification to an Act, Justice Date-Bah overlooked the entirety of Article 75(2) which provides two modes of ratification: an Act or a parliamentary resolution. Second, in the course of this unsatisfactory interpretative exercise, Justice Date-Bah harks back to a long line of English cases to argue that Ghana follows the dualist position.[86] In what appears to be his vaunted regard for dualism, he held that the 1992 Constitution cannot be interpreted as altering Ghana's dualist standpoint[87] else the Executive can "bypass Parliament in changing the rights and obligations of the citizens of Ghana."[88]

In analysing the first criticism, it is important to note that the Constitution neither distinguishes between ratification by an Act or

---

[81] *CIBA* Case, 444.

[82] *CIBA* Case, 412.

[83] *Republic v. High Court (Commercial Division); ex parte Attorney-General (NML Capital Ltd 1st Interested Party)* Supreme Court Suit No. J5/10/2013 (unreported) [*ARA Libertad* Case].

[84] *ARA Libertad* Case, 2–3.

[85] *ARA Libertad* Case, 4; As used by Justice Date-Bah, "appropriate language" suggests an Act of Parliament. This misapprehension that ratification is *only* possible through legislation to the exclusion of parliamentary resolutions continues to feature prominently in Ghanaian legal commentaries on the subject. *See* George Sarpong and Emmanuel Benneh, "The Doctrine of Sovereign Immunity in International Law: The ARA Libertad Case (Argentina v. Ghana)," *University of Ghana Law Journal* 28 (2015): 149–151.

[86] *ARA Libertad* Case, 5–6.

[87] *ARA Libertad* Case, 6 (interpreting 1992 Constitution, arts. 40 and 73).

[88] *ARA Libertad* Case, 7.

parliamentary resolution, nor does it place them in a hierarchical order where one assumes preeminence over the other. As used in Article 75(2) (b), a resolution appears as a legislative device of no less value than an Act. Regrettably, the learned judge's misapprehension of the ratification process creates some uncertainty regarding the effect of complying with Article 75 of the Constitution. Particularly, his silence over the applicability of Article 75(2)(b) suggests an inferred exclusion of parliamentary resolutions as a mode of treaty ratification. Yet, ratification in Ghana contemplates a legislative procedure; thus, whether as an Act or a resolution, it implies a Parliament-backed process not an exclusive Executive affair as wrongly suggested by Justice Date-Bah's interpretation.[89]

With respect to the second criticism, Justice Date-Bah's decision in the *ARA Libertad* Case failed to account for the significant changes introduced into Ghana's treaty jurisprudence beginning with the 1969 Constitution and continued till date. This historical variation empowers Parliament to ratify treaties; effectively ensuring that Parliament, the expression of the people's legislative will, is assured that the executed treaty is consistent with municipal law.[90] This power endows Parliament with the legal authority to vet treaty content as part of the ratification process, and not merely mechanical concurrence with an Executive act. Thus, when a rights-conferring treaty passes this constitutional muster, assessed to be consistent with municipal law and subsequently ratified, it ought to be construed as incorporated. Moreover, as a safeguard measure, Parliament may require that ratification is accompanied with

---

[89] Mawuse Barker-Vormawor, "Five Years On: A Requiem for the Ex Parte Attorney-General, NML Capital Ltd 1st Interested Party Decision," Ghana Law Hub (2018), accessed January 3, 2019, https://ghanalawhub.com/five-years-on-a-requiem-for-the-ex-parte-attorney-general-nml-capital-ltd-1st-interested-party-decision/. In defence of Justice Date-Bah, there is a general misapprehension that ratification by resolution does not carry equal weight as ratification by an Act. Therefore, the Constitution Review Commission in its final report suggested Parliament passes a law to distinguish between treaties to be ratified by either an Act or resolution. Constitution Review Commission, *Report of the Constitution Review Commission: From a Political to a Developmental Constitution* (2011), para. 284; Chief Justice Akuffo in her majority opinion in *Margaret Banful and Henry Nana Boakye v. Attorney-General and Ministry of Interior* Suit No. J1/7/2016 (unreported) reiterated that treaties must be ratified by an Act or resolution [*GITMO Case*].

[90] Ghana ratified the Statute of the International Criminal Court by a resolution: Parliamentary Debates (November 11, 1999), vols. 23: cols. 1033.

a reservation to restrict or deny the application of parts of the treaty it considers inconsistent with municipal law.[91]

Justice Date-Bah's excessive regard for dualism is an unwitting reification of dualism's Eurocentrism. In addressing this issue, I note, with caution that, customary international law is somewhat accepted to be directly applicable with little query, as opposed to a treaty which is deemed to be domestically applicable only when ratified.[92] Considering the emerging consensus is that the monist–dualist dichotomy is of little practical contemporary consequence to the reception and applicability of international law within municipal law,[93] it is extremely surprising that Ghana's courts would actively seek to reify colonial legacies that have actually undergone constitutional modification as far back as the 1969 Constitution. Thus, Justice Date-Bah's acquiescence has been described by some as an unquantifiable cost to Ghana's own fledgling treaty jurisprudence.[94]

However, I must point out that the Supreme Court is not bound by its previous decisions.[95] The court may decide cases and reach different conclusions as it deems fit without being constrained to abide by its previous decisions. However, as it relates to the incorporation of rights contained in international legal instruments, my suggestion is that the better approach is one that corresponds to Chief Justice Archer's view in the *IGP* Case.[96] In contradistinguishing Chief Justice Archer and Justice Atuguba's positions on one hand with the views of Justice Ampiah and especially Justice Date-Bah's decision in the *ARA Libertad* Case, it is apparent Justice Date-Bah did not adequately consider the general rules governing the law of treaties and Ghana's own peculiar position on the reception of treaties into municipal law. To this end, the VCLT enjoins a state that has signed or ratified a treaty not to act in a manner that is

---

[91] VCLT, art. 19.

[92] Bhupinder Chimni, "Customary International Law: A Third World Perspective," *American Journal of International Law* 112, no. 2 (2018): 9–13.

[93] Takele Bulto, "The Monist-Dualist Divide and the Supremacy Clause: Revisiting the Status of Human Rights Treaties in Ethiopia," *Journal of Ethiopian Law* 23, no. 1 (2009): 134.

[94] Barker-Vormawor, "Five Years On."

[95] 1992 Constitution, art. 129(3).

[96] *IGP* Case, 466.

inconsistent with the treaty's purpose.[97] Additionally, ratification is the primary means by which a state indicates its consent to other state parties that it is bound by a treaty.[98] Therefore, Justice Date-Bah's decision failed to contemplate what the practical utility of ratification would be if a state does not intend to act out the object of a treaty it has ratified.

Finally, it is trite learning a state cannot invoke its domestic law to justify non-performance of its treaty obligations.[99] While it may be argued that the obligations contemplated at international law are generally between states, the intended beneficiaries of rights-conferring treaties are, quite often, individuals within the state. When states proceed to enter into treaties, they ought to understand the enormity of that responsibility, both home and abroad. Thus, the suggestion that interpreting the Constitution in a manner that gives effect to an unincorporated treaty would negatively affect the rights of the citizens, as urged by Justice Date-Bah, overlooks the potentially progressive dividends of such incorporation[100]; as it could be positive, and conceivably enhance human rights jurisprudence.

4   De-schematising Dualism

In examining dualism's utility, I adopt a TWAIL framework to critique dualism's application to the incorporation of human rights treaties. TWAIL is associated with postcolonial theory which, in turn, is interested in how historical colonial rule continues to shape and dictate to the postcolonial state in a "disruptive" fashion.[101] In this regard, TWAIL scholars understand that the international legal system is predominantly an extension of European imperialism[102]; a system "set up to accommodate the former imperial powers."[103] Consequently, postcolonial states like Ghana are 'impelled' to continue inherited legal rules, including

---

[97]VCLT, art. 18.

[98]VCLT, arts. 2, 11, 14 and 16.

[99]VCLT, art. 27; Mattias Kumm, "The Legitimacy of International Law: A Constitutionalist Framework of Analysis," *European Journal of International Law* 15, no. 5 (2004): 910.

[100]*ARA Libertad* Case, 7.

[101]Robert Young, *Empire, Colony, Postcolony* (West Sussex: Wiley-Blackwell, 2015), 144.

[102]Ibid., 138.

[103]Ibid.

dualism, without adequately scrutinising the domestic suitability of these rules.

As TWAIL's corollary, postcolonial theory's influence is prominent in several disciplines, including law.[104] It serves as a reminder of colonial legacies and the influence of imperialism embedded in political and legal structures designed to continue the exploitation of (de)colonised peoples.[105] Consequently, postcolonial legal theory is concerned with providing insights into the material conditions and law-making processes in the colonial period and the legacies those law-making systems bequeathed to the postcolonial state.[106]

4.1   On TWAIL: Between Law and Politics

TWAIL builds on postcolonial legal theory by layering a critical outlook of international legal analysis.[107] More closely, TWAIL seeks to develop an alternative approach to international law praxis.[108] From this, we can discern TWAIL's mission as threefold: to deconstruct international law's role in the creation and entrenchment of systemic discrimination by the Global North against the Global South; to construct an alternate vision of international law that conspicuously gives visibility to the Global South and its unique legal perspective; and finally to do away with legal, policy and political constraints inhibiting the Global South's progress.[109] TWAIL's enduring influence as a mode of international legal analysis is

---

[104] Edward Said, *Orientalism* (New York: Pantheon Books, 1978); Edward Said, *Culture and Imperialism* (New York: Knopf, 1994); Lufti Hamadi, "Edward Said: The Postcolonial Theory and the Literature of Decolonization," *European Scientific Journal* 2 (2014): 39.

[105] Homi Bhabha, *The Location of Culture* (London: Routledge, 1994); Eve Darian-Smith, "Postcolonial Law," in *International Encyclopedia of the Social and Behavioral Sciences*, ed. James D. Wright, 2nd ed. (Amsterdam: Elsevier, 2015), 18: 647.

[106] Sally Merry, "Colonial and Postcolonial Law," in *The Blackwell Companion to Law and Society*, ed. Austin Sarat (Malden: Blackwell, 2004), 573.

[107] Alpana Roy, "Postcolonial Theory and Law: A Critical Introduction," *Adelaide Law Review* 29, no. 1/2 (2008): 315.

[108] Obiora Okafor, "Critical Third World Approaches to International Law (TWAIL): Theory, Methodology or Both?" *International Community Law Review* 10 (2008): 378.

[109] Makau Mutua, "What Is TWAIL," *American Society of International Law Proceedings* 94 (2000): 31–32.

undergirded by its inherently polycentric vision.[110] While TWAIL scholars are animated by a variety of concerns, they are bound together by the central logic that the global community as a political space and global justice as a legal concept are tilted in favour of the Global North.[111] Thus, TWAIL acknowledges the law–politics nexus and how that relationship mutually strengthens each domain, either as law or as politics.[112] For example, in a recent TWAIL-inspired critique of international criminal law, it is argued that this branch of international law is at once dependent and divorced from politics. This distinction is important in how we understanding international criminal law's patently apolitical character in its pursuit of international justice, when in fact its methods for achieving this end are deeply political.[113] Consequently, it is important to test TWAIL's utility in unravelling (colonial) legal technologies like dualism.

4.2   TWAIL-ing Dualism

While TWAIL developed as an oppositional stance to classical conceptions of international law, its utility cannot be confined to the international domain as the international is in constant interaction with the local; influencing and complementing each other in the development of legal norms.[114] TWAIL's significance to the critique of this interaction ought to interest international law scholars because of the long-term effects of "received law" and dominant (colonial) political practices that have metamorphosed to assume legal permanence.[115] Consequently,

---

[110]James Gathii, "TWAIL: A Brief History of Its Origins, Its Decentralized Network, and a Tentative Bibliography," *Trade, Law and Development* 3 (2011): 34.

[111]David Fidler, "Revolt Against or from Within the West? TWAIL, the Developing World and the Future of International Law," *Chinese Journal of International Law* 2, no. 1 (2003): 30.

[112]Jalia Kanjave, "A TWAIL Analysis of Foreign Investment and Development-Induced Displacement Resettlement: Lessons from Uganda's Bujagali Hydroelectric Project," *Ottawa Law Review* 44, no. 2 (2013): 218.

[113]Michelle Burgis-Kasthala, "Scholarship as Dialogue? TWAIL and the Politics of Methodology," *Journal of International Criminal Justice* 14, no. 4 (2016): 928.

[114]Bhupinder Chimni, "The World of TWAIL: Introduction to the Special Issue," *Law, Trade and Development* 3, no. 1 (2011): 25.

[115]Victor Essien, "Sources of Law in Ghana," *Journal of Black Studies* 24, no. 3 (1994): 249.

TWAIL praxis must engage with the deceptive objectivity of the commingling of law and politics, both inherited as part of the postcolonial process.

Dualism, to begin with, is a deeply "political practice."[116] The language, structure and normative value of dualism are central features in the reception and application of international law in the postcolonial context. It is instructive to note, here, that due to its elusive character, attempts at analysing dualism's "deep structures" in contemporary international law have been largely unsuccessful.[117] Our inability to fully comprehend dualism's influence reveals the structurally Eurocentric and intensely imperialised nature of the postcolonial state. For example, it has been recently acknowledged that while India (a former British colony) is theoretically dualist, it is monist-like in practice as its courts are willing to give effect to human rights obligations arising from treaties that are yet to be domesticated.[118]

From an African perspective, TWAIL scholarship argues for international law reforms from a post-independence viewpoint.[119] In this regard, it is argued that international law's universality requires an African re-evaluation.[120] Therefore, I find it unsurprising that international law's perceived universality continues to characterise every aspect of the postcolonial state, manifesting in the vestigial influences of colonialism like dualism which are expressed in subtle, routine processes that should invite the scrutiny of TWAIL scholarship.[121]

---

[116]Obiora Okafor, "Newness, Imperialism and International Legal Reform in Our Time: A TWAIL Perspective," *Osgoode Hall Law Journal* 43 (2005): 172 argued that the application of the concept of "newness" as basis for the US unilateral counterterrorism response to post-9/11 events was simply "a political manoeuvre" by dominant states in the Global North to carry out own agenda of extending control over the world by drawing undue significance to this singular act of terror which took place in the US. I describe dualism as political practice in similar sense.

[117]Bhupinder Chimni, "International Law Scholarship in Post-colonial India: Coping with Dualism," *Leiden Journal of International Law* 23 (2010): 24.

[118]Aparna Chandra, "India and International Law: Formal Dualism, Functional Monism," *Indian Journal of International Law* 57, nos. 1–2 (2017): 25.

[119]James Gathii, "A Critical Appraisal of the International Legal Tradition of Taslim Olawale Elias," *Leiden Journal of International Law* 21 (2008): 319.

[120]Ibid.

[121]Luis Eslava and Sundhya Pahuja, "Beyond the Post (Colonial): TWAIL and the Everyday Life of International Law," *Verfassung und Recht in Übersee* 45, no. 2 (2012): 199.

4.3   Overcoming Dualism's (Imaginary) Barrier

TWAIL's reconstructive interest in reforming international law agrees with the call to transcend dualism. As noted earlier, TWAIL scholars argue international law is replete with reformulated neocolonial technologies such as dualism.[122] Yet, TWAIL scholarship can equally argue that dualism, as a screening mechanism, enables states to scrutinise wholesale reception of international law into their municipal legal systems. However, in my view, an attempt by TWAIL scholars to rely on dualism to redress the neocolonial content of international law will amount to seeking remedy in an inherently faulty legal technology.

Consequently, I find that a more appropriate way to vet treaty content is during treaty negotiations. In this regard, a state can make reservations in respect of treaty provisions at the time of ratification.[123] More radically, some states have denounced treaties altogether so they can lodge reservations when they re-accede to these treaties.[124] This radical option has been criticised by the Global North, yet some states in the Global South continue to use it in furtherance of their national interests.[125] In my opinion, in an international power structure that is overbearing on Southern states (and their interests) and severely compromises how the will of states is formed and expressed, it is crucial that these states creatively use existing mechanisms within the international legal order. If sovereignty, and its attendant freedom to contract presume that states can accede to and withdraw from treaties at will, Southern states need to test this logic. By withdrawing from unfavourable treaties and re-acceding to them with reservations, these states will be doing no more than what the international system promises them is possible. Thus, there is no reason why Ghana cannot explore this approach to re-vet the content

---

[122] Muthucumaraswamy Sornarajah, "Power and Justice: Third World Resistance in International Law," *Singapore Yearbook of International Law* 10 (2006): 29.

[123] VCLT, art. 19.

[124] Laurence Helfer, "Not Fully Committed: Reservations, Risks, and Treaty Design," *Yale Journal of International Law* 31, no. 2 (2006): 371.

[125] Palitha Kohona, "Reservations: Recent Developments in the Practice of the Secretary-General of the United Nations as Depositary of Multilateral Treaties," *Georgia Journal of International and Comparative Law* 33 (2005): 433–435; Björn Arp, "Denunciation Followed by Re-accession with Reservations to a Treaty: A Critical Appraisal of Contemporary State Practice," *Netherlands International Law Review* 61, no. 2 (2014): 144.

of treaties so that once ratified, a treaty would be considered as consistent with municipal law hence directly applicable. As TWAIL's reconstructive focus is to correct the prevailing inequities in the international legal order, rediscovering the "Nyerere doctrine" and recalibrating it as appropriate within the present neoliberal structures and postcolonial milieu would allow states to vet their international commitments; thus, ensuring they are less likely to excuse themselves from the performance of obligations they have ratified or acceded to.[126]

4.4 Indirect Incorporation: Courts to the Rescue?

The overarching test will be how to go past the veil of domestication? A plausible framework is indirect incorporation. But, that equally raises a collateral concern: whether such treaties should be persuasive or determinative. The challenge posed by indirect incorporation is not uniquely Ghanaian. In the US, the courts employ unincorporated treaties as aids for interpreting the constitution and federal laws.[127] Variations in this interpretative outlook is found elsewhere.[128] In Tanzania, the courts have held that the constitution is consistent with the provisions of the African Charter although the Charter is unincorporated domestically.[129] On the strength of these comparative judicial experiences, I suggest that in interpreting the interaction between international human rights obligations and municipal law, the reasonable construction that the courts should adopt is that which accords with the preservation of the state's international obligations within domestic law.[130] Conceivably, the courts can adopt a restrictive approach in respect of treaties that do not confer rights, similar to the US dichotomy of self-executing and non-self-executing treaties. This suggestion echoes Chief Justice Archer's position in

---

[126]Nasila Rembe, "The Vienna Convention on State Succession in Respect of Treaties: An African Perspective on Its Applicability and Limitations," *Comparative and International Law Journal of Southern Africa* 17, no. 2 (1984): 135.

[127]Paust, "Basic Forms," 263–264.

[128]Constitution (Consequential, Transitional and Temporal Provisions) Act 16 (1984), section 5(1).

[129]*DPP v. Daudi Pete* (TZCA) 1 (1991).

[130]Amos Enabulele, "Incompatibility of National Law with the African Charter on Human and Peoples' Rights: Does the African Court on Human and Peoples' Rights Have the Final Say?" *African Human Rights Journal* 16 (2016): 18–19.

the *IGP* Case where he noted that the African Charter was still applicable in Ghana despite its non-incorporation.[131] Such an approach also supports virtual incorporation of international human rights instruments under the auspices of Articles 33(5) and 37(3).[132] Conversely, an approach founded on Justice Ampiah's position in the *CIBA* Case, and especially Justice Date-Bah's decision in the *ARA Libertad* Case, would amount to tacit continuation of obstructive colonial legacies.

Dualism, therefore, as conceived and adhered to in Ghana is a colonial inheritance that has become a pliable device in the state's toolkit. Ghana is quick to ratify treaties yet unwilling to domesticate these treaties based on a supposed mechanical adherence to this politico-legal technology with its correspondingly subtle immobilising effects which ultimately denies Ghana's peoples the purpose, benefits and rights in these treaties.[133] Accordingly, the combined effect of Chief Justice Archer's position and Kludze's virtual incorporation is one plausible way for the courts to engage with ratified but yet-to-be incorporated human rights treaties. Interestingly, what is less obvious is that these jurists had laid the foundation for this kind of TWAIL-oriented analysis without being self-aware that they were speaking in the TWAIL *langue*. My argument is not that such interpretation should be for persuasive effect; rather, that it should be determinative and as a matter of judicial principle, the courts should endeavour to interpret domestic law to accord with a state's international (treaty) obligations, especially where domestic obligations coincide with justifiable international human rights expectations arising from such ratified treaties.[134]

---

[131] *IGP* Case, 466.

[132] Kludze, "Constitutional Rights," 682.

[133] Ernest Y. Ako, "Re-thinking the Domestication of International Treaties in Ghana," in *A Commitment to Law, Development and Public Policy: A Festschrift in Honour of Nana Dr. S.K.B. Asante*, ed. Richard F. Oppong and Kissi Agyebeng (Wildy, Simmonds and Hill Publishing, 2016), 597.

[134] Gib van Ert, "Canada," in *The Role of Domestic Courts in Treaty Enforcement: A Comparative Study*, ed. David Sloss (Cambridge: Cambridge University Press, 2009), 204–206.

4.5 Functional Transcendence

Pressing forward, the remaining question is, how does Ghana overcome this colonial dominance regarding the integration of its obligations under unincorporated treaties like the African Charter into municipal law? The most obvious reaction would be a constitutional amendment; but that is unlikely to happen anytime soon.[135] A second choice is for the courts to adopt transjudicial communication to transcend dualism.[136] This approach is quite innovative; however, I need to point out that it is not entirely new to African courts as other jurisdictions apply it in their interpretative functions.[137] There is another way to approach this conundrum. As noted earlier, state parties are required to implement the African Charter by adopting legislative or *other measures*.[138] Evidently, the first avenue for asserting rights arising from treaties is in national courts, failing which the aggrieved party may seek redress beyond the state.[139] In this respect, states are required to provide a local framework for the vindication of rights.[140] Here, the Charter's use of "legislative" suggests it is only one of possibly several modes of incorporating treaties as the phrase "other measures" is used disjunctively with "legislative"; thereby suggesting the drafters contemplated enforcement should not be inhibited by the constraints of an enactment.[141] This reflects the OAU/AU practice that a treaty becomes binding on the state once it is ratified.[142]

---

[135] Kenya's 2010 Constitution did away with dualism, effectively permitting the domestic application of previously ratified but unincorporated treaties and prospectively incorporating treaties upon ratification: Tom Kabau and Chege Njoroge, "The Application of International Law in Kenya and the 2010 Constitution: Critical Issues in the Harmonisation of the Legal System," *The International and Comparative International Law Journal of South Africa* 44, no. 3 (2011): 293.

[136] Transjudicial communication is the direct application of international law by national or supranational courts irrespective of whether they are binding, domesticated or unincorporated: Anne-Marie Slaughter, "A Typology of Transjudicial Communication," *University of Richmond Law Review* 29 (1994): 101.

[137] Adjami, "African Courts," 112.

[138] African Charter, art. 1.

[139] Appiagyei-Atua, Ghana at 50, 198.

[140] Ibid.

[141] VCLT, art. 27.

[142] Maluwa, "Ratification of African Union Treaties," 8.

The doctrine of legitimate expectation provides yet another avenue for making unincorporated treaties domestically applicable. This doctrine "significantly relaxes the rule that unincorporated treaties cannot confer rights or impose duties in domestic law."[143] Again, I return to Chief Justice Archer's position in the *IGP* Case as it accords with this doctrine.[144] The doctrine also endorses the importance of rights conferred by unincorporated treaties and how these rights should not be overlooked in adjudicating rights-related causes.[145] In the recent past, Ghana has indicated its readiness to apply unincorporated human rights treaties.[146] Yet, this promise has gone past a decade and half with no commitment to match the this promise. If Ghana is willing to translate this commitment into actionable deeds, it could reasonably be joined to the judicial obligation to interpret the Constitution and other laws in a manner that promotes human rights and effectuates analogous obligations under unincorporated treaties.[147] However, it is not my proposition that the courts usurp Parliament's functions nor dictate how the Executive exercises its constitutional power to execute treaties; rather, in my view, a proactive judiciary will impel the Executive and Parliament to begin to take treaty negotiation, ratification and incorporation more seriously.[148]

5   CONCLUSION

Ghana is at a historic moment requiring a reconsideration of its treaty law and practice. As discussed in this chapter, dualism emerged at a time of strict separation between international and municipal law.[149] But today, there is a functional congruence leading to a complementary relationship between the two legal domains.[150] The emerging trend strongly suggests a blurring of lines between monism and dualism with

---

[143] Oppong, "Reimagining International Law," 314.

[144] *IGP* Case, 466.

[145] Oppong, "Reimagining International Law," 314–315.

[146] Seventeenth Periodic Report of State Parties Due in 2002: Ghana. 01/10/2002. CERD/C/431/Add.3.

[147] Interpretation Act 2009 (Act 792), section 10(4); 1992 Constitution, art. 129(3).

[148] Ako, "Re-thinking Domestication," 603; Ako and Frimpong, "Foreign Relations Law," 593–595.

[149] Bulto, "The Monist-Dualist Divide," 137.

[150] Ibid.

a shift in favour of a monist-like attitude in dualist states.[151] It is in this respect that Ghana's inconsistent domestication approach invites a necessary functional transcendence of dualism which is nothing more than an unhelpful colonial bequest that continues to frustrate the applicability of the panoply of rights provided under the African Charter.

More than sixty years after independence, Ghana's treaty law and practice must consciously evolve away from the unhelpful fetters of its colonial heritage. Ghana ought to recognise that rights conferred by unincorporated human rights treaties can have a positive impact on municipal law. In this regard, my argument is that the jurisprudential significance of functional transcendence continues to receive wider academic and practical endorsement for its pragmatism. Thus, it is evident that the continuing orthodoxy of dualism, as conceived in UK law and politics, and inherited by Ghana, must be critically reassessed to permit a reformulation along the lines suggested by Chief Justice Archer that domestic legislation is not necessarily required to activate rights in ratified-but-unincorporated human rights treaties, including the African Charter.

Since treaty incorporation is slow or almost non-existent, it is important to look to the redemptive power of the courts where the Executive and Parliament are failing in their duties. Justifiably, there are matters that would require deliberate legislative expression. For example, treaties that can fundamentally alter the structure of government or override fundamental constitutional provisions must be expressly incorporated. Substantially, I am not proposing monism as the uncritical replacement for dualism. What I am suggesting is that Ghana should consider distinguishing between indirect incorporation of human rights treaties on the basis of legitimate expectation and transjudicial communication, and other treaties requiring explicit legislative expression; thus, creating a self-executing and non-self-executing treaty categorisation as exists elsewhere. This proposition invites the Supreme Court to reappraise its recent position in the *GITMO* Case that in Ghana, there is no distinction between treaties as exists in other jurisdictions.[152] This suggestion,

[151]Walters, "Creeping Monism", 643; Chandra, "India and International Law," 25.

[152]Ernest Yaw Ako and Richard Frimpong Oppong, "Foreign Relations Law in the Constitutions and Courts of Commonwealth African Countries," in *The Oxford Handbook of Comparative Foreign Relations Law*, ed. Curtis A. Bradley (Oxford: Oxford University Press, 2019), 593–596.

however, must not be misconstrued as grovelling for homogeneity with other jurisdictions or a credulous call to replace dualism with monism, but rather seen as a conscious attempt at defining and protecting Ghana's interests through targeted reform of its treaty law and practice. Thus, these seemingly unobtrusive matters are the places TWAIL scholarship must begin invest itself if TWAIL's resistance to the enduring influence of Eurocentrism is to make desired progress.

Acknowledgments Doctoral Candidate, Allard School of Law, University of British Columbia (Canada); LLM (Harvard); QCL (Gh. Sch. Law); LLB, BA (Univ. of Ghana). I gratefully acknowledge Gideon Gabor and Mawuse Barker-Vormawor for their probing questions and invaluable feedback. I would also like to thank the Canadian Council on International Law for supporting my research through the award of the John Peters Humphrey Fellowship.

REFERENCES

Adjami, Mirna. "African Courts, International Law, and Comparative Case Law: Chimera or Emerging Human Rights Jurisprudence." *Michigan International Law Journal* 24 (2002–2003): 103–167.
Ako, Ernest Yaw. "Re-thinking the Domestication of International Treaties in Ghana." In *A Commitment to Law, Development and Public Policy: A Festschrift in Honour of Nana Dr. S.K.B. Asante*, edited by Richard Frimpong Oppong and Kissi Agyebeng, 587–604. London: Wildy, Simmonds and Hill Publishing, 2016.
Ako, Ernest Yaw, and Richard Frimpong Oppong. "Foreign Relations Law in the Constitutions and Courts of Commonwealth African Countries." In *The Oxford Handbook of Comparative Foreign Relations Law*, edited by Curtis A. Bradley, 583–600. Oxford: Oxford University Press, 2019.
Appiagyei-Atua, Kwadwo. "Ghana at 50: The Place of International Human Rights Norms in Ghana's Courts." In *Ghana Law Since Independence: History, Development and Prospects*, edited by Henrietta J.A.N. Mensa-Bonsu, 179–215. Accra: Black Mask, 2007.
Arp, Björn. "Denunciation Followed by Re-accession with Reservations to a Treaty: A Critical Appraisal of Contemporary State Practice." *Netherlands International Law Review* 61, no. 2 (2014): 141–165.
Barker-Vormawor, Mawuse. "Five Years On: A Requiem for the Ex Parte Attorney-General, NML Capital Ltd 1st Interested Party Decision." Ghana Law Hub (2018). Accessed July 20, 2018. https://ghanalawhub.com/five-years-on-a-requiem-for-the-ex-parte-attorney-general-nml-capital-ltd-1st-interested-party-decision/.

Barrett, Jill. "The United Kingdom and Parliamentary Scrutiny of Treaties: Recent Reforms." *International Comparative Law Quarterly* 60, no. 1 (2011): 225–245.

Benneh, Emmanuel Y. "The Sources of Public International Law and their Applicability to the Domestic Law in Ghana." *University of Ghana Law Journal* 26 (2013): 67–143.

Bennion, Francis. *Constitutional Law of Ghana*. London: Butterworths, 1962.

Bhabha, Homi. *The Location of Culture*. London: Routledge, 1994.

Boczek, Boleslaw. *International Law: A Dictionary*. 2 vols. Lanham, MD: Scarecrow Press, 2005.

Borchard, Edwin. "The Relationship Between International Law and Municipal Law." *Virginia Law Review* 27, no. 2 (1940): 137–148.

Bulto, Takele. "The Monist-Dualist Divide and the Supremacy Clause: Revisiting the Status of Human Rights Treaties in Ethiopia." *Journal of Ethiopian Law* 23, no. 1 (2009): 132–160.

Burgis-Kasthala, Michelle. "Scholarship as Dialogue? TWAIL and the Politics of Methodology." *Journal of International Criminal Justice* 14, no. 4 (2016): 921–937.

Chandra, Aparna. "India and International Law: Formal Dualism, Functional Monism." *Indian Journal of International Law* 57, nos. 1–2 (2017): 25–45.

Chimni, Bhupinder. "Customary International Law: A Third World Perspective." *American Journal of International Law* 112, no. 2 (2018): 1–46.

———. "International Law Scholarship in Post-Colonial India: Coping with Dualism." *Leiden Journal of International Law* 23 (2010): 23–51.

———. "The World of TWAIL: Introduction to the Special Issue." *Law, Trade and Development* 3, no. 1 (2011): 14–25.

Chitty, Joseph. *A Treatise on the Law of the of the Prerogatives of the Crown: And the Relative Duties and Rights of the Subject*. London: J. Butterworth and Son, 1820.

Constitution Review Commission. *Report of the Constitution Review Commission: From a Political to a Developmental Constitution*. 2011.

Darian-Smith, Eve. "Postcolonial Law." In *International Encyclopedia of the Social and Behavioral Sciences*, edited by James D. Wright, 2nd ed., vol. 18, 647–651. Amsterdam: Elsevier, 2015.

Da Rocha Ferreira, Andre, Cristieli Carvalho, Fernanda G. Machry, and Pedro B.V. Rigon. "Formation and Evidence of Customary International Law." *UFRGS Model United Nations Journal* 1 (2013): 182–201.

De Smith, Stanley. "The Independence of Ghana." *Modern Law Review* 20 (1957): 347–363.

Dixon, Martin. *Textbook on International Law*, 3rd ed. London: Blackstone Press, 1996.

Enabulele, Amos. "Incompatibility of National Law with the African Charter on Human and Peoples' Rights: Does the African Court on Human and Peoples' Rights Have the Final Say?" *African Human Rights Journal* 16 (2016): 1–28.

Eslava, Luis, and Sundhya Pahuja. "Beyond the Post(Colonial): TWAIL and the Everyday Life of International Law." *Verfassung und Recht in Übersee/Law and Politics in Africa, Asia and Latin America* 45, no. 2 (2012): 195–221.

Essien, Victor. "Ghana." In *Sources of State Practice in International Law*, edited by Ralph Gaebler and Alison Shea, 2nd revised ed., 253–261. Leiden: Brill, 2014.

———. "Sources of Law in Ghana." *Journal of Black Studies* 24, no. 3 (1994): 246–262.

Fidler, David. "Revolt Against or from Within the West? TWAIL, the Developing World and the Future of International Law." *Chinese Journal of International Law* 2, no. 1 (2003): 29–76.

Gathii, James. "TWAIL: A Brief History of Its Origins, Its Decentralized Network, and a Tentative Bibliography." *Trade, Law and Development* 3 (2011): 26–64.

———. "A Critical Appraisal of the International Legal Tradition of Taslim Olawale Elias." *Leiden Journal of International Law* 21 (2008): 317–349.

Gonidec, P.F. "Relationship Between International Law and National Law in Africa." *African Journal of International and Comparative Law* 10 (1998): 244–249.

Hamadi, Lufti. "Edward Said: The Postcolonial Theory and the Literature of Decolonization." *European Scientific Journal* 2 (2014): 39–46.

Helfer, Laurence. "Not Fully Committed: Reservations, Risks, and Treaty Design." *Yale Journal of International Law* 31, no. 2 (2006): 367–382.

Hollis, Duncan B., and Carlos M. Vasquez. "Treaty Self-Execution as "Foreign" Foreign Relations Law." In *The Oxford Handbook of Comparative Foreign Relations Law*, edited by Curtis A. Bradley, 467–484. Oxford: Oxford University Press, 2019.

Jackson, John. "Status of Treaties in Domestic Legal Systems." *American Journal of International Law* 86, no. 2 (1992): 310–340.

Kabau, Tom, and Chege Njoroge. "The Application of International Law in Kenya and the 2010 Constitution: Critical Issues in the Harmonisation of the Legal System." *The Comparative and International Law Journal of South Africa* 44, no. 3 (2011): 293–310.

Kanjave, Jalia. "A TWAIL Analysis of Foreign Investment and Development-Induced Displacement Resettlement: Lessons from Uganda's Bujagali Hydroelectric Project." *Ottawa Law Review* 44, no. 2 (2013): 213–260.

Khaitan, Tarunabh. "Directive Principles and the Expressive Accommodation of Ideological Dissenters." *International Journal of Constitutional Law* 16 (2018): 389–420.

Kennedy, David. "Sources of International Law." *American University Law Review* 2, no. 1 (1987): 1–96.

Klabbers, Jan. *International Law.* Cambridge: Cambridge University Press, 2013.

Kludze, A.K.P. "Constitutional Rights and Their Relationship with International Human Rights in Ghana." *Israel Law Review* 41, no. 3 (2008): 677–702.

Kohona, Palitha. "Reservations: Recent Developments in the Practice of the Secretary-General of the United Nations as Depositary of Multilateral Treaties." *Georgia Journal of International and Comparative Law* 33 (2005): 433–450.

Kumm, Mattias. "The Legitimacy of International Law: A Constitutionalist Framework of Analysis." *European Journal of International Law* 15, no. 5 (2004): 907–931.

Lang, Arabella. "Parliament's Role in Ratifying Treaties." *House of Commons Briefing Paper* 5855 (2017): 1–27.

Maluwa, Tijanyawa. "Ratification of African Union Treaties by Member States: Law, Policy and Practice." *Melbourne Journal of International Law* 13, no. 2 (2012): 636–684.

Merry, Sally. "Colonial and Postcolonial Law." In *The Blackwell Companion to Law and Society,* edited by Austin Sarat, 569–588. Malden: Blackwell, 2004.

Mutua, Makau. "What Is TWAIL." *American Society of International Law Proceedings* 94 (2000): 31–38.

Nyarko, Michael. "The Impact of the African Charter and Maputo Protocol in Ghana." In *The Impact of the African Charter and Maputo Protocol in Selected African States,* edited by Victor Ayeni, 95–113. Pretoria: Pretoria University Law Press, 2016.

Okafor, Obiora. "Critical Third World Approaches to International Law (TWAIL): Theory, Methodology or Both?" *International Community Law Review* 10 (2008): 371–378.

———. "Newness, Imperialism and International Legal Reform in Our Time: A TWAIL Perspective." *Osgoode Hall Law Journal* 43 (2005): 171–191.

Okeke, Christian. "The Use of International Law in the Domestic Courts of Ghana and Nigeria." *Arizona Journal of International and Comparative Law* 32, no. 2 (2015): 371–430.

Oppong, Richard. "The High Court of Ghana Declines to Enforce an ECOWAS Judgment." *African Journal of International and Comparative Law* 25, no. 1 (2017): 127–132.

———. "Re-imagining International Law: An Examination of Recent Trends in the Reception of International Law into National Legal Systems in Africa." *Fordham International Law Journal* 30, no. 2 (2006): 296–345.

Paust, Jordan. "Basic Forms of International Law and Monist, Dualist, and Realist Perspectives." In *Basic Concepts of International Law: Monism and*

Dualism, edited by Marko Novakovic, 244–265. Belgrade: University of Belgrade, 2013.

Quansah, Emmanuel. "An Examination of the Use of International Law as an Interpretative Tool in Human Rights Litigation in Ghana and Botswana." In *International Law and Human Rights Litigation in Africa*, edited by Magnus Killander, 37–57. Pretoria: Pretoria University Law Press, 2010.

Qureshi, Shazia, and Ernest Owusu-Dapaa. "The International Human Right to Health: What Does It Mean for Ghana and Pakistan?" *Journal of Political Studies* 21, no. 1 (2014): 315–334.

Rembe, Nasila. "The Vienna Convention on State Succession in Respect of Treaties: An African Perspective on Its Applicability and Limitations." *Comparative and International Law Journal of Southern Africa* 17, no. 2 (1984): 131–143.

Roy, Alpana. "Postcolonial Theory and Law: A Critical Introduction." *Adelaide Law Review* 29, no. 1/2 (2008): 315–357.

Said, Edward W. *Culture and Imperialism*. New York: Knopf, 1994.

———. *Orientalism*. New York: Pantheon Books, 1978.

Sarpong, George, and Emmanuel Benneh. "The Doctrine of Sovereign Immunity in International Law: The ARA Libertad Case (Argentina v. Ghana)." *University of Ghana Law Journal* 28 (2015): 138–158.

Shaw, Malcolm. *International Law*, 5th ed. Cambridge: Cambridge University Press, 2003.

Slaughter, Anne-Marie. "A Typology of Transjudicial Communication." *University of Richmond Law Review* 29 (1994): 99–137.

Sloss, David. "Domestic Application of Treaties." In *The Oxford Guide to Treaties*, edited by Duncan Hollis, 367–398. Oxford: Oxford University Press, 2012.

Sornarajah, Muthucumaraswamy. "Power and Justice: Third World Resistance in International Law." *Singapore Yearbook of International Law* 10 (2006): 19–57.

Stern, W.B. "Kelsen's Theory of International Law." *American Political Science Review* 30, no. 4 (1936): 736–741.

Stewart, Robert. "Treaty-Making Procedure in the United Kingdom." *American Political Science Review* 32, no. 4 (1938): 655–669.

Thompson, William. *Ghana's Foreign Policy, 1957–1966: Diplomacy Ideology, and the New State*. Princeton: Princeton University Press, 1969.

Triepel, Heinrich. "Les Rapports entre Le Droit Interne et Le Droit International." *Recueil des Cours* 1 (1923): 73–121.

Twitchett, Kenneth. "Colonialism: An Attempt at Understanding Imperial, Colonial and Neo-colonial Relationships." *Political Studies* 13, no. 3 (1965): 300–323.

Van Ert, Gib. "Canada." In *The Role of Domestic Courts in Treaty Enforcement: A Comparative Study*, edited by David Sloss, 166–208. Cambridge: Cambridge University Press, 2009.

————. "The Domestic Applicability of International Law in Canada." In *The Oxford Handbook of Comparative Foreign Relations Law*, edited by Curtis A. Bradley, 501–518. Oxford: Oxford University Press, 2019.

Vazquez, Carlos. "The Four Doctrines of Self-Executing Treaties." *American Journal of International Law* 89 (1995): 695–723.

Walters, Melissa. "Creeping Monism: The Judicial Trend toward Interpretive Incorporation of Human Rights Treaties." *Columbia Law Review* 107 (2007): 628–705.

Young, Robert. *Empire, Colony, Postcolony.* West Sussex: Wiley-Blackwell, 2015.

CHAPTER 7

Human Rights-Based Reform of Criminal Law in Africa

Emma Charlene Lubaale

1   Introduction

The violence and atrocities characterizing the history of African states are well documented.[1] Human rights violations were a major feature of this history, a period many are not comfortable reminiscing about. This history may be viewed from two angles, one pertaining to the colonial period and that after colonialism, but characterized by dictatorial regimes. During the colonial era, African states were subjected to colonial rule, their independence obviously being compromised. In the late 1950s and 1960s, Africa breathed a sigh of relief, for during this period, the struggles of Africa for independence begun to bear fruit with decolonization taking its course. But many states would be far from seeing the dawn of democracy as shortly after, many of the regimes that took

---

[1] Obaid A. EI-Obaid and Kwadwo Appiagyei Atua, "Human Rights in Africa—A New Perspective on Linking the Past to the Present," *McGill Law Journal* 41 (1996): 819–854; Rollin F. Tusalem, "The Colonial Foundations of State Fragility and Failure," *Polity* 48 (2016): 445–495.

E. C. Lubaale (✉)
University of Venda, Thohoyandou, South Africa

© The Author(s) 2020
M. Addaney et al. (eds.), *Governance, Human Rights, and Political Transformation in Africa*,
https://doi.org/10.1007/978-3-030-27049-0_7

over the reins were largely dictatorial with, amongst others, one civil war after another. Over the years, however, African states have and continue to commit themselves to building free and democratic societies. The shackles of the unpalatable past are slowly falling off and a perusal through African states' constitutional frameworks suggests that African states are determined to rebuild democratic regimes, with human rights as a cornerstone.

Colonialism impacted on African systems including their legal structures and systems. Suffice it to note that even prior to the establishment of colonial rule in African states, African states had their own legal systems.[2] Precolonial law across African states was customary law and unwritten. It would therefore be misleading to aver that the colonial regime ushered in legal systems into Africa. What is indisputable, however, is that the colonial regime contributed immensely to the establishment of formal legal structures in Africa,[3] a contribution that is seldom acknowledged. The need to formalize the legal system saw the introduction of written laws, amongst which were criminal codes. As colonial states such as Britain already had established legal structures including written criminal codes in place, the laws of these states become a point of reference for the adjudication of justice in Africa during the colonial era.[4] Of course, African states attained independence, nonetheless, the legal structures introduced during the colonial regime, including the criminal codes, remained part and parcel of the laws of African states. At the time these codes were transplanted to Africa, the human rights movement had not gained as much momentum and as such, although the content of some of these codes was at odds with human rights standards, they were hardly challenged.

African states have since gained independence and are now major players on the international plane. To this end, African states have made a number of international commitments including ratifying a host of international human rights treaties, many of which put into question

---

[2] Henry Francis Morris, *Some Perspectives of East African Legal History*, §§1–28 (1970); Manfred O. Hinz, *Traditional Governance and African Customary Law: Comparative Observations from a Namibian Perspective* (2009). https://pdfs.semanticscholar.org/cad2/49ee6eb777ff90be5c0fa21d58862d6ed116.pdf.

[3] Leslie Sebba, "The Creation and Evolution of Criminal Law in Colonial and Postcolonial Societies," *Crime, History & Societies* 3 (1993): 71–91.

[4] Ibid.

the criminal codes inherited from the regime of colonialism.[5] African states have taken the notion of human rights seriously, going as far as to domesticate a host of international human rights treaties. A perusal through the constitutions of African states clearly reveals that a section of the constitutions of African states is devoted to the Bill of Rights, many of which mirror the rights entrenched in various international human rights treaties to which most African states are party.[6] Worthy to note, amongst the crimes proscribed in the inherited criminal law codes are sodomy, attempted suicide, unnatural offences, sedition, being idle and disorderly, to mention but a few. Years after independence, there is no doubt that African states have full dominion over their national criminal justice systems. But, in light of African states' commitment to human rights, would it be said that the wave of human rights has effectively swept across their criminal law frameworks? This question forms the crux of this chapter and to provide answers to it, two crimes as contained in the criminal codes of randomly selected African states are placed at the heart of the discussion. The crimes selected are the crime of sodomy and that of attempted suicide. These crimes are randomly selected as it is impractical to canvass all archaic offences under the various criminal codes. Thus, the choice of the two crimes is merely to demonstrate the implication of all archaic offences for human rights. These offences are analyzed in light of current human rights standards. Based on this analysis, it is concluded that despite the fact that these offences are at odds with human rights standards, the pace at which African states have taken steps to bring their criminal codes up to speed with prevailing international human rights standards has been extremely slow, with the criminal codes of most African states mirroring the codes left behind by former colonizers at the time of independence.

---

[5] Gerry Holt, "When Suicide Was Illegal," http://www.bbc.com/news/magazine-14374296. See also Suicide Act 1961, Chapter 60/9 and 60/10 of England and Wales, based on which the crime of attempting suicide ceased to be a crime in England and Wales.

[6] See e.g. United Nations Convention on the Rights of the Child, November 20, 1989, http://www.ohchr.org/en/professionalinterest/pages/crc.aspx; International Covenant on Civil and Political Rights, December 16, 1996, http://www.refworld.org/docid/3ae-6b3aa0.html; International Covenant on Economic, Social and Cultural Rights, December 16, 1966, http://www.refworld.org/docid/3ac6b36c0.html; United Nations Convention Against Torture, March 13, 1985, http://www.refworld.org/docid/3b00f040c.html; and African Charter on Human and Peoples' Rights, June 27, 1981, http://www.refworld.org/docid/3ae6b3630.html; etc. The status of ratification of these treaties suggests that African states have committed to adhering to international standards on human rights.

2   THE CRIME OF ATTEMPTED SUICIDE AND HUMAN RIGHTS

The offence of attempting suicide cannot be understood in the abstract. For this purpose, suicide and its historical and philosophical underpinnings are briefly discussed. Though not conclusive, various authors have given meaningful content to the term suicide. According to Schlebusch, suicide connotes "a wide range of self-destructive or self-damaging acts in which people engage, owing to varying degrees of levels of distress, psychopathology … awareness and expectations of the deleterious consequences or outcome of the behaviour."[7] In the words of Shneidman "[it] is a conscious act of self-induced annihilation, best understood as a multidimensional malaise in a needful individual who defines an issue for which the suicide is perceived as the best solution."[8] Schlebusch and Shneidman's definitions introduce a very important perspective on the subject of suicide—the mental health of an individual. From these definitions, it can be inferred that there is a nexus between mental health and suicidal behaviour. In fact, the World Health Organisation (WHO) has observed that suicide is a public and mental health problem ranking high on the list of causes of death.[9] This reality opens to question the issues— does the criminalisation of attempting suicide transgress the rights of persons suffering for mental disorders?

Suicide is a complex and hotly debated subject. Throughout the ages, most societies considered the act of suicide a taboo. From a philosophical point of view, several philosophers weighed in on the status of the act of suicide. Some grounded their non-acceptability of suicide on the sacredness of life. Plato's lack of support for the act of committing suicide can be gleaned from his comments on this issue as follows: "the gods are our keepers and we men are one of their possessions."[10] He went on, "[i]f one of your possessions were to destroy itself without intimation from you that you wanted it to die, wouldn't you be angry with it and punish it, if you had any means of doing so? Certainly."[11] Aristotle on

---

[7] Lourens Schlebusch, *Suicidal Behaviour in South Africa*, §179 (2005).

[8] Edwin Shneidman, *Definition of Suicide*, §203 (1985).

[9] World Health Organisation, *Preventing Suicide: A Global Imperative*, §2–5 (2014).

[10] Edith Hamilton and Huntington Cairns, eds., *The Collected Dialogues of Plato*, §45 (1961).

[11] Ibid.

his part anchors his argument in the state's duty to punish transgressors. To him, to commit suicide is to offend the state.[12] Some commentators have grounded their argument in religious books including the Bible and the Khoran, the argument being that suicide usurps God's power over life and death.[13] Others, however, take a contrary view, contending that "[the Bible] does not directly forbid suicide."[14] Considered together, despite contrary views, arguments on the unacceptable nature of suicide have often been anchored in the immoral nature of taking one's life. Throughout the ages, therefore, societies have been powerfully opposed to the act of suicide. Within the context of traditional Africa, resentment to suicide was evident in the manner in which individuals who committed suicide were dealt with. In some societies, such individuals were denied decent burials as their conduct was considered an affront to the Gods.[15]

Despite the general disapproval of acts of suicide in most societies, the act was not criminalized for the obvious reason that the would-be accused person would be deceased, thus, no one to charge. The general resentment of suicide was therefore demonstrated by punishing those who attempted to commit suicide but did not succeed. England was one of the countries whose criminal codes explicitly criminalized the act of attempting to commit suicide, categorizing it as a misdemeanour.[16] With the wave of colonialism, England's written criminal code became relevant in establishing formal legal structures of criminal law in British colonies. This explains why the criminal codes of most former British colonies are similar in terms of content. Notable in this regard are the criminal codes of Uganda, Kenya, Tanzania, Nigeria, Ghana and

---

[12] Aristotle, "Nicomachean Ethics," in *The Basic Works of Aristotle*, §977, ed. Richard McKeon (1941).

[13] See e.g. B.S. Yadwad and H.S. Gouda, "Is Attempted Suicide an Offence?" *JIAFM* 27 (2005): 108–111; Antoon A. Leenaars, "Suicide and Human Rights: A Suicidologist's Perspective," *Health and Human Rights* 6 (2003): 128.

[14] Leenaars, "Suicide and Human Rights," 137–138.

[15] See e.g. Mensah Adinkrah, "Suicide and Mortuary Beliefs and Practices of the Akan of Ghana," *Journal of Death and Dying* 74 (2015): 138–163.

[16] See Holt, when suicide was illegal, and the Suicide Act 1961, Chapter 60/9 and 60/10 of England and Wales which only abolished this crime in 1961.

Malawi.[17] Far afield, examples include the criminal code of India. These criminal codes proscribed the act of attempting to commit suicide in a similar manner. Under section 206 of the Gambian Penal Code, "[a]ny person who attempts to kill himself is guilty of a misdemeanour." Under section 57 of the Ghanaian criminal code, "whoever attempts to commit suicide shall be guilty of a misdemeanour." Similar provisions are evident in the criminal codes of other jurisdictions including Kenya,[18] Uganda,[19] Tanzania[20] Nigeria[21] and Malawi,[22] all of which are former British colonies.

The criminalisation of suicide is, amongst others, premised on the claim that criminalisation has a deterrent effect.[23] The argument, therefore, is that if the crime of attempting suicide is decriminalized, cases of suicide will escalate.[24] Cases abound in which the laws against attempting suicide have been enforced to the letter. In Ghana, for example, a man who attempted to commit suicide on account of the social rejection he faced from his community, was arrested, charged, tried, convicted and sentenced to a three-month term of imprisonment.[25] Pertinent to note, law enforcement officers were cognizant of his distressed condition as evident in the steps taken to have him receive medical attention prior to being charged.[26] Yet, soon after recovery, he was charged despite the circumstances surrounding his action. In Kenya, a man who attempted to kill himself by hanging was convicted and sentenced to a three-year

---

[17] See generally the criminal codes of these states. A perusal through these codes reveals a number of similarities in terms of the offences proscribed. This is based on the fact that these laws have similar backgrounds.

[18] See Kenya's Penal Code Act, Chapter 63, §225.

[19] See Uganda's Penal Code Act, Chapter 120, §209. Despite being adopted in 1950, before Uganda attained independence, it remains operational to this day with very minimal amendments.

[20] See Tanzania's Penal Code Act, Chapter 16, §217.

[21] See Nigeria's Criminal Code Act, Chapter 77, §327.

[22] See Malawi's Penal Code Act, Chapter 7, §22.

[23] Charles Wendo, "Suicide Cases on the Rise-Survey" (2007), http://psychrights.org/countries/uganda/thenewvisionsuicidecasesontherise070831.pdf.

[24] Ibid.

[25] A. Osei, "Jailing of Suicide Man—Time to Review Our Criminal Code" (2011).

[26] Ibid.

term of imprisonment.[27] The circumstances leading to his conduct pertained to a misunderstanding between his brother and himself which left him frustrated.[28] In Malawi, a case of a 17-year-old girl who attempted suicide by hanging, is a typical example of the rigorous enforcement of the law on attempts to commit suicide.[29] The circumstances surrounding her action pertained to her parents' intimation to withhold financial support from her on account of her alleged misbehaviour.[30] Frustrated by her parents' decision, she attempted to commit suicide. She was charged with attempting to commit suicide in terms of section 229 of the Malawian Penal Code. It is unfeasible to exhaust all relevant cases, nonetheless, similar decisions abound in other African states.

Much can be deduced from the brief summaries on the implementation of these laws in these states. Perhaps most importantly, the mental state of the accused in all these cases was a major trigger of their conduct. The fact that no regard was accorded to the accused's mental state is unfortunate. It is to be noted that scientific research abounds, in demonstration of the direct nexus between suicidal behaviour and mental health.[31]

[27] Health Kenya, "Attempted Suicide and Kenyan Law" (2013), http://healthkenya. wordpress.com/2013/10/10/attempted-suicide-and-kenyanlaw/.

[28] Ibid.

[29] *Nyasa Times*, "Police Arrest Student for Attempting Suicide" (2012), https://www. nyasatimes.com/police-arrest-student-for-attempting-suicide/.

[30] Ibid.

[31] Mariam S. Schotte and George Clum, "Problem-Solving Skills in Suicidal Psychiatric Patients," *Journal of Consulting and Clinical Psychology* 55 (1987): 49–54; Hilda N. Shilubane, Robert A. Ruiter, Arjan E. Bos, Bert H. Van den Borne, Shamagonam James, and Priscilla S. Reddy, "Psychosocial Determinants of Suicide Attempts Among Black South African Adolescents: A Qualitative Analysis," *Journal of Youth Studies* 15 (2012): 177–189; Edwin Shneidman, *Suicide as Psychache: A Clinical Approach to Self-Destructive Behaviour* (1993); E.C. Harris and B. Barraclough, "Suicide as an Outcome for Mental Disorders: A Meta-analysis," *British Journal of Psychiatry* 70 (1997): 205–228; Mark J. Williams, *Suicide and Attempted Suicide: Understanding the Cry of Pain* (2001); Mark J. Williams, *The Cry of Pain: Understanding Suicide and Self-Harm* (1997); M.D. Clarke, "Autonomy, Rationality and the Wish to Die," *Journal of Medical Ethics* 25 (1999): 457–462; Jouko K. Lönnqvist, "Psychiatric Aspects of Suicidal Behaviour: Depression," in *The International Handbook of Suicide and Attempted Suicide*, §107–120, ed. Keith Hawton and Kees van Heeringen (2000); Rory C. O'Connor, "Suicidal Behaviour as a Cry of Pain: Test of a Psychological Model," *Archives of Suicide Research* 7 (2003): 279–308; J.M. Bertolote, A. Fleischmann, D. De Leo, and D. Wasserman, "Psychiatric Diagnoses and Suicide: Revisiting the Evidence," *Crisis* 25 (2004): 147–155; Thomas Joiner, *Why People Die by Suicide* (2005); L. Khasakhala, K.R. Sorsdahl, V.S. Harder, D.R. Williams,

Mental health scholars have also interpreted the mental state of individuals who attempt suicide as falling within the ambit mental disorders.[32] Yet, despite such research, cases, such as those above, abound, thus a clear demonstration of African criminal justice systems' failure to appreciate the mental health issues surrounding the act of attempting suicide. Not surprisingly, mental health commentators are of the opinion that these states' criminalization of the act of attempting suicide accords no regard for the mental health needs of those accused, describing such a stance as a violation of human rights.[33] Pickard, for instance, is of the opinion that criminalizing individuals without regard to their mental state "allows discrimination on grounds of mental disorder."[34] Pertinent to note, a number of African states are party to the International Convention on the Rights of Persons with Disabilities.[35] This treaty mandates states to, amongst others, afford persons with disabilities equal protection of the law.[36] The Committee on the Rights of Persons With Disabilities

D.J. Stein, and D.M. Ndetei, "Lifetime Mental Disorders and Suicidal Behaviour in South Africa," *African Journal of Psychiatry* 14 (2011): 134–139; Eugene Kinyanda, Heidi Hjelmeland, and Seggane Musisi, "Psychological Factors in Deliberate Self-Harm as Seen in an Urban African Population in Uganda: A Case-Control Study," *Suicide Life Threat Behaviour* 55 (2005): 468–477; Jessica D. Ribeiro and Thomas Joiner, "The Interpersonal-Psychological Theory of Suicidal Behaviour: Current Status and Future Directions," *Journal of Clinical Psychology* 65 (2009): 1291–1299; and L.J. Oliffe, J.S. Ogrodniczuk, J.L. Bottorff, J.L. Johnson, and K. Hoyak, "'You Feel Like You Can't Live Anymore': Suicide from the Perspectives of Canadian Men Who Experience Depression," *Social Science & Medicine* 74 (2012): 505–514.

[32] Hanna Pickard, "Choice, Deliberation, Violence: Mental Capacity and Criminal Responsibility in Personality Disorder," *International Journal of Law and Psychiatry* 40 (2015): 15–25.

[33] See e.g. Yadwad and Gouda, "Is Attempted Suicide an Offence?" 108–111; Leenaars, "Suicide and Human Rights," 128–148; Sree Latha and N. Geetha, "Criminalizing Suicide Attempts: Can It Be a Deterrent?" *Medicine, Science and the Law* 4 (2004): 343–347.

[34] Pickard, "Choice," 15–25.

[35] See United Nations Convention on the Rights of Persons with Disabilities, January 24, 2007, http://www.refworld.org/docid/45f973632.html. On status of ratification, visit, https://www.un.org/development/desa/disabilities/convention-on-the rights-of-persons-with-disabilities.html. Currently, there are 177 parties to this treaty, the majority of them being African states.

[36] See §5 of the United Nations Convention on the Rights of Persons with Disabilities on the right to equality and non-discrimination.

(CRPWD), through its general comments, has given detailed content to the rights enshrined in the CRPWD.[37] As a starting point, the Committee is cognizant of the fact that "[m]any national laws and policies perpetuate the exclusion and isolation of and discrimination and violence against persons with disabilities."[38] A notable area of concern for the Committee is the limited commitment of states to ensure equal protection of the law for persons with disabilities. Against this backdrop, the Committee has implored states' national legislatures to review national laws, and where necessary to repeal them, with a view to eliminating all forms of discrimination against persons with disabilities.[39] Other General Comments by this Committee buttress the call for reforms to current national legislation.[40] With the current emphasis on due regard to equal protection of the law for persons with disabilities, the tendency of states to punish persons who attempt suicide, often on account of mental disorders, is not only cruel, inhuman and degrading, but also, an affront to the ethos of equality and other fundamentally guaranteed rights such as dignity.[41] Moreover, the argument that criminalizing the act of attempting suicide deters cases of suicide has also been punctured, with some commentators contending that reduction of rates of suicide should lie in addressing the causes of suicide rather than punishing those who attempt it since the

---

[37] See e.g. Committee on the Rights of Persons with Disabilities, General Comment No. 6 (2018) on equality and non-discrimination, April 26, 2018, http://tbinternet.ohchr.org/_layouts/treatybodyexternal/Download.aspx?symbolno=CRPD/C/GC/6&Lang=en.

[38] Ibid.

[39] Ibid.

[40] See e.g. Committee on the Rights of Persons with Disabilities, General Comment No. 1 (2014) on Article 12: Equal recognition before the law, May 19, 2014, https://documents-dds-ny.un.org/doc/UNDOC/GEN/G14/031/20/PDF/G1403120.pdf?OpenElement.

[41] On the implication of criminalisation of attempting suicide for human rights, see Leenaars, "Suicide and Human Rights," 137–138; Pat Carlen, "Crime, Inequality, and Sentencing," in *A Reader on Punishment*, ed. Anthony Duff and David Garland (1994), 306–332; Heidi Hjelmeland, Eugene Kinyanda, and Birthe L. Knizek, "Mental Health Workers' Views on the Criminalisation of Suicidal Behaviour in Uganda," *Medicine, Science and the Law* 52 (2012): 148–151; Emma C. Lubaale, *The Crime of Attempted Suicide in Uganda: The Need for Reforms to the Law*, forthcoming in 2018 in *Journal of Law Society and Development*. Lubaale argues that criminalizing attempting to commit suicide is problematic not only on account of its disregard of fundamental human rights, but also, its incompatibility with the principles of criminal law on the notion of "attempts."

mental health challenges of individuals are the major triggers of suicidal behaviour.[42]

The laws criminalizing the act of attempting suicide continue to rest uncomfortably alongside human rights regimes that African states have willingly subscribed to by way of ratification of international human rights treaties and the entrenchment of these rights in national constitutions. For so long, Africa's problems, including those pertaining to the legal framework, have been partly attributed to colonialism.[43] But can these claims continue to hold weight in light of African states' independence and human rights obligations? In fact, one commentator raises the question, "[h]ow is it that the white settlers, the African tribesmen, the Jews and the Arabs, having thrown off the yoke of imperial domination, have been so slow to repeal the modified version of the English criminal law so arbitrarily imposed upon them?"[44] Incidentally, Britain, a country where most of these laws find their origin has since repealed the crime of attempting suicide.[45] Far afield, India is particularly instructive. In 2014, India, a former British colony just like many African states made reforms to its Penal Code.[46] These reforms had the effect decriminalizing the crime of attempting suicide. In Africa, Zambia exemplifies this

[42] Yadwad and Gouda, "Is Attempted Suicide an Offence," 110; Mensah Adinkrah, "Anti-suicide Laws in Nine African Countries: Criminalization, Prosecution and Penalization," *African Journal of Criminology and Justice Studies* 9 (2016): 287–288; and Hjelmeland, "Mental Health Workers," 148–151.

[43] Daniel Englander, "Protecting the Human Rights of LGBT People in Uganda in the Wake of Uganda's Anti-homosexuality Bill, 2009," *Emory International Law Review* 25 (2011): 1268–1269; Naveen K. Gautam, *Decriminalisation of Attempt to Commit Suicide* (2014), https://www.lawctopus.com/academike/decriminalization-attempt-commit-sui- cide/. In this regard the author, Gautam, as the case is for African commentators attributes India's archaic criminal Code to British colonialism, contending that "[India's] penal laws are nothing but the handiwork of Britishers." Gautam, however, criticizes the practice in India in light of the fact that "Britishers have themselves amended their penal laws and decriminalised attempt to commit suicide."

[44] Sebba, "The Creation and Evolution," 85.

[45] Britain struck the offence of attempting suicide as far back as 1961 as evident in Suicide Act 1961, Chapter 60/9 and 60/10 of England and Wales, yet, in 2018, former British colonies are yet to table discussions on the decriminalization of archaic criminal laws.

[46] The Indian Penal Code 1860, §309, as struck down, stated: "Whoever attempts to commit suicide and does any act towards the commission of such offence, shall be punished with simple imprisonment for a term which may extend to one year or with fine or both."

practical dynamic. In this state, the crime of attempting suicide has been struck off the law books.[47] The fact that some states are taking action suggests that arguments for decriminalization of this crime in alignment with human rights standards are certainly not farfetched.

3   The Crime of Sodomy and Human Rights

The crime of sodomy, just like attempting suicide, is a legacy of colonialism. States in Africa criminalize it differently. Some states' criminal codes have explicit provisions on the crime of sodomy whilst others rely on general provisions to proscribe sodomy or what has elsewhere been referred to as homosexual conduct. With regard to the criminal codes of former British colonies, the crime found its way in these codes during the colonial era. Currently, the majority of African states criminalize homosexuality. Though the wording of the specific sections varies from country to country, a golden thread that runs through these provisions is that the interpretation and application of these sections is geared towards punishing individuals who engage in homosexual conduct. Worthy to note, the private nature of homosexual conduct often leaves law enforcement officers with no concrete evidence to prosecute individuals for it. The practice, therefore, has been to rely on criminal provisions on homosexual conduct to punish individuals for their sexual orientation.[48]

It is unnecessary to discuss all the sections proscribing homosexual conduct since the provisions on this issue are similar in many respects across criminal codes which find their roots in British colonialism. For this purpose, a few countries' provisions will suffice to drive the point made home. Uganda, for instance, does not have a specific provision

---

[47] As far back as 1967, Zambia abrogated the offence of attempting suicide as evident in The Suicide Act, Chapter 89 of the Laws of Zambia 1967, §3. Under §3 of this Act, "[t]he rule of law whereby it is an offence against the common law for a person to kill himself is hereby abrogated."

[48] Human Rights Awareness and Promotion Forum, *Protecting "Morals" by Dehumanizing Suspected LGBTI Persons? A Critique of the Enforcement of the Laws Criminalizing Same Sex Conduct in Uganda*, §57–72 (2013) (hereinafter HRAPF). See argument with regard to the status of these laws in Uganda. Although the laws are not enforced, they are relied to discriminate against LGBTI people on account of their orientation. This category of individual suffer a number of violations including the violation of their right to privacy, freedom from cruel, inhuman and degrading treatment, freedom from torture, human dignity, to mention but a few.

proscribing homosexual conduct under its criminal code. However, various sections have been relied on to discriminate against lesbian, gay, bisexual, transgender and intersex (LGBTI) people. The Penal Code Act proscribes unnatural offences under section 145.[49] In terms of this section "[a]ny person who has carnal knowledge of any person against the order of nature; has carnal knowledge of an animal; or permits a male person to have carnal knowledge of him or her against the order of nature, commits an offence and is liable to imprisonment for life."[50] The phrase "against the order of nature" under Uganda's criminal justice system has no clear definition but has generally been interpreted to target those whose sexual orientation does not conform to heterosexual orientation.[51] As such, this section has been relied on to charge individuals suspected to be of homosexual orientation. Although the provision has thus far not been the subject of constitutional scrutiny, its continued presence in Uganda's penal laws continues to found a basis for undermining the rights of LGBTI people in Uganda including their right to dignity, life and privacy. Cases abound in which the rights of LGBTI people were undermined based on their sexual orientation.

In the case *Victor Mukasa v. Yvonne Ooyo*,[52] officials of the Local Council where Victor Mukasa (a known LGBTI rights adherent in Uganda) resided arrested her along with a colleague for allegedly being idle and disorderly. The conduct of being idle and disorderly is proscribed in terms of section 167 of Uganda's Penal Code Act and it constitutes one of the vague provisions that law enforcement authorities have relied on harass LGBTI people. Mukasa was taken to a nearby police station and whilst at this station, she was subjected to a number of violations including having her breasts fondled with a view to, amongst others, confirm her gender. She was ultimately released without being charged with any crime. Such a practice clearly depicts the tendency of community members and law enforcement officials to rely on the criminal nature of homosexual conduct under section 145 and other vague provisions under Uganda's Penal Code Act to undermine the rights of LGBTI people. It was therefore hardly surprising for the Court in this case to

---

[49] See the Penal Code Act of Uganda, Chapter 120, §145.

[50] Ibid.

[51] HRAPF, *Protecting "Morals"*, 29.

[52] *Victor Juliet Mukasa and Yvonne Oyo v. The Attorney General of Uganda*, Misc. Cause No. 247 (2006).

rule that the rights of Mukasa, including her right to dignity and privacy were violated. Despite this ruling, no mention was made of the constitutionality of the crime of unnatural offences under section 145, one of the bases on which the rights of LGBTI people are undermined. Another especially notorious example is the case of *Kasha Jacqueline, David Kato and OnziemaPatience v Rolling Stone Publications Limited and Giles Muhame*,[53] where again, the violation of the rights of LGBTI people in this instance was anchored in the criminal nature of the accused's sexual orientation. In this case, a Ugandan newspaper tabloid (*Rolling Stone*) published a list of individuals known to this tabloid to be homosexuals. The tabloid carried a headline which called for the hanging of the individuals listed in the tabloid. This publication was challenged in court, with the court ruling amongst others, that it was a violation of the rights of these individuals including their right to life and privacy. Commentators argued that the act of publishing the name of these individuals exposed them to further risk in a society that was largely homophobic.[54]

Malawi, also a former British colony, categorizes homosexual conduct within the ambit of unnatural offences and other general provisions. The Malawian Penal Code Act makes provision for the offence of indecent practices between males.[55] In terms of this section "[a]ny male person who, whether in public or private, commits any act of gross indecency with another male person, or procures another male person to commit any act of gross indecency with him, or attempts to procure the commission of any such act by any male person with himself or with another male person, whether in public or private, shall be guilty of a felony and shall be liable to imprisonment for five years, with or without corporal punishment."[56] This constitutes one of the general and vague provisions

---

[53] *Kasha Jacqueline, David Kato and Onziema Patience v. Rollingstone Publications Limited and Giles Muhame*, Miscellaneous Application No. 163 (2010).

[54] Adrian Jjuuko, "The Incremental Approach: Uganda's Struggle for the Decriminalisation of Homosexuality," in *Sexual Orientation and Gender Identity in the Commonwealth*, ed. Institute of Common Wealth Studies (2013), 381–408.

[55] See the Malawian Penal Code, Chapter 7, §156.

[56] Ibid. See also §157 with regard to indecent practices between females. Under this provision, "Any female person who, whether in public or private, commits any act of gross indecency with another female person, or procures another female person to commit any act of gross indecency with her, or attempts to procure the commission of any such act by any female person with herself or with another female person, whether in public or private, shall be guilty of an offence and shall be liable to imprisonment for five years."

relied on to criminalize homosexual conduct. The phraseology of the Malawian section in so far as unnatural offences in Malawi are concerned mirrors that of Uganda. Under the Malawian section, it is a criminal offence for a person to have "carnal knowledge of any person against the order of nature."[57] It is equally an offence for a person to permit "a male person to have carnal knowledge of him or her against the order of nature."[58] The maximum penalty for a person found guilty of the crime of unnatural offences is "imprisonment for fourteen years, with or without corporal punishment."[59] This latter provision has found the basis for the prosecution of individuals on account of their sexual orientation. Despite the fact that the crime of unnatural offences under section 153 does not proscribe sexual orientation, but rather, carnal knowledge, this provision continues to pose a threat to LGBTI people in Malawi.

The Malawian case of *Chimbalanga and Monjeza*,[60] is a standard reference point in understanding the plight of LGBTI people in Malawi. In this case, Chimbalanga (a transgender woman) and Monjeza (a man) were arrested after the police got wind of their engagement party which had taken place a few days prior to their arrest. They were detained and whilst in detention, their application for bail was denied.[61] In addition, their motion to have sections 153 and 157 of the Malawian Penal Code subjected to constitutional scrutiny by the Constitutional Court of Malawi was denied with no justification.[62] On 18 May 2010, the accused were convicted in terms of sections 153 and 156 of the Penal Code Act for unnatural offences and "indecent practices between males" respectively. They were sentenced to a 14-year term of imprisonment with hard labour, the maximum sentence for this category of offence in

---

[57] See the Malawian Penal Code Act, Chapter 7, §153.

[58] Ibid.

[59] Ibid.

[60] BBC News, "Malawi Gay Couple Get Maximum Sentence of 14 Years" (2010), http://www.bbc.com/news/10130240. For a commentary on this case, see Louise Price, "The Treatment of Homosexuality in the Malawian Justice System: R v Steven Monjeza Soko and Tiwonge Chimbalanga Kachepa," *African Human Rights Law Journal* (2017): 524–533.

[61] *The Guardian*, "Malawi Gay Wedding Couple Denied Bail for 'Own Protection'" (2010), https://www.theguardian.com/world/2010/jan/04/malawi-gay-wedding-couple-bail.

[62] Eldson Chagara, "Malawi Court Dismisses Gay Couple's Appeal Case" (2010), https://uk.reuters.com/article/ozatp-malawi-court-idAFJOE61M03O20100223.

terms of the Penal Code Act.[63] The homophobic nature of the judicial officer who presided over this case was evident. Justice Lovemore, without mincing words ruled as follows: "I will give you a scaring sentence so that the public be protected from people like you so that we are not tempted to emulate this horrendous example. We are sitting here to represent the Malawi society, which I do not believe is ready at this point in time to see its sons getting married to other sons or conducting engagement ceremonies."[64]

This decision, of course, was the subject of scathing criticism from, inter alia, civil society organizations including the International Bar Association's Human Rights Institute, Amnesty International and the International Gay and Lesbian Human Rights Commission.[65] The pressure exerted on the government of Malawi, coupled with other factors including the withholding of donor funds and aid by Malawi's donors,[66] led to the ultimate release of Chimbalanga and Monjeza.[67] Pertinent to note, however, sections 153 and 156, based on which they were convicted remain alive and well and continue to be a threat to the LGBTI community in Malawi and to reinforce the culture of homophobia. Uganda and Malawi have been placed at the heart of the discussion. This, however, is just the tip of the iceberg in so far as the plight of LGBTI people in Africa is concerned as similar or worse examples hold true in other African states.

What is especially disheartening is that African states have pledged allegiance to the respect of human rights for all individuals including LGBTI people. In terms of international human rights treaties and instruments, there is an established framework lending impetus to the cause for reforms to the criminal law codes of African states in regard to these crimes. These treaties cannot be exhausted but a few will suffice to demonstrate this reality. Article 2 of the International Convention

---

[63] BBC News, "Malawi Gay Couple."

[64] Ibid.

[65] On this see Corinne Lennox, "The LGBT Situation in Malawi: An Activist Perspective" (2013), 365, http://sas-space.sas.ac.uk/4824/9/13Mwakasungula_LGBT MalawiActivist.pdf.

[66] David Smith, "Malawi to Review Homosexuality Ban After US Aid Threat" (2011), https://www.theguardian.com/world/2011/dec/09/malawi-homosexuality-ban-review.

[67] BBC-News, "Malawi Gay Couple Released After Presidential Pardon" (2010), http://www.bbc.com/news/10194057.

on Civil and Political Rights (ICCPR), for instance, mandates states to treat all individuals within their territory without distinction.[68] The Human Rights Committee has also given meaningful content to the provisions contained in the ICCPR as it pertains to LGBTI rights.[69] This Committee has adjudicated on cases, arriving at decisions that mandate states to put in place mechanisms that address the challenge of discrimination against LGBTI people.[70] Similar stances are evident in General Comments of regulatory committees of other international instruments including the International Covenant on Social Economic Rights,[71] the United Nations Conventions on the Rights of the Child[72] and the United Nations Convention Against Torture.[73] Significantly, although

[68] §2 of the ICCPR provides that "[e]ach State Party to the present Covenant undertakes to respect and to ensure to all individuals within its territory and subject to its jurisdiction the rights recognized in the present Covenant, without distinction of any kind, such as race, colour, sex, language, religion, political or other opinion, national or social origin, property, birth or other status."

[69] See, for example, the 1994 case of *Toonen v. Australia*, Communication No. 488/1992, U.N. Doc. CCPR/C/50/D/488/1992 (1994).

[70] Ibid. At §8.7 of its decision, the Committee ruled that references to "sex" under article 2 of the ICCPR includes "sexual orientation." For this reason, the Human Rights Committee ruled that the ICCPR envisages sexual orientation as a ground based on which an individual cannot be discriminated against. Although the Human Rights Committee focused on the notion of "sex," an argument could be advanced to the effect that the phrase "other status" as used in article 2 of the ICCPR, encompasses sexual orientation.

[71] For example, the Committee on Economic, Social and Cultural Rights has interpreted §2(2) of the International Convention on Economic, Social and Cultural Rights in General Comment No. 20, to recognize sexual orientation against which an individual should not be discriminated against. The Committee makes reference to the phrase "other status" under §2(2) of the ICESCR to buttress this position. On this see UN Committee on Economic, Social and Cultural Rights (CESCR), General Comment No. 20: Non-dis-crimination in economic, social and cultural rights (§2(2), of the International Covenant on Economic, Social and Cultural Rights), July 2, 2009, E/C.12/GC/20, http://www.refworld.org/docid/4a60961f2.html.

[72] United Nations Committee on the Rights of the Child, General Comment No. 4 (2003): Adolescent Health and Development in the Context of the Convention on the Rights of the Child, July 1, 2003, CRC/GC/2003/4, http://www.refworld.org/docid/4538834f0.html. The United Nations Committee on the Rights of the Child has observed that article 2 of the Convention of the Rights of the Child encompasses sexual orientation.

[73] United Nations Committee Against Torture (CAT), General Comment No. 2: Implementation of §2 by States Parties, January 24, 2008, CAT/C/GC/2, http://www.refworld.org/docid/47ac78ce2.html. The United Nations Committee Against Torture has

these treaties do not explicitly speak to the issue of LGBTI rights or sexual orientation in general, their progressive interpretation makes a strong case for African states to revisit their criminal codes on the crime sodomy, unnatural offences and all provisions having the effect of discriminating against LGBTI people. It is, however, unfortunate that despite African states' ratification of these treaties, the laws on proscription of homosexual conduct continue to rear their ugly heads.

It is indeed indisputable that these criminal codes are a legacy of colonialism. But the question is—for how long shall Africa play this card knowing full well it is independent and has human rights obligations to meet? African states yearned for independence, with the promise of addressing the failings of the unpalatable colonial past ringing loud at the time of their struggles for freedom. The overarching question however is—has the freedom that came with independence been exercised for the benefit of all including the most marginalized in society who include sexual minorities? In so far as striking down laws on the crime of sodomy is concerned, African states cannot claim that the idea is farfetched. South Africa, even whilst faced with challenges such as homophobia across sections of its society, took the step to strike down the crime of sodomy.[74] Homophobia is a real obstacle to LGBTI peoples' enjoyment of human rights, but comparative examples from states such as South Africa suggest that it is a surmountable one. The crime of sodomy could no more rest comfortably alongside South Africa's very own Constitution. Of course, South Africa's is one that makes explicit provision for sexual orientation as a ground against which a person cannot be discriminated,[75] an advantage that not many African Constitutions enjoy. However, it is to be remembered that despite the fact that most African Constitutions lack such an explicit provision in their constitutions, they are party to international treaties which impose obligations on them to enforce LGBTI rights.[76]

also weighed in, noting that in fulfilling the provisions of the CAT, all persons must be taken into account, regardless of their sexual orientation or transgender identity.

[74] See decision in *National Coalition for Gay and Lesbian Equality v. Minister of Justice* 1998 (12) BCLR 1 (CC).

[75] See section 9(3) of the Constitution of the Republic of South Africa 1996, which encompasses sexual orientation as a prohibited ground for discrimination.

[76] A perusal through the status of ratification of the various international treaties suggests that most African states have committed to these treaties by virtue of their ratification.

4   CONCLUSION

Prior to independence, the criminal codes in place had provisions that, without a doubt, were an affront to human rights. Notable are the offences of attempting suicide and sodomy. African states have since attained independence and in addition, made commitments to uphold human rights. Yet, African societies continue to suffer the brunt of colonial laws. The pace at which African states are aligning their criminal codes with prevailing human rights standards remains extremely slow. Archaic laws have for so long been attributed to colonialism. In the British Prime Minister, Theresa May's words: "[a]s the United Kingdom's Prime Minister, I deeply regret the fact that such laws [including sodomy laws] were introduced, and the legacy of discrimination, violence and even death that persists today," the implication of colonialism for African criminal structures is indisputable.[77] That acknowledged, however, it is time for African states to step up to the plate and to make reforms to their criminal codes. Of course, the success of reforms to the criminal codes is by no means an assured way to improving the rights of categories of individuals such as sexual minorities and those who attempt suicide. This is because societies remain sentimental about some of these age-old laws. The task therefore goes beyond reforming the text of criminal codes but implicates broader issues such as societal attitudes. That said, however, decriminalization cannot be downplayed. It certainly is one of the many strategies that states need to invoke to attain the much desired free and democratic societies. Colonialism has carried its fair share of the blame as it pertains to archaic laws. The gaps in the criminal law framework of African states should now be traced not to colonialism but to the lack of commitment on the part of African states to align their laws with prevailing human rights standards.

---

[77] Nick Duffy, "Theresa May Tells Commonwealth Leaders: We Deeply Regret Colonial-Era Anti-gay Laws" (2018), https://www.pinknews.co.uk/2018/04/17/theresa-may-commonwealth-anti-gay-laws/.

BIBLIOGRAPHY

Adinkrah, Mensah. "Suicide and Mortuary Beliefs and Practices of the Akan of Ghana." *Journal of Death and Dying* 74 (2015): 138–163.

Adinkrah, Mensah. "Anti-suicide Laws in Nine African Countries: Criminalization, Prosecution and Penalization." *African Journal of Criminology and Justice Studies* 9 (2016): 287–288.

African Charter on Human and Peoples' Rights, June 27, 1981. Accessed May 14, 2018. http://www.refworld.org/docid/3ae6b3630.html.

Aristotle. "Nicomachean Ethics." In *The Basic Works of Aristotle*, edited by Richard McKeon. New York: Random House Publishers, 1941.

BBC News. "Malawi Gay Couple Get Maximum Sentence of 14 Years" (2010). Accessed May 14, 2018. http://www.bbc.com/news/10130240.

BBC News. "Malawi Gay Couple Released After Presidential Pardon" (2010). Accessed May 14, 2018. http://www.bbc.com/news/10194057.

Bertolote, J.M., A. Fleischmann, D. De Leo, and D. Wasserman. "Psychiatric Diagnoses and Suicide: Revisiting the Evidence." *Crisis* 25 (2004): 147–155.

Carlen, Pat. "Crime, Inequality, and Sentencing." In *A Reader on Punishment*, edited by Anthony Duff and David Garland. Portland: William Publishing, 1994.

Chagara, Eldson. "Malawi Court Dismisses Gay Couple's Appeal Case" (2010). Accessed May 14, 2018. https://uk.reuters.com/article/ozatp-malawi-court-idAFJOE61M03O20100223.

Clarke, M.D. "Autonomy, Rationality and the Wish to Die." *Journal of Medical Ethics* 25 (1999): 457–462.

Committee on the Rights of Persons with Disabilities, General Comment No. 1 (2014) on Article 12: Equal Recognition Before the Law, May 19, 2014. Accessed May 14, 2018. https://documents-dds-ny.un.org/doc/UNDOC/GEN/G14/031/20/PDF/G1403120.pdf?OpenElement.

Committee on the Rights of Persons with Disabilities, General Comment No. 6 (2018) on Equality and Non-discrimination, April 26, 2018. Accessed May 14, 2018. http://tbinternet.ohchr.org/_layouts/treatybodyexternal/Download.aspx?symbolno=CRPD/C/GC/6&Lang=en.

Criminal Code Act, Chapter 77, Nigeria.

Duffy, Nick. "Theresa May Tells Common-Wealth Leaders: We Deeply Regret Colonial-Era Anti-gay Laws" (2018). Accessed May 14, 2018. https://www.pinknews.co.uk/2018/04/17/theresa-may-commonwealth-anti-gay-laws/.

El-Obaid, Obaid A., and Kwadwo Appiagyei-Atua. "Human Rights in Africa—A New Perspective on Linking the Past to the Present." *McGill Law Journal* 41 (1996): 819–854.

Englander, Daniel. "Protecting the Human Rights of LGBT People in Uganda in the Wake of Uganda's Anti-homosexuality Bill 2009." *Emory International Law Review* 25 (2011): 1263–1316.

Gautam, K. Naveen. "Decriminalisation of Attempt to Commit Suicide" (2014). Accessed May 14, 2018. https://www.lawctopus.com/academike/decriminalization-attempt-commit-suicide/.

Hamilton, Edith, and Huntington Cairns, eds. *The Collected Dialogues of Plato.* Princeton, NJ: Princeton University Press, 1961.

Harris, E.C., and B. Barraclough. "Suicide as an Outcome for Mental Disorders: A Meta-Analysis." *British Journal of Psychiatry* 70 (1997): 205–228.

Health Kenya. "Attempted Suicide and Kenyan Law" (2013). Accessed May 14, 2018. http://healthkenya.wordpress.com/2013/10/10/attempted-suicide-and-kenyanlaw/.

Hinz, Manfred O. *Traditional Governance and African Customary Law: Comparative Observations from a Namibian Perspective* (2009). Accessed May 14, 2018. https://pdfs.semanticscholar.org/cad2/49ee6eb777ff90be5c-0fa21d58862d6ed116.pdf.

Hjelmeland, Heidi, Eugene Kinyanda, and L. Birthe Knizek. "Mental Health Workers' Views on the Criminalisation of Suicidal Behaviour in Uganda." *Medicine, Science and the Law* 52 (2012): 148–151.

Holt, Gerry. "When Suicide Was Illegal." Accessed May 14, 2018. http://www.bbc.com/news/magazine-14374296.

Human Rights Awareness and Promotion Forum. *Protecting "Morals" by Dehumanizing Suspected LGBTI Persons? A Critique of the Enforcement of the Laws Criminalizing Same Sex Conduct in Uganda* (2013). Accessed May 14, 2018. www.lgbtnet.dk/…/230-a-critique-of-the-enforcement-of-the-laws-criminalising-same.

International Covenant on Civil and Political Rights, December 16, 1996. Accessed May 14, 2018. http://www.refworld.org/docid/3ae6b3aa0.html.

International Covenant on Economic, Social and Cultural Rights, December 16, 1966. Accessed May 14, 2018. http://www.refworld.org/docid/3ae6b36c0.html.

Joiner, Thomas. *Why People Die by Suicide.* Chicago: Harvard University Press, 2005.

Jjuuko, Adrian. "The Incremental Approach: Uganda's Struggle for the Decriminalisation of Homosexuality." In *Sexual Orientation and Gender Identity in the Commonwealth*, edited by Institute of Common Wealth Studies. London: Institute of Commonwealth Studies, 2013.

Kasha Jacqueline, David Kato and Onziema Patience v. Rollingstone Publications Limited and Giles Muhame, Miscellaneous Application No. 163 (2010).

Khasakhala, L., K.R. Sorsdahl, V.S. Harder, D.R. Williams, D.J. Stein, and D.M. Ndetei. "Lifetime Mental Disorders and Suicidal Behaviour in South Africa." *African Journal of Psychiatry* 14 (2011): 134–139.

Kinyanda, Eugene, Heidi Hjelmeland, and Seggane Musisi. "Psychological Factors in Deliberate Self-Harm as Seen in an Urban African Population in

Uganda: A Case-Control Study." *Suicide Life Threat Behaviour* 55 (2005): 468–477.

Latha, Sree, and N. Geetha. "Criminalizing Suicide Attempts: Can It Be a Deterrent?" *Medicine, Science and the Law* 4 (2004): 343–347.

Leenaars, A. Antoon. "Suicide and Human Rights: A Suicidologist's Perspective." *Health and Human Rights* 6 (2003): 128–148.

Lennox, Corinne. "The LGBT Situation in Malawi: An Activist Perspective" (2013). Accessed May 14, 2018. http://sas-space.sas.ac.uk/4824/9/13M-wakasungula_LGBTMalawiActivist.pdf.

Lönnqvist, K. Jouko. "Psychiatric Aspects of Suicidal Behaviour: Depression." In *The International Handbook of Suicide and Attempted Suicide*, edited by Keith Hawton and Kees van Heeringen. Winchester: Wiley, 2000.

Lubaale, C. Emma. "The Crime of Attempted Suicide in Uganda: The Need for Reforms to the Law." *Journal of Law Society and Development* 4 (2017): 1–19.

Morris, Henry Francis. *Some Perspectives of East African Legal History*. Uppsala: The Scandinavian Institute of African Studies, 1970.

National Coalition for Gay and Lesbian Equality v. Minister of Justice 1998 (12) BCLR 1 (CC). Constitution of the Republic of South Africa 1996.

Nyasa Times. "Police Arrest Student for Attempting Suicide" (2012). Accessed May 14, 2018. https://www.nyasatimes.com/police-arrest-student-for-attempting-suicide/.

O'Connor, C. Rory. "Suicidal Behaviour as a Cry of Pain: Test of a Psychological Model." *Archives of Suicide Research* 7 (2003): 279–308.

Oliffe, L.J., J.S. Ogrodniczuk, J.L. Bottorff, J.L. Johnson, and K. Hoyak. "You Feel Like You Can't Live Anymore: Suicide from the Perspectives of Canadian Men Who Experience Depression." *Social Science & Medicine* 74 (2012): 505–514.

Osei, A. "Jailing of Suicide Man—Time to Review Our Criminal Code" (2011). Penal Code 1860, India.

Penal Code Act, Chapter 63, Kenya.

Penal Code Act, Chapter 7, Malawi.

Penal Code Act, Chapter 16, Tanzania.

Penal Code Act, Chapter 120, Uganda.

Pickard, Hanna. "Choice, Deliberation, Violence: Mental Capacity and Criminal Responsibility in Personality Disorder." *International Journal of Law and Psychiatry* 40 (2015): 15–25.

Price, Louise. "The Treatment of Homosexuality in Malawian Justice System: R v Steven Monjeza Soko and Tiwonge Chimbalanga Kachepa." *African Human Rights Law Journal* 10 (2010): 524–533.

Ribeiro, R. Jessica, and Thomas Joiner. "The Interpersonal-Psychological Theory of Suicidal Behaviour: Current Status and Future Directions." *Journal of Clinical Psychology* 65 (2009): 1291–1299.

Schlebusch, Lourens. *Suicidal Behaviour in South Africa*. Durban: University of KwaZulu-Natal Press, 2005.

Schotte, S. Mariam, and George Clum. "Problem-Solving Skills in Suicidal Psychiatric Patients." *Journal of Consulting and Clinical Psychology* 55 (1987): 49–54.

Sebba, Leslie. "The Creation and Evolution of Criminal Law in Colonial and Post-colonial Societies." *Crime, History & Societies* 3 (1993): 71–91.

Shilubane, Hilda N., Robert A. Ruiter, Arjan E. Bos, H. Bert Van den Borne, Shamagonam James, and Priscilla S. Reddy. "Psychosocial Determinants of Suicide Attempts Among Black South African Adolescents: A Qualitative Analysis." *Journal of Youth Studies* 15 (2012): 177–189.

Shneidman, Edwin. *Definition of Suicide*. New York: Wiley, 1985.

Shneidman, Edwin. *Suicide as Psychache: A Clinical Approach to Self-Destructive Behaviour*. Northvale, NJ: Jason Aronson, 1993.

Smith, David. "Malawi to Review Homosexuality Ban After US Aid Threat" (2011). Accessed May 14, 2018. https://www.theguardian.com/world/2011/dec/09/malawi-homosexuality-ban-review.

Suicide Act 1961, Chapter 60/9 and 60/10 of England and Wales.

Suicide Act, Chapter 89 of the Laws of Zambia 1967.

The Guardian. "Malawi Gay Wedding Couple Denied Bail for 'Own Protection'" (2010). Accessed May 14, 2018. https://www.theguardian.com/world/2010/jan/04/malawi-gay-wedding-couple-bail.

Toonen v. Australia, Communication No. 488/1992, U.N. Doc. CCPR/C/50/D/488/1992 (1994).

Tusalem, Rollin F. "The Colonial Foundations of State Fragility and Failure." *Polity* 48 (2016): 445–495.

United Nations Committee Against Torture (CAT), General Comment No. 2: Implementation of Article 2 by States Parties, January 24, 2008, CAT/C/GC/2. Accessed May 14, 2018. http://www.refworld.org/docid/47ac78ce2.html.

United Nations Committee on Economic, Social and Cultural Rights (CESCR), General Comment No. 20: Non-discrimination in Economic, Social and Cultural Rights (Article 2(2), of the International Covenant on Economic, Social and Cultural Rights), July 2, 2009, E/C.12/GC/20. Accessed May 14, 2018. http://www.refworld.org/docid/4a60961f2.html.

United Nations Committee on the Rights of the Child, General Comment No. 4 (2003): Adolescent Health and Development in the Context of the Convention on the Rights of the Child, July 1, 2003, CRC/GC/2003/4. Accessed May 14, 2018. http://www.refworld.org/docid/4538834f0.html.

United Nations Convention Against Torture, March 13, 1985. Accessed May 14, 2018. http://www.refworld.org/docid/3b00f040c.html.

United Nations Convention on the Rights of the Child, November 20, 1989. Accessed May 14, 2018. http://www.ohchr.org/en/professionalinterest/pages/crc.aspx.

United Nations Convention on the Rights of Persons with Disabilities, January 24, 2007. Accessed May 14, 2018. http://www.refworld.org/docid/45f973632.html.

Victor Juliet Mukasa and Yvonne Oyo v. The Attorney General of Uganda, Misc. Cause No. 247 (2006).

Wendo, Charles. "Suicide Cases on the Rise-Survey" (2007). Accessed May 14, 2018. http://psychrights.org/countries/uganda/thenewvisionsuicidecasesontherise070831.pdf.

Williams, J. Mark. *Suicide and Attempted Suicide: Understanding the Cry of Pain.* London: Diane Pub Co., 2001.

Williams, J. Mark. *The Cry of Pain: Understanding Suicide and Self-Harm.* London: Penguin Books, 1997.

World Health Organisation. *Preventing Suicide: A Global Imperative.* Geneva: WHO Press, 2014.

Yadwad, B.S., and H.S. Gouda. "Is Attempted Suicide an Offence?" *JIAFM* 27 (2005): 108–111.

PART III

Civil Engagement in Governance and Human Rights

CHAPTER 8

Advancing the Right to Demonstrate in Kenya Through Negotiated Management

Mariam Kamunyu and Edward Kahuthia Murimi

1 INTRODUCTION

The right to demonstrate is recognised internationally as well as in Kenya. The fact of the recognition of the right in theory has not translated to substantive actualisation in the case study country; instead a presumption of limitation is the norm and all too often the right to protest is freely dispensed with or counterbalanced at the altar of public order. This chapter identifies a practical solution to this long-standing status quo by evaluating the viability of the negotiated management model, which is premised on a presumption in favour of holding demonstrations. It begins by outlining the essential ingredients of this model and similarly examines what exactly the right to demonstrate entails, including positive and negative obligations of the State in relation to this right. This is followed by a discussion on guiding principles to implementation of

M. Kamunyu (✉)
Centre for Human Rights, University of Pretoria, Pretoria, South Africa

E. K. Murimi
University of Nairobi, Nairobi, Kenya

© The Author(s) 2020
M. Addaney et al. (eds.), *Governance, Human Rights,
and Political Transformation in Africa*,
https://doi.org/10.1007/978-3-030-27049-0_8

the negotiated management approach to policing demonstrations. The chapter then turns to the legal framework regulating the right to demonstrate in Kenya and attendant limitations to the right. It further analyses the current practices regarding exercise of the right to demonstrate and responses to demonstrations by state agents. The authors interrogate how implementation of the negotiated management model would address challenges for those who seek to exercise the right to demonstrate, namely, disproportionate restrictions including total bans, 'public order justifications' advanced by the state to infringe on the right and excessive use of force. Soft law standards developed by the African Commission on Human and Peoples' Rights in the form of Guidelines on freedom of association and assembly as well as policing of assemblies in Africa are discussed. A case is made that these standards are a useful reference point in reforming Kenya's law and practice on exercise of the right to demonstrate. The paper concludes, having established the utility of the model to address these challenges, with an analysis of practical considerations of how the model would be anchored in Kenya's legal framework.

2   CONTEXT OF DEMONSTRATIONS IN KENYA

According to a joint report by Amnesty International and Human Rights Watch, in the period between 9 August and 12 September 2017, as many as 67 people were killed following Kenya's general elections of August 2017. Most of these deaths were as a result of police action and hundreds of others suffered gunshot wounds, broken bones and extensive bruising resulting from police violence.[1] In the period preceding the general election, the police had repeatedly engaged opposition supporters who were demanding resignation of allegedly partisan election officials. The police were accused of using excessive force to handle the demonstrators through, inter alia, use of tear gas and batons. Nothing better describes the government attitude and policing approach to these demonstrations than remarks by the then Interior Minister, Joseph Nkaissery: 'I said the other day we have enough tear gas, plus there are those who come to the

---

[1] Amnesty International and Human Rights Watch, *"KILL Those Criminals"—Security Forces Violations in Kenya's August 2017 Elections* (New York: Amnesty International/ Human Rights Watch, 2017), 1, accessed April 11, 2018, https://www.hrw.org/sites/ default/files/report_pdf/kenya1017_web.pdf.

streets after taking too long without taking a shower. We have acquired special equipment to give them a bath.'[2] Strong-armed responses to protesters in Kenya are not a recent phenomenon, particularly before and after elections.

In the infamous post-election violence of 2007/2008, the Kenya National Commission on Human Rights observed that there were multiple instances where Kenya's security forces 'used excessive and lethal force in actual or apparent endeavours to quell violence.'[3] This chapter seeks to contribute to the existing body of knowledge by proposing the negotiated management approach to handling protests in Kenya. This, it is hoped, will aid the efforts to reverse the apparent trend where the state perceives demonstrators as a nuisance as opposed to right holders who should be facilitated to exercise a fundamental human right.

3   THE NEGOTIATED MANAGEMENT MODEL: MEANING, PRINCIPLES AND PROSPECTS

The negotiated management model of policing protests has been defined as one that is based on greater cooperation between the police and demonstrators and an effort to avoid violence.[4] The model is premised on a constructive relationship between police and demonstrators and emphasises the right to protest. The negotiated solutions in this regard include facilitating protests and tolerating disruption to public life. As a policing philosophy, it is an attempt to maintain public order while at the same time retaining legitimacy and democratic freedom.[5] This model has in

[2] Aislinn Laing, "Mayhem in Kenya as Police Tackle Protest Over 'Corrupt' Poll Officials," *The Telegraph*, May 16, 2016, accessed April 11, 2018, https://www.telegraph.co.uk/news/2016/05/16/mayhem-in-kenya-as-police-tackle-protest-over-corrupt-poll-offic/.

[3] Kenya National Commission on Human Rights, *On the Brink of the Precipice: A Human Rights Account of Kenya's Post-2007 Election Violence* (Nairobi. KNCHR, 2008), 8, accessed April 11, 2018, https://kenyastockholm.files.wordpress.com/2008/08/pev-report-as-adopted-by-the-commission-for-release-on-7-august-20081.pdf.

[4] Alex Vitale, "From Negotiated Management to Command and Control: How the New York Police Department Polices Protests," *Policing and Society* 15, no. 3 (2006): 286.

[5] Michael Rosie and Hugo Gorringe, "What a Difference a Death Makes: Protest, Policing and the Press at the G20," *Sociological Research Online* 14, no. 5 (2009): 2, accessed April 28, 2018, https://www.researchgate.net/publication/46559303_What_a_Difference_a_Death_Makes_Protest_Policing_and_the_Press_at_the_G20.

the recent past been predominantly employed in the United States and Europe.[6] It has been observed that in the late 1980s the police in these regions had, for the most part, adopted a 'negotiated management bundle of crowd control strategies.'[7] In the wake of clashes between the police and demonstrators in the 1960s, most western democracies began to explore the negotiated management approach.[8] This was informed by the recognition that it was more productive to work with crowds rather than against them[9] The Special Rapporteur on extrajudicial, summary or arbitrary executions has lauded negotiated management and succinctly highlighted its key feature[10]:

> Under this approach, the task of the police is to protect rights and to facilitate, rather than frustrate, demonstrations. Some community disruption by protesters is tolerated, and force is used only where violence occurs, and then only in moderation.

In a nutshell, this model has been described as focusing on minimising violence and balancing the rights of companies, governments and the general public with those of workers and special interest groups and therefore enables the possibility of a win-win situation for all parties involved.[11]

In stark contrast, in Kenya, protests are predominantly handled using the escalated force model of protest policing that preceded negotiated management. The escalated force model is primarily defined by the use of force to disperse demonstrators where police begin by confronting demonstrators with a show of force and this is followed by increasing levels of force until demonstrators disperse.[12] Some of the other identified

---

[6] UN Human Rights Council, *Report of the Special Rapporteur on Extrajudicial, Summary or Arbitrary Executions* A/HRC/17/28 (2011), 18.

[7] John McCarthy, "The Policing of Transnational Protest by Donatella Della Porta, Abby Peterson, Herbert Reiter," *Acta Sociologica* 50, no. 4 (2007): 441.

[8] n. 6 above, 17.

[9] Ibid.

[10] Ibid.

[11] David Baker, "From Batons to Negotiated Management: The Transformation of Policing Industrial Disputes in Australia," *Policing: A Journal of Policy and Practice* 1, no. 4 (2007): 391, accessed October 10, 2014, http://policing.oxfordjournals.org.

[12] David Schweingruber, "Mob Sociology and Escalated Force: Sociology's Contribution to Repressive Police Tactics," *The Sociological Quarterly* 41, no. 3 (2000): 378.

features of this model include massive use of force to deter even minor violations, intimidating use of relations with organisers and generalised and indiscriminate information gathering.[13] At its worst, 'the militancy of protestors [is] met by increased militancy by the police. Any show of force or violence by the protestors [is] met with overwhelming force in return.'[14] From an escalated force model stand-point, crowds are best understood as irrational, monolithic units that are dangerous and prone to violence. In contrast, the negotiated management model regards such stereotypes as wrong and potentially dangerous.[15] Stated differently, the latter approach appreciates that force (from the police) begets force (from the protesters).

Demonstrations in Kenya, as will be demonstrated, bear the clear marks of an escalated force model. This is notwithstanding that the right to freedom of peaceful assembly is recognised in the International Covenant on Civil and Political Rights (ICCPR), the African Charter on Human and Peoples' Rights and Kenya's national laws. The African Commission on Human and Peoples' Rights (African Commission) has observed that 'exercising this right [of protest], even peacefully, is often met with repression and brutality from the state and its apparatus.'[16]

This was also the case for western democracies in decades past. 'In response to the growing violence at demonstrations... [the] new doctrine of "negotiated management" emerged based on greater cooperation between police and demonstrators and an effort to avoid violence.'[17] Given the gains realised in countries that have adopted it, it is time for Africa to move towards negotiated management of demonstrations. The African Commission shares this conviction[18]:

---

[13] Donatella Porta, Abby Peterson, and Herbert Reiter, "The Policing of Transnational Protest" cited in John McCarthy "The Policing of Transnational Protest by Donatella Della Porta, Abby Peterson, Herbert Reiter," *Acta Sociologica* 50, no. 4 (2007): 441.

[14] n. 4 above, 286.

[15] n. 6 above, 17.

[16] African Commission on Human and Peoples' Rights, Danish Institute for Human Rights and African Policing Civilian Oversight Forum, "Police and Human Rights in Africa," *Newsletter on Police and Human Rights in Africa*, no. 4 (2014): 3.

[17] n. 4 above.

[18] n. 16 above.

As Africa witnesses an increase in the number of protests, the challenges of implementation of known and accepted standards has injected a new urgency into the public order policing debate. The African Commission on Human and Peoples' Rights is currently developing its focus on the critical area of Police and Human Rights. In this context, the Commission may be well served to consider the development of its own African guidelines on facilitating peaceful protest.

The African Commission's assessment of a public order management approach is in line with and in fact describes negotiated management. This is discernible from their view that '[p]olicing protest action and specifically peaceful protest must put dialogue, communication and negotiation at the core. These are fundamental values in any democratic and community centred policing paradigm.'[19]

3.1   The Effect of Negotiated Management on the Right to Demonstrate

The negotiated management approach bestows obligations and duties on the part of the state and its apparatus in the handling of demonstrations. Scholars, practitioners, rights holders and duty bearers are always concerned with the nature of obligation that a right imposes as this has a direct correlation to its realisation. With regards to the right to demonstrate, it has been said that[20]:

> Complying with the right to protest in the context of freedom of assembly entails both the negative obligation of refraining from interfering with peaceful protests and the positive obligation of protecting rights holders, including human rights defenders, in the exercise of their right to protest.

Negative Obligation
The right to demonstrate is understood as a civil and political right. Civil and political rights usually conjure a negative duty on the part of the state, i.e. the general duty to refrain. This obligation requires the state and its apparatus to refrain from interfering with the exercise of the right

---

[19] Ibid.

[20] UN General Assembly, *Report of the Special Representative of the Secretary-General on Human Rights Defenders* A/62/225 (2007), 2.

to protest. Towards this, the Special Rapporteur on the rights to freedom of peaceful assembly and of association 'considers as a best practice the presumption in favour of holding peaceful assemblies, as stressed by the OSCE/ODIHR Panel of Experts on Freedom of Peaceful Assembly.'[21] From a negotiated management view, this presumption has two key implications. The first is that '[a]nything not expressly forbidden by law should be presumed to be permissible, and those wishing to assemble should not be required to obtain permission to do so.'[22] The second is that the said presumption in favour of protest 'should be clearly and explicitly established in law.'[23]

The Special Rapporteur reiterates that 'States... have a negative obligation not to unduly interfere with the right to peaceful assembly.'[24] He proposes the following test towards limiting prohibition of protests[25]:

> Prohibition should be a measure of last resort and the authorities may prohibit a peaceful assembly only when a less restrictive response would not achieve the legitimate aim(s) pursued by the authorities.

The ultimate test proposed by the Special Rapporteur is that 'any restrictions imposed must be necessary and proportionate to the aim pursued.'[26]

In view of the above, the Kenyan State has a negative obligation not to unduly interfere with the rights to assemble and demonstrate. The fundamental duty to respect rights and fundamental freedoms as captured in article 21(1) of the Constitution includes the State's duty to refrain from such undue interference. Agents of the State such as the police must have reasonable and justifiable grounds for limiting, interfering, curtailing or infringing on fundamental rights such as the rights to assemble and demonstrate.

---

[21] UN Human Rights Council, *Report of the Special Rapporteur on the Rights to Freedom of Peaceful Assembly and of Association, Maina Kiai* A/HRC/20/27 (2012), 8.

[22] OSCE Office for Democratic Institutions and Human Rights, *Guidelines on Freedom of Peaceful Assembly* (2010), 15.

[23] n. 22 above.

[24] n. 20 above, 11.

[25] Ibid.

[26] Ibid.

Positive Obligation

Traditionally, civil and political rights were thought to engender negative obligations while socio-economic rights beget positive obligations. The negotiated management approach predominantly invokes a positive obligation on the part of states despite the classification of the right to protest as a civil and political right. This positive obligation should not be seen as an anomaly or an innovation. The traditional approach which rigidly classified human rights into distinct classes of civil and political rights engendering only negative obligations; and socio-economic and cultural rights engendering only positive obligations has long been jettisoned. The 1993 Vienna Declaration on Human Rights adopted in 1993 affirms that '[a]ll human rights [civil and political, socio-economic and cultural) are universal, indivisible and interdependent and interrelated.'[27]

The key manifestation of the state's positive obligation in the protection of rights and to facilitate demonstrations is seen in 'the role of law-enforcement officials [which] goes beyond recognizing the existence of fundamental rights and includes positively safeguarding those rights.'[28] Best practice in this regard suggests that[29]:

> This [duty to protect] should be expressly stated in any relevant domestic legislation pertaining to freedom of assembly and police and military powers. This positive obligation requires the state to protect the participants of a peaceful assembly from any persons or groups (including *agents provocateurs* and counter-demonstrators) that attempt to disrupt or inhibit them in any way.

As can be observed, this obligation necessarily informs an approach that is different from the approach taken in an escalated force model evident in Kenya where police treat the protesters not as the persons deserving of protection, rather as the offenders. Aiming to correct this preconceived bias, the negotiated management approach emphasises that governments must comprehend protest as rational behaviour; democratic expression of dissent or displeasure by members of the citizenry. Most modern

---

[27] UN World Conference on Human Rights, *Vienna Declaration and Programme of Action* A/CONF.157/24 (1993), para. 5.

[28] n. 22 above, 75.

[29] n. 22 above, 36.

governments are coming to this realisation and are seeking to improve their protest policing infrastructure. For instance, the UK, through a parliamentary process conducted an inquiry into protest policing and subsequently recommended various legal and operational changes in order to enhance the right to protest. Their overall conclusion was that: 'Peaceful protest should be facilitated and protected: to fail to do so would jeopardise a number of rights.'[30]

Equally of note is that, the success of the negotiated management approach largely depends on communication and cooperation between the police and protesters and importantly, restraint on the part of the police. A departure from the old ways of policing protest inescapably calls for the government to take positive measures to ensure that the police are well trained and equipped to handle protest. Researchers in this area recommend[31]:

> Governments must ensure that law-enforcement officials receive adequate training in the policing of public assemblies. Training should equip law-enforcement agencies to act in a manner that avoids escalation of violence and minimizes conflict, and should include "soft skills", such as negotiation and mediation. Training should also include relevant human rights issues and should cover the control and planning of policing operations, emphasizing the imperative of minimizing recourse to force to the greatest extent possible.

The UN High Commissioner for Human Rights has underscored this view, highlighting that 'management of demonstrations, in practice, also requires knowledge of crowd behaviour, adequate equipment – including a range of less-than-lethal weapons – and appropriate training of law enforcement officials, including in human rights.'[32] This serves to reiterate the fact that this duty on the part of government is now an accepted view.

---

[30] House of Lords and House of Commons Joint Committee on Human Rights, *Demonstrating Respect for Rights? A Human Rights Approach to Policing Protest* (Seventh Report of Session 2008–2009), 56.

[31] n. 22 above, 75–76.

[32] UN Human Rights Council, *Effective Measures and Best Practices to Ensure the Promotion and Protection of Human Rights in the Context of Peaceful Protests. Report of the United Nations High Commissioner for Human Rights*, A/HRC/22/28 (2013), 8.

3.2   Guiding Principles

There are some deducible principles that capture the key philosophy of the negotiated management approach.

The Safety Triangle

Negotiated management encompasses the safety triangle principle, which emphasises dialogue and communication among the three key parties to a protest, i.e. the protesters, police and relevant authorities with the ultimate objective being to facilitate the right to peaceful protest. The safety triangle has been brought to prominence by the Special Rapporteur on extrajudicial, summary or arbitrary executions in his report on demonstrations[33]:

> A number of countries that follow this approach [negotiated management] have formalised the role of the "safety triangle" during demonstrations, that is, the organisers, local or State authorities, and the police, who are required to communicate with each other in order to avert safety risks and diffuse conflict.

In fact, the Special Rapporteur has lauded this as one of the key norms in the policing of protest by stating that '[t]he proper management of demonstrations depends on… the so-called "safety triangle"'.[34] This approach has also been recognised by the UN High Commissioner for Human Rights who listed it as one of the effective measures and best practices to ensure the promotion and protection of human rights in peaceful protest.[35]

Leading scholars and researchers in protest management have recently recommended that 'National regulations should adopt the "safety triangle" approach to promote the negotiated management of protests.'[36] This formalisation is in recognition of the indispensable role that the safety triangle plays to the negotiated and effective management of demonstrations.

---

[33] n. 4 above, 18.

[34] n. 6 above, 19.

[35] n. 33 above, 8.

[36] Geneva Academy of International Humanitarian Law and Human Rights, *Facilitating Peaceful Protests* (Academy Briefing no. 5, 2014), 30.

The authors, however, envisages that there may be some instances where the fourth group of stakeholders may need to be represented in the safety triangle, which may implicate a change of terminology to 'safety square.' A case in point is that there is a remainder of the public that is not dissenting but may be affected by the protest. Perhaps it is fair to say that such an interest will be represented by the state, but as depicted by cases of counter-demonstration involving anti-abortion or pro-death penalty and anti-death penalty protesters; harmonisation of all interests within one safety triangle can be difficult. Irrespective of this, the police have 'a duty to protect and facilitate each event where counter-demonstrations are organised or occur, and the state should make available adequate policing resources to facilitate such related simultaneous assemblies.'[37]

Dialogue and Communication

Dialogue and communication are some principal pillars of the negotiated management approach and are collectively discussed here owing to their interdependent nature. Among the government's positive obligations is 'the need to facilitate peaceful protest through dialogue and communication.'[38] The Special Rapporteur on the rights to freedom of peaceful assembly and of association 'stresses the utmost importance of genuine dialogue, including through negotiation, between law enforcement authorities and organisers in order to ensure the smooth conduct of the public assembly.'[39]

Dialogue is relevant both before and during the protest. In order for the police to play their facilitative role, there should be 'good dialogue, communication and co-operation between police and protestors; police and third parties; and protestors and those against whom they are protesting'[40] It has been found that 'effective dialogue in both directions was more likely to lead to a peaceful and trouble-free protest.'[41]

---

[37] n. 22 above, 18.

[38] Hugo Gorringe, Clifford Stott, and Michael Rosie, "Dialogue Police, Decision Making, and the Management of Public Order During Protest Crowd Events," *Journal of Investigative Psychology and Offender Profiling* 9 (2012): 111.

[39] n. 21 above, 11.

[40] n. 31 above, 48.

[41] As above, 48.

Effective communication between the police and protesters is important in exchanging information that will enable facilitation of the protest and protection of the protesters. In line with a negotiated management approach, protesters should not be treated as an unreasonable monolithic entity. This therefore calls for what is known as a 'no surprises' approach of policing. One of the features of this approach is that '[l]aw-enforcement officers should allow time for people in a crowd to respond as individuals to the situation they face, including any warnings or directions given to them.'[42] For instance, the police in the UK have adopted this 'no surprises' approach as the extract from the manual on public order policing indicates[43]:

> A 'no surprises' communication philosophy should be adopted: ongoing communication should be maintained with all relevant stakeholders throughout the operational planning strategies and during the event itself. Protesters and the public should be made aware of likely police action in order to make informed choices and decisions.

Negotiation and Mediation

Under the traditional escalated force model, if tensions are high during a protest, the police response has customarily been to call-off the protest. However, under negotiated management, '[i]f a stand-off or dispute arises during the course of an assembly, negotiation or mediated dialogue may be an appropriate means of trying to reach an acceptable resolution.'[44] Doing so prevents the eruption of violence and thereby serving both protesters' and police interests. In Warsaw for instance, there has been a practice to deploy 'civil servants with previous experience in dealing with assemblies who may be present at an assembly and who can facilitate communication between the organisers and law-enforcement officials.'[45]

Negotiation and mediation are not only useful during the protest but also at the planning stages before the protest. For instance, for mutual

---

[42] n. 22 above, 77.

[43] National Policing Improvement Agency, Association of Chief Police Officers and Association of Chief Police Officers in Scotland, *Manual of Guidance on Keeping the Peace* (2010), 92.

[44] n. 22 above, 78.

[45] Ibid.

agreement as to when, where and how the assembly is conducted. This opportunity should not be used by the government to impose undue restrictions as to the time, place and manner of protest. Rather negotiation and mediation become particularly important when there is disagreement on these factors relating to the protest and 'may help reach a mutually agreeable accommodation in advance of the date provided in the notification for the assembly.'[46]

Tolerance
Under the negotiated management approach, keeping the peace is given the highest premium. The people's right to express dissent is considered more paramount than the fastidious upholding of the law for minor infractions. One of the key features of negotiated management has been described as embracing 'coercive intervention as a last resort; tolerance of minor breaches; [p]artnership aimed at ensuring the right to demonstrate; [and] [i]nformation gathering focused on punishing offenses.'[47] The Special Rapporteur on extrajudicial, summary or arbitrary executions concurs with this principle, when he notes that[48]:

> The negotiated management approach entails accepting some of the spillover effect of the protest in return for assurances as to the peaceful nature of the event. The emphasis of this approach is therefore on ensuring peace, rather than enforcing law. In this paradigm of "under-enforcement" of the law, force should be used by the police in self-defence, rather than to assert the authority of the law in the abstract.

The foregoing is not in fact an outlandish submission and is comparable to the justification for civil disobedience which is permissible in a democracy. This notion has been identified as having received backing from the US Supreme Court, for instance in *Cox v Louisiana*, where the Court stated that '[t]here is... a strong case for the protection of protests, demonstrations of civil disobedience under the first amendment.'[49] The First Amendment constitutionally guarantees 'the freedom of speech, or

---

[46] n. 22 above, 70.

[47] n. 7 above, 441.

[48] n. 6 above, 18.

[49] *Cox v Louisiana* 379 U.S. 559 (1965) as cited in Harrop Freeman, "The Right of Protest and Civil Disobedience," *Indiana Law Journal* 41 (1966): 246.

of the press; or the right of the people peaceably to assemble, and to petition the Government for a redress of grievances.'[50] In further justification for tolerance, one may also venture that the offences committed during protest are based on a pure democratic motive and not the intention to break the law.

This chapter does not suggest that the justification for protest or civil disobedience calls for blanket exoneration on all offences committed in the course of a protest. On this issue the US Supreme Court has recommended that the state should exercise a balanced approach depending on the violation; a holding which yet again lends credence to the tolerance principle[51]:

> The Court has also several times stated that there is a distinction between violation of law where a third person is injured and one where merely the State is incommoded, and has required the State to adjust itself to the citizens' conscience and first amendment interests.

The principle of tolerance also calls for a presumption of peacefulness of the demonstration. Where there are sporadic incidents, the police are required to simply identify and if possible single out the violent elements without necessarily calling off the whole protest. This has received support from scholars in the area who have insisted that tolerance is one of the prevailing traits of the negotiated management approach as it is practiced in the United States and Europe[52]:

> The new approach called for the protection of free speech rights, toleration of community disruption, on-going communication between police and demonstrators, avoidance of arrests, and limiting the use of force to situations where violence is occurring...

Ultimately, the principle of tolerance finds justification in furtherance of democratic expression as established below[53]:

---

[50] U.S Const. amend. I.

[51] n. 49 above, 245.

[52] n. 4 above.

[53] n. 49 above, 247.

[S]ociety might take the position that the individual has a *right* of dissent (and civil disobedience) because of the advantages accruing to society from free and open discussion. Here "tolerance" becomes "justified"-i.e. "jurid-ified" on principle.

The European Court of Human Rights, whose decisions would be of persuasive value in Kenya's judicial context, has had occasion to pro-nounce itself on the issue of tolerance. In the case of *Ashughyan v. Armenia* the Court held that:

> any demonstration in a public place may cause a certain level of disruption to ordinary life, including disruption of traffic, and where demonstrators do not engage in acts of violence it is important for the public authorities to show a certain degree of tolerance towards peaceful gatherings if the freedom of assembly guaranteed by Article 11 of the Convention is not to be deprived of all substance.[54]

The authors submit that such perspective is particularly relevant to Kenya where authorities have in the recent past banned demonstrations for reasons that they result in, inter alia, 'serious disruption of normal business.'[55]

Akin to the four guiding principles discussed above, Amnesty International has highlighted a six-pronged perspective to good practices for law-enforcement officials policing demonstrations, which the authors find suitable for adoption by the Kenyan State.[56] Firstly, they should facilitate and not restrict peaceful public assemblies and this includes not using force in unlawful but non-violent assemblies. Secondly, law-en-forcement officials should protect peaceful assemblies, including against violent individuals or smaller groups. Here, minor violations of the law such as billposting and littering should not lead to dispersing of an assembly. In addition, where a small minority tries to turn a peaceful assembly to a violent one, officers should protect peaceful protesters and not use the acts of a few as a pretext to curtail the rights of the majority.

---

[54] *Application no. 33268/03*, ECHR, Judgment, 17 July 2008, para. 90.

[55] "Kenya Bans Opposition Protests as Election Crisis Deepens," *The Guardian*, October 12, 2017, accessed April 12, 2018, https://www.theguardian.com/world/2017/oct/12/kenya-bans-opposition-protests-as-election-crisis-deepens.

[56] Amnesty International, *Policing Demonstrations in the European Union* (2012), 6, accessed April 12, 2018, https://www.amnesty.org.uk/files/eu-police.pdf.

Thirdly, law-enforcement officials should de-escalate tense or volatile situations through, among other things, communication with organisers and demonstrators before and during protests. This is particularly crucial in contexts such as sensitive anniversaries or popular public outcry. Fourthly, use of police powers should only be for lawful aims, for example, arrests and detentions should only be in accordance with legal procedures and not used as a means of punishment for participation. Fifthly, law-enforcement officials should minimise damage, preserve and respect life and protect uninvolved people. They should use force only to the extent necessary, and only when non- or less-violent means have failed or are unlikely to achieve the legitimate objective. Lastly, the officials should be accountable to the public and the judiciary for all operations.[57]

4   Towards the Negotiated Management Model in Kenya

The discussion in the section that follows will examine public order management in Kenya, the legal framework governing such management and how the present arrangements are interacting with the right to protest. The chapter will also undertake an assessment of implementation of the negotiated management approach in the country. This will be done by illustrating how a negotiated management model can address practical concerns affecting demonstrations in Kenya. Finally, the chapter will identify an entry point for the incorporation of this model in Kenya.

4.1   The Legal Framework Governing the Management of Demonstrations in Kenya

The Law on Public Order Management and Policing
The management of public order and demonstrations are inextricably interlinked. This assertion emanates from an analysis of the legal attitude to demonstrations and a practical perspective on the nature of protest[58]:

---

[57]n. 56 above, 7.

[58]David Pollard, Neil Parpworth, and David Hughes, *Constitutional and Administrative Law: Text with Materials* (Oxford: Oxford University Press, 2007), 631.

Protests which have … more limited objectives such as the end of an unpopular government policy or the improvement of conditions in the workplace, may actually achieve those objectives without seriously imping-ing upon public order. More often than not, however, some form of dis-turbance is a corollary of the protest.

Negotiated management is in itself a public order and policing man-agement model. It is therefore imperative to interrogate the public order management arrangements in place in Kenya in the context of demonstrations.

Public order management falls under the legislative scope of two Acts of Parliament; the Public Order Act (POA)[59] and the National Police Service Act.[60] The POA concerns itself with the regulation of public gatherings and processions including demonstrations. A public gather-ing is defined as, 'a public meeting, a public procession, and any other meeting, gathering or concourse of ten or more persons in any public place.'[61] A public procession is defined as 'any procession in, to or from a public place.'[62] Part III of the POA is dedicated to public gatherings and its exclusive jurisdiction in the management of demonstrations is illustrated by the provision that: 'No person shall hold a public meet-ing or a public procession except in accordance with the provisions of this section.'[63] The primary requirement for persons intending to hold demonstrations is notice which is 'at least three days but no more than fourteen days before the proposed date of the public meeting or proces-sion.'[64] The notice should entail the organiser's contact details, the date and time of the procession as well as the proposed route.[65]

The regulating authority in Kenya in matters of demonstrations is the Kenya Police. The National Police Service Act in its part VII vests vari-ous functions, powers, obligations and rights on police officers. It specif-ically obligates police to maintain order on roads and other places during demonstrations. Section 54(1) provides that '[t]he Kenya Police Service

---

[59] Public Order Act, Chapter 56 of the Laws of Kenya.

[60] National Police Service Act No. 11A of 2011.

[61] n. 59 above, section 2.

[62] n. 59 above, section 2.

[63] n. 59 above, section 5(1).

[64] n. 59 above, section 5(2).

[65] n. 59 above, section 5(3).

shall – (b) prevent unnecessary obstruction during assemblies, meetings and processions on public roads and streets....'[66] From the phrasing of this section, it is clear that demonstrations are merely tolerated when convenient rather than facilitated. This deduction is informed by current practices in Kenya where there is little or no tolerance to disruption of public life to allow protests. Based on the wording of the law, the police have unfettered discretion to construe what constitutes 'unnecessary obstruction' and therefore interfere with the right to demonstrate. An example of how such discretion can negatively impact on the right to demonstrate is the ban of protests by the Interior Minister in October 2017 on the ground that the protests 'were hurting business.'[67]

Legal Limitations on the Right to Demonstrate
The right to demonstrate is not absolute in nature. Limitations on rights, including human rights are not necessarily ill-founded and may be necessary in a democratic society. What is important, however, is that they are imposed and implemented in strict compliance with the law and in a manner that does not defeat the very essence of the right or the spirit of the law. This section seeks to examine the parameters for the lawful limitation of the right to demonstrate in Kenya.

The Kenyan Constitution provides that '[e]very person has the right, peaceably and unarmed, to assemble, to demonstrate, to picket, and to present petitions to public authorities.'[68] The qualifier, to the right is immediately apparent: 'as long as the assemblies are peaceful and unarmed. Actions or laws aimed at quelling armed or violent assemblies will therefore not constitute an infringement of this right.'[69] The High Court of Kenya has referred to these qualifiers under article 37 as 'clawbacks' and clarified as follows regarding non-peaceful protests: 'If they consist of violence to or intimidation of the public then the assembly or

---

[66]n. 60 above, section 54(1)(b).

[67]Nation Team, "Matiang'i Ban on Demos Sparks Storm," *Daily Nation*, October 13, 2017, accessed April 24, 2018, https://mobile.nation.co.ke/news/politics/Matiang-i-ban-on-demos-sparks-storm-/3126390-4137380-format-xhtml-9q2qwaz/index.html.

[68]Constitution of Kenya, 2010, art. 37.

[69]Vincent Nmehielle, *The African Human Rights System: Its Laws, Practice and Institutions* (Martinus: Nijhoff Publishers, 2001), 113 cited in Morris Mbondenyi and John Ambani, *The New Constitutional Law of Kenya: Principles, Government & Human Rights* (LawAfrica, 2012), 182.

the demonstration ought to be stopped. Likewise, participants in assemblies, picketers and demonstrators must not be armed. Weapons as well as defensive or protective contraptions which breed or stimulate aggression ought not to be possessed by the demonstrators or picketers.'[70]

On this qualifier, the UN offers some useful interpretive guidance noting that an 'assembly should be deemed peaceful if its organisers and participants have peaceful intentions and do not use, advocate or incite violence; such features should be presumed.'[71] It has further been suggested that the term *peaceful* 'should be interpreted to include conduct that may annoy or give offence, and even conduct that temporarily hinders, impedes or obstructs the activities of third parties.'[72]

In addition to the internal qualifier at article 37, the right to demonstrate in Kenya is also subject to the general limitation clause in the Constitution which provides that[73]:

> A right or fundamental freedom in the Bill of Rights shall not be limited except by law, and then only to the extent that the limitation is reasonable and justifiable in an open and democratic society based on human dignity, equality and freedom, taking into account all relevant factors.

The foregoing constitutional limitations in Kenya adhere to international standards and are acceptable on paper. However, as will be illustrated in this chapter, in practice the limitations are arbitrarily and excessively invoked. This is contrary to aspirations underpinning the affirmation and guarantees of the right to protest and international human rights jurisprudence which posit that, '[f]reedom to hold and participate in peaceful protests is to be considered the rule, and limitations thereto considered the exception.'[74]

---

[70] *Ferdinand Ndung'u Waititu & 4 others vs the Attorney General & 9 others*, Petition No. 169 of 2016, accessed April 28, 2018, http://kenyalaw.org/caselaw/cases/view/122806/.

[71] n. 32 above, 6.

[72] n. 22 above, 15.

[73] n. 68 above, art. 24.

[74] n. 33 above.

4.2   The State of the Right to Protest in Kenya

This section undertakes a practical discussion of the experience of demonstrations in Kenya. We contend that the wide legal berth afforded to the state to restrict protest is not unwitting; rather it is by design as deducible from the colonial history of Kenya. In colonial times, rights were not celebrated and the coloniser was not about creating laws that empowered subjects to express dissent. On the contrary, the coloniser was more committed to suppressing of dissent and the colonial history of Kenya is one of repressive laws and repressive policing. It is this negative culture that has persisted and continues to pervade the postcolonial experiences. One scholar notes that[75]:

> Actually, during the colonial era the right to assembly and to associate in any form was strictly controlled. The colonialists were afraid that the African people could effectively organise against colonial domination if they were allowed to assemble and associate.

The culture of restricting the right to assembly is a colonial vestige that the government adheres to. Successive governments have retained these repressive methods as highlighted by a study undertaken in 2000 on the state of democracy in Kenya during the Moi[76] era. The study report notes that '[o]ver the years, the country has witnessed repeated examples of meetings and demonstration critical of the government being dispersed by the police, often with violence.'[77] This dismal state of affairs persists as illustrated in the 2014 report on the state of demonstrations in Kenya, excerpted below[78]:

> Since 2011, there have been a number of demonstrations involving clashes between demonstrators and police and military personnel. The police have

---

[75] Kivutha Kibwana, *Fundamental Rights and Freedoms in Kenya* (1990) cited in Chris M. Peter, "Fundamental Rights and Freedoms in Kenya—A Review Essay," *African Journal of International and Comparative Law* 3 (1991): 79.

[76] Daniel Toroitich Arap Moi is the second president of Kenya who served an unbroken 24-year term in office from 1978 to 2002.

[77] Njuguna Ng'ethe et al., *Democracy Report for Jamhuri ya Kenya* (IDEA & SAREAT, 2000), 17, accessed September 22, 2014, http://www.idea.int/publications/sod/upload/Kenya.pdf.

[78] The International Center for Not-for-Profit Law, *NGO Law Monitor: Kenya*, accessed September 22, 2014, http://www.icnl.org/research/monitor/kenya.html.

been accused of using excessive power to intimidate Kenyans who protest. This been affirmed by videos of police abusing protestors, particularly vulnerable groups, such as internally displaced persons (IDPs).

More recently, Amnesty International in its 2017/2018 report stated that 'Kenyan police used excessive force against opposition protesters following the general election – including with live ammunition and tear gas, leaving dozens dead, at last 33 of whom were shot by police, including two children.'[79] In what is an apparent application of double standards, while the police dispersed opposition protesters, the report notes that pro-government protesters were permitted to demonstrate without interference.[80] Even more worrying is the report by Human Rights Watch that documented raping of women and girls in the process of responding to protests in opposition strongholds, most of whom claimed to have been raped by 'police officers or men in uniform who often carried guns, batons, tear gas canisters, whips, or wore helmets and other anti-riot gear.'[81]

From the foregoing, it is apparent that the dismal state of the right to demonstrate is as a result of the gaps and limitations created by the law as well as institutionalisation of an authoritarian culture throughout most facets of government. This status quo on demonstrations compels an alternative approach to the management of demonstrations. The next section accordingly proposes how to resolve the challenges to demonstrations in Kenya via the negotiated management approach.

4.3   Can Negotiated Management Address Current Challenges on the Exercise of the Right to Demonstrate?

The aim in this section is twofold. The first is to interrogate the present concerns about demonstrations in Kenya and the second is to explore the prospects of an alternative reality by means of the negotiated

---

[79] Amnesty International, *Amnesty International Report 2017/18—The State of the World's Human Rights* (London: Amnesty International Limited, 2018), 19, accessed April 12, 2018 https://www.amnesty.org/download/Documents/POL1067002018ENGLISH.PDF.

[80] n. 79 above, 223.

[81] Human Rights Watch, *"They Were Men in Uniform" Sexual Violence Against Women and Girls in Kenya's 2017 Elections* (New York: Human Rights Watch, 2017), 14, accessed April 12, 2018, https://www.hrw.org/sites/default/files/report_pdf/kenya1217_web.pdf.

management model. The concerns that will be elucidated include those that arise from the failings of the legal framework while others emanate from practice that is at variance with law.

Disproportionate Restrictions in Practice

Disproportionate restrictions are those that atrophy or completely defeat the actualisation of the right to demonstrate. The Human Rights Committee (HRC)[82] has identified gaps that affect the implementation of freedom of assembly to include '(a) bans on demonstrations; (b) unjustified restrictions on demonstrations; [and] (c) unnecessary requirements to obtain authorizations that affect the enjoyment of freedom of assembly.'[83] These gaps are briefly discussed below under the Kenyan context.

(a) **Total bans**

Kenyan laws do not envisage a total ban on demonstrations; this has however come to be the police practice. The Constitution of 2010 provides an express constitutional right to demonstrate, yet the culture of blanket bans has persisted in spite of the new constitutional dispensation. After the general election in 2013 and the presidential election petition that followed, there was a countrywide blanket ban on demonstrations. The day before the petition was determined by the Supreme Court, the Inspector General of the National Police Service (IG) 'warned that the police would not permit political gatherings, reminding the population of a countrywide directive issued earlier that month that banned all forms of demonstrations, celebrations, political rallies and gatherings.'[84] A group of human rights organisations that evaluated and reported on protest incidents around this time concluded that[85]:

---

[82] HRC is the treaty body that oversees the implementation of the International Covenant on Civil and Political Rights.

[83] UN General Assembly, *Report of the Special Representative of the Secretary-General on Human Rights Defenders* A/62/225 (2007), 7.

[84] International Network of Civil Liberties Organisations, *Take Back the Streets: Repression and Criminalization of Protest Around the World* (2013), 39.

[85] As above.

[T]he directive clearly contravened Article 37 of the Constitution, which guarantees everyone "the right, peaceably and unarmed, to assemble, to demonstrate, to picket and to present petitions to public authorities." Nevertheless, media reports quoted the Inspector General as stating that the ban "should not be construed as denial of right to association, but a precaution to ensure criminal elements do not hijack such demonstrations to engage in lawlessness."

In defending the ban, the police stated that it was 'necessary to maintain security.' The Kenya Human Rights Commission maintained that 'the exceedingly broad ban was not founded on a legitimate security threat.'[86] In 2014, the IG continued to rationalise total bans on demonstrations: 'I have cancelled all political parties' rallies until further notice due to security reasons. Cancellation of all political rallies also applies to processions & demonstrations, as criminals may take advantage of these gatherings.'[87] One can however question the sincerity of the security concerns as the IG reversed his decision soon after members of the opposition sought a lift on the ban to hold a welcome rally for the former Prime Minister, Raila Odinga, who was returning from a hiatus abroad.[88] The foregoing events point to an arbitrariness, and therefore unlawfulness, in the imposition of bans.

More recently, following the annulment of Uhuru Kenyatta victory in the August 2017 presidential elections and subsequent demonstrations by opposition protesters, the Interior Minister banned demonstrations in the central business districts of Nairobi, Mombasa and Kisumu (Kenya's three largest cities). His justification for this directive was 'disruption of business and alleged looting.'[89]

The foregoing narratives reveal some of the worst-case scenarios in terms of the restrictions being manifestly unlawful.

Under a negotiated management model, a total ban would be difficult to justify. The model imposes a negative obligation on the part of the

---

[86] n. 84 above.

[87] "Kimaiyo Bans Political Rallies, Reverses Ban to Allow CORD Rally," *allafrica*, May 28, 2014, accessed April 28, 2018, http://allafrica.com/stories/201405290256.html.

[88] As above.

[89] Cyrus Ombati and Protus Onyango, "Controversy Over Matiang'i Ban on Demos in CBD," *The Standard*, October 13, 2017, accessed April 28, 2018.

state to refrain from interfering with the right to demonstrate. Further, a total ban goes against several of the model's tenets such as the presumption in favour of holding protests. In addition, the negotiated management model embraces conciliatory principles such as dialogue, negotiation, mediation and tolerance all of which would certainly prevent the imposition of a blanket ban.

> The former Special Rapporteur on the rights to freedom of peaceful assembly and of association has averred that 'blanket bans are intrinsically disproportionate and discriminatory measures as they impact on all citizens willing to exercise their right to freedom of peacefully assembly.'[90] This is similarly the view of the negotiated management model which calls for a case by case assessment of each demonstration thereby precluding a blanket ban approach.

The High Court of Kenya has adopted the position that cancelling demonstrations and total bans requires intense scrutiny before they can be clothed with legality and that if there are less stringent restrictions then these should be preferred. The Court has held as follows in this regard[91]:

> However, the ban of the demonstration by the police was illegal and clearly constituted a denial or violation of a right which had "the effect of imposing greater restrictions than are necessary to achieve its purpose." A restriction that goes beyond what is necessary in a modern democratic society to achieve its purpose must be unconstitutional. If the restriction goes beyond what is necessary, it is unconstitutional. It is my finding that the cancellation of the demonstrations went beyond what is reasonably necessary. Less stringent restrictions would have catered for the concerns of the police such as providing security to ensure that the demonstration was peaceful. The imposition of lesser restrictions was an option. The level of justification required to warrant a limitation upon a right depends on the extent of the limitation. The more invasive the infringement, the more powerful the justification must be. This is undoubtedly the correct

---

[90] UN Human Rights Council, *Report of the Special Rapporteur on the Rights to Freedom of Peaceful Assembly and of Association, Maina Kiai* A/HRC/23/39 (2013), 17.

[91] *Wilson Olal & 5 others v Attorney General & 2 others*, Constitutional Petition No. 323 of 2014. Accessed April 12, 2018, http://kenyalaw.org/caselaw/cases/view/137643/.

approach. In a modern constitutional state courts must subject bans on demonstrations – particularly blanket bans on demonstrations – to intensive scrutiny. As Woolman notes, courts must "require the state to demonstrate that no other means of dealing with a threat of public order ... is available."

(b) Unjustified restrictions and unnecessary notice requirements

The HRC has also flagged unjustified requirements to obtain authorisation as some of the factors that impede the implementation and enjoyment of the freedom of assembly. Our discussion of the legal limitations on the right to demonstrate reveals that there is a notice obligation in Kenya, without which an assembly would be unauthorised. An assembly outside of this notice regime is termed an 'unlawful assembly' by the POA. This is further compounded by a provision in the Act which stipulates that taking part in such an assembly amounts to an offence.[92]

This mandatory notification requirement is problematic for two key reasons. To begin with, its effect is to make spontaneous protests impossible or immediately unlawful should they occur. This is manifestly unjust and 'impede[s] enjoyment of an essential character of the freedom of assembly whereby people may come together spontaneously and immediately following a triggering event.'[93] The nature of spontaneous assemblies is such that 'there may be events of urgent or special significance to which an immediate response by way of a spontaneous assembly would be entirely justified.'[94] In these circumstances, delay occasioned by waiting for authorisation would render the response obsolete.[95] Indeed Kenya's law is presently couched in terms that do not envisage or permit spontaneous demonstrations. Section 5(2) of the POA stipulates that

---

[92] Section 5(10) of the Act.

[93] Michael O'Flaherty, "Effective Measures and Best Practices to Ensure the Promotion and Protection of Human Rights in the Context of Peaceful Protests: A Background Paper," 10, accessed September 22, 2014, http://www.ohchr.org/EN/Issues/AssemblyAssociation/Pages/Seminar2December2013.aspx.

[94] OSCE Office for Democratic Institutions and Human Rights, *Guidelines on Freedom of Peaceful Assembly* (2010), 69.

[95] As above.

'Any person intending to convene a public meeting or a public procession shall notify the regulating officer of such intent at least three days but not more than fourteen days before the proposed date of the public meeting or procession' (emphasis added). This essentially eliminates the possibility of lawful spontaneous demonstrations.

The second challenge with the authorisation requirement in Kenya derives from the automatic inference of an 'unlawful assembly' where authorisation is not obtained and even worse the creation of an affiliated offence. Such an approach is highly discouraged in practice and in law in other jurisdictions. The European Court of Human Rights has held that[96]:

> A decision to disband the ensuing, peaceful assembly solely because of the absence of the requisite prior notice, without any illegal conduct by the participants, amounts to a disproportionate restriction on freedom of peaceful assembly.

The negotiated management takes on a different and more progressive approach in respect of authorisations. Under this model, the only mandatory qualification for a demonstration is that it must be peaceful. The negotiated management model imposes a positive obligation on the part of the state to facilitate protest. Therefore notice requirements such as those in Kenya should only be in place to enable facilitation. But the most important point is that fundamentally, the law should require the organiser of an assembly to submit a notice of intent rather than a request for permission. The negotiated management approach in this regard is succinctly captured in international guidelines as below[97]:

> It is not necessary under international human rights law for domestic legislation to require advance notification about an assembly. Indeed, in an open society, many types of assembly do not warrant any form of official

---

[96] *Bukta and others v Hungary* European Court of Human Rights, 17 July 2007, para. 36 cited in Geneva Academy of International Humanitarian Law and Human Rights, *Facilitating Peaceful Protests* (Academy Briefing no. 5, 2014), 13.

[97] n. 96 above, 17.

regulation. Prior notification should, therefore, only be required where its purpose is to enable the state to put in place necessary arrangements to facilitate freedom of assembly.

Viewed as such, a notice requirement 'may not necessarily violate the right to peaceful assembly.'[98] Even where such a notice requirement is in place, the Special Rapporteur on the rights to freedom of peaceful assembly and of association has asserted that[99]:

> Should the organisers fail to notify the authorities, the assembly should not be dissolved automatically … and the organisers should not be subject to criminal sanctions, or administrative sanctions resulting in fines or imprisonment.

The same approach applies to government response to spontaneous assemblies. A negotiated management approach entails that: '[e]ven where no such exemption for spontaneous assemblies exists in the law, the authorities should still protect and facilitate any spontaneous assembly so long as it is peaceful in nature.'[100]

The present regulatory regime in Kenya entails several disproportionate restrictions which impinge upon the right to demonstrate. Negotiated management proposes a more viable and suitable alternative that will enhance the realisation of the right to demonstrate. Moreover, as relates to total bans and unjustified authorisations; the negotiated management approach is more in line with recognised international standards on protest management. In this respect, South Africa is leading the way on this progressive trajectory and should provide inspiration for Kenya. The High Court of South Africa recently held that section 12(1)(a) of the Regulation of Gatherings Act which criminalised convening a gathering of more than 15 people without notice violates section 17 of the South African Constitution as it deters people from exercising their fundamental constitutional right to assemble peacefully unarmed.[101]

---

[98] n. 37 above, 10.

[99] n. 21 above, 9.

[100] n. 96 above.

[101] *Phumeza Mlungwana & 9 Others vs The State & Minister of Police*, Case No. A431/15, 24 January 2018.

Examining the Public Order Justification

As seen above, the legal limitations on the right to demonstrate are allowed to the extent that they are reasonable and justifiable in a democratic society. In Kenya, public order is not constitutionally provided but in the Kenyan POA. Where there is a 'clear, present or imminent danger of a breach of the peace or public order,'[102] a demonstration may be barred. The foregoing public order justifications are acceptable if the limitation to the right to demonstrate falls within the legal parameter and is exercised in good faith. In fact, the authors concur with the view that 'even where the underlying causes of a particular protest action are clearly meritorious, the State has a residual obligation to maintain public order.'[103] Public order as understood in this legitimate sense is therefore not the bone of contention in the present instance.

Germane to the present discussion are the instances where disproportionate restrictions on demonstrations are imposed under the guise of public order. Being a country that observes an escalated force model of policing, Kenya has a typical obsession with the maintenance of public order. This preoccupation with public order can be seen to explain the wide, excessive and indiscriminate powers given to the police by the POA in the regulation of demonstrations. The Special Rapporteur on extrajudicial, summary or arbitrary executions in his oft-quoted report on demonstrations is concerned about countries like Kenya when he observes that 'in a troubling number of instances, the police are given explicit, unfettered discretion to prohibit demonstrations.'[104] This sentiment receives corroboration from a report in Kenya[105]:

> "The license should be used to inform the government about public meetings so that the authorities can provide security," noted opposition MP Martha Karua, "to facilitate, not to obstruct legitimate activity." In practice, however, the law gives local authorities sweeping powers to interpret whether a meeting might "prejudice the maintenance of public order." This discretionary power is misused.

[102] n. 59 above, section 5(8)(b).

[103] UN Human Rights Council, *Report of the Special Rapporteur on Extrajudicial, Summary or Arbitrary Executions* A/HRC/17/28 (2011), 5–6.

[104] UN Human Rights Council, *Report of the Special Rapporteur on Extrajudicial, Summary or Arbitrary Executions'* A/HRC/17/28 (2011), 15.

[105] Human Rights Watch, *Multipartyism Betrayed in Kenya: Continuing Rural Violence and Restrictions on Freedom of Speech and Assembly* (1994), 22.

It is surprising that in spite of a relatively new Constitution in Kenya, there is 'an alarming tendency on the part of the state security apparatus to seek to roll back the constitutional gains realized... under the guise of preserving "peace and security".'[106] While the democratic space has certainly improved, security apparatus nevertheless retain a propensity for arbitrary invocation of the 'public order' justification in seeking to restrain protest activities. They have accordingly been cautioned[107]:

> Security forces must operate within the structures of accountability, rule of law, respect for human rights and other core values established by the Constitution, and avoid the temptation to revert to old habits of acting as an arm of the regime in power and a tool for political repression and persecution.

The preoccupation and misappropriation of the 'public order' justification in Kenya is one of the manifestations of the escalated force model. 'The escalated force approach reflects a preference for the protection of public order.'[108] In contrast, 'the negotiated management approach, which focuses on the preservation of peace, hinges the question as to whether protest should be curtailed on whether the rights of others are threatened.'[109]

Researchers on the right to protest have observed that just like in Kenya, currently there is a 'tendency in many countries to treat public demonstrations as a threat to public order or national security and to criminalize or forcefully repress protests even when they are peaceful.'[110] A negotiated management approach is more reasonable as the 'duty to facilitate peaceful protests implies that protests are not per se a threat to public order.'[111] This model recognises that, '[w]hen protests occur, the authorities should therefore engage in an open, inclusive, and meaningful dialogue with those who protest.'[112]

---

[106] n. 105 above, 42.

[107] Ibid.

[108] n. 104 above, 15.

[109] Ibid.

[110] n. 37 above, 7.

[111] Ibid.

[112] Ibid.

Excessive Use of Force

Policing of demonstrations in Kenya is characterised by excessive use of force particularly through police violence and brutality as well as firing of live ammunition and teargas on more often than not peaceful protesters. Unlike the other constraints to demonstrations, the excessive use of force is particularly egregious because in addition to impinging on the right to protest; it also violates the rights to life, freedom and security of the person and the right to dignity. It has been empirically established that '[t]he incidence of police violence in breaking up peaceful demonstrations, and in treating suspects in the course of arrest and while in custody, is a recurrent and disturbing phenomenon.'[113]

In Kenya, elections seem to always provide the trigger for the police to go into overdrive. This is in line with an observation that 'the use of excessive force by law enforcement officers [is] prompted by the belief that it is expected of them, in curbing political demonstrations.'[114] For instance, after the 2007 general elections, Human Rights Watch reported that[115]:

> Since the disputed December 27, 2007 presidential elections, Kenyan police in several cities have used live ammunition to disperse protesters and disperse looters, killing and wounding dozens. Some observers and even police have described the police response as an unofficial "shoot to kill" policy. For example, Human Rights Watch received credible reports that in Kisumu dozens of people were shot dead by police while demonstrating against the election result announced on December 31.

The above is particularly pertinent for the reason that the post-election violence of 2007/2008 was subsequently found to be in the scale of crimes against humanity and consequently a situation that warranted the attention of the International Criminal Court (ICC). The post-election violence resulted in the death of almost 1162 people and the police accused of using excessive and lethal force.[116] Similarly,

---

[113] n. 77 above, 8.

[114] n. 104 above, 7.

[115] Human Rights Watch, *Kenya: End Police Use of Excessive Force* (2014), accessed September 22, 2014, http://www.hrw.org/news/2008/01/12/kenya-end-police-use-excessive-force.

[116] n. 3 above.

after the 2013 general elections and the announcement of the results, 'demonstrations erupted in Kisumu, a city in western Kenya and a stronghold of support for Odinga.' A report that documented this incident found that[117]:

> Five people were shot dead and more than twenty injured when police used live ammunition to disperse protesters. These atrocities were committed in total disregard for the letter and spirit of the Constitution of Kenya, which is anchored on the principles of respect for human rights.

The same report further noted that, 'as many of the protesters were unarmed, the police actions violated the POA, which requires that the police should use no more force than is reasonably necessary.'[118] These incidents point to a worrying and grounded practice in protest policing in the country where protesters are treated as 'potentially violent.' However, the irony is that this approach is not useful at all nor does it succeed in keeping the peace as research has observed that, 'if a crowd is treated like an irrational group of criminals who only understand the language of force, that is how they will behave.'[119] Owing to its principles particularly of tolerance, the negotiated management model is necessarily different[120]:

> This milder approach represents a shift towards a more active use of communication, negotiation, cooperation, information gathering and emphasis on preventive police policies. The new approach regard[s] stereotypes associated with the classical understanding of crowd behaviour as wrong and potentially dangerous, because the police could misunderstand the situation and use excessive force, which could escalate the conflict.

Premised on this, the negotiated management model invokes various facilitative obligations that are useful in mitigating the escalated use of force. To start with, the state 'has a positive duty to take reasonable and appropriate measures to enable peaceful assemblies to take place without

---

[117] n. 105 above, 38.
[118] n. 84 above, 39.
[119] n. 104 above, 17.
[120] Ibid.

participants fearing physical violence.'[121] This includes 'a positive obligation to protect the right to life... [and] the right to freedom from inhuman or degrading treatment.'[122]

Further, implementation of the safety triangle feature of negotiated management means that dialogue has likely been established between protesters and police before the protest thereby heightening the chances of successful mediation on ground to resolve tension that could lead to violence. Indeed, *via* the negotiated management approach 'violence can often be averted by the skilful intervention of law-enforcement officials.'[123]

5   Soft Law Standards from the African Commission as Sources of Inspiration for Reforms in Kenya

Frans Viljoen has described the term 'soft law' as referring to rules that are not legally binding on states but which nonetheless can be of important persuasive value, particularly in domestic courts, depending on their quality, dissemination and use.[124] Two sets of such rules, relevant to the subject under consideration in this chapter, were recently adopted by the African Commission on Human and Peoples' Rights (African Commission). These are the Guidelines on Freedom of Association and Assembly in Africa (adopted in May 2017)[125] and the Guidelines for the Policing of Assemblies by Law-Enforcement Officials in Africa (adopted in March 2017).[126] The African Charter on Human and Peoples' Rights, to which Kenya is a State Party, mandates the African

---

[121] n. 94 above, 75.

[122] Ibid.

[123] n. 94 above, 73.

[124] Frans Viljoen, *International Human Rights Law in Africa* (Oxford: Oxford University Press, 2012), 30.

[125] African Commission on Human and Peoples' Rights, *Guidelines on Freedom of Association and Assembly in Africa*, accessed April 28, 2018, http://www.achpr.org/files/instruments/freedom-association-assembly/guidelines_on_freedom_of_association_and_assembly_in_africa_eng.pdf.

[126] African Commission on Human and Peoples' Rights, *Guidelines for the Policing of Assemblies by Law Enforcement Officials in Africa*, accessed April 28, 2018, http://www.achpr.org/files/instruments/policing-assemblies-in-africa/achpr_guidelines_on_policing_assemblies_eng_fre_por_ara.pdf.

Commission at article 45(1)(b) to 'formulate and lay down, principles and rules aimed at solving legal problems relating to human and peoples' rights and fundamental freedoms upon which African Governments may base their legislation.' It is on the strength of these provisions that the African Commission led the process of developing and adopting these Guidelines. Their content is highlighted below not only for their utility as a persuasive interpretive tool in Kenyan courts but also because they encapsulate the core ingredients of the negotiated management model. They can thus be a basis or inspiration for amending existing law or drafting new laws to ensure that the country's legal framework facilitates enjoyment of the right to demonstrate.

The Guidelines on Freedom of Association and Assembly in Africa sets out ten fundamental principles that should guide interpretation of freedom of association and assembly. The principles are relevant to the right to demonstrate which is inextricably yoked to freedom of assembly. The principles particularly relevant to freedom of assembly are: (1) a presumption in favour of exercising the right, (2) that the primary role of the legal framework is to enable the exercise of the right, (3) that participation of individuals in the political, social and cultural life of their communities must be enabled, (4) that constitutional, legislative and administrative measures on the right must comply with regional and international human rights obligations, (5) that authorities with governance oversight shall conduct their work impartially and fairly and (6) that procedures relating to the governance of assemblies shall be clear, simple and transparent.

Besides the above principles, the Guidelines on Freedom of Association and Assembly in Africa have clarified that freedom of assembly extends to peaceful assemblies and that an assembly should be deemed peaceful if the organisers have expressed peaceful intentions and if the conduct of participants is generally peaceful.[127] This conceptualisation of the term 'peaceful' is akin to that adopted by the UN High Commissioner for Human Rights.[128] As already discussed, Kenya has a notification regime, which is preferred to an authorisation regime for regulating assemblies/demonstrations/processions. The Guidelines have

---

[127] n. 125 above, clause 70.
[128] See n. 71 above.

clarified that even where a notification regime exists, such prior notification should be for purposes of facilitating exercise of the right and take necessary measures to protect public safety and rights of other citizens.[129] Importantly, the Guidelines provide that notification procedures should not be burdensome and that no notification need be submitted for small assemblies, assemblies unlikely to generate disturbance or spontaneous assemblies.[130] Such provision, if adopted in Kenya, would cure the current legal deficiency that mandates organisers of assemblies to notify the authorities at least three days prior to the event and thus by default making spontaneous assemblies 'unlawful.'

The Guidelines for the Policing of Assemblies by Law-Enforcement Officials in Africa are equally progressive. They include provisions that closely mirror the negotiated management model of policing protests/assemblies. Regarding communication between the authorities and organisers/participants of assemblies for example, these Guidelines are particularly spot-on. They provide that[131]:

> Law enforcement agencies should engage in continuous dialogue and negotiation with assembly organisers and participants to proactively address any issues that may arise during the conduct of an assembly operation. Law enforcement agencies should deploy specially trained negotiators to assembly operations for this purpose, based on any need identified during risk assessment and contingency planning.

The Guidelines also make provisions for de-escalation. Specifically, with respect to assemblies where participants are not acting peacefully, law enforcers are required to ensure that all actions taken in response satisfy the requirements of legality, necessity, proportionality, freedom from discrimination and equality before the law. In addition, such actions must conform to regional and international human rights standards.[132] Further, the Guidelines stipulate that use of force must be a measure of last resort and that law-enforcement officers must as far as is possible use non-violent means before resorting to the use of force and firearms. Even where force and firearm are used, this can only be with the aim

---

[129] n. 125 above, clause 71.

[130] n. 125 above, clause 72 and 75.

[131] n. 126 above, clause 13.1.

[132] n. 126 above, clause 20.1.

of achieving a legitimate law-enforcement objective.[133] Similarly, dispersing an assembly should be a measure of last resort and law enforces are required to act on the presumption that although they have the power to intervene in an assembly, they only do so in circumstances that are legal, necessary, proportionate and non-discriminatory. The section that follows will discuss the possibilities of anchoring the negotiated management model in Kenya's legal framework and as seen above, provisions in the two sets of Guidelines from the African Commission are a good starting or reference point.

6   Exploring Legal Entries for the Negotiated Management Model

In the previous section, the suitability and necessity of the negotiated management approach in Kenya has been ascertained. Here we consider which legal avenues exist for the adoption of the model. As noted earlier, public order management in the context of demonstrations is vested in police authorities. The negotiated management is therefore suitable for application as it is, in fact a policing model. Nonetheless, given the present policing culture and context of Kenya, it is unlikely that the principles of negotiated management will be embraced by the policing outfit without legal intervention. In a different context, mere guidelines encapsulating the negotiated management model of policing would perhaps suffice. Indeed, authoritative best practices have recommended that: 'These rules need not be elaborated in legislation but should be expressed in domestic law-enforcement guidelines, and legislation should require that such guidelines be developed.'[134] However, the police apparatus in Kenya is obviously lacking in political will or know-how in human rights policing. These realities necessitate adopting a more aggressive legal approach. Moreover, for practical reasons, guidelines would not suffice because there is already 'bad' law in place by way of the POA that needs reform. Since guidelines cannot repeal or amend extant laws, the express repeal or amendment by way of enactment of new legislation is needed.

---

[133] n. 126 above, clause 21.1.2.

[134] n. 94 above, 81.

Legislation is additionally suitable since its primary essence is to address a societal need by introducing new provisions or changing the law.[135] A distinct legislation on the management of demonstrations is also in line with global trends as captured by the Special Rapporteur on extrajudicial, summary or arbitrary executions in his report on demonstrations[136]:

> Around one third of the 76 countries considered have specialised legislation in place on demonstrations. In other countries, demonstrations are regulated together with other public order issues or in the countries' penal codes. Some countries recognise a positive duty to facilitate demonstrations.

Such legislation should be guided by the negotiated management model while mindful of the Kenyan context. The proposed legislation should have as its primary goal the facilitation of protests. The spirit of the law that should illuminate all provisions is that; at the heart of all its principles, negotiated management seeks to facilitate and not to circumscribe protest and a presumption in favour of holding protests should be assumed and expressly articulated. The phrasing and duties of the police in relation to policing protest should also reflect this position capturing not only negative but positive obligations.

In light of the restrictions to demonstrations in Kenya and the poor policing culture; the proposed legislation will need to unequivocally enact that 'the dispersal of assemblies should be a measure of last resort.'[137] In addition, the proposed law should express the, 'circumstances that warrant dispersal and who is entitled to issue dispersal orders (for example, only police officers of a specified rank and above).'[138]

Finally, in addition to the content, appropriate titling of such legislation is a critical issue for consideration. As has been argued, the success of the negotiated management approach rests on the trust levels or dynamics among the safety triangle parties, i.e. state, police and

---

[135] WorldatWork, *Public Policy Tool Kit: The Difference Between Legislation and Regulation*, accessed September 22, 2014, http://www.worldatwork.org/waw/adimLink?id=33051.

[136] n. 104 above, 14.

[137] n. 94 above, 81.

[138] Ibid.

protesters. The name of the legislation therefore needs to signify a clear turnaround in approach by affirming the right to protest and the intention to uphold it. Featuring familiar terminology of public order in the new legislative piece would likely do no more than conjure up the old perspectives which have been impugned. Titling the legislation also provides an opportunity to settle the debate as to whether there is a presumption in favour of or against the right to protest. It is against this backdrop that the authors propose the title: 'Freedom of assembly and right to public protest (Protection and Enforcement) Act.'

7 CONCLUSION

This chapter has laid out the practical concerns that are plaguing the management of demonstrations in Kenya. These concerns range from a legal framework that has atrophied the right to demonstrate; to challenges that have emerged from authoritarian policing practice handed over from colonial times and persisting to date. The discussion has illustrated how negotiated management can address all the present restrictions in the handling of protests; thereby emerging as a suitable and much-needed protest policing alternative. The enactment and genuine implementation of the negotiated management model will undoubtedly enhance the right to demonstrate in Kenya.

REFERENCE

African Commission on Human and Peoples' Rights. "Guidelines on Freedom of Association and Assembly in Africa." Accessed April 28, 2018. http://www. achpr.org/files/instruments/freedom-association-assembly/guidelines_on_ freedom_of_association_and_assembly_in_africa_eng.pdf.

African Commission on Human and Peoples' Rights. "Guidelines for the Policing of Assemblies by Law Enforcement Officials in Africa." Accessed April 28, 2018. http://www.achpr org/files/instruments/policing-assemblies-in-africa/achpr_guidelines_on_policing_assemblies_eng_fre_por_ara.pdf.

African Commission on Human and Peoples' Rights, Danish Institute for Human Rights and African Policing Civilian Oversight Forum. "Police and Human Rights in Africa." *Newsletter on Police and Human Rights in Africa* no. 4 (2014).

Amnesty International and Human Rights Watch. *"Kill Those Criminals"— Security Forces Violations in Kenya's August 2017 Elections.* New York: Amnesty International/Human Rights Watch, 2017. Accessed April 11, 2018. https:// www.hrw.org/sites/default/files/report_pdf/kenya1017_web.pdf.

Amnesty International. *Amnesty International Report 2017/18—The State of the World's Human Rights.* London: Amnesty International Limited, 2018. Accessed April 12, 2018. https://www.amnesty.org/download/Documents/POL1067002018ENGLISH.PDF.

Amnesty International. *Policing Demonstrations in the European Union* 2012. Accessed April 12, 2018. https://www.amnesty.org.uk/files/eu-police.pdf.

Application no. 33268/03, European Court of Human Rights, Judgment, July 17, 2008.

Baker, David. "From Batons to Negotiated Management: The Transformation of Policing Industrial Disputes in Australia." *Policing: A Journal of Policy and Practice* 1, no. 4 (2007): 390–402. Accessed October 10, 2014. http://policing.oxfordjournals.org.

Bukta and others v Hungary European Court of Human Rights, 17 July 2007, para 36 cited in Geneva Academy of International Humanitarian Law and Human Rights. *Facilitating Peaceful Protests* (Academy Briefing no. 5 2014).

Constitution of Kenya, 2010.

Cox v Louisiana 379 U.S. 559 (1965).

Davide, Pollard, Parpworth Neil, and Hughes David. *Constitutional and Administrative Law: Text with Materials.* Oxford: Oxford University Press, 2007.

Donatella, Porta, Peterson Abby, and Reiter Herbert. "The Policing of Transnational Protest" cited in John McCarthy "The Policing of Transnational Protest by Donatella Della Porta, Abby Peterson, Herbert Reiter," *Acta Sociologica* 50, no. 4 (2007): 441–442.

Ferdinand Ndung'u Waititu & 4 others vs the Attorney General & 9 others. Petition No. 169 of 2016. Accessed April 28, 2018. http://kenyalaw.org/caselaw/cases/view/122806/.

Freeman, Harrop. "The Right of Protest and Civil Disobedience." *Indiana Law Journal* 41 (1966): 228–254.

Geneva Academy of International Humanitarian Law and Human Rights. *Facilitating Peaceful Protests.* Academy Briefing no. 5, 2014.

Hugo, Gorringe, Stott Clifford, and Rosie Michael. "Dialogue Police, Decision Making, and the Management of Public Order During Protest Crowd Events." *Journal of Investigative Psychology and Offender Profiling* 9 (2012): 111–125.

Human Rights Watch. Multipartyism Betrayed in Kenya: Continuing Rural Violence and Restrictions on Freedom of Speech and Assembly. *Human Rights Watch Short Report* 6, no. 5 (1994).

House of Lords and House of Commons Joint Committee on Human Rights. *Demonstrating Respect for Rights? A Human Rights Approach to Policing Protest* (Seventh Report of Session 2008–2009).

Human Rights Watch. "Kenya: End Police Use of Excessive Force" (2014). Accessed September 22, 2014. http://www.hrw.org/news/2008/01/12/kenya-end-police-use-excessive-force.

Human Rights Watch. *"They Were Men in Uniform" Sexual Violence Against Women and Girls in Kenya's 2017 Elections*. New York: Human Rights Watch, 2017. Accessed April 12, 2018. https://www.hrw.org/sites/default/files/report_pdf/kenya1217_web.pdf.

International Network of Civil Liberties Organisations. *Take Back the Streets: Repression and Criminalization of Protest Around the World*. New York: International Network of Civil Liberties Organisations, 2013.

Kenya National Commission on Human Rights. *On the Brink of the Precipice: A Human Rights Account of Kenya's Post-2007 Election Violence*. Nairobi: KNCHR, 2008. Accessed April, 11, 2018. https://kenyastockholm.files.wordpress.com/2008/08/pev-report-as-adopted-by-the-commission-for-release-on-7-august-20081.pdf.

"Kenya Bans Opposition Protests as Election Crisis Deepens." *The Guardian*, October 12, 2017. Accessed April 12, 2018. https://www.theguardian.com/world/2017/oct/12/kenya-bans-opposition-protests-as-election-crisis-deepens.

Kibwana, Kivutha. *Fundamental Rights and Freedoms in Kenya*. Nairobi: Oxford University Press, 1990.

"Kimaiyo Bans Political Rallies, Reverses Ban to Allow CORD Rally." allafrica, May 28, 2014. Accessed April 28, 2018. http://allafrica.com/stories/201405290256.html.

Laing, Aislinn. "Mayhem in Kenya as Police Tackle Protest Over 'Corrupt' Poll Officials." *The Telegraph*, May 16, 2016. Accessed April 11, 2018. https://www.telegraph.co.uk/news/2016/05/16/mayhem-in-kenya-as-police-tackle-protest-over-corrupt-poll-offic/.

Mbondenyi, Morris, and Ambani John. *The New Constitutional Law of Kenya: Principles, Government & Human Rights*. Nairobi, LawAfrica, 2012.

McCarthy, John. "The Policing of Transnational Protest by Donatella Della Porta, Abby Peterson, Herbert Reiter." *Acta Sociologica* 50, no. 4 (2007).

Ng'ethe, Njuguna, Owiti Jeremiah, Nasongo Shadrack, Beetham David, and Bracking Sarah. *Democracy Report for Jamhuri ya Kenya*. International Institute for Democracy and Electoral Assistance (IDEA) & Series on Alternative Research in East Africa (SAREAT), 2000. Accessed September 2, 2014. http://www.idea.int/publications/sod/upload/Kenya.pdf.

National Policing Improvement Agency, Association of Chief Police Officers & Association of Chief Police Officers in Scotland. *Manual of Guidance on Keeping the Peace*, 2010.

National Police Service Act No. 11A of 2011.

Nation Team. "Matiang'i Ban on Demos Sparks Storm." *Daily Nation*, October 13, 2017. Accessed April 24, 2018. https://mobile.nation.co.ke/news/politics/Matiang-i-ban-on-demos-sparks-storm-/3126390-4137380-format-xhtml-9q2qwaz/index.html.

Nmehielle, Vincent. *The African Human Rights System: Its Laws, Practice and Institutions.* Leiden: Martinus Nijhoff Publishers, 2001.

O'Flaherty, Michael. "Effective Measures and Best Practices to Ensure the Promotion and Protection of Human Rights in the Context of Peaceful Protests: A Background Paper." Accessed September 22, 2014 http://www.ohchr.org/EN/Issues/AssemblyAssociation/Pages/Seminar2December2013.aspx.

Ombati, Cyrus, and Protus Onyango. "Controversy Over Matiang'i Ban on Demos in CBD." *The Standard*, October 13, 2017. Accessed April 28, 2018.

OSCE Office for Democratic Institutions and Human Rights. *Guidelines on Freedom of Peaceful Assembly.* Warsaw, Poland: OSCE/ODIHR, 2010.

Peter, Chris. "Fundamental Rights and Freedoms in Kenya—A Review Essay." *African Journal of International and Comparative Law* 3 (1991): 61.

Phumeza Mlungwana & 9 Others vs The State & Minister of Police, Case No. A431/15, January 24, 2018.

Public Order Act, Chapter 56 of the Laws of Kenya.

Rosie, M., and H. Gorringe. "What a Difference a Death Makes: Protest, Policing and the Press at the G20." *Sociological Research Online* 14, no. 5 (2009): 4. Accessed April 28, 2018. https://www.researchgate.net/publication/46559303_What_a_Difference_a_Death_Makes_Protest_Policing_and_the_Press_at_the_G20.

Schweingruber, David. "Mob Sociology and Escalated Force: Sociology's Contribution to Repressive Police Tactics." *The Sociological Quarterly* 41, no. 3 (2000): 371–389.

The International Center for Not-for-Profit Law. "NGO Law Monitor: Kenya." Accessed September 22, 2014. http://www.icnl.org/research/monitor/kenya.html.

UN General Assembly. *Report of the Special Representative of the Secretary-General on Human Rights Defenders* A/62/225 (2007).

UN Human Rights Council. *Report of the Special Rapporteur on Extrajudicial, Summary or Arbitrary Executions* A/HRC/17/28 (2011).

UN Human Rights Council. *Report of the Special Rapporteur on the rights to freedom of peaceful assembly and of association, Maina Kiai* A/HRC/20/27 (2012).

UN Human Rights Council. *Report of the Special Rapporteur on the Rights to Freedom of Peaceful Assembly and of Association, Maina Kiai* A/HRC/23/39 (2013).

UN Human Rights Council. *Effective Measures and Best Practices to Ensure the Promotion and Protection of Human Rights in the Context of Peaceful Protests. Report of the United Nations High Commissioner for Human Rights.* A/HRC/22/28 (2013).

UN World Conference on Human Rights. *Vienna Declaration and Programme of Action* A/CONF.157/24 (1993).

U.S. Const. amend. I.

Viljoen, Frans. *International Human Rights Law in Africa.* Oxford: Oxford University Press, 2012.

Vitale, Alex. "From Negotiated Management to Command and Control: How the New York Police Department Polices Protests." *Policing and Society* 15, no. 3 (2006): 283–304.

Wilson Olal & 5 others v Attorney General & 2 others, Constitutional Petition No. 323 of 2014, accessed April 12, 2018. http://kenyalaw.org/caselaw/cases/view/137643/.

WorldatWork. *Public Policy Tool Kit: The Difference Between Legislation and Regulation.* Accessed September 22, 2014. http://www.worldatwork.org/waw/adimLink?id=33051.

CHAPTER 9

The Right to Peaceful Assembly in a Chaotic Democracy: An Analysis of Nigerian Law

Bamisaye Olutola

1 INTRODUCTION

The right of people to assemble and to demonstrate on issues of common concern to them is a fundamental human right,[1] as it is regarded as the people's 'way of exercising direct democracy'.[2] Asides from this being a right, demonstrations are a communication tool for those who feel the state is giving no serious attention to their demands.[3] Protesters have not only historically shaped the course of governmental policies, in

---

[1] HREA, "Freedom of Assembly and Association," available at http://www.hrea.org/erc/Library/display_doc.php?url=%3A%2F%2Fwww.osce.org%2Fnode%2F24525&external=N, accessed March 28, 2018.

[2] Report of the United Nations High Commissioner for Human Rights on Seminar on effective measures and best practices to ensure the promotion and protection of human rights in the context of peaceful protests, A/HRC/25/32 (29 January 2014), 18.

[3] Stuart Woolman, "Assembly, Demonstration and Petition," in *The Bill of Rights Handbook*, 6th ed., ed. Iain Currie and Johan De Waal (Cape Town: JUTA, 2013), 378.

B. Olutola (✉)
Faculty of Law, University of Lagos, Lagos, Nigeria

Centre for Human Rights, University of Pretoria, Pretoria, South Africa

© The Author(s) 2020
M. Addaney et al. (eds.), *Governance, Human Rights, and Political Transformation in Africa*,
https://doi.org/10.1007/978-3-030-27049-0_9

recent times, they have been perceived to be 'prime makers of history'.[4] Moreover, everyone should be able to exercise his or her right to peaceful demonstrations on issues of concern to them without fear of intimidation or threat of being killed while exercising the same.[5] The right of everybody to peaceful assembly which also includes the right to peaceful demonstration is widely recognised by various international and regional human right instruments.

Nigeria is a party to various international human rights treaties, principal among which are the International Covenant on Civil and Political Rights (ICCPR) and the African Charter on Human and Peoples' Rights (African Charter), which place an unwavering three-tier obligation on Nigeria to respect, protect and fulfil those rights contained in those treaties. Nigeria has however not taken any concrete and targeted step to ensure that these unlawful killings are abated, by reviewing its use of force laws.[6]

This study aims to propose practical approaches that are based on international human rights standards, so as to ensure the highest standard of protection of the right to life of participants in peaceful assembly or demonstration in Nigeria. This is because, '[h]uman rights standards on the use of force derive from the understanding that the irreversibility of death justifies stringent safeguards for the right to life, especially in relation to due processes'.[7] The chapter unpacks the laws governing the use of force in Nigeria as they relate to demonstrations, the reasons being that respect for human rights which includes right to peaceful assembly is regarded as one of the hallmarks of good governance in any society or state.

---

[4] Michael O'Flaherty, "Effective Measures and Best Practices to Ensure the Promotion and Protection of Human Rights in the Context of Peaceful Protests: A Background Paper," (2013) 3, available at www.ohchr.org/Documents/Issues/FAssociation/Seminar2013/BackgroundPaperSeminar.doc, accessed March 27, 2018.

[5] Preamble to the UN Human Rights Council Resolution on "The Promotion and Protection of Human Rights in the Context of Peaceful Protests" A/HRC/25/L.20 (March 25, 2014).

[6] Wade M. Cole, "Mind the Gap: State Capacity and the Implementation of Human Rights Treaties," *International Organization* 69, spring (2015): 405–441, 412.

[7] Report of Philip Alston, UN Special Rapporteur on Extrajudicial, summary or arbitrary executions, A/61/311 (2006), 33.

2 Peaceful Assembly Under Siege: The Conceptual Issues

A plethora of authors have written on the legitimate right of everybody to demonstrate peacefully and the state's corresponding duty to protect demonstrators in addition to respect for the right to peaceful demonstration. Heyns argues that legitimate resistance which could also be demonstration is the flipside of the human rights coin.[8] He further argues that people across the world have shown the readiness to fight and take matters into their hands when their core interests are not respected or protected.[9]

Crashaw and Holmstrom in arguing for the state to recognise the right of citizens to demonstrate posited that police needs to protect the right to life of demonstrators, based on the fact that the right to freedom of assembly is necessary to secure other rights.[10] Kalin and Kunzli argue that right to life of demonstrators should be protected because 'freedom to gather together with other persons is fundamental for the exercise of any form of democracy'.[11] O'Flaherty, states that the human right of the people to protest though not contained in any international human rights instrument is 'an amalgam of different rights, including, the right to freedom of peacefully assembly (Art. 21 ICCPR), the right to freedom of association (Art. 22 ICCPR), the right to freedom of expression (Art. 19 ICCPR) and the right to participate in the conduct of political affairs (Art. 25 ICCPR)'.[12] He however, decried the excessive use of force by states during such times and argues that appropriate legal regimes recognising the right to peaceful protest at state level can create an enabling environment.[13] He is of the view that, while international

---

[8] Cristof Heyns, "A 'Struggle Approach' to Human Rights," in *Law and Pluralism*, ed. Arend Soeteman (New York: Springer, 2001), 171–190.

[9] Heyns, "A 'Struggle Approach' to Human Rights."

[10] Ralph Crawshaw and Leif Holmström, *Essential Cases on Human Rights for the Police: Review and Summaries of International Cases* (Leiden, the Netherlands: Brill Nijhoff, 2006), 487.

[11] Jörg Künzli and Walter Kälin, *The Law of International Human Rights Protection* (London: Oxford, 2009), 474.

[12] O'Flaherty, "Effective Measures and Best Practices to Ensure the Promotion and Protection of Human Rights in the Context of Peaceful Protests: A Background Paper," 11.

[13] Ibid., 18.

law offers protection to demonstrators, the scale of the threat they face calls for intensified focus on the need for the protection of public space for peaceful protest.[14] Boyle and Shah argue that the scope of the right to peaceful assembly under international law extends to demonstrations and the state has an obligation not to interfere with this right, and to ensure the right to peaceful assembly is protected.[15]

However, this study argues that challenges with the right to demonstrate and the way(s) the right to life of demonstrators in Nigeria can be protected, is yet to be critically considered. Sampson argues that there exists the people's right to demonstrate in Nigeria based on international instruments which Nigeria has validly ratified, and on the fact that demonstration is central to any democratic state.[16] However, Sampson criticised the fact that the Nigeria police officials favour the traditional method of security which emphasises on national security rather than the liberal security approach which favours human-centred demonstrations.[17] Sampson further suggested the need for the state to protect demonstrators, the Public Order Act (POA) be reviewed, and the police better equipped on managing demonstrations. He however, did not discuss the various uses of force laws and how these laws impact the right to life of demonstrators.[18]

Falana contends that the right to protest in Nigeria is guaranteed by the constitution by virtue of section 40 of the Constitution of the Federal Republic of Nigeria (CFRN) which guarantees the right to peaceful assembly, but does not focus on the use of force law during demonstration.[19] Similarly, Chinweze argues on the constitutionality of the POA and how the police officials have used it unjustifiably to stifle the right to peaceful assembly of Nigerians. Chinweze further calls

[14] Ibid., 21.

[15] Kevin Boyle and Sangeeta Shah, "Thought, Expression, Association, and Assembly," in *International Human Rights Law*, edited by Daniel Moeckli et al., 2nd ed. (London: Oxford University Press, 2014), 234–235.

[16] Isaac Sampson, "The Right to Demonstrate in a Democracy: An Evaluation of Public Order Policing in Nigeria," *African Human Rights Law Journal* 10, no. 2 (2010): 446

[17] Ibid., 438.

[18] Ibid., 451–456.

[19] Femi Falana, "Nigerians' Right to Protest Is Constitutionally guaranteed," available at http://saharareporters.com/2012/01/08/nigerians%E2%80%99-right-protest-constitutionally-guaranteed, accessed March 27, 2019.

for the abrogation of the POA either by the legislature or the court.[20] Eruaga argues that Nigerians have the right to protest or demonstrate, since the term assembly as guaranteed by the CFRN, includes intentional gathering of people for a particular purpose which also includes public protest or demonstrations.[21] Eruaga further contends that since Nigeria is a signatory to various international treaties, it has the obligation to protect peaceful demonstrators from violence and refrain from undermining the right.[22]

3   THE RIGHT TO FREEDOM OF ASSEMBLY UNDER INTERNATIONAL LAW

At the global level, the right to peaceful assembly first found its way into the first codified international human rights document, the Universal Declaration on human rights (Universal Declaration).[23] Article 20(1) of the Universal Declaration guarantees the right to peaceful assembly and association to everyone.[24] As a result of the need to make states accountable for their respective human rights obligations as far as international human rights law are concerned, the UN adopted two binding human rights instruments, which are the ICCPR[25] and the International Covenant on Economic and Social Cultural Rights (CESCR).[26] The ICCPR, is a document that guarantees numerous civil and political rights and has an expansive definition on the right to peaceful assembly. Article 21 of the ICCPR mandates state parties to recognise the right to

[20] Chinelo Chinweze, "The Constitutionality of the Public Order Act in a Democracy: 'A Square Peg in a Round Hole'," available at http://www.gamji.com/article5000/NEWS5960.htm, accessed March 29, 2018.

[21] Osatohanmwen Eruaga, "The Right to Protest: A Review of the Law and Empirics in Nigeria," in *Freedom of Protest*, ed. Epiphany Azinge and Laura Ani (Abuja: NIALS Press, 2013), 35.

[22] Sampson, "The Right to Demonstrate in a Democracy," 36.

[23] Universal Declaration of Human Rights (UDHR), G.A. Res. 217A, U.N. Doc A/810 (10 December 1948).

[24] Ibid.

[25] International Covenant on Civil and Political Rights, Mar. 23, 1976, 999 U.N.T.S. 172.

[26] International Covenant on Economic, Social and Cultural Rights, Dec. 16, 1966, 993 U.N.T.S. 3.

peaceful assembly of everyone, and that this right can only be restricted on some of the listed grounds under the Covenant. The express guarantee of the right to peaceful assembly presupposes a negative obligation on state parties, which is to the effect that there should be a presumption of the right to peaceful assembly.[27]

Despite the indisputable nature of the right to peaceful demonstrations, several states all over the world have over the years made various laws that give an impression of upholding the right to peaceful demonstration which this study argues limits and sometimes outrightly stifled its enjoyment.[28] Peaceful demonstration helps those at the margin of the society to be heard and it '…serve[s] as a very important correction and a tool to highlight situations where human rights are violated or at risk'.[29] Since democracy entails contestation and participation, the right to oppose government policies and programmes through peaceful demonstration is inevitable.[30]

Notwithstanding the recognition of this right under international law, there are limitations and derogations to this right. Similar to other human rights, the rights to peaceful assembly, is not absolute, as it can be limited and derogated from in certain circumstances. In terms of article 21 of the ICCPR the right can be limited through legislation which are in 'conformity with law, necessary in a democratic state, national security or public safety, public order (*ordre public*), the protection of public health or morals or the protection of rights and freedom of others'. It can also be lawfully derogated from during times of public emergencies under article 4 of the ICCPR. However, in an attempt to limit this right, states usually invoke national laws, which have a grave impact on the right to peaceful assembly and other rights.

---

[27] Kevin Boyle and Sangeeta Shah, "Thought, Expression, Association, and Assembly," in *International Human Rights Law*, 2nd ed., ed. Daniel Moeckli et al. (London: Oxford University Press, 2014), 234.

[28] *'The Global Suppression of Protest'* by the International Network of Civil Liberties Organizations (10 October 2013), available at https://www.aclu.org/blog/free-speech/global-suppression-protest, accessed March 28, 2019.

[29] Jonas Støre, "Paper Delivered at the Seminar on Human Rights Defenders and Peaceful Protest on 6 June 2012," available at http://www.regjeringen.no/en/archive/Stoltenbergs-2nd-Government/Ministry-of-Foreign-Affairs/taler-og-artikler/2012/hr_defenders.html?id=684851, accessed March 27, 2019.

[30] Makau Mutua, "Human Rights in Africa: The Limited Promise of Liberalism," *African Studies Review* 51, no. 1 (2008): 21.

At the regional level, the right to peaceful assembly is guaranteed under article 11 of the European Convention for the Protection of Human Rights and Fundamental Freedom (European Convention), and article 15 of the American Convention on Human Rights (American Convention).

In the African Human rights system, the African Charter on Human and Peoples' Rights (African Charter)[31] guarantees the right to peaceful assembly under article 11 and the African Commission on Human and Peoples' (African Commission), has, through its numerous decisions, breathed life into this provision. The African Commission at its 55th Session in 2014, in recognition of the need to address the threat posed by many state parties to the right to peaceful demonstration, adopted a resolution on the right to peaceful demonstrations.[32] According to the resolution, the Commission '[c]ondemns serious restrictions imposed by some states to fundamental rights and freedoms specifically freedom of expression and the rights to information and peaceful demonstration'. In addition to expressing one's view, demonstration entails a citizens' continued participation subsequent to elections and is the hallmark of democratic and pluralist states.

There is no provision for derogation of any of the rights under the Charter.[33] The silence on derogation by the African Charter, according to Viljoen, may constitute a 'normative innovation' but, at the same time, puts it at loggerhead with domestic constitutional regimes of many African states.[34] Derogation connotes total (though temporary) suspension of a right as guaranteed in international human rights instrument or the constitution of a state while limitation denotes a withholding of a part or fraction of a right.[35] Derogation is invoked by states in

---

[31] African Charter on Human and Peoples' Rights adopted on 27 June 1981 at Nairobi, Kenya and entered into force on 21 October 1986, OAU Doc. CAB/LEG/67/3 Rev. 5, 21 ILM 58 (1982).

[32] 281: Resolution on the Right to Peaceful Demonstrations, at the Commission meeting at its 55th Ordinary Session held from 28 April to 12 May 2014, in Luanda, Angola.

[33] *Constitutional Rights Project and Others v Nigeria* (2000) African Human Rights Law Report 227 (ACHPR 1999), 41.

[34] Frans Viljoen, *International Human Rights Law in Africa*, 2nd ed. (London: Oxford University Press, 2012), 333.

[35] Abdi Ali, "Derogation from Constitutional Rights and Its Implication Under the African Charter on Human and Peoples' Rights," *Law Democracy & Development* 17 (2013): 80.

exceptional circumstances to allow states depart from their treaty obligations for that material time.[36] Some authors view the non-inclusion of a derogation clause in the Charter as a fundamental omission,[37] while others view it as a welcome development.[38] It has even been suggested that the absence of derogation clause in the Charter has lifted all rights in Charter to a status of 'regional *jus cogens*'.[39] The African Commission has held in plethora of its decisions that derogation is not allowed under the Charter,[40] even in times of war.[41]

It must be pointed out here that, article 11 of the Charter provides for a possible limitation to the right to peaceful assembly, when it states that:

> ...The exercise of this right shall be subject only to necessary restrictions provided for by law in particular those enacted in the interest of national security, the safety, health, ethics and the rights and freedoms of others.

Thus, unlike the ICCPR which uses the phrase 'in a democratic society'; the African Charter uses 'necessary restriction'. A state may fail in justifying its limitation of this right sanctioned by domestic law if it cannot show that, such restriction/ law is 'necessary', as the claw-back clause is not a leeway for states to breach their obligations under the Charter.[42] The Commission's decision in the case of *Civil Liberty Organisation*

---

[36] Ibid., 80.

[37] Christof Heyns, "The African Regional Human Rights System: In Need of Reform?" *African Human Rights Law Journal* 1 (2001): 155; Fatsah Ouguergouz, *The African Charter on Human and Peoples' Rights: A Comprehensive Agenda for Human Dignity and Sustainable Development* (Leiden, the Netherlands: Brill; Nijhoff 2003); Laurent Sermet, "The Absence of a Derogation Clause from the African Charter on Human and Peoples' Rights: A Critical Discussion," *African Human Rights Law Journal* 7 (2007): 142.

[38] Ali, "Derogation from Constitutional Rights and Its Implication Under the African Charter on Human and Peoples' Rights," 87.

[39] Viljoen, *International Human Rights Law in Africa*, 334.

[40] *Media Rights Agenda and Others v Nigeria* (2000) AHRLR 200 (ACHPR 1998), 67; *Article 19 v Eritrea* (2007) AHRLR 73 (ACHPR 2007), 87; *Constitutional Rights Project and Others v Nigeria* (2000) AHRLR 227 (ACHPR 1999), 41; *Jawara v The Gambia* (2000) AHRLR 107 (ACHPR 2000), 49.

[41] *Commission Nationale des Droits de l'Hommeet des Libertés v Chad* (2000) AHRLR 66 (ACHPR 1995), 21.

[42] *Amnesty International v Zambia* (2000) AHRLR 325 (ACHPR 1999), 50.

v Nigeria which pertains to the taking over of the structures of the Nigerian Bar Association by the government, resonate the idea that constitutional provisions should not be overridden by regulatory authorities so as to downplay rights guaranteed in the constitution and international instruments.[43]

Therefore, any limitation which undermines international human rights standards will fail the limitation threshold of the African Charter. Similarly, for a limitation under national law to pass the international human rights standards, such limitation must not render the right illusory,[44] and must not be discriminatory in nature.[45]

4   SECURING THE RIGHT TO ASSEMBLY IN NIGERIA: THE ROLE OF INTERNATIONAL HUMAN RIGHTS LAW

Nigeria is a party to several international instruments, including the ICCPR and the African Charter. Section 12(1) of the CFRN which encapsulates the status of treaties under Nigerian law provides that:

> [n]o treaty between the Federation and any other country shall have any force of law except to the extent to which any such treaty has been enacted into law by the National Assembly.

The African Charter is among the treaties that have passed through the process contained in the above section.[46] The validity of section 12(1) of the CFRN has been upheld in the case of *Abacha v Fawehinmi*, where the Supreme Court of Nigeria held that 'an international treaty entered into by the government of Nigeria does not become binding until enacted into law by the National Assembly'.[47] The court further held that, while the provisions of the Charter are superior to other laws, they are inferior to the CFRN. Ali argues that the position of the court on the superiority of CFRN to the African Charter is against Nigeria's

---

[43](2000) AHRLR 186 (ACHPR 1995), 15.

[44]*Media Right Agenda* case, 70.

[45]*Constitutional right project* case, 44.

[46]The African Charter on Human and Peoples' Rights (Ratification and Enforcement) Act 1983.

[47]*Abacha and Others v Fawehinmi* (2001) AHRLR 172 (NgSC 2000), 12.

obligations under the Charter[48]; Durojaye argues in favour of the decision, as he asserts that '[t]he mere fact that an international treaty has been incorporated into domestic law does not necessarily elevate the treaty above the constitution. This is particularly true of a dualist state like Nigeria'.[49]

Without any doubt, the CFRN will be declared to be the supreme law in Nigerian court, but the reverse will definitely be the case in an international forum, as Nigeria will not be allowed to evade its international obligations based solely on the provisions of its constitution. A classic example is the 'Bakassi Peninsula' case, where Nigeria obeyed the decision of the International Court of Justice (ICJ) to cede the Peninsula to the Republic of Cameroun, notwithstanding that 'Bakassi' is among the listed local government areas in the Nigerian Constitution.[50]

A treaty is a source of obligation on parties that have freely entered into it.[51] Viljoen rightly noted that, once a state has ratified a human rights treaty, what is expected of such state is to '…adapt its national law and policies to square with its obligation under the treaty'.[52] The obligations of states under international human rights law can be broadly categorised into: (i) obligation to respect the rights (which entails the state refraining from interfering with the enjoyment of the rights); (ii) obligation to protect the rights (state is required to ensure that third-parties do not interfere with the enjoyment of the rights); (iii) obligation to fulfil the rights (this requires state to put in mechanisms in place to facilitate the enjoyment of the rights); and (iv) obligation to promote the rights (state must make conscious efforts to educate the people on these rights).[53] The UN has noted that '[t]he responsibility to respect, protect and fulfil human

---

[48]Ali, "Derogation from Constitutional Rights and Its Implication Under the African Charter on Human and Peoples' Rights," 98.

[49]Ebenezer Durojaye, "Litigating the Right to Health in Nigeria: Challenges and Prospect," in *International Law and Domestic Human Rights Litigation in Africa*, ed. Magnus Killander (Pretoria: PULP, 2010), 160.

[50]Part 1 to the first schedule of the CFRN (under Cross River State).

[51]David J. Harris, *Cases and Materials on International Law*, 6th ed. (London: Oxford University Press, 2004), 42.

[52]Frans Viljoen, "The African Charter on the Rights and Welfare of the Child," in *Introduction to Child Law in South Africa*, ed. C.J. Davel (Cape Town: Juta Law, 2000), 215.

[53]Ibid., 6; *SERAC and Another v Nigeria* (2001) AHRLR 60 (ACHPR 2001), 45–47.

rights lies with States. They ratify international human rights instruments and are required to create mechanisms to safeguard human rights'.[54]

Nigeria having freely ratified both the ICCPR and the African Charter, has an unwavering and unimpeachable obligation to bring its domestic laws (including its constitution) in conformity with both treaties, and must not act against the tenor of the treaties. During ratification of either the ICCPR or the African Charter, Nigeria did not enter any reservation which could have excused Nigeria from some of the obligations under the treaties.[55]

4.1 Right to Peaceful Assembly Under the Nigerian Law: A Paper Tiger?

The right to peaceful assembly is guaranteed under section 40, though peaceful assembly is only provided in its side note and not in the main provision. Section 40 provides that:

> Every person shall be entitled to assemble freely and associate with other persons, and in particular he may form or belong to any political party, trade union or any other association for the protection of his interest...

The above provision leaves no one in doubt of the rights of every person (both citizen and non-citizen) to enjoy the right to peaceful assembly. The fact that the section does not specifically mention demonstrations is immaterial[56]; as I have pointed out that the right to peaceful assembly carries with it, a concomitant right to peaceful demonstration.[57] Olarenwaju has rightly noted in the Nigeria context that '[w]hile no human rights instrument or national constitution grants the absolute right to protest [demonstrate], such right to protest [demonstrate] is an expression of the right to freedom of assembly...'[58] Nigerians have

---

[54] UN publication on "National Human Rights Institutions History, Principles, Roles and Responsibilities" (2010), 1; also the General Guidelines of the UN Nairobi Declaration on the Administration of Justice (2008).

[55] Article 21 of Vienna Convention on the Law of Treaties.

[56] Unlike section 17 of the 1996 Constitution of the Republic of South Africa.

[57] Boyle and Shah, "Thought, Expression, Association, and Assembly," 234.

[58] Adegoke Olarenwaju, "Right to Protest and Right to Strike: An Overview," in *Freedom of Protest*, ed. Epiphany Azinge and Laura Ani (Abuja: NIALS Press, 2013), 3.

in recent times invoked the above provision to express their displeasure over government laws and policies by way of protest or demonstrations; which they believe to be anti-masses, and this in no doubt has brought the right to protest into our legal jurisprudence.[59]

Similarly, in the decision of *Inspector General of Police v All Nigerian Peoples' Party and Others* (ANPP case),[60] the Court of Appeal had to determine whether the requirement of licence prior to exercising the right to demonstrating under the POA is constitutional in the light of express provision of section 40 of the CFRN. The court in upholding the express right of Nigerians to participate in peaceful assembly, protest and demonstrations without any permit,[61] stated that '[t]he power given to the governor of a state to issue permit under the POA cannot be used to attain the unconstitutional result of deprivation of the right to freedom of speech and freedom of assembly'.[62]

Many Nigerians have in recent times placed more demands on the right since Nigeria returned to democratic rule on 29 May 1999. This was after the dark ages of military (mis)rule.[63] However, as the citizens demand for their right to peaceful assembly by way of protest, demonstrations and picketing; the state has been invoking some undemocratic legislation to deny citizens of this right based on the permissible limitations under the CFRN.[64] The various limitations of this right under the Nigerian law are discussed in the subheadings below.

4.2   Limitations of the Right to Peaceful Assembly Under Nigerian Law

The CFRN, makes provisions for a general limitation section for major fundamental rights; and the right to peaceful assembly is among such rights. Section 45(1) has on its side note the phrase '[r]estriction and

---

[59]Osatohanmwen Eruaga, "The Right to Protest: A Review of the Law and Empirics in Nigeria," Azinge and Ani (n. 58 above), 39.

[60](2007) AHRLR 179 (NgCA 2007).

[61]Ibid., 32.

[62]Ibid., 31.

[63]Ogadimma Arisukwu, "Policing Trends in Nigeria Since Independence (1960–2012)." *The Police Journal* 55 (2012): 151.

[64]Akin Ibidapo-Obe. *In the Public Interest: A Study of the Legal Interventions of Femi Falana* (Lagos: Concept Publications, 2008), 1.

derogation from fundamental rights'. The section provides that: '[n]oth-ing in sections 37, 38, 39, 40 and 41 of this Constitution shall invalidate any law that is reasonably justifiable in a democratic society- (a) in the interest of defence, public safety, public order or public morality or pub-lic health; or (b) for the purpose of protecting the rights and freedom of other persons'.

Notwithstanding, the above provision, there exist in the CFRN, a supremacy clause under section 1(3) which provide that '[i]f any law is inconsistent with the provisions of this constitution, this constitution shall prevail, that other law shall to the extent of the inconstancy be void'.

Therefore, in order to appreciate the power of the National Assembly to make laws limiting the various rights under the CFRN, the suprem-acy clause must be equally borne in mind The valid logic that could be deduced from the above two provisions is that, while the constitution empowers the National Assembly to lawfully limit or derogate from the right through the instrumentality of laws, such legislative power must be balanced with the need to respect the supremacy of the constitution.[65] It suffices to say that since the supreme law of the land is the constitu-tion; any law that purports to limit the rights against the tenor of the constitution will not pass constitutional muster under section 1(3). The court in the *ANPP* case noted that '[t]he Constitution of any country is the embodiment of what the people desire to be their guiding light in governance, their supreme law and the *grundnorm* of all their laws'.[66]

The CFRN empowers the National Assembly to limit certain rights which includes the right to assemble based on laws that are 'reasonably justifiable in a democratic society'. Notably, section 318 of the CFRN, which is the interpretation section, offers no assistance as to determine what it contemplates by the phrase. However, in the case of *Castells* v *Spain*, it was held that, there cannot be a democratic society without 'pluralism, tolerance and broadmindedness'.[67] While it is the duty of the government to ensure the defence, safety and order of its country, it can-not do this without regards to the rights of its citizens. Therefore, laws

[65] Ibikunle v Adaralode (2000) 23 WRN 86 (NgSC); Kotoye v Central Bank of Nigeria & Others (2000), 16 WRN 1 (NgSC).

[66] ANPP Case, 17.

[67] European Court of Human Rights, judgment, 23 April 1992, 42.

may be justified under these headings '...when they are objectively reasonable and necessary to protect public order, safety and the rights and freedoms of others'.[68]

As noted earlier, popular desires are not enough to derogate or limit a right. Equally popular morality cannot take the place of 'society's morality'. What should determine whether a limitation under the heading passes both constitutional muster and human rights standard; is to be determined among others by the general application test, non-discrimination test and the proportionality test. The CFRN makes provision for the limitations of the right to peaceful assembly on the above ground. Similarly, the proportionality test will be applied to determine whether the limitation is justifiable. There are several laws that have impact on the right to peaceful assembly in Nigeria. However, among these pieces of legislation in this chapter, will consider the Same-Sex Marriage (Prohibition) Act of 2014 (same-sex Act).

Securing rights: Protection of right to life in the context of demonstrations in a chaotic democracy

The discussion presented in this section aims to determine the level of compliance of Nigeria's use of force laws in the context of demonstration with that of the international human rights regimes. This is based on the fact that the right to life is endangered when state either tries to quell or control demonstrations or assemblies through the use of force (either lethal or non-lethal). The first step to ensuring the effective protection of the right to life of demonstrators is by putting to good use of force laws in place which mirror the international best practices.

It will be instructive to state from the outset that, Nigeria being a Federal Republic has one Police Force, known as the Nigerian Police Force (NPF) as provided for under the CFRN, but with various Commands or divisions in all the 36 states of the Federation.[69] Furthermore, the words arbitrary/unlawful/extrajudicial killings as used in this research; extend to situations where the right to life is gravely threatened as a result of the use of force by the police during times of assemblies or demonstrations. The waves of demonstrations, protests

---

[68] Geneva Academy, *Facilitating Peaceful Protests* (2014), 11.

[69] Section 214(1); section 3 of the Nigerian Police Act, Cap. P19, Laws of the Federal Republic of Nigeria (2004).

and assemblies across the world in recent time (in Africa and across the world),[70] and the use of law enforcement agencies to quell, stop or manage such assemblies re-enforces the need for a closer examination of the position of international human rights law, on these issues. While it is an indisputable fact that one of the duties of the states is to maintain law and order during demonstrations, this duty must be coupled with the state's obligations to respect human rights; most especially the right to life of demonstrators.[71]

The right to life has been universally acknowledged and guaranteed in various international human rights instruments and has also been entrenched at the domestic levels among states. Article 3 of the Universal Declaration of Human Rights (Universal Declaration) provides that '[e]veryone has the right to life, liberty and security of his person'.[72] Similarly, article 6 of the ICCPR has a wide provision on the right to life. However, the provision of article 6(1) is instructive in this regard, as it does not only guarantee the right to life but demands its protection by law and prohibits its arbitrary deprivation. Article 6(1) provides that '[e]very human being has the inherent right to life. This right shall be protected by law. No one shall be arbitrarily deprived of his life'.[73] The African Charter on Human and Peoples' Rights (African Charter) in article 4 has a similar provision.

The right to life is not only irreplaceable when violated; it is the right that gives life to other rights and it is indeed a 'sacrosanct right'[74] According to Heyns

---

[70]Thomas Probert, ed., "Unlawful Killings in Africa: A Study Prepared for the UN Special Rapporteur on Extrajudicial, Summary or Arbitrary Execution" (2014); Anne Peters and Isabelle Ley, *Comparative Study: Freedom of Peaceful Assembly in Europe* (2014), available at http://www.venice.coe.int/files/Assemblies_Report_12March2014.pdf, accessed 27 March 2018.

[71]Resolution of the Human Rights Council on the promotion and protection of human rights in the context of peaceful protests, U.N. Doc A/HRC/22/L.10 (March 2013), 2.

[72]Universal Declaration of Human Rights, G.A. Res. 217A, U.N. Doc A/810 (Dec. 10, 1948).

[73]International Covenant on Civil and Political Rights, Mar. 23, 1976, 999 U.N.T.S. 172.

[74]Wahab Egbewole and Azubike Onuora-Oguno, "Weeping for the Innocent," *University of Benin Law Journal* 15, no. 1 (2014): 63.

[t]he right to life has two components. The first and material component is that every person has a right to be free from the arbitrary deprivation of life: it places certain limitations on the use of force. The second and more procedural component is the requirement of proper investigation and accountability where there is reason to believe that an arbitrary deprivation of life may have taken place.[75]

The above quotation drives home the point that, besides the state's obligation not to arbitrarily kill demonstrators through its agents, it must ensure their protection from non-state actors, and where death or violation occurs, the failure of state to take proactive actions against such perpetrators amounts to breach of its obligation under international human rights law.[76] The right to life stands tall among other rights under the ICCPR, as it is a non-derogable right even in times of public emergencies.[77] Similarly, under the American Convention[78] and the European Convention,[79] the right to life enjoys non-derogable status during times of public emergencies. The African Charter provides that the right to life can only be limited through due process of the law, which must be in accordance with the general limitation clause of article 27(2) of the Charter. The Africa Commission on human and peoples' rights (African Commission), recognises that '[t]he right to life is the fulcrum of all rights. It is the fountain through which other rights flow, and any violation of this right without due process amounts to arbitrary deprivation'.[80]

During times of demonstrations, protest and peaceful assemblies, there is usually a conflict of interests among bystanders, demonstrators

---

[75] Christof Heyns' Report, UN Special Rapporteur on extrajudicial, summary or arbitrary executions (1 April 2014) A/HRC/26/36, 46.

[76] Communication 323/2006 *Egyptian Initiative for Personal Rights & INTERIGHTS v Egypt*, 174.

[77] Article 4(2) of ICCPR, UN Human Rights Committee (HRC), CCPR General Comment No. 29: Article 4: Derogations during a State of Emergency, 31 August 2001, CCPR/C/21/Rev.1/Add.11, 11; Human Rights Committee, General Comment 31, Nature of the General Legal Obligation on States Parties to the Covenant, U.N. Doc. CCPR/C/21/Rev.1/Add.13 (2004), 6–8.

[78] Article 27(2).

[79] Article 15(2).

[80] *Forum of Conscience v Sierra Leone* (2000) AHRLR 293 (ACHPR 2000), 19.

and law enforcement officials; which often poses a threat to the right to life.[81] While demonstrators usually insist on their inherent right to protest or assemble peacefully, law enforcement officials on the other hand, assert their duty to maintain law and order. This confrontation usually results in the loss of lives, as more often than not, lethal force is used by the police and results in loss of innocent lives.[82] It is beyond controversy that the prime duty of every state is to protect the lives of its citizen.[83] It therefore becomes an 'apparent paradox',[84] when the state on the basis of maintaining law and order, turns itself into predator of the right to life. There are several instances where security operatives in Nigeria have used excessive force which resulted in loss of lives and/or injury are discussed further in this chapter. While sometimes, spontaneous demonstration may call for serious issues of security, the state must maintain its security with regards to the 'larger freedom'[85] of its citizens and must recognise that effective security does not start with the killing of innocent demonstrators but with the upholding of their basic rights.[86] In recent times, the UN and the AU have in addition to condemning unnecessary killings of peaceful protesters; regarded such act as a crime against humanity. It is to be noted that the 2011 case on the killings of the peaceful Libyan protestors is currently before the International Criminal Court (ICC). The perpetrators are facing charges bothering on crimes against humanity on the referral of the UN Security Council.[87]

[81] Michael O'Flaherty, "Effective Measures and Best Practices to Ensure the Promotion and Protection of Human Rights in the Context of Peaceful Protests: A Background Paper," (2013), 8.

[82] Heyns, A/HRC/26/36, 43.

[83] Ibid., 26.

[84] Abdullahi An-Na'im, "Possibilities and Constraints of the Legal Protection of Human Rights Under Constitutions of African Countries," in *Universal Rights, Local Remedies: Implementing Human Rights in the Legal Systems of Africa*, ed. Abdullahi An-Na'im (London: Interights, 1999).

[85] Kofi Annan, "'In Larger Freedom': Decision Time at the UN" (2005), 1, available at http://www.unis.unvienna.org/pdf/freedom_annan.pdf, accessed March 27, 2019.

[86] The Final Report of the Commission on Human Security (2003), 11, available at http://www.unocha.org/humansecurity/chs/finalreport/English/FinalReport.pdf, accessed March 29, 2019.

[87] UN Security Council Resolution 1970, S/RES/1970 (2011); The AU Peace and Security Council Resolution, PSC/MIN/COMM.2(CCLXXV) (2011).

Though there are no binding international instruments regulating the use of force by law enforcement officials on the international plane, there exist two 'soft laws' instruments that have received widespread acceptance across nations. They are *the Basic Principles on the Use of Force and Firearms by Law Enforcement Officials* (Basic Principles)[88] and *Code of Conduct for Law Enforcement Officials* (Code).[89] The Code has commentary that augments its provisions. However, the main principle on the use of force among these Basic Principles is contained in principle 9 which provides:

> Law enforcement officials shall not use firearms against persons except in self-defence or defence of others against the imminent threat of death or serious injury, to prevent the perpetration of a particularly serious crime involving grave threat to life, to arrest a person presenting such a danger and resisting their authority, or to prevent his or her escape, and only when less extreme means are insufficient to achieve these objectives. *In any event, intentional lethal use of firearms may only be made when strictly unavoidable in order to protect life.* (Emphasis added).

While the state has an obligation to regulate and maintain public order in time of assembly, the Basic Principles and the Code require that law enforcement officials must comply with their provisions.[90] The general rule on the use of force in the context of demonstration is that, where assembly is lawful and peaceful, then the use of force is strictly limited.[91]

Where the assembly is 'unlawful' but peaceful; the law enforcement officials are prohibited from using force, and where this is not practicable, shall only use force to the minimum extent necessary. However, lethal force (which is the force that can lead to death or life-threatening injury) cannot be used,[92] and states are expected to show a certain

---

[88] Adopted by the Eighth United Nations Congress on the Prevention of Crime and the Treatment of Offenders, Cuba, 1990. United Nations General Assembly resolution 45/111 adopted without a vote the same year welcomed the Basic Principles.

[89] Adopted by the General Assembly in its resolution 34/169 (1979); also, Principles on the Effective Prevention and Investigation of Extra-legal, Arbitrary and Summary Executions, E.S.C Res. 1989/65, 24 May 1989.

[90] Article 9 of the code.

[91] Geneva Academic, "Facilitating Peaceful Assembly," (2014).

[92] Principle 13.

degree of tolerance towards peaceful gatherings if the right to assembly will be meaningful.[93] Where an assembly is lawful but turns violent, the law enforcement officials shall avoid the use of force, and where its use is unavoidable, or where other means remain ineffective, such force must be proportionate to the legitimate objective pursued.[94]

Where an assembly is both unlawful and violent, the law enforcement officials are expected in dispersing such an assembly to only use firearm where less forceful means are not practicable, and only to the minimum extent necessary.[95] It must be noted, that a violent assembly is not an opportunity for law enforcement officials to 'shoot and kill'. This principle suggests that an incremental level of force should be applied. That is, the officials must proceed from a lesser force to higher force, and this Principle requires officials to comply with Principle 9 that protects the rights of demonstrators during such time.[96] Sporadic or isolated violent act in the midst of a peaceful assembly does not alter the nature of an assembly to a violent one. An assembly remains peaceful once the intentions of the organisers are peaceful and the organisers are not inciting the public to violence.[97] Failure to obtain the requisite notification for peaceful assembly does not equally make it a violent assembly.[98] Two apparent features under the Basic Principles and the Code for the legitimate use force are 'necessity and proportionality'.

However, the principles of 'necessity and proportionality' deserve close scrutiny. The principle of necessity presupposes that firearm or, lethal or, any force must not be used except in a situation where such force is unavoidable and to pursue a legitimate objective.[99] In the context of the right to life, a legitimate objective will only be justified, if it is used to either save a life ('protect life principle') or protect someone from a life-threatening injury.[100] Necessity in turn has three components

---

[93] *Balçik and others v Turkey*, European Court of Human Rights, Judgment, 29 February 2008, 52.

[94] Principles 4 and 5.

[95] Principles 13 and 14.

[96] Heyns, A/HRC/26/36, 42.

[97] O'Flaherty, "Effective Measures and Best Practices to Ensure the Promotion and Protection of Human Rights in the Context of Peaceful Protests," 9.

[98] Ibid., 10.

[99] Heyns A/HRC/26/36, 59.

[100] Ibid., 58

and they are: qualitative necessity, quantitative necessity and temporal necessity. Necessity in qualitative context means that the use of potential force is unavoidable to achieve the legitimate objective; while quantitative necessity demands that the amount of force used must not exceed the required force to achieve the desired objective, and temporal necessity implies that force should only be used against the person who poses the immediate threat. However, absolute necessity is required where lethal or potential lethal force is to be used.[101]

On the other hand, proportionality prescribes the amount of force to be used where the use of force is unavoidable. While the principle of necessity allows a law enforcement official to use force when unavoidably necessary, the principle of proportionality dictates the extent of force which an official can apply. These require that only a proportionate force must be applied.[102]

Conclusively, under international human rights law, the use of force in the context of demonstration should be an exception rather than the norm. Unavoidable use of force should be necessary and proportionate, while lethal force should only be used to protect life or prevent loss of life and limb.

4.3   Taming the Law: Right to Life and Its Derogations Under the Nigerian Law

The right to life is guaranteed under section 33 of the CFRN which provides that:

1. Every person has a right life, and no one shall be deprived intentionally of his life, save in execution of the sentence of a court in respect of a criminal offence of which he has been found guilty in Nigeria.
2. A person shall not be regarded as having being deprived of his life in contravention of this section, if he dies as a result of the use, to such extent and in such circumstances as are permitted by law, of such force as is reasonably necessary-

---

[101] Ibid., 60.
[102] Ibid., 66.

(a) for the defence of any person from unlawful violence or for the defence of property;
(b) in order to effect lawful arrest or to prevent the escape of a person lawfully detained; or
(c) for the purpose of suppressing a riot, insurrection or mutiny.

These above provisions reveal four instances where the right to life can be derogated from. These instances are: death sentence, defence of property or person, to effect a lawful arrest and to suppress a riot, insurrection or mutiny. Although, demonstration is not mentioned, officials of the NFP have always reacted to demonstrations as a riot. Since death sentence and lawful arrest are not within the scope of this chapter, I shall concentrate on other derogations to the right life. An apparent defect that exists from the provisions, is regrettably the omission of the principle of proportionality in the amount of force to be used, and secondly the absence of the 'protect life principle', as the section makes 'defence of property' a ground for the derogation of the right to life. The ripple effects of these fundamental omissions (is discussed further in this chapter). The use of the phrase 'reasonably necessary' force is vague and imprecise enough to determine the reasonability of the necessity of the use of force.[103] To say the least, it is problematic and subject to a catalogue of meanings. Similarly, 'unlawful violence' cannot meet the threshold of 'protect life' principle because; all forms of criminal assault may constitute unlawful violence.

The implication of the above omissions from CFRN gives the impression that a police officer has the right to shoot and kill either to suppress riots or defend property, even where no life is in danger. This has a grave implication for the right to life of demonstrators in Nigeria, as the attitude of the officers of the NPF to demonstrators is hostile because demonstrators are considered to be opposition and are dealt with accordingly.[104] This they do by firing life ammunition, robber bullets or tear gas to disperse demonstrators, in the name of maintaining law and order, even where such demonstrations pose no threat and are peaceful. The

---

[103] Ibid., 97.

[104] Uchechukwu Ngwaba, "Right to Protest and the Politics of Opposition," in *Freedom of Protest*, ed. Epiphany Azinge and Laura Ani (Abuja: NIALS Press, 2013), 147.

attitude of the NPF is not only consistently violent but 'anti-people'.[105] This faulty notion of taking life for the protection of property has unfortunately received judicial approval.[106] Due to the irreplaceability of the right to life once violated, it defies good reasoning to allow it to be taken arbitrarily for the purpose of protecting or preserving a property, irrespective of the worth of such a property.[107] This has a practical impact on the right to life of demonstrators in the face of modern-day shrinking and privatisation of public space.[108]

Besides the above section of CFRN that gives the police power to use force in the context of demonstrations, there are some legislations that have such provisions, including the Nigerian Police Act (NPA); the Police Code of Conduct (PCC); the Force Order 237 (Order 237); Nigerian Criminal Code (NCC); and the POA. The NPF is basically saddled with the responsibility of maintaining law and order in Nigeria, as such they have extensive powers on the use of force. Section 4 of the NPA provides that:

> The police shall be employed for the prevention and detection of crime, the apprehension of offenders the preservation of law and order; the protection of life and property and the due enforcement of all laws and regulations with which they are directly charged, and shall perform such military duties within or without Nigeria as may be required by them by, or under the authority of this or any other Act.[109]

In the course of trying to do all its core duties contained in the above provision, the officers of the NFP invoke the use of force in most instances. Force Order 237 regulates the use of firearms by the police. Section 3 allows a police officer to use a firearm to save his life or that of another, but can also use a firearm against rioters in order to prevent

---

[105] Isaac Sampson, "The Right to Demonstrate in a Democracy: An Evaluation of Public Order Policing in Nigeria," *African Human Rights Law Journal* 10, no. 2 (2010): 434.

[106] *R v Ebi* (1936) 3 West African Court of Appeal 36; *Joseph Adebayo v The Republic* (1967) Nigeria Monthly Law Report 391 (NgSC).

[107] Heyns A/HRC/26/36, 61.

[108] Geneva Academic, "Facilitating Peaceful Assembly" (2014), 14.

[109] Also section 10(2).

'them from committing serious offences against lives and property'.[110] Section 4, rather than providing for an outright prohibition of the use of firearm against an 'unarmed' person, merely states that it 'would be most difficult to justify' its use, thereby giving an opportunity for the justification of the use of firearms against an unarmed person, and also allows such an officer to shoot if attacked with a stick or machete, but the officer has to prove that he could not disable the assailant. Section 6 empowers a police officer to shoot at the knees of rioters, and also authorises the police to single out and kill the leader of the rioters. Section 6 is rather unfortunate, as it derogates from the 'protect life' principle by authorising the killing of a rioter who poses no threat to the life of anyone. Similarly, the PCC prohibits police officers from using 'unnecessary force or violence', but only force which is 'reasonable' in discharging their duties.[111] Both the Order 237 & PCC leave the amount of force to be used and what amounts to its reasonableness to the discretion of the officer. This is not only dangerous to the life of demonstrators but arrogates excessive power to members of the NPF, who have a long history of using excessive force against harmless Nigerians and demonstrators.[112]

The Nigerian Criminal Code (NCC) which is applicable to only Southern parts of Nigeria,[113] and has been in force since 1904, contains some provisions on the use of force.[114] Several of its provisions are not only obsolete but are not in tandem with the lived realities of modern-day Nigeria. Chapter 10 of the NCC deals with '*Unlawful Assemblies: Breaches of Peace*'. Section 69 of the NCC regards assembly to be unlawful, if three or more persons gather, and they conduct themselves in a way that 'will tumultuously disturb the peace, or will by such assembly needlessly and without any reasonable occasion provoke other persons tumultuously to disturb the peace'. It is immaterial if the assembly was lawful from the outset; it states that; such an unlawful assembly will become a 'riot' when it starts acting 'tumultuously'.

---

[110] Section 3A, B, and C.

[111] Rule 2 of the Nigeria Police Code of Conduct.

[112] Matthias Ojo, "The Nigeria Police and the Search for Integrity in the Midst of Diverse Challenges: An Effective Police Management Approach," *Open Journal of Industrial and Business Management* 1, no. 1 (2013), 11.

[113] While the Penal Code is in operation in the Northern parts of Nigeria.

[114] Criminal Code Act, CAP C38 Laws of the Federation of Nigeria, Volume 4, 2004.

What the NCC terms as 'riot', in the widest stretch of imagination can never be one, as a riot is defined as 'a wide violent disturbance by a crowd of people'.[115] This makes riots a violent assembly rather than one with a loud noise as the NCC erroneously put it. Participation in an 'unlawful' assembly or 'riot' is punished with one and three years of imprisonment respectively.[116] The word 'tumultuously' means 'making loud confused noise or excited or confused'.[117] Since most demonstrations come with the usual noise and excitement, the NCC inadvertently and unfortunately criminalises public demonstrations, notwithstanding whether they are peaceful but with loud noise, thereby not only stifling the right but rendering it non-existent. This runs contrary to international human rights standards on the regulation of peaceful demonstrations.[118]

The most worrisome and problematic provisions of the NCC, has to do with issues of proclamation and dispersal of demonstrators. Section 72 of NCC allows either a Magistrate or, a police officer above the rank of an Assistant Superintendent, or any commissioned officer of the Nigerian Navy, Army or Air forces who in 'his or her view' perceives that a 'riot' is being committed or about to be committed by rioters or persons assembled, to issue a proclamation in the name of the Federal Republic of Nigeria, asking the rioters or persons so assembled, to disperse peaceably. Section 73 empowers the said officer to 'do all things necessary for dispersing the persons so continue to assemble', after a reasonable time following the proclamation. It further states that in cases of 'any resistance'; such an official may 'use all such force as is reasonably necessary to overcome such resistance, and shall not be liable in any criminal or civil proceeding for having, by the use of such force, caused harm or death to any person'.

The vivid implication of section 73 of the NCC is that, it does not only give the officials a very wide and unchecked discretion but goes ahead to authorise such an official to 'shoot-to-kill' at the instance

---

[115] *Oxford Student's Dictionary*, 3rd ed. (London: Oxford University Press, 2012), 895.

[116] Section 70 and 71 of the Criminal Code.

[117] *Oxford Student's Dictionary*, 1135.

[118] Report of the UN Special Rapporteur on the rights to freedom of peaceful assembly and of association, MainaKiai (24 April 2013), 47.

of 'any resistance'.[119] This provision is overbroad, pays no attention to the irreversibility in the violation of the right to life of demonstrators, and runs contrary to the principles on the use of force under international human rights law.[120] Maintenance of public order ought not to be a valid ground for the violation of the right to life.[121] Excluding such officers who arbitrarily kill demonstrators on the account of mere resistance, from criminal or civil liability, is not only against Nigeria's obligation to ensure proper accountability of unlawful killings resulting from the use of excessive force but also entrenches the culture of impunity among members of the NPF.[122] This is because, where there is no proper accountability of arbitrary killings among state officials, then, impunity becomes the order of the day.[123] Members of the NPF, are hitherto synonymous with impunity.[124]

4.4   Excessive Use of Force by the Nigerian Police

The lack of proper legal frameworks and accountability mechanisms on the excessive use of force, has not ceased to pose grave threats to the right to life of demonstrators in Nigeria. The use of excessive force by members of the NPF has become a 'widespread phenomenon'.[125] For instance on 30 June 2003, there were demonstrations (*2003 increase in fuel price demonstration case*) across the country over the 50% increase in the fuel prices by the government. The police force's response to the protests was brutal; as more than twenty (20) peaceful demonstrators lost their lives through the use of live bullet by the police.[126] Similarly,

---

[119] Report of Philip Alston, UN Special Rapporteur on extrajudicial, summary or arbitrary executions (28 May 2010), 33.

[120] Principles 9, 10, 2, 3, 4 and 5 (Basic Principles) and Articles 2 and 3 (the code).

[121] Geneva Academic, "Facilitating Peaceful Assembly," 26.

[122] Principles 22, 23 and 24 (Basic Principles).

[123] Probert, "Unlawful Killings in Africa: A Study Prepared for the UN Special Rapporteur on Extrajudicial, Summary or Arbitrary Execution," 17

[124] Egbewole and Onuora-Oguno, "National Security, Impunity and Justice in Nigeria," 69.

[125] Amnesty International report, *Killing at Will: Extrajudicial Executions and Unlawful Killings by the Nigeria Police Force*, AFR44/038/2009, 8.

[126] Human Rights Watch Report, *Nigeria: Renewed Crackdown on Freedom of Expression* (December 2003), vol. 15, no. 19(A), 8.

on 12 October 2009 (*demolition demonstration case*), during a peaceful demonstration against a planned demolition of their homes in Bundu community, Port Harcourt, by the River State's government, at least six (6) demonstrators were killed. Till date, no investigation has been carried out nor has anyone been held responsible for the arbitrary killings.[127]

Also, on 1 January 2012, after the President's broadcast on the introduction of the new fuel pump price (*subsidy removal protest*), several people across the country went out in the streets to peacefully protest against it. The members of the police used excessive force in attempting to disperse the crowds and several innocent demonstrators' lives were lost.[128] Although in Lagos state some officers who were involved in the shooting are currently undergoing criminal trial, the lives of those who have been killed cannot be replaced.[129] If there had been proper accountability of the incidences of 2003 and 2009, the 2012 incidence could have been averted.[130]

In the same vein, the police force's total disregard for the right to life of demonstrators was played out again on 12 January 2014 (*Rivers rally case*). This was a peaceful rally in Rivers state which had in attendance the Governor of the state. During the course of the dispersal by the police, a rubber bullet was fired at a serving Senator, who almost lost his life, but for the fact that he was urgently flown abroad for treatment.[131] No investigation has been carried out on the excessive use of force by the police regarding this incidence.

5   CONCLUSION

This chapter discusses the extent to which the current Nigerian legal regimes comply with international human right standards on the protection of right to life of demonstrators. This chapter further highlights

---

[127] Amnesty International report, *Port Harcourt Demolitions: Excessive Use of Force Against Demonstrators* (2011), 5.

[128] Benu Nwanne, "Government Propaganda and the Fuel Subsidy Protests in Nigeria: Matters Arising," *European Journal of Business and Social Sciences* 2, no. 10 (2014): 118.

[129] "Lagos Begins Prosecution of Subsidy Protest Killer Cop," *Premium Times*, 15 May 2013.

[130] Olusola Osunyikanmi and Foluke Adebukola, "A Comparative Analysis of Police Accountability in Nigeria and United States," *International Journal of Humanities and Social Science* 2, no. 11 (2012): 56.

[131] Jimitota Onoyume and Egufe Yafugborhi, "Rivers Crisis: Senator Abe Shot, Flown to London," *The Vanguard*, January 13, 2014.

that t despite Nigeria's ratification of various human rights instruments, there exist a lag between its laws and institutions, and that of international norms as far as protection of the right to life of demonstrators is concerned. The aim of this chapter is to proffer viable and practical recommendations that will have an impact on the current unpleasant trends. It is contended that the main impediment to the protection of the right to life of demonstrators in Nigeria is the constitutional permissible derogations on the right to life. The various grounds for derogations of the right to life as provided in section 33(2), which includes defence of property, unlawful violence and quelling of insurrection without the corresponding 'protect life' principle. This chapter asserts that Nigeria has a long way to go in this regard. Some of the laws analysed in this chapter are old, ineffective and unnecessary in a democratic society like Nigeria. Based on these findings and my insight on the workings of the Nigerian society, some recommendations shall be made. These recommendations are inspired by best practices across the world and from international legal order on the protection of the right to life of demonstrators.

This chapter recommends that the right to life provision in the constitution should be reviewed by removing the various derogations that are 'anti-protect-life principle'. Additionally, the right to life provision in the Nigerian Constitution should be 'unqualified' similar to the wordings of the 1996 South African Constitution. The Nigerian government should create State Police for each State of the Federation that will only work in collaboration with the Federal Police Force. Where necessary, the new police for each State should be changed from 'Police Force' to 'Police Service' in order to reflect that the police are employed to serve and not kill or oppress the people. These reforms will contribute to a change in perception of state-centred law enforcement approach (reactive) to people and demonstrators-friendly approach by the police (proactive).

References

Books

Ali, A. "Derogation from Constitutional Rights and Its Implication Under the African Charter on Human and Peoples' Rights." *Law Democracy & Development* 17 (2013): 78–110.

An-Na'im, A. "Possibilities and Constraints of the Legal Protection of Human Rights Under Constitutions of African Countries." In *Universal Rights,*

Local Remedies: Implementing Human Rights in the Legal Systems of Africa. London: Interights, 1999.

Boyle, K., and S. Shah. "Thought, Expression, Association, and Assembly." In *International Human Rights Law,* edited by Daniel Moeckli, Sangeeta Shah, and Sandesh Sivakumaran, 2nd ed., 234–235. London: Oxford University Press, 2014.

Crawshaw, R., and L. Holmstrom. *Essential Cases on Human Rights for the Police: Review and Summaries of International Cases.* Leiden: Martinus Nijhoff, 2006.

Durojaye, E. "Litigating the Right to Health in Nigeria: Challenges and Prospect." In *International Law and Domestic Human Rights Litigation in Africa,* edited by M. Killander. Pretoria: Pretoria University Press, 2010.

Eruaga, O. "The Right to Protest: A Review of the Law and Empirics in Nigeria." In *Freedom of Protest,* edited by E. Azinge and L. Ani. Abuja: NIALS Publications, 2013.

Harris, D.J. *Cases and Materials on International Law,* 6th ed. London: Sweet and Maxwell, 2004.

Heyns, C.H. "A 'Struggle Approach' to Human Rights." In *Law and Pluralism,* edited by A. Soeteman. Dordrecht, the Netherlands: Springer, 2001.

Ibidapo-Obe, A. *In the Public Interest: A Study of the Legal Interventions of Femi Falana.* Lagos: Concept Publications, 2008.

Kalin, W., and J. Kunzli. *The Law of International Human Rights Protection.* London: Oxford University Press, 2009.

Ngwaba, U. "Right to Protest and the Politics of Opposition." In *Freedom of Protest,* edited by E. Azinge and L. Ani. Abuja: NIALS Publications, 2013.

Olarenwaju, A. "Right to Protest and Right to Strike: An Overview." In *Freedom of Protest,* edited by E. Azinge and L. Ani. Abuja: NIALS Publications, 2013.

Ouguergouz, F. *The African Charter on Human and Peoples' Right: A Comprehensive Agenda for Human Dignity and Sustainable Development.* The Hague; London and New York: Martinus Nijhoff, 2003.

Peters, A., and I. Ley. *Comparative Study: Freedom of Peaceful Assembly in Europe.* London: Hart Publishing, 2016.

Viljoen, F. *International Human Rights Law in Africa,* 2nd ed. London: Oxford University Press, 2012.

Viljoen, F. "The African Charter on the Rights and Welfare of the Child." In *Introduction to Child Law in South Africa,* edited by C.J. Davel. Cape Town: JUTA, 2000.

Woolman, S. "Assembly, Demonstration and Petition." In *The Bill of Rights Handbook,* edited by I. Currie and J. De Waal, 6th ed. Cape Town: JUATA, 2013.

Journal Articles

Arisukwu, O. "Policing Trends in Nigeria Since Independence (1960–2012)." *The Police Journal* 55 (2012): 151.

Cole, W. "Mind the Gap: State Capacity and the Implementation of Human Rights Treaties." *International Organization* 69, no. 2 (2015): 405–441.

Egbewole, W., and A. Onuora-Oguno, "National Security, Impunity and Justice in Nigeria: Weeping for the Innocent." *University of Benin Law Journal* 15, no. 1 (2014): 63.

Heyns, C.H. "The African Regional Human Rights System: In Need of Reform?" *African Human Rights Law Journal* 1, no. 2 (2001): 155–174.

Mutual, M. "Human Rights in Africa: The Limited Promise of Liberalism." *African Studies Review* 51, no. 1 (2008): 21.

Nwanne, B. "Government Propaganda and the Fuel Subsidy Protests in Nigeria: Matters Arising." *European Journal of Business and Social Sciences* 2, no. 10 (2014): 117–127.

Ojo, M. "The Nigeria Police and the Search for Integrity in the Midst of Diverse Challenges: An Effective Police Management Approach." *Open Journal of Industrial and Business Management* 1, no. 1 (2013): 87–100.

Osunyikanmi, O., and A. Foluke. "A Comparative Analysis of Police Accountability in Nigeria and United States." *International Journal of Humanities and Social Science* 2, no. 11 (2012): 250–257.

Sampson, I. "The Right to Demonstrate in a Democracy: An Evaluation of Public Order Policing in Nigeria." *African Human Rights Law Journal* 10, no. 2 (2010): 432–456.

Sermet, L. "The Absence of a Derogation Clause from the African Charter on Human and Peoples' Rights: A Critical Discussion." *African Human Rights Law Journal* 7, no. 1 (2007): 142–161.

Online Articles/Materials

Alemika, E. "History, Context and Crises of the Police in Nigeria." Presentation at the Biennial Retreat of the Police Service Commission on the theme, Repositioning the Nigeria Police to Meet the Challenges of the Policing a Democratic Society in the twenty-First Century and Beyond, held at the Le Meridian Hotel, Uyo, Akwa Ibom State, Nigeria (November 1–4, 2010). Available at https://psc.gov.ng/wp-content/uploads/2017/11/HISTORY-AND-CONTEXT.pdf. Accessed June 16, 2019.

Chinweze, C. "The Constitutionality of the Public Order Act in a Democracy: 'A Square Peg in a Round Hole'." Available at http://www.gamji.com/article5000/NEWS5960.htm. Accessed August 24, 2018.

Falana, F. "Nigerians' Right to Protest Is Constitutionally Guaranteed." Available at http://saharareporters.com/2012/01/08/nigerians%E2%80%99-right-protest-constitutionally-guaranteed. Accessed June 16, 2018.

Geneva Academy Briefing No. 5. "Facilitating Peaceful Protests" (January 2014). Available at https://www.geneva-academy.ch/joomlatools-files/docman-files/Facilitating%20Peaceful%20Protests%20.pdf. Accessed June 16, 2019.

Kiai, M. "Making It Safer to Express Dissenting Views Through Peaceful Assembly and Association." Available at http://www.ohchr.org/EN/NewsEvents/Pages/Makingitsafertoexpressdissentingpeacefulassemblyassociation.aspx. Accessed September 4, 2018.

O'Flaherty, M. "Effective Measures and Best Practices to Ensure the Promotion and Protection of Human Rights in the Context of Peaceful Protests: A Background Paper" (2013) 3. Available at www.ohchr.org/Documents/Issues/FAssociation/Seminar2013/BackgroundPaperSeminar.doc. Accessed October 1, 2018.

Probert, T., ed. "Unlawful Killings in Africa: A Study Prepared for the UN Special Rapporteur on Extrajudicial, Summary or Arbitrary Executions" (2014). Available at http://www.cghr.polis.cam.ac.uk/research-themes/right_to_life/unlawful_killings_in_africa/unlawful_killings_report/Unlawful_Killings_Africa.pdf. Accessed October 10, 2018.

"Seven Dead as Yemeni Police Open Fire on Anti-government Protesters in Sanaa." Available at http://english.al-akhbar.com/node/21443. Accessed October 28, 2018.

Støre, J. "Paper Delivered at the Seminar on Human Rights Defenders and Peaceful Protest on 6 June 2012." Available at http://www.regjeringen.no/en/archive/Stoltenbergs-2nd-Government/Ministry-of-Foreign-Affairs/taler-og-artikler/2012/hr_defenders.html?id=684851. Accessed September 4, 2018.

"The Global Suppression of Protest" by the International Network of Civil Liberties Organizations (10 October 2013). Available at https://www.aclu.org/blog/free-speech/global-suppression-protest. Accessed September 4, 2018.

News Articles

Ezeamalu, Ben. "Lagos Begins Prosecution of Subsidy Protest Killer Cop." *Premium Times*, May 15, 2013. https://www.premiumtimesng.com/news/134380-lagos-begins-prosecution-of-subsidy-protest-killer-cop.html. Accessed June 16, 2019.

Onoyume, Jimitota, and Egufe Yafugborhi. "Rivers Crisis: Senator Abe Shot, Flown to London." *The Vanguard*, January 13, 2014. https://www.vanguard-ngr.com/2014/01/rivers-crisis-senator-abe-shot-flown-london/. Accessed June 16, 2019.

CHAPTER 10

The Role of the Judiciary in Safeguarding the Right to Assembly and Public Protest in Ghana

Michael Gyan Nyarko

1 Introduction

The right to freedom of assembly is one of the foundations of a functioning democracy.[1] It was described by John Rawls as one of the basic liberties.[2] The right to freedom of assembly, together with the right to association and freedom of expression are essential for the exercise of many other rights.[3] Its importance therefore cannot be overemphasized. It was at the heart of some of the most influential social movements in

---

[1] *Inspector-General of Police v All Nigeria Peoples Party and Others* (2007) AHRLR 179 (NgCA 2007), para. 12.

[2] John Rawls, *A Theory of Justice* (Cambridge: Harvard University Press, 1971), 53.

[3] Human Rights Council, Report of the Special Rapporteur on the Rights to Freedom of Peaceful Assembly and of Association, Maina Kiai, May 21, 2012, UN Doc. A/HRC/20/27 (hereafter Maina Kiai, 2012), para. 12.

M. G. Nyarko (✉)
Centre for Human Rights, University of Pretoria, Pretoria, South Africa

© The Author(s) 2020
M. Addaney et al. (eds.), *Governance, Human Rights, and Political Transformation in Africa*,
https://doi.org/10.1007/978-3-030-27049-0_10

247

the last four centuries[4]; it was instrumental to the claim for women's suffrage in the eighteenth and nineteenth centuries and the civil rights movement in the United States[5]; the independence struggle in many African countries; the anti-apartheid liberation struggle in South Africa[6] and the 'Arab spring'.[7] Participation in peaceful assemblies ensures that people have the opportunity to express their opinion in community with others.[8] Consequently the right to peaceful assembly 'facilitates dialogue within civil society and among civil society, political leaders and government'.[9] It provides a forum for public debate and the open expression of protest.[10] The right to freedom of assembly can serve many purposes including providing a medium for collective social or political engagement, celebration of culture or tradition and expression of disagreement or protest. It is the exercise of the right to freedom of assembly including through public protests that is the focus of this chapter. Consequently, the discussion on the right to freedom of assembly in this chapter will mainly focus on public protests and or demonstrations even though ocassional reference will be made to the right to freedom of assembly broadly. On many occasions, the right to assembly and protest are used interchangeably.

The right to freedom of assembly has a transformational power and has been used as a tool to stand against tyranny and influence decision-making. In recent years the transformational power of the right to assembly, including demonstration and public protest has been witnessed

---

[4] John D. Inazu, "The Forgotten Freedom of Assembly," *Tulane Law Review* 84 (2010): 565 at 566.

[5] Inazu (as above).

[6] Stuart Woolman, "Assembly, Demonstration and Petition," in *The Bill of Rights Handbook*, ed. Ian Currie and Johan De Waal (Cape Town: Juta, 2013), 377.

[7] Notably, the Arab Spring pro-democracy protests led to the toppling of authoritarian governments in Tunisia, Egypt and Libya; see Lisa Anderson, "Demystifying the Arab Spring: Parsing the Differences Between Tunisia, Egypt and Libya," *Foreign Affairs*, May/June (2011), accessed September 4, 2018, https://www.foreignaffairs.com/articles/libya/2011-04-03/demystifying-arab-spring?fa_anthology=1116900.

[8] Organisation for Security and Co-operation in Europe (OSCE) Office for Democratic Institutions and Human Rights (ODIHR), *Guidelines on the Freedom of Peaceful Assembly* (2010), 24.

[9] OSCE Guidelines (as above).

[10] *Éva Molnár v Hungary*, Application no. 10346/05, European Court of Human Rights (2008), para. 42.

across the world: Across the Middle East, North Africa, Ukraine, Hong Kong and the United States. Sub-Saharan Africa has also not escaped the trend, as people have recently taken to the streets to demand change in Burkina Faso, Democratic Republic of Congo, Cameroun, Sudan and Ethiopia, to mention a few. In Tunisia, Egypt, Libya, Ethiopia, Sudan and Burkina Faso change has come. However, in many other countries across the world; from Azerbaijan to Syria, China to Venezuela, Nigeria to Uganda, there exist severe constraints on the freedom of assembly, often preventing citizens from coming together to collectively express, promote, pursue and defend their interests. In many instances, protesters are arrested or subjected to brutal and sometimes lethal force by law enforcement agencies. Problems relating to restraints on the right to assembly and protest are not limited to authoritarian regimes alone. Many well-established democracies such as Canada, USA and Denmark[11] and recently Spain,[12] amongst others have also been criticized by human rights groups for their response to street protests.

In sub-Saharan Africa, almost all countries within the region formally recognize the right to freedom of assembly in their constitutions.[13] These constitutional guarantees have however, often not translated into the enjoyment of the freedom of assembly. There appear to be at least two reasons for this. First, the laws that are supposed to give effect to this constitutional right are inadequate. Second, oppressive conduct of ruling governments against opposition parties through the use of the police and repressive public order laws.[14] The Ghanaian case of *New Patriotic Party (NPP) v Inspector-General of Police (NPP Case)*[15] provides a good illustration of how constitutional guarantee of the right to freedom of assembly can be frustrated by public order laws. This chapter analyzes the decision of the Supreme Court of Ghana in the *NPP Case* with the

[11]International Centre for Non-profit Law (ICNL), "Freedom of Assembly," *Global Trends in NGO Law* 2 (2011): 1.

[12]Sam Jones and Stephen Burgen, "Catalonia Responds to Police Violence: 'People Are Angry, Very Angry,'" *The Guardian*, October 3, 2017, accessed March 4, 2018, https://www.theguardian.com/world/2017/oct/03/catalonia-tensions-rise-as-strikes-held-over-police-violence-during-referendum.

[13]Article 19, "Freedom of Association and Assembly" (2001), 3, accessed March 3, 2018, https://www.article19.org/data/files/pdfs/publications/sub-saharan-africa-freedom-of-association-and-assembly.pdf.

[14]Article 19 (as above).

[15](2001) AHRLR 138 (GhSC 1993); [1993–1994] 2 GLR 459; [2000] 2 HRLRA 1.

aim of examining its consistency with international human rights law and principles on the right to freedom of assembly and the contribution the decision has made toward the enjoyment of the freedom of assembly in Africa. Even though the case was decided more than two decades ago, it provided a backbone for critical reform regarding the right to freedom of assembly and particularly public protests in Ghana, and events following it provide a good template of what role the judiciary can play in protecting public protests in Africa. The chapter also highlights how lower courts were utilized by the police to stifle the inroads made by the *NPP Case*, culminating in a recent decision of the High Court which further bolsters the protection of the right to protest in Ghana.

The rest of the chapter is organized as follows; before delving into the analysis of the case, Sect. 2 provides an overview of the normative framework of the right to assembly under international human rights law taking into consideration normative developments at the UN level and within the various regional human rights systems. Section 3 briefly highlights the permissible limitations of the right. Section 4 then provides a summary of the decision of the court in the *NPP Case*, providing a basis for and an evaluation of the *NPP Case* vis-à-vis the international legal framework in Sect. 5. Section 6 proceeds to provide a brief assessment of the contribution of the *NPP Case* to the protection of the right to freedom of assembly in Africa. Section 7 discusses how the police used the lower courts to circumvent the gains made through the *NPP case* and subsequent law reform. Section 8 provides concluding remarks.

2   Normative Framework for the Right to Peaceful Assembly

Many international human rights instruments, both general and group-based, as well as several regional human rights instruments, guarantee the right to freedom of assembly. Like all other human rights, the right to freedom of assembly can be traced to the Universal Declaration of Human Rights (UDHR) which is often described as the cornerstone of modern international human rights law.[16] A chronological evaluation of the right to freedom of assembly under international human rights

---

[16]William A. Schabas, *The Universal Declaration of Human Rights: The Travaux Préparatoires, volume 1, October 1946 to November 1947* (New York: Cambridge University Press, 2013), xxxvii.

law must therefore commence with the UDHR. Whilst Declarations are generally nonbinding documents, the UDHR which together with the International Covenant on Civil and Political Rights (ICCPR) and the International Covenant on Economic Social and Cultural Rights (ICESCR) are often referred to as the 'International Bill of Rights'[17] is a strong expression of international human rights law principles. The UDHR has been proclaimed as 'a common understanding of the peoples of the world concerning the inalienable and inviolable rights of all members of the human family and constitutes an obligation for the members of the international community'.[18] Consequently, some scholars have argued that the UDHR has evolved into customary international law through periodic reaffirmation by the United Nations General Assembly (UNGA) and other international institutions.[19] Whether or not the UDHR has indeed evolved into customary international law, it has without doubt incontestable 'political standing and symbolic importance'[20] as an authoritative enumeration of universally recognized human rights.[21] The contents of UDHR have subsequently being codified in the ICCPR and ICESCR as well as many other international and regional human rights instruments.

That said, article 20(1) of the UDHR provides that '[e]veryone has the right to freedom of peaceful assembly and association'. This is also mirrored in article 21 of the ICCPR which provides that

---

[17] Henry J. Steiner, Philip Alston, and Ryan Goodman, *International Human Rights in Context: Law, Politics, Morals—Texts and Materials* (Oxford: Oxford University Press, 1996), 142; John P. Humphrey, "International Bill of Rights: Scope and Implementation," *William and Mary Law Review* 17, no. 3 (1976): 527 at 528–540.

[18] Proclamation of Teheran, Final Act of the International Conference on Human Rights, UN Doc. A/CONF. 32/41 at 3 (1968), para. 2.

[19] Hurst Hannum, "The Status of the Universal Declaration of Human Rights in National and International Law," *Georgia Journal of International and Comparative Law* 25 (1995): 287.

[20] Klaus Decker, Siobhán McInerney-Lankford, and Caroline Sage, "Human Rights and Equitable Development: 'Ideals', Issues and Implications," Background Paper for the World Development Report (2006), 10, accessed September 4, 2018, http://siteresources.worldbank.org/INTWDRS/Resources/477365-1327693659766/8397901-1327773323392/Human Rights_and_Equitable_Development Ideals Issues_and_Implications.pdf.

[21] Louis Henkin, "The International Bill of Rights: The Universal Declaration and the Covenants," in *International Enforcement of Human Rights*, ed. Rudolf Bernhardt and John A. Jolowizc (Berlin: Springer, 1987), 1 (1987), 1–6.

[t]he right to peaceful assembly shall be recognized. No restrictions may be placed on the exercise of this right other than those imposed in conformity with the law and which are necessary in a democratic society in the interest of national security or public safety, public order, the protection of public health or morals or the protection of the rights and freedoms of others.

The right to freedom of assembly is also guaranteed by the International Convention on the Elimination of All Forms of Racial Discrimination,[22] Convention on the Right of the Child,[23] European Convention for the Protection of Human Rights and Fundamental Freedoms,[24] African Charter on Human and Peoples' Rights,[25] African Charter on the Rights and Welfare of the Child,[26] Arab Charter on Human Rights,[27] American Convention on Human Rights[28] and Declaration on Human Rights Defenders.[29]

The right to freedom of assembly has been further elaborated upon by international and regional human rights bodies. It must be emphasized that only 'peaceful assembly' is protected and not all assemblies.[30] Peaceful assembly would, thus exclude assemblies that involve the use of force, the threatened use of force or incitement of people to use force.[31] An individual's right to peaceful assembly is however not affected by the acts of violence of others.[32] Similarly, the right to peaceful assembly is not undermined by the possibility that other members of the society may oppose the assembly or the message it sends,[33] or sporadic violence

---

[22] Article 5(d)(ix).

[23] Article 15.

[24] Article 11.

[25] Ibid.

[26] Article 8.

[27] Article 28.

[28] Article 15.

[29] Articles 5 and 12.

[30] OSCE Guidelines (n. 8 above), 16.

[31] *Osmani and Others v FYR of Macedonia*, Application no. 50841/99, European Court of Human Rights (2001).

[32] *Ezelin v. France*, Application no. 11800/85, European Court of Human Rights (1991); (1992) 14 EHRR 362.

[33] *Christians Against Racism and Fascism v United Kingdom*, Application no. 8440/78, European Commission of Human Rights (1980).

committed by others.[34] States therefore have an obligation to protect those exercising their right to peaceful assembly from attack or aggression by others.[35] The Human Rights Council has repeatedly stressed that 'peaceful protests should not be viewed as a threat, and therefore encourage[s] all States to engage in an open, inclusive and meaningful dialogue when dealing with peaceful protests and their causes'.[36]

In a bid to ensure the maximum enjoyment of the right to freedom of assembly, many international human rights mechanisms including the Organisation for Security and Co-operation in Europe (OSCE) Office for Democratic Institutions and Human Rights (ODIHR) Panel of Experts on Freedom of Peaceful Assembly and Council of Europe's European Commission for Democracy through Law (the Venice Commission),[37] the UN Special Rapporteur on right to freedom of assembly and association, the UN Special Rapporteur on arbitrary, summary and extrajudicial killings and the African Commission on Human and Peoples' Rights have provided some instructive guides which are regarded as international best practice. A brief summary of some of these principles is provided below.

2.1   Presumption in Favor of Peaceful Assembly

Given the importance of the right to peaceful assembly as a fundamental human right, the right should in so far as possible not be subject to regulation.[38] As freedom of assembly is a right and not a privilege, persons intending to exercise the right to assembly do not need

---

[34] *Ziliberberg v Moldova*, Application no. 61821/00, European Court of Human Rights (2004); Maina Kiai, 2012 (n. 3 above), para. 25; African Commission on Human and Peoples' Rights, "Guidelines on Freedom of Association and Assembly in Africa" (2017), para. 70(b).

[35] *Ouranio Toxo and Others v Greece*, Application no. 74989/01, European Court of Human Rights (2005), para. 43.

[36] Human Rights Council resolutions 19/35 (preambular, para. 11) and 22/10 (preambular, para. 16).

[37] These organizations are the authors of the OSCE Guidelines (n. 8 above).

[38] Report of the United Nations High Commissioner for Human Rights, "Effective Measures and Best Practices to Ensure the Promotion and Protection of Human Rights in the Context of Peaceful Protest," UN Doc. A/HRC/22/28, January 21, 2013, para. 21.

authorization of the state in the form of obtaining permission to do so,[39] as permission requirements undermine the enjoyment of the right. This should be clearly spelt out in law to ensure the optimum enjoyment of the right.[40] Notification of the police or relevant authority is not required under international human rights law and its requirement should therefore be sparingly used. Prior notification should therefore be only required in large assemblies where a certain degree of disruption is anticipated, to enable the state to make the necessary arrangements to facilitate the enjoyment of the right to freedom of assembly and must under no circumstance amount to permission.[41] Notification procedures should not be cumbersome such as requiring notifications too far in advance. Notification periods should be as short as possible, as is reasonably necessary to enable exchange of views between the organizers and authorities and should by no means involve the payment of a fee.[42] Notification procedures should be flexible enough when it comes to issues such as late filing of notification or incomplete documentation, with the ultimate aim of facilitating the enjoyment of the right rather than stifling it.[43] On the other hand, a failure of authorities to respond to a notification is deemed as acknowledgement that the assembly may go ahead as planned without any modifications.[44] Where notifications are required, spontaneous assemblies where organizers cannot reasonably comply with the notice requirement or where no organizer can be identified should be exempted from notification requirements.[45]

---

[39] Report of the UN High Commissioner for Human Rights (as above), para. 11; African Commission (n. 34 above), para. 71.

[40] OSCE Guidelines (n. 8 above), 15.

[41] OSCE Guidelines (n. 8 above), 18; Human Rights Council, Report of the Special Rapporteur on the Rights to Freedom of Peaceful Assembly and of Association, Maina Kiai, April 24, 2013, UN Doc. A/HRC/23/39 (hereafter Maina Kiai, 2013), para. 52; African Commission (n. 38 above), para. 75; *Kivenmaa v. Finland*, Communication No. 412/1990, UN Human Rights Committee, UN Doc. CCPR/C/50/D/412/1990 (1994).

[42] African Commission (n. 34 above), para. 72.

[43] As above.

[44] As above, para. 73.

[45] Maina Kiai, 2012 (n. 3 above), para. 29; African Commission (n. 34 above), para. 75.

Failure to give notification in itself should not automatically amount to disbandment of a peaceful assembly unless there is some other illegal conduct by participants of the assembly.[46]

2.2   State Obligation to Protect Peaceful Assembly

Apart from the states negative obligation not to arbitrarily interfere with peaceful assembly; states also have a positive obligation to facilitate the enjoyment of the right to peaceful assembly which should be explicitly indicated in the laws regulating peaceful assembly.[47] In this regard, states have the obligation to provide protection to persons engaging in peaceful assembly from attackers or counter-demonstrators who aim to disrupting such assembly, especially where the assembly espouses views that are unpopular.[48] This must be provided at the expense of the state without any charge to the organizers or persons partaking in the assembly. Even in the event that demonstrations become violent 'participants retain their rights to bodily integrity and other rights and force may not be used except in accordance with the principles of necessity and proportionality'.[49] The African Commission further recommends that firearms should never be used merely to disperse assemblies as this could potentially endanger the right life of the participants.[50]

2.3   Nondiscrimination

The right to peaceful assembly should be enjoyed by all persons equally. Regulating authorities should not discriminate amongst groups on any ground.[51] States therefore shall not prohibit an assembly based on

---

[46] *Bukta and Others* v. *Hungary*, Application No. 25691/04, European Court of Human Rights (2007); Maina Kiai, 2012 (n. 3 above), 29; African Commission (n. 34 above), para 71(h)

[47] OSCE Guidelines (n. 8 above), 36.

[48] OSCE Guidelines (n. 8 above), 36; Maina Kiai, 2012 (n. 3 above), paras. 33–38; African Commission (n. 34 above), paras. 94–98.

[49] African Commission on Human and Peoples' Rights, "General Comment No. 3 on the African Charter on Human and Peoples' Rights: The Right to Life (article 4)" (2015), para. 28.

[50] As above.

[51] OSCE Guidelines (n. 8 above), 16.

what views are suspected will be expressed, except in instances where such views bother on hate speech and incitement to violence, which may be prohibited by states.[52] For instance, states cannot discriminate against assemblies that are likely to criticize government officials or policy or which may even be offensive or provocative, except where they amount to hate speech or incitement to violence.[53] Similarly, states cannot prohibit an assembly based on other illegitimate grounds such as sex, race, social status, religion, disability, sexual orientation or gender identity.[54] This ensures that governments do not utilize regulatory authorities to suppress dissenting views or political opposition.

3 PERMISSIBLE LIMITATIONS ON THE RIGHT TO FREEDOM OF ASSEMBLY

Like many other human rights, the right to freedom of assembly is not absolute. There are limited conditions under which the limitation of the right to peaceful assembly may be permissible under international human rights law.[55] Such restrictions must be within the limitation provisions of article 21 of the ICCPR[56] and corresponding provisions of other human rights treaties. Under article 21 of the ICCPR a limitation must fulfill the following requirements:

3.1 Legality

To avoid arbitrary restriction on the right to freedom of assembly, any limitation must be enshrined in a law of general application.[57] The laws

---

[52] African Commission (n. 34 above), paras. 77 at 78.

[53] As above, paras. 78 and 79.

[54] As above, para. 80.

[55] ICNL (n. 11 above), 2.

[56] *Kivenmaa v Finland*, Communication No. 412/1990, UN Human Rights Committee, UN Doc. CCPR/C/50/D/412/1990 (1994), para. 9.2.

[57] *Media Rights Agenda & Others v Nigeria* (2000) AHRLR 200 (ACHPR 1998), para. 71; *Prince v South Africa*, Communication 255/2002, para. 44 reprinted in Christof Heyns and Magnus Killander, *Compendium of Key Human Rights Documents of the African Union* (2013), 239.

must be specific, have sufficient clarity and be accessible to enable the individual to assess and foresee the likely consequences of her conduct.[58] No limitation can be imposed that is not prescribed by law. The law itself must be in conformity with international human rights standards and not arbitrary.[59]

3.2 Necessity

Not all limitations prescribed by law are permissible. In terms of article 21 of the ICCPR a prescribed limitation is only permissible if it is necessary in a democratic society. These include limitations necessary in the 'interests of national security or public safety, the prevention of disorder or crime, the protection of health or morals, or the protection of the rights and freedoms of others'.[60] The mere allegation of any of the above grounds per se is not enough to ground a limitation of the right to protest. Any such allegation 'must be duly substantiated'.[61] The onus is therefore on the state or its relevant agency to provide evidence to support any such allegation with ascertainable facts that demonstrate for instance, the real risk of public insecurity.

3.3 Proportionality

'Any limitations imposed shall be in accordance with the principle of legality, have a legitimate public purpose, and be necessary and proportionate means of achieving that purpose within a democratic society, as

---

[58] *Gillan and Quinton v. the United Kingdom*, Application no. 4158/05, European Court of Human Rights (2010), para. 77.

[59] *Article 19 v Eritrea* (2007) AHLR 73 (ACHPR 2007), para. 92; *Civil Liberties Organisation (in respect of the Bar Association) v Nigeria* (2000) AHRLR 186 (ACHPR 1995), para. 16; *Open Door and Dublin Well Woman v Ireland*, Application no. 14234/88, European Court of Human Rights (1992), paras. 69 and 70.

[60] Article 21 of ICCPR; *Samut Karabulut v Turkey*, Application no. 16999/04, European Court of Human Rights (2009), paras. 37–38; *Belyazeka v Belarus*, Communication no. 1772/2008, Human Rights Committee (2012), para. 11.7.

[61] *Primov and Others v Russia*, Application no. 17391/06, European Court of Human Rights (2014), para. 150; *Lashmankin and Others v Russia*, Applications nos. 57818/09 and 14 others, European Court of Human Rights (2017), paras. 421–424; *Chumak v Ukraine*, Application no. 44529/09, European Court of Human Rights (2018), para. 50.

these principles are understood in the light of regional and international human rights law'.[62] A law that prescribes a limitation must therefore justify the legitimate purpose the limitations serves which must proportionately outweigh the full enjoyment of the right.[63] As the Human Rights Committee has observed:

> When a State party imposes restrictions ... it should be guided by the objective to facilitate the right, rather than seeking unnecessary or disproportionate limitations to it. The State party is thus under the obligation to justify the limitation of the right protected by article 21 of the Covenant.[64]

The African Commission has also observed regarding the limitation of rights, that, '[t]he reasons for possible limitation must be founded in a legitimate State interest and the evils of limitation of rights must be strictly proportionate with, and absolutely necessary for, the advantages which are to be obtained. In this regard, states must recognize that the exercise of the right to protest by its nature may cause nuisance to the general public or a section of it, but the mere existence of that possibility or its actual occurrence is not enough justification to prohibit peaceful protests. As the European Court of Human Rights noted in a recent case "peaceful assemblies require the public authorities to show a certain degree of tolerance, even if they cause some inconvenience for everyday life".[65] In such instances, state authorities must strike a fair balance between protecting the interest of the general public and upholding the rights of the protesters by adopting measures to "minimise the disruption, while at the same time accommodating the organisers' legitimate interests in assembling within sight and sound of their target audience".[66] Even more important, a limitation may never have a consequence that the right itself becomes illusory'.[67] In any event the least

---

[62]African Commission (n. 34 above), para. 85.

[63]*Rassemblement Jurassien Unite Jurassienne v. Switzerland*, Application no. 8191/78, European Commission of Human Rights (1979).

[64]*Denis Turchenyak and others v Belarus*, Comm. No. 1948/2010, Human Rights Committee, UN Doc. CCPR/C/108/D/1948/2010, September 2013, 10, para. 7.4.

[65]*Chumak v Ukraine* (2018), para. 53.

[66]As above; see also African Commission (n. 34 above), paras. 87–88.

[67]*Media Rights* v *Nigeria*, paras. 69–70; *Prince* v *South Africa*, para. 43; see also African Commission (n. 34 above), paras. 85–88.

restrictive means of achieving the legitimate purpose of the limitation should be preferred to one that curtails the right further.[68] The African Commission also highlights that states must seek to facilitate the right to protest by ensuring that their urban planning is designed in a manner that does not unnecessarily prevent access to public spaces such as historical locations which may be regularly utilized by protesters.[69]

In terms of sanctions for noncompliance, states are enjoined to refrain from employing criminal sanctions to enforce compliance with protest laws. Where criminal sanctions are necessary they must be proportionate to the alleged misconduct and only be exacted by an impartial court of competent jurisdiction.[70]

The subsequent sections evaluate the decision in the *NPP Case* and assess its consistency with the right to freedom of assembly under international human rights law as espoused above.

4   FACTS OF THE CASE

The plaintiff, New Patriotic Party (NPP), a registered political party in Ghana was granted a permit to hold a political rally on 3 February 1993 in accordance with the Public Order Decree, 1972 (NRCD 68). However the police withdrew the permit before the rally could be held. Subsequently, on 16 February 1993, the plaintiff and other opposition political parties embarked on peaceful demonstration in Accra, protesting against the budget of 1993. The demonstration was broken up by the police and some demonstrators arrested and arraigned before court for demonstrating without police permit contrary to sections 8, 12(c) and 13 of the Public Order Decree, 1972 (NRCD 68).[71] The following

---

[68] Human Rights Committee, *General Comment No. 31: The Nature of the General Legal Obligation Imposed on States Parties to the Covenant* (2004), CCPR/C/21/Rev 1/Add.13, para. 6; *Ezelin v France* (1991), paras. 48–53; *Chorherr v. Austria*, Judgment, Application no. 13308/87 European Commission of Human Rights (1993), para. 33; *Interights & Others v Mauritania* (2004) AHRLR 87 (ACHPR 2004), paras. 82–85.

[69] African Commission (n. 34 above), para. 87.

[70] African Commission (n. 34 above), paras. 99–103.

[71] Section 8 of National Redemption Council Decree (NRCD) 68 required that the holding of all public processions and meetings and the public celebration of any traditional custom should be subject to obtaining the prior police permit; section 12 empowered a

day 17 February 1993, the plaintiff obtained a permit to hold another political rally in commemoration of the 28th anniversary of the death of Dr. J.B. Danquah, the political idol of the plaintiff. This permit was also withdrawn and the police prohibited the rally.

The plaintiff being dissatisfied with the actions of the police commenced legal action in the Supreme Court for a declaration that sections 7, 8, 12(a) and 13 of NRCD 68 were inconsistent with article 21(1) (d) of the 1992 Constitution of Ghana which guarantees the 'freedom of assembly including freedom to take part in processions and demonstration' and therefore void and unenforceable. The plaintiffs argued that under article 21(1)(d) of the 1992 Constitution no permit was required from the police or any individual or entity for the exercise of the right to freedom of assembly including holding a rally, demonstration, procession or the public celebration of any traditional custom. The requirement of permit to exercise the constitutionally guaranteed right was therefore a derogation of the rights of the plaintiffs. The defendant admitted the facts but argued in response that the freedom of assembly was not an absolute right and could therefore be limited in terms of article 21(4) (c)[72] of the Constitution. Sections 7, 8, 12(c) of NRCD 68 were therefore reasonable restrictions in terms of article 21(4) of the Constitution.

The Supreme Court unanimously held in favor of the plaintiff and nullified section 7 of NRCD 68 which empowered the Minister of Interior to prohibit the holding of public meetings or processions in a specified area or for a specified time, section 8 which required that the holding of all public processions and meetings and the public celebration of any traditional custom should be subject to the obtaining of a prior police permit, section 12(*a*) which empowered a police officer an unfettered power to stop and disperse any meeting or processions in

---

superior police officer to stop or disperse such a procession or meeting conducted without permit; and section 13 made it an offense to hold such processions, meetings and public celebrations without such police permission.

[72]Article 21(4)(c) provides as follows: '21(4) Nothing in, or done under the authority of, a law shall be held to be inconsistent with, or in contravention of, this article to the extent that the law in question makes provision – (c) for the imposition of restrictions that are reasonably required in the interest of defense, public safety, public health or the running of essential services, on the movement or residence within Ghana of any person or persons generally, or any class of persons; or...'.

any public place in contravention of sections 7 and 8 and section 13(*a*) which made it an offense to hold such procession, meetings and public celebration without prior police permit.

5 APPRAISAL OF THE NPP DECISION VIS-À-VIS THE INTERNATIONAL FRAMEWORK

It is always difficult balancing the right to freedom of assembly with the need to maintain public order, peace and security and courts are therefore usually cautious about security issues. The court in this case achieved this balance by protecting the fundamental right to assembly whilst noting that reasonable limitations may be placed on the right. The decision of the court is evaluated under the presumption in favor of the enjoyment of the right and proportionality.

5.1 Presumption in Favor of Enjoyment of the Right

The decision of the Court represents a paradigm shift from the require-ment of permission to the enjoyment of a fundamental right without unnecessary restriction. Throughout the judgment the Court recognizes that the requirement of police permission is incompatible with the enjoyment of the right to freedom of assembly. It also recognizes that restrictions on the enjoyment of rights generally are inconsistent with democratic norms.[73] Justice Amua-Sekyi for instance remarks that

> I would have thought that it was self-evident that the continued enjoy-ment by any community of fundamental human rights was incompatible with any requirement that a permit or license be first obtained. Whoever has power to grant a permit or license has power to refuse it... Any such restriction on the right to freedom of assembly would make it meaningless and a sham.[74]

Similarly in her judgment, Justice Bamford-Addo remarked that the

---

[73] *NPP Case* 471.
[74] *NPP Case* 469.

Freedom to act therefore means the absolute right to do something without preconditions and admits of no obligation to obtain permission of anyone before acting. Freedom to act and the obligation to obtain a permit before acting are contradictory and direct opposites and they cannot coexist. If one is not free to act without permission, the reset is that one is not free.[75]

Justice Hayfron-Benjamin also notes further

...that human rights are inalienable being the birthright of the individual as a human being, they cannot be derogated from nor can anyone deprive one of his or her human rights. Therefore these rights are to be enjoyed freely without any impediments or preconditions.[76]

This conforms to the provisions of article 21 of the ICCPR and various jurisprudence of the Human Rights Committee, the European Court of Human Rights and the African Commission as has been expatiated above. The Court recognized the need for the presumption in favor of the enjoyment of the right to freedom of assembly as against its restriction. The Court also emphasized that given unfettered discretion to the police to decide whether fundamental rights can be exercised are inherently prohibitive, and such a rule even though provided by law is arbitrary and therefore void. The concept of presumption in favor of the right is therefore well recognized by the court.

5.2   Proportionality

Whilst upholding the constitutional right to freedom of assembly, the Court was also careful not to lay down an open-ended permanent injunction that would render the police powerless to ensure public safety or the protection of the right of others. As expatiated above, international human rights law supports reasonable limitations that are necessary in a democratic society to amongst others ensure public safety, public health and protect the rights of others. Thus in his Judgment, Justice Charles Hayfron-Benjamin emphasized that

[75] *NPP Case* 478.
[76] *NPP Case* 481.

[t]he necessary limitations which are inherent in the exercise or enjoyment of any "right" of assembly, procession or demonstration are that the citizen must observe the law—in particular ...which deals with the preservation of the public peace.[77]

Justice Bamford-Addo also emphasized that

...in the enjoyment of these rights, regard must be had for the rights of others and for the public interest. The public interest demands that the police maintain law and order in society. Therefore the police will continue to maintain law and order and to ensure that there are no infringements of the criminal laws of the land by those exercising their rights.[78]

These remarks aptly conform to the proportionality test under article 21 of the ICCPR. The court acknowledges the need for the relevant agencies of the state, particularly the police to ensure public safety, order and protection of the rights of others. To hold otherwise would amount to encouraging disorderly conduct. As Justice Aikins noted

It is possible that a lawful procession or demonstration may be obstructed or defeated by counter-demonstrations, or aggressive provocation from hangers on, and it is doubtless with this in mind that the framers of the Constitution, 1992 allowed that a law could be made for the imposition of restrictions that are reasonably required, for example giving directions and conditions, in the interest of defence, public safety, public order, public health or the running of essential services. It should be noted that this provision does not give any power to the police or anyone else to forbid the holding of any meeting, procession or demonstration.[79]

As aptly expressed, the police still retain the power to maintain public peace and order. The caveat, however, is that, for the police to interfere with the right to assembly they must provide satisfactory justification that reasonable grounds exist for exercising such powers.

It is submitted that overall, even though the Supreme Court of Ghana did not make reference to international human rights instruments nor decisions of regional or UN human rights bodies, save a remark about

---

[77] *NPP Case* 508.

[78] *NPP Case* 484.

[79] *NPP Case* 476.

the UN Declaration on the right to development, the decision reached in the NPP Case clearly articulates the provisions of international and regional human rights law on the right to freedom of assembly. The case generally observes the principles that have been articulated under international human rights law and therefore conforms with the basic human rights standards on the right to freedom of assembly. The next section briefly provides some remarks on the contribution of the case to the protection of the right to freedom of assembly in Ghana.

6   Contribution of the *NPP Case* to the Protection of the Right to Freedom of Assembly and Right to Protest

The Contributions of the *NPP Case* to the right to freedom of assembly are manifold, the most pertinent of which are briefly discussed below. The decision in the *NPP Case* led to the repeal of the Public Order Decree[80] which was replaced with the Public Order Act, 1994 (Act 491). The new Act does not require prior police permit as a condition for public assembly or celebration. It rather requires the organizers to notify the police of the assembly at least five days prior to the event.[81] The police may request the organizers (with written justification) to postpone to another date or relocate the assembly to another location where the officer is satisfied that it is likely to occasion violence or endanger public safety or the rights of others.[82] The organizers are however not bound to follow the request of the police officer and have to notify the police within 48 hours of the request of their willingness or otherwise to follow the request.[83] Where the organizers refuse to comply with the request of the police officer, the law places the onus on the police to procure an injunctive order from a court of competent jurisdiction to stop the assembly.[84] The Court in prohibiting the assembly must justify that the order is reasonably required in the interest of public safety, public health

---

[80]Benjamin Kumbor, "Epistolary Jurisdiction of the Indian Courts and Fundamental Human Rights in Ghana's 1992 Constitution: Some Jurisprudential Lessons," *Law, Social Justice & Global Development* 9 (2001): 2.

[81]Public Order Act, section 1(1).

[82]Public Order Act, section 1(4).

[83]Public Order Act, section 1(5).

[84]Public Order Act, section 1(6).

or for the protection of the rights of others.[85] The Act also requires police officers to take all reasonable steps to facilitate the enjoyment of the right to freedom of assembly by directing the routes and vehicular traffic to ensure the orderly enjoyment of the right.[86]

The Act is, however, by no means perfect and has its own shortcomings. For instance, notification is seemingly required for all protest, contrary to international best practice. As discussed earlier, international best practice dictates that notification should only be required for large assemblies or for assemblies at which a certain degree of disruption is anticipated.[87] This is because the essence of notification is to ensure that the police or other relevant authority are prepared to provide protection to the protestors or to ensure that there is as minimal disruption as possible to the general public. In terms of the express provisions of the Act, all protests 'shall' be preceded by the submission of notification to the police, without any exceptions as to the number of persons involved in a particular protest. Ideally, small protests which pose no threat to the public order should not be subject to notification requirements. For instance, under South Africa's Regulation of Gatherings Act, notification is only required if the assembly or protest involves more than fifteen people.[88] In Kenya, a minimum of ten or more people must be present at an assembly or protest for the notification requirements to be triggered.[89]

Similar to the above concern, Ghana's Public Order Act also fails to make provision for spontaneous protests, which should generally be excused from notification requirements as earlier highlighted. Spontaneous protests are by their nature not planned ahead of time and therefore are excused from notification requirements because of the element of non-foreseeability. As a consequence of the strict notification requirements of the Act, spontaneous protests would be considered illegal. The Act's failure to provide a threshold for the minimum number of

[85] Public Order Act, section 1(7).

[86] Public Order Act, section 2.

[87] OSCE Guidelines (n. 8 above), 18; Maina Kiai, 2013 (n. 41 above), para. 52; African Commission (n. 34 above), para. 75; see also Jacob Zenn, "Freedom of Assembly: Procedures of Permission and Notification" (2013), 3, http://www.icnl.org/research/resources/assembly/Permission-Notification%20article.pdf.

[88] Sections 1 and 3 of Regulation of Gatherings Act.

[89] Sections 5(1) and 5(2) of the Public Order Act; see also Woolman (n. 6 above); Zenn (n. 87 above), 7.

participants in a protest which should trigger a notification requirement and its exclusion of spontaneous protests from notification requirements is therefore a shortfall which needs to be addressed.

Related to the above, criticism could be also laid against the inflexible time period within which notification for a protest must be submitted to the police. In terms of the provisions of the Act, organizations must at all cost give at least five days' notice to the police before engaging in a protest action. There are no exceptions to this requirement and therefore one cannot give a shorter notice even where there are legitimate reasons why the organizers of an assembly or protest cannot comply with the notice period. Here too, the South African Regulation of Gatherings Act provides an important example of flexibility with regards to notification requirements. For instance, even though the South African Act, recommends a notice period of seven days for assemblies or protests, the law allows organizers to give notification shorter than seven days but not less than 48 hours, where there are legitimate reasons that justify the organizers' inability to notify the relevant authorities in time.[90] It must therefore be remarked that the inflexibility of Ghana's Act regarding the notice period has the potential to stifle the enjoyment of the right. As discussed earlier, whilst periods for notification may be provided in law, they are not supposed to be so rigid as to frustrate the exercise of the right in some instances. The above shortcomings nonetheless, the *NPP Case* led to the enactment of quite progressive legislation which ensures the enjoyment of the right rather than restricting it and provides judicial oversight over the limitation of the right rather than the discretion of law enforcement officers. This has provided better protection of the right. Its application for twenty years has not led to public disorder or caused safety issues which many African countries are legislating against. It therefore serves as an example to relieve African countries of the apprehension they have about the full enjoyment of the right to freedom of assembly.

---

[90] Section 3(2) of Regulation of Gatherings Act; see also Woolman (n. 6 above); South African Human Rights Commission, "Human Rights in Community Protests," https://www.sahrc.org.za/home/21/files/SAHRC%20Community%20Protest%20Pamphlet%20revised%2020%20March%202018.pdf; Simon Delaney, "The Right to Freedom of Assembly, Demonstration, Picket and Petition Within the Parameters of South African Law," in *Socio-economic Rights—Progressive Realisation?* ed. Foundation for Human Rights (2016), 595.

Additionally, the decision has also become a precedent that courts in other African countries can draw, and have drawn, inspiration from to strike down repressive 'public order' laws in a bid to provide better protection of the right to freedom of assembly. For instance in the Nigerian case of *Inspector-General of Police v All Nigeria Peoples Party and Others*[91] the Court of Appeal of Nigeria relied on amongst others the *NPP Case* in reaching the conclusion that the public order laws of Nigeria which required that police permit be sought in order to exercise the right to freedom of assembly was neither consistent with 1999 Constitution of Nigeria nor the African Charter on Human and Peoples' Rights.

7 BEYOND 1994: POLICE ABUSE OF PUBLIC ORDER ACT AND MATTERS ARISING

As the previous sections highlight, the *NPP Case* provided the basis for the adoption of the Public Order Act of 1994, which provides for a reasonable basis for the effective realization of the right to freedom of assembly, including through protests. Over the years, however, the Act has been manipulated in various ways by the police to censor assemblies and protests in particular. For instance, manhandling of protesters by the police continue to be a very regular occurrence in Ghana,[92] most times with total impunity. Boateng and Darko ascribe the brutal nature of policing in Ghana primarily to a hangover from a colonial system that treated the police as 'property' of the ruling class to suppress the rest of the society.[93]

Beyond police brutality of protesters, arguably the most pertinent way in which the police has manipulated the Public Order Act to stifle the exercise of the right to peaceful assembly and protest is through the use of the courts. As highlighted in the preceding section, the Act requires the police to approach a court to request an order to curtail or

---

[91] *Inspector-General of Police v. All Nigeria Peoples Party and others* (2007) AHRLR 179 (NgCA 2007), para. 23.

[92] Francis D. Boateng and Isaac N. Darko, "Our Past: The Effect of Colonialism on Policing in Ghana," *International Journal of Police Science & Management* 18 (2016): 13; See also Nana A. Anyidoho, "Review of Rights Discourse—Ghana" (2009), which highlights how the police has treated protesters over the years.

[93] As above.

postpone an assembly or protest if they cannot procure the agreement of the organizers to do same. The practice of the police over the years has been to apply to the Circuit Court for ex parte injunctions to curtail protests. These ex parte applications were easily granted by the courts because the protesters were never given notice of such applications to enable them to challenge the reasons canvassed by the police as the justification for the order.[94] Quashigah had warned in 1999 that given the time period within which notifications for protests are to be made, the only reasonable order that the Act envisages could be granted by a court is one made ex parte by the police, given that the Civil Procedure Rules at the time required at least two clear days between the service of a motion (for an injunction in this case) and the hearing.[95] Given the short notice period of five days required by the Act and the clear provisions of the Civil Procedure Rules, he concluded that only an ex parte motion was possible under the circumstances. He, however, cautions that utilizing ex pate injunctions to curtail constitutional rights without giving the affected persons the right to be heard would not only jeopardize the right to assembly and protest but would also be contrary to the fair trial provisions of the constitution.[96] Consequently, he concluded that the whole procedure contemplated by the Public Order Act for handling judicial oversight over a decision of the police to curtail an assembly or protest is not in conformity with the spirit of the constitution.[97]

Whilst I agree with Quashigah that resorting to the ex parte injunctions to curtail the right to peaceful assembly or protest would be contrary to the constitutional guarantee of the right, it is submitted that the current Civil Procedure Rules which have been in force since 2004

---

[94] "Occupy Ghana Condemns Abuse of Ex Parte Injunction by Police," Myjoyonline, accessed September 5, 2018, https://www.myjoyonline.com/news/2015/September-29th/occupyghana-condemns-abuse-of-ex-parte-injunction-by-police.php; "Let My Vote Count Alliance Wins Historic Case Against Police, Attorney-General," Ghanapoliticsonline, accessed September 5, 2018, http://ghanapoliticsonline.com/let-my-vote-count-alliance-wins-historic-case-against-police-attorney-general/; and "NPP Hits Streets Over Dumsor," Ghana Today, accessed September 5, 2018, http://www.ghanatoday.com/news/politics/item/2813.

[95] Edward K. Quashigah, "The Constitutional Right to Freedom of Assembly and Procession in Ghana in the Light of the Decision in the Public Order Case and the Public Order Act," *University of Ghana Law Journal* 20 (1996–1999): 1.

[96] As above.

[97] As above.

allows a judge the discretion to abridge the time if the urgency of the case demands.[98] There is therefore no reasonable justification for the police to continue to resort the use of ex parte injections.

The police, however, continued this practice until November 2015 when the High Court ruled in *Ex parte Gifty Oware-Aboagye*[99] that the use of ex parte injunctions to curtail peaceful assemblies and protest is in violation of the Public Order Act. The applicant in this case invoked the supervisory jurisdiction of the High Court to quash an order ex parte injunction that had been granted by the Circuit Court restraining the applicant from organizing a protest. The applicant requested the High Court to declare that the Circuit Court had no jurisdiction to grant the ex parte injunction and also that the order was granted in contravention of the fair hearing rule of *audi alterem partem* and therefore should be quashed. The facts that necessitate this application were as follows: on 1 September 2015 a notification was given to the police about an intended protest action. The police invited the applicant for discussion after which a second notification was sent to the police about an intended peaceful picket at the Parliament House and Electoral Commission, which was initially agreed to by the police. The police all of a sudden went to the Circuit Court on 14 September 2015 to obtain an ex parte interim injunction when there was no substantive suit pending. The interim injunction was granted on 28 September 2015. It is against this order that the applicant sought the intervention of the High Court, as it has supervisory jurisdiction over the Circuit Court pursuant to which an application may be made to the High Court to quash a decision of the Circuit Court.[100]

Three issues were set down for determination by the High Court, namely (1) whether the Circuit Court has jurisdiction to grant an injunction restraining an assembly or protest in terms of the Public Order Act; (2) whether an ex parte application for an interim injunction not premised on an substantive suit is valid; and (3) whether the grant of

---

[98] See Order 19 Rule 2 and Order 80 Rule 4 of High Court (Civil Procedure) Rules 2004.

[99] *Republic v Circuit Court Accra, ex parte Gifty Oware-Aboagye (Inspector General of Police & Attorney General Intervening as Interested Parties)*, Suit No: HRCM 4/2016, Human Rights Court, Accra.

[100] See article 141 of the 1992 Constitution of Ghana; see also section 16 of the Courts Act 1993 (Act 459) and Order 55 Rules 1 and 2 of the High Court (Civil Procedure) Rules 2004 (CI 47).

the ex parte injunction violated the right to fair hearing of the applicant. Regarding the first issue, the High Court held that the Circuit Court is not competent to issue an injunction against an intended assembly or protest because the Public Order Act does not expressly confer jurisdiction on the Circuit Court. The Court highlighted that under the Constitution of Ghana the Circuit Court is a lower court and therefore can only exercise jurisdiction expressly conferred on it.[101] Consequently, since neither the Courts Act, which establishes the Circuit Court and outlines its jurisdiction nor the Public Order Act, expressly confers jurisdiction on the Circuit Court to entertain actions brought under the Public Order Act, the Circuit Court had no jurisdiction.[102]

On the second and third issues, the High Court held that an ex parte application which is filed when there is no substantive suit pending is only allowed when expressly provided by legislation. Since the Public Order Act does not expressly provide that an application to restrain an assembly can be made ex parte, such applications must always be on notice to the parties who will be affected by the order. The Court consequently declared that ex parte applications filed under the Public Order Act are void, since they are contrary to the Act and in breach of the rules of natural justice. In the words of the Court '[i]t would be unfair to use an ex-parte application to initiate an action whose outcome would affect the rights of other people and once it is granted, the action terminates'.[103] The Court also remarked that the practice of the police in circumventing the provisions of the Public Order Act through the use of ex parte applications for injunctions before the Circuit Court is a 'crude approach [that] should not be encouraged in a democratic society'.[104]

The decision of the High Court is an important follow-up to the *NPP Case* and ensures that the gains that were made through the adoption of the Public Order Act are not arbitrarily undermined by the police through 'backdoor' judicial proceedings. It is also particularly important that the Court ruled that the only the High Court or Regional Tribunal, which has the same jurisdiction as the High Court can entertain actions

---

[101] *Ex parte Gifty Oware-Aboagye*, 8.

[102] As above.

[103] As above, 12.

[104] As above.

under the Public Order Act. The Public Order Act exist to regulate the enjoyment of the fundamental right to assembly, and it is therefore logical that only a court constitutionally mandated to enforce fundamental rights has jurisdiction to entertain a process that seeks to limit the enjoyment of fundamental rights.

The proscription of ex parte applications also provides an important protection to the right to assembly and protest because persons who intend to engage in protest action would have to be notified of any action by the police before the High Court seeking to restrain them from protesting. This provides an opportunity for the affected persons to challenge the police on the justifications. This ensures that a Court exercising judicial oversight is seized with all the facts and competing interests in other to make a fair assessment of the case before pronouncing its judgement. This in theory provides further protection to the rights to protest. It however, remains to be seen in practice how the High Court will act differently from the Circuit Court.

8   Conclusion

Every nation has the duty under international law to protect the rights and liberties of persons within its jurisdiction. Liberal legal frameworks and strong courts are necessary for the protection of these rights and to challenge arbitrary executive action where necessary. People can better protect their rights if they can freely come together to express their opinions including through assembly and public protests. The *NPP Case* is a ray of light for the enjoyment of the freedom of assembly in Ghana and Africa as a whole. In an era where many governments continue to use repressive public order laws to suppress and sometimes even deny the enjoyment of this right, it is refreshing that the Supreme Court of Ghana was bold to make a human rights compliant decision that has been a true torch bearer of the right to freedom of assembly in the region. However, as the example of Ghana has shown, liberal interpretation by courts alone is not sufficient to protect the right to peaceful assembly from illiberal policing tactics. Police in Ghana used lower courts to stifle assemblies until a recent intervention by the High Court requiring police to procure restraining orders only from the High Court, on notice to the organizers of the assembly sought to be curtailed. This is to ensure that organizers of assemblies are given the opportunity to be heard and counter the allegations of state officials and ultimately prevent state authorities from using ex parte judicial processes to stifle the right to peaceful assembly. Civil society and other relevant actors therefore need to constantly be on the lookout for these kinds of police maneuvering to ensure that judicial and legislative gains are not circumvented.

REFERENCES

Books, Book Chapters and Articles

Anderson, Lisa. "Demystifying the Arab Spring: Parsing the Differences Between Tunisia, Egypt and Libya." *Foreign Affairs*, May/June (2011). Accessed September 4, 2018. https://www.foreignaffairs.com/articles/libya/2011-04-03/demystifying-arab-spring?fa_anthology=1116900.

Anyidoho, Nana A. "Review of Rights Discourse—Ghana" (2009).

Article 19. "Freedom of Association and Assembly" (2001), 3. Accessed March 3, 2018. https://www.article19.org/data/files/pdfs/publications/sub-saharan-africa-freedom-of-association-and-assembly.pdf.

Boateng, Francis D., and Isaac N. Darko. "Our Past: The Effect of Colonialism on Policing in Ghana." *International Journal of Police Science & Management* 18 (2016): 13.

Decker, Klaus, Siobhán McInerney-Lankford, and Caroline Sage. "Human Rights and Equitable Development: 'Ideals', Issues and Implications." Background Paper for the World Development Report (2006). Accessed September 4, 2018. http://siteresources.worldbank.org/INTWDRS/Resources/477365-1327693659766/8397901-1327773323392/Human_Rights_and_Equitable_Development_Ideals_Issues_and_Implications.pdf.

Delaney, Simon. "The Right to Freedom of Assembly, Demonstration, Picket and Petition Within the Parameters of South African Law." In *Socio-economic Rights—Progressive Realisation?* edited by Foundation for Human Rights, 595. Johannesburg: Foundation for Human Rights, 2016.

Hannum, Hurst. "The Status of the Universal Declaration of Human Rights in National and International Law." *Georgia Journal of International and Comparative Law* 25 (1995): 287–396.

Henkin, Louis. "The International Bill of Rights: The Universal Declaration and the Covenants." In *International Enforcement of Human Rights*, edited by Rudolf Bernhardt and John A. Jolowizc, 1–6. Berlin: Springer, 1987.

Humphrey, John P. "International Bill of Rights: Scope and Implementation." *William and Mary Law Review* 17, no. 3 (1976): 527–541.

Inazu, John D. "The Forgotten Freedom of Assembly." *Tulane Law Review* 84 (2010): 565.

International Centre for Non-profit Law (ICNL). "Freedom of Assembly." *Global Trends in NGO Law* 2 (2011): 1.

Kumbor, Benjamin. "Epistolary Jurisdiction of the Indian Courts and Fundamental Human Rights in Ghana's 1992 Constitution: Some Jurisprudential Lessons." *Law, Social Justice & Global Development* 9 (2001): 2.

Quashigah, Edward K. "The Constitutional Right to Freedom of Assembly and Procession in Ghana in the Light of the Decision in the Public Order Case and the Public Order Act." *University of Ghana Law Journal* 20 (1996–1999): 1.

Rawls, John. *A Theory of Justice*. Cambridge, MA: Harvard University Press, 1971.

Schabas, William A. *The Universal Declaration of Human Rights: The Travauxx Préparatoires, volume 1, October 1946 to November 1947*, xxxvii. New York: Cambridge University Press, 2013.

South African Human Rights Commission. "Human Rights in Community Protests." https://www.sahrc.org.za/home/21/files/SAHRC%20Community%20Protest%20Pamphlet%20revised%2020%20March%202018.pdf.

Steiner, Henry J., Philip Alston, and Ryan Goodman. *International Human Rights in Context: Law, Politics, Morals—Texts and Materials*. Oxford: Oxford University Press, 1996.

Woolman, Stuart. "Assembly, Demonstration and Petition." In *The Bill of Rights Handbook*, edited by Ian Currie and Johan De Waal, 377. Cape Town: Juta, 2013.

Zenn, Jacob. "Freedom of Assembly: Procedures of Permission and Notification" (2013). http://www.icnl.org/research/resources/assembly/Permission-Notification%20article.pdf.

Reports and Guidelines

Organisation for Security and Co-operation in Europe (OSCE) Office for Democratic Institutions and Human Rights (ODIHR). *Guidelines on the Freedom of Peaceful Assembly* (2010).

Report of the United Nations High Commissioner for Human Rights. "Effective Measures and Best Practices to Ensure the Promotion and Protection of Human Rights in the Context of Peaceful Protest." UN Doc. A/HRC/22/28, January 21, 2013.

UN Human Rights Committee. *General Comment No. 31: The Nature of the General Legal Obligation Imposed on States Parties to the Covenant*, CCPR/C/21/Rev.1/Add.13 (2004).

Universal Declaration of Human Rights (UDHR).

UN Human Rights Council. Report of the Special Rapporteur on the Rights to Freedom of Peaceful Assembly and of Association, Maina Kiai, May 21, 2012, UN Doc. A/HRC/20/27 (hereafter Maina Kiai, 2012), para. 12.

UN Human Rights Council. Report of the Special Rapporteur on the Rights to Freedom of Peaceful Assembly and of Association, Maina Kiai, April 24, 2013, UN Doc. A/HRC/23/39.

Websites

Jones, Sam, and Stephen Burgen. "Catalonia Responds to Police Violence: 'People Are Angry, Very Angry.'" *The Guardian*, October 3, 2017. Accessed March 4, 2018. https://www.theguardian.com/world/2017/oct/03/catalonia-tensions-rise-as-strikes-held-over-police-violence-during-referendum.

"Let My Vote Count Alliance Wins Historic Case Against Police, Attorney-General." Ghanapoliticsonline. Accessed September 5, 2018. http://ghanapoliticsonline.com/let-my-vote-count-alliance-wins-historic-case-against-police-attorney-general/.

"NPP Hits Streets Over Dumsor." Ghana Today. Accessed September 5, 2018. http://www.ghanatoday.com/news/politics/item/2813.

"Occupy Ghana Condemns Abuse of Ex Parte Injunction by Police." Myjoyonline. Accessed September 5, 2018. https://www.myjoyonline.com/news/2015/September-29th/occupyghana-condemns-abuse-of-ex-parte-injunction-by-police.php.

International cases

Article 19 v Eritrea (2007) AHLR 73 (ACHPR 2007).

Belyazeka v Belarus, Communication no. 1772/2008, Human Rights Committee (2012).

Bukta and Others v. Hungary, Application No. 25691/04, European Court of Human Rights (2007).

Chorherr v. Austria, Judgment, Application no. 13308/87 European Commission of Human Rights (1993).

Christians Against Racism and Fascism v United Kingdom, Application no. 8440/78, European Commission of Human Rights (1980).

Chumak v Ukraine, Application no. 44529/09, European Court of Human Rights (2018).

Civil Liberties Organisation (in respect of the Bar Association) v Nigeria (2000) AHRLR 186 (ACHPR 1995).

Denis Turchenyak and others v Belarus, Comm. No. 1948/2010, Human Rights Committee, UN Doc. CCPR/C/108/D/1948/2010, September 2013.

Éva Molnár v Hungary, Application no. 10346/05, European Court of Human Rights (2008).

Ezelin v. France, Application no. 11800/85, European Court of Human Rights (1991); (1992) 14 EHRR 362.

Gillan and Quinton v. the United Kingdom, Application no. 4158/05, European Court of Human Rights (2010).

Interights & Others v Mauritania (2004) AHRLR 87 (ACHPR 2004)

Kivenmaa v. Finland, Communication No. 412/1990, UN Human Rights Committee, UN Doc. CCPR/C/50/D/412/1990 (1994).

Lashmankin and Others v Russia, Applications nos. 57818/09 and 14 others, European Court of Human Rights (2017).

Media Rights Agenda & Others v Nigeria (2000) AHRLR 200 (ACHPR 1998).

Open Door and Dublin Well Woman v Ireland, Application no. 14234/88, European Court of Human Rights (1992).

Osmani and Others v FYR of Macedonia, Application no. 50841/99, European Court of Human Rights (2001).

Ouranio Toxo and Others v Greece, Application no. 74989/01, European Court of Human Rights (2005).

Primov and Others v Russia, Application no. 17391/06, European Court of Human Rights (2014).

Prince v South Africa, Communication 255/2002.

Rassemblement Jurassien Unite Jurassienne v. Switzerland, Application no. 8191/78, European Commission of Human Rights (1979).

Samut Karabulut v Turkey, Application no. 16999/04, European Court of Human Rights (2009).

Ziliberberg v Moldova, Application no. 61821/00, European Court of Human Rights (2004).

Domestic cases

Inspector-General of Police v All Nigeria Peoples Party and Others (2007) AHRLR 179 (NgCA 2007).

New Patriotic Party (NPP) v Inspector-General of Police (2001) AHRLR 138 (GhSC 1993).

Republic v Circuit Court Accra, ex parte Gifty Oware-Aboagye (Inspector General of Police & Attorney General Intervening as Interested Parties), Suit No: HRCM 4/2016, Human Rights Court, Accra.

CHAPTER 11

The Role of Election Management Bodies in Advancing Democracy in Ghana

Bright Sefah

1 INTRODUCTION

We live in a time when the call for freedom and democracy in governance echoes across continents. Democracy is rooted in governments whose supreme power is vested in its people and exercised directly by them or by their designated agents.[1] A prominent feature of democracy is elections. Elections are managed by Electoral Management Bodies (EMBs) which are expected to deliver free, fair and periodic elections as their role in promoting democracy. EMBs are today seen as 'the linchpin of effective electoral governance in new and established democracies'.[2] Undeniably, there is a worldwide trend of creating EMBs

[1] Alfred Amedeker, "An assessment of Ghana's Democratic Consolidation Since 1992 and the Implications for International Relations" (MA dissertation, University of Ghana, 2013), 8–9.

[2] Shaheen Mozaffar, "Patterns of Electoral Governance in Africa's emerging democracies," *International Political Science review* 23 (2002): 85.

B. Sefah (✉)
African Union Commission (AUC), Addis Ababa, Ethiopia

© The Author(s) 2020   277
M. Addaney et al. (eds.), *Governance, Human Rights,
and Political Transformation in Africa,*
https://doi.org/10.1007/978-3-030-27049-0_11

as 'independent and permanent electoral commissions'.[3] However, the role of these EMBs sometimes turns to cause what the election itself intends to prevent as their credibility and independence is sometimes called into question. Structure and appointment to power positions in these institutions as well as their electoral processes are just a few of the areas of contention upon which some of the EMBs lose their credibility. One cannot overemphasize the important role elections play with regards to entrenching democracy as elections find itself at the heart of democracy.[4] This is because democratically elected governments derive their 'authority' on the basis of the approval of the governed through well-organized, free and fair elections.[5] Jean Kirkpatrick argues that:

> democratic elections are not merely symbolic [...] but rather competitive, periodic and inclusive elections in which the chief decision-makers in government are selected by citizens who enjoy broad freedom to criticize governments, to publish their criticisms and to present alternatives.[6]

It is for such reasons that the role of the Electoral Commission of Ghana (EC), in a nation considered to be the model of democracy in a region where political instability is common,[7] in enhancing the democracy of Ghana is discussed.

This chapter considers the relationship between the EMBs and democracy. The EC of Ghana will be assessed on its qualities and roles to ascertain whether the EC conforms to the standards set by International IDEA, in promoting democracy in Ghana.

2   ELECTION MANAGEMENT BODIES (EMBS)

EMBs are institutions that are established with the mandate of organizing and managing elections. The following models of EMBs can be distinguished.

---

[3] Mcebisi Ndletyana, *Institutionalizing Democracy: The Story of the Electoral Commission of South Africa 1993–2014* (South Africa: Africa Institute of South Africa, 2015), 14.

[4] Howard Cincotta, *What Is Democracy* (1998), para. 1, http://www.ait.tw/infousa/zhtw/DOCS/whatsdem/homepage.htm.

[5] Ibid.

[6] Cincotta, *What Is Democracy* (1998), para. 1.

[7] Omar Mohammed, "The Six African Elections to Watch Out for in 2016" (2016), para. 5, http://qz.com/585357/the-six-africans-elections-to-watch-out-for-in-2016-and-why/.

2.1   The Independent Model

This is the most common form of EMB found in many parts of the world.[8] In this model, the management and the organization of elections are conducted by an institution that does not depend on, and has autonomy from, the executive arm of government. Although, primarily financially supported by the government, management of budgets is solely done by the EMB, which is financially accountable to parliament.[9] These EMBs have various levels of 'financial accountability and autonomy and to some extent accountability related to performance'.[10] This model can be found such as Burkina Faso, Nigeria, Mauritius, South Africa, Ghana and Liberia, among others.

2.2   The Government Model

This model is the direct contrast of the independent model. Here, the organization and management of the electoral process are entrusted in the executive arm of government through any of its ministries for instance the interior ministry and local authorities. At the national level, this model is headed by a minister or civil servant, who reports to a cabinet minister.[11] The government model is primarily financially supported by the Ministry of Local Government or Local Authority.[12] Prominent among states that employ the government model are the United States of America (USA), Singapore, The United Kingdom (UK), Denmark and Switzerland. The implementation of elections is done by the local authorities in countries such as Switzerland, UK and USA whereas the assumption of the 'duty of policy coordination' is done by the Central EMB in countries such as Switzerland and Sweden.[13] Per its name one

[8] Lawrence LeDuc Richard et al., *Comparing Democracies 3: Election and Voting in the 21st Century* (London: Sage, 2010), 42.

[9] Financing EMBs are major problems in Africa. As an independent body serving the need of citizens, EMBs do not have programs of raising their own money and so are supported by governments. In as much as the government funds the EMBs doesn't guarantee partiality toward them as this governmental duty are mostly constitutionally backed. Foreign donors also play prominent roles in financing EMBs.

[10] Deluc et al., *Comparing Democracies 3: Elections and voting in the 21st Century*, 42.

[11] Richard et al., *Comparing Democracies 3: Election and Voting in the 21st Century*, 44.

[12] Pippa Norris, *Why Elections Fail* (New York: Cambridge University Press, 2015), 143.

[13] The fact that the government model is employed does not guarantee partiality toward the government as in many cases. A closer looks at countries that are mentioned above

may assume bias in such models, but countries like Sweden, USA, UK and Denmark have proved that the government model can be effective if there are institutional checks and balances that fundamentally ensure its independence. This model is rarely practiced in Africa.

2.3   The Mixed Model

This model is a double component EMB with a twofold structure. The first fold is an independent institution that manages policies, supervises and monitors the EMB's activities similar to the independent model, whereas the second fold implements activities and is situated in any of the state's departments or local government.[14] Here, the election is organized by the second component with partial observation by the independent component.[15] This model is employed in Japan, Spain and France including French colonies in Africa like Senegal, Republic of Congo and Mali. Although this model has to an extent worked in some countries, has shortcomings such as overlap in their duties. For instance, while applying the mixed model in 1999, the effectiveness and credibility of Guinea's elections were questioned because of conflicting roles played by both independent and government components.[16]

3   THE DEMOCRACY ENHANCING' QUALITIES AND ROLES OF EMBs

3.1   Qualities of EMBs

Elections have proved to be a very important platform for the enhancement of democracy and in other instances the cause of unrests.[17] Either way, the EMBs that organize and manage elections are expected to portray certain qualities for parties and the public to have confidence

---

have little to no problems with regards to elections and electoral violence. It is rather some countries with the independent model that have shown uncertainties and mistrust in their systems.

[14] International IDEA, "Electoral Management Design" (2014), 8.

[15] IDEA, "Electoral Management Design," 8.

[16] Ibid.

[17] Stan Chullo, *The Face of Africa: Looking Beyond the Shadows* (UK: Author House, 2006), 110.

in them. Although, there are no internationally recognized standards for assessing the qualities EMBs must possess, the criteria set by International IDEA stands as a good measure for assessing the quality of EMBs. This criterion is briefly discussed below.

Independence
The above discussion on the models of EMBs revealed that the government model and the mixed model are imbedded and semi-imbedded respectively in the government. However, its attachment must not defeat its purpose of managing quality, free and fair elections. It must structurally prove to be independent as has been shown in the USA, Singapore and UK.[18] In light of this EMBs are expected not to favor governments or incumbents or any other political party. Independence of EMBs is mostly asserted constitutionally and through other legal documents.[19] Therefore it is imperative to provide a legal framework to buttress the independence of the EMB.[20] The appointment of leadership must come from a competent and impartial source, like the Judiciary or civil society organization and persons appointed to the leadership should ideally not be affiliated with a political party to avoid unwarranted meddling of the EMBs activities.[21]

Impartiality
To institute integrity and be lauded as credible, the EMB must conduct its electoral mandate with impartiality.[22] In this regard, the EMB must ensure total independence of its actions to maintain its integrity. The EMB must treat all those who partake in elections equally, with

---

[18]The structural independence emanates from the independent Model of EMBs where the EMB is supposed to be separate entity from other arm of government, especially the Executive whereas the fearless comes from the normative expectations of EMBs where they must do their work diligently without fear or favor.

[19]IDEA, "Electoral Management Design," 8.

[20]This is evident in countries like Mexico, South Africa, Kenya, Mauritius and Zambia. This system works better with the independent Model than the other Models.

[21]Some countries like Brazil, Zambia and Australia have proved that the use of Justices or Judges as heads or chairpersons of EMBs can be very good. Burkina Faso also appointed the leader of a civil society organization.

[22]Charles Lasham, "Transparency and Impartiality of the Electoral Administration on Election Day: The Importance of the Management of the Elections and the Role of the Electoral Administrator" (2005), 3.

fairness and without handing advantage to any party or interest group. The appointment of the chairperson and staff must also be put under consideration in order to avoid appointing party affiliates who will serve their parties interests other than their mandates. Although, appointments of chairpersons for the mixed model like in Spain and the governmental model like in Sweden and Finland are usually said to be partial they have proved to be fair and impartial whereas the some EMBs which structurally conform to the independent model have independence only by name. The appointments of chairpersons in most cases raises eyebrows as appointees may be known to be a member of the government or political parties. Impartiality, therefore, has to be evident from the practices of the EMB and the electoral process supervised by the EMB.

Transparency

To maintain credibility on its mandate, transparency is paramount. The awareness and participation in deliberations that surround the EMBs activities by government, civil societies, media and political parties should be an important element of well-functioning EMBs.[23] If stakeholders are aware of the deliberations on the EMB's activities it breeds openness and transparency. For this reason, stakeholders of elections must constantly be invited and briefed on decisions that are being taken by the EMB as well as electoral reforms. This will require regular communication between the EMB, the stakeholders and the media.[24] Financial transparency is also one of the major areas that attracts the scrutiny of the public. This can help to combat negative public perceptions, detect and stop financial or electoral fraud. Electoral laws can be used to provide mechanisms for transparency.[25]

Professionalism

The people at the helm of affairs at any EMB are very important to the realization of integrity and the efficiency of the body. The recruitment

[23] Carl W. Dundas, *Electoral Essays and Discourses* (UK: Author House, 2014), 233.

[24] Commonwealth, *Election Management: A Compendium of Commonwealth Good Practices* (2016), 15.

[25] Transparency also covers the EMBs finances. This could be enforced by electoral laws requiring EMBs to update the public on its financial activities as practiced in Indonesia. This could be through media briefings, releases and stakeholder consultations like the Liberian EMB for their 2011 elections.

of qualified and competent staff is important. Professionalism will be realized through officials diligently executing their mandate fairly and accurately.[26] The management of elections should be undertaken by dedicated, well-trained people, both temporary[27] and permanent, who have committed to apply higher professionalism toward the process of elections and its technicalities.[28] In as much as professionalism depends highly on the training and the higher qualification of the personnel, it also hinges on the attitude of the staff. If the qualified and competent staff that are employed are diligent, accurate and generally committed to their tasks, it automatically breeds professionalism.

3.2   The Role of EMBs in Enhancing Democracy

Electoral Reforms
One of the most important obligations of EMBs is the implementing reforms of electoral regulations that guide the electoral processes.[29] This could be provided for in either 'national constitutions or other legal frameworks' like electoral laws.[30] In many cases, reforms originate after an election has been conducted, assessed and evaluated. The purpose of this function of EMBs is to analytically bring out the best practices and the challenges in the process of election. It further unearths what caused the challenges for improvement in future elections. This could be done internally by staff assessments and appraisals or externally by other experts to bring out their conclusions on the electoral process.[31]

In this regard, some undertakings are expected of the EMB, which includes planning research, stakeholder engagement, policy development and the presentation of drafts bills to the legislature and/or the executive.[32] Subsequently, if the law is adopted, the operationalization

---

[26] IDEA, "Electoral Management Design," 258.

[27] EMBs employ temporary people to support them during elections as a result of the work overload during elections.

[28] IDEA, "Electoral Management Design," 258.

[29] International IDEA, *Electoral Law Reforms in Africa: Insight into the Role of EMBs and Approaches to Engagement* (Sweden: Bulls Graphic, 2014), 13.

[30] IDEA, *Electoral Law Reforms*, 13.

[31] Ibid., 16.

[32] Ibid., 14.

of the law, informing and educating interest groups on changes and the implementation of such changes are part of the functions of the EMB.[33]

The Conduct of Elections

The conduct of trustworthy and integrity based free, fair and transparent elections is the main function expected of every EMB. It is not just about conducting elections but rather, seeing to the well expected democratic and constitutional changes of government, a vehicle for giving the populace the opportunity to choose a leader and a government.

The EMB periodically administers the registration of eligible voters, the registration of political parties that wish to contest for political positions, educating the populace on the need to vote, providing logistics for the voting exercise, ensuring a transparently free and fair voting, counting and tabulating the votes cast and announcing the winner for the conducted elections.[34] The registration of eligible voters is one of the key areas that is misunderstood as the voters register decides who votes and who does not vote. There must therefore be periodic registrations to clean the voters register.[35] The EMB must be transparent and allow all political parties and interest groups the opportunity to observe the process in order to avoid misunderstandings and misconceptions.[36]

Candidate's registrations must also be conducted in accordance with the laws governing the registration of candidates and must not favor the government or any other political party.[37] A rule that qualifies one candidate must also apply to the other candidates. Rules that disqualify one but qualifies another breeds partiality and can make the electoral process lose credibility.[38] Logistics must be diligently catered for by the EMB. Shortage of election materials in particular stations should be avoided

[33] Ibid.

[34] Johnson Olaniyi, "Enhancing Democracy and Surmounting the Challenges of Election Management in Africa: Insights from Nigeria," in *Myths of Peace and Democracy? Towards Building Pillars of Hope, Unity and Transformation in Africa*, ed. Munyaradzi Mawere and Ngonidzashe Marongwe (Cameroon: African Books Collective, 2016), 124.

[35] Carl Dundas, *The Lag of 21st Century Democratic Elections: In Africa Union Member States* (USA: Author House, 2011), 158.

[36] Dundas, *The Lag of 21st Century Democracy*, 158.

[37] Dietar Nohlen et al., *Elections in Africa: A Data Handbook* (New York: Oxford University Press, 1999), 427.

[38] UN Economic Commission for Africa, "African Governance Report III: Elections and the Management of Diversity" (2013), 7.

to give every voter the opportunity to vote. Where there is the use of biometric machines, measures must be put in place for assurance of replacements when there are breakdown of machines and other related problems.[39]

Announcement of winners is crucial. The officer in charge must be firm in announcing the results and declaring the winner. For these reasons the competence of the officer in charge should be instrumental in the appointment or selection process. He or she must not give an impression of partiality and must firmly announce and declare the winner(s) accurately as the acceptance of the declaration will result in improving democracy and good governance.

Women's Political Participation

For many decades, there have been efforts to promote and improve women's political participation. This can be seen through provisions of international instruments such as declarations, conventions and reports of international bodies, resolutions, charters and policies.[40] Despite all these, we fail to acknowledge the important role EMBs can play in the promotion of women's political participation. Irrespective of the model, EMBs are responsible for the conduct of elections as well as the management of electoral processes which includes making and amending electoral laws. In reference to their thorough acquaintance and familiarity with the laws governing elections and electoral activities, EMBs are in an advantageous position to support and promote the empowerment of women in the process of elections.

Challenges such as social and cultural beliefs, biases and stereotypes are among the problems that women face.[41] Excessive registration fees for candidacy with the EC and the kilometric processes one must go through in the course of registering as a candidate for elections

---

[39] Ravindra Das, *Adopting Biometric Technology: Challenges and Solutions* (USA: Author House, 2016), 47.

[40] Regarding right to vote and be voted for, most instruments are general in nature as it does not mention men or women. However the patriarchal nature of our societies does not give women the same opportunities. The CEDAW and the Maputo Protocol are just few of the instruments that promote women's rights.

[41] Bright Joe Sefah and Kennedy Kariseb, "Women's Political Participation in Decision Making Processes and Organs: Trends, Practices and Social Realities," in *Ghana @ 60: Governance and Human Rights in Twenty First Century Africa*, ed. Michael Addaney and Michale Gyan Nyarko (Pretoria: Pretoria University Law Press, 2017), 117.

sometimes constrain women's involvement in electoral processes.[42] The UNDP policy paper for EMBs on the promotion of gender equality and women's participation proposes ways of ensuring gender equality. These include the use of the integration of gender mainstreaming perspectives in departments and institutions that handle electoral process by introducing 'inclusive electoral processes' that gives women equal opportunities.[43] This also includes integrating 'gender specific or gender target interventions' for tackling areas, including 'affirmative actions'.[44]

The Involvement of Civil Society Organizations
Civil society organizations (CSOs) often have mandates of promoting activities that seek to build platforms for the improvement of governance and human rights. Through international and local CSOs, the electoral process benefits greatly in ways which may assist the EMB to provide 'election, voter and civic education'.[45] CSOs sometimes assist with funding EMBs and training NGOs whose work relates to the electoral process for quality and integrity-based elections.[46] The conduct of elections demands extra staff, which is usually resolved through the employment of temporary staff during elections to supplement the permanent staff. These temporal staffs can be financed or trained by CSOs for the success of the electoral process.

Furthermore, reports on electoral processes, challenges and best practices, are prominently reported by CSOs which serves as independent observers. This has an impact on the improvement of the work of EMBs.[47] In this regard, the collaboration between EMBs and CSOs has a beneficial impact on elections.

Election Observation
Election observation involves consistent information gathering on electoral processes aimed at making 'informed judgments' by professionals without

---

[42] Sefah and Kariseb, *Women's Political Participation*, 117.

[43] UNDP and UN Women, *Inclusive Electoral Process: A Guide for Electoral Management Bodies on Promoting Gender Equality and Women's Participation* (UN: UNDP and UN Women, 2015), 2.

[44] UNDP, *Inclusive Electoral Process* (2015), 2.

[45] Dundas, *Electoral Essays and Discourses*, 241.

[46] Dundas, *Electoral Essays and Discourses*, 241.

[47] Dundas, *Electoral Essays and Discourses*, 242.

inherent authority for intervening in the process.[48] Professionals' participation in mediation or technical assistance should not interfere in the electoral process to avoid placing these professionals' core responsibility in jeopardy. Election Observers may include international CSOs consisting of human rights and democracy focused organizations such as International IDEA, the Democracy and Electoral Assistance Unit (DEAU) of the African Union as well as community focused CSOs serving as an oversight mechanism for electoral processes. Election observers serve as machineries that strengthen electoral transparency and credibility and facilitate the acceptance of the results of elections.[49] Election observers are primarily institutions whose works are greatly respected worldwide. Thus, a partnership and allowing election observations strengthens the work of EMBs.

4   THE ELECTORAL COMMISSION OF GHANA: AN APPRAISAL

4.1   *The History and Setup of the Electoral Commission of Ghana*

Evolution of the Electoral Commission of Ghana
The EC of Ghana is the only body mandated with the organization of elections for the democratic transfer and changes in government in Ghana.[50] The evolution of the EC was as a result of the institutional inheritance of colonial rule. The EC started as a department within the Ministry of Local government, mandated to supervise elections conducted by the British rulers.[51] Opposition parties raised suspicion about interference by the ruling government in elections held immediately subsequent to the March 1957 independence, which they suggested were void of fairness and respect for the electoral laws.[52] Subsequent to the overthrow of Kwame Nkrumah in 1966, the independent model of EMB was adopted by succeeding governments. The authority for conducting elections shifted to an independent commission, headed by

---

[48] Arne Tostensen, "Elections Observation as an Informal Means of Enforcing Political Rights," *Nordsk Tidsskrift for Menneskerettigheter* 22 (2004): 330.

[49] Carl Dundas, *The Lag of 21st Century Democratic Elections*, 20.

[50] Article 45 of the 1992 Constitution of Ghana.

[51] Emmanuel Gyimah-Boadi, "Modeling Success: Governance and Institution-Building in Africa: The Case of Ghana's Electoral Commission" (2007), 6.

[52] Gyimah-Boadi, *Modeling Success* (2007), 6.

a single commissioner.[53] The commission under the first Republic was seen as not credible as there were influences from the government.[54] However, with elections under the second and third Republic, the Commission was touted by the media and election observers as autonomous and impartial, although the oppositions were unconvinced about its autonomy.[55]

Ushering in the fourth Republic, there were several impediments as the public perceived the hastily appointment of the Interim National Electoral Commission (INEC) as being manipulated and interfered by the then government, led by Ft Ltd. Jerry John Rawlings.[56] However, many saw the system after 1992 as generally able to hold credible elections for the reason that there was a general agreement of a suitable system that will support multiparty elections, which resulted in the establishment of the Electoral Commission of Ghana. Progressively transforming through NCD, INEC and finally to the EC, it heightened and enriched its integrity and effectiveness. The EC has had minimal negative interference or manipulation from CSOs and benefactors.

The Setup of the Electoral Commission of Ghana
The independence of the EC is guaranteed by the Constitution.[57] Furthermore, the EC is 'established under the Electoral Commission Act of 1993'.[58] Regarding its composition, the EC is made up of seven members. These are the chairperson, two deputy chairpersons as well as four additional members. All members are appointed by the president in 'consultation with the Council of State'.[59] There are no term limits for any of the commissioners.[60] The functions of the EC include compiling

---

[53] Gyimah-Boadi, *Modeling Success* (2007), 7.

[54] Gyimah-Boadi, *Modeling Success* (2007), 7.

[55] Gyimah-Boadi, *Modeling Success* (2007), 8.

[56] Ibid.

[57] Article 46 of the 1992 Constitution of Ghana.

[58] The preparations and conducting elections is established for the EC of Ghana under articles 43–46 of the 1992 Constitution. The rest of the mandate it further detailed in the Electoral Commission Act of 1993.

[59] Article 43 and 70 of the 1992 Constitution of Ghana.

[60] The Constitution does not provide for term limits. Chairpersons serve until they are found in a position where they cannot serve any more or they retire. The president appoints a new commissioner to that effect.

the voter's register, delimitations of constituencies, conducting and supervising elections and referenda, educating electorates on the electoral process and its aims, expanding voters' registrations and other functions which the law prescribes.[61]

Structure, Financing and Staffing

Apart from its headquarters in Accra, the EC also has offices in regional and district capitals. The head of the district office report to the regional office and regional offices report to the national secretariat of the Commission.[62] The appointment of officers at all levels is done by the Commission with guidance from the Public Service Commission.[63] The EC in performing its functions hires temporary staff for the period of elections to support the commission at offices and polling stations.[64] Previously, temporary staffs were civil servants, however the role is currently open to qualified Ghanaians.[65] With regard to funding, the EC's budget is from the Consolidated Fund[66] approved by parliament and the government.

Parliament serves as an accountability mechanism while the executive gives approval for funding. This breeds conflict of interest as the executive arm of government which grants funding is a competitor in elections. In addition, every ruling party in the fourth republic has had the majority in parliament and controls parliament. Therefore, the executive and its majority in parliament can interfere with the activities of the EC by cutting down the EC's budget should the EC disagree to proposals from the government. In the same vein, it breeds agitation and mistrust from the opposition as the belief that the group of people who provide and oversee the EC's funds cannot compete fairly without interfering in the elections.

---

[61] Article 45 of the 1992 Constitution of Ghana.

[62] Article 52 of the 1992 Constitution of Ghana.

[63] Article 53 of the 1992 Constitution of Ghana.

[64] EC, "Online Recruitment System" (2016), www.ec.gov.gh/.../115-recruitment-temporary-election-officials.html.

[65] Electoral Institute for Sustainable Democracy in Africa, "Ghana: Electoral Commission of Ghana" (2012), para. 7, accessed October 22, 2016, https://www.eisa.org.za/wep/gha3.htm.

[66] The consolidated fund is one of the public funds of Ghana as provided for under article 175 and 176 of the 1992 Constitution of Ghana. Funds in the Consolidated Fund include revenues and monies received on behalf of the government.

4.2   The Democracy Enhancing Qualities of the Electoral Commission of Ghana

Independence

The EC is operated under the Independent Model.[67] Citizens largely recognize its autonomy and believe the government or interested parties do not interfere or manipulate it.[68] This was expressed in a survey where respondents confirmed their satisfaction with its independence based on previous elections conducted.[69] The satisfaction and recognition given to the EC stems from the fact that its independence is constitutionally guaranteed.[70] In shielding it from government or external influence, the constitution and other legislations provide for its autonomy regarding finances and institutional operations.[71] Even though Commissioners are appointed by the President, checks and balance sexist to ensure unbiased and impartial processes that disallow party affiliation.[72] The experience of the candidate and investigations into his or her background are also considered.

Despite the general perception of impartiality of the EC, the legislative framework which entrusts the appointment of the commissioners in the president and his selected Council of State raises questions around the potential for partiality. For instance, President John Mahama appointed Ms Charlotte Osei as the Electoral Commissioner.[73] Although, Osei supervised the 2016 elections in which the incumbent president lost, the opposition alleged her involvement with the defeated

---

[67] Shola Omotola, "The Electoral Commission of Ghana and the Administration of the 2012 Elections," *Journal of African Elections* 2 (2014): 12, 37.

[68] Omotola, "Electoral Commission of Ghana and the Administration of the 2012 Elections," 36.

[69] Ernest Adu-Gyamfi, "Assessment of Citizens Perception on the Independence of the Electoral Commission of Ghana," in *Public Policy and Administration Research* 4 (2014): 67.

[70] Article 46 of the 1992 Constitution of Ghana.

[71] Articles 44, 46, 51, 53, 54 of the 1992 Constitution of Ghana.

[72] The current chairperson's diverse experiences such as proven civil servant who headed the NCCE, a company lawyer for Unibank Ghana LTD, lectured at the University of Ghana and advisory board member for the Ministry of Gender, Children and Social Protection but her political affiliation is also questionable.

[73] Government of Ghana, "Charlotte Osei Appointed New EC Chairperson," June 2015, http://www.ghana.gov.gh/index.php/news/1523-charlotte-osei-appointed-new-ec-chairperson.

government.[74] Following allegations of procurement irregularities and conflict between her and her deputies, the current president removed her from office and appointed Ms. Jeanne Mensah as the current Electoral Commissioner, fueling further accusations partiality from the current opposition.[75]

Commissioners must be selected or elected through a competitive merit-based process involving other independent bodies such as national human rights institutions, civil society organizations and parliament are involved. Namibia's selection of commissioners is a shining example for Ghana to follow. Applications are received from the general public with specific criteria to be met for selection. The selected number is interviewed publicly by a selected committee of experts from various institutions and the public. The committee selects a number which finally goes to the president for final appointment with at least two women.[76]

Commissioners' conditions of service are equivalent to that of higher court justices for financial security.[77] Recruiting temporary and permanent staff as well as drafting essential legislative instruments for regulating electoral processes are all under the ambit of the EC.[78] Their independence is further proven by their function of setting dates for elections and determining the modality for results' declaration.

Additionally, the creation of the Inter-Party Advisory Committee (IPAC) is another way the EC promotes its democratic quality of impartiality as it gives an equal platform to all political parties to table their concerns for redress.[79] The IPAC comprises of the EC and all political

---

[74]Citifmonline, "NDC Appointed Charlotte Osei to Rig Elections-Martin Amidu," August 2017, http://citifmonline.com/2017/08/07/ndc-appointed-charlotte-osei-to-rig-election-martin-amidu/.

[75]Government of Ghana, "New EC Chairperson, Two Deputies and Executive Member Sworn into Office," August 2018, http://www.ghana.gov.gh/index.php/news/4900-new-ec-chairperson-two-deputies-and-executive-member-sworn-into-office.

[76]Sections 5, 6, 7 and 8 of the Namibian Electoral Act 5, 2014; This was informed by cases such as *Rally for Democracy and Progress and Others v Electoral Commission of Namibia and Others* 2011 (12) SA NASC 21; *Maletsky v The Electoral Commission of Namibia* 2014 (326) NAHCMD 365.

[77]Article 44 of the 1992 Constitution of Ghana.

[78]Articles 51 and 53 of the 1992 Constitution of Ghana.

[79]IPAC is a platform for dialogues between the registered political parties and the EC.

parties. It was created as a link or platform for bridging the gap between the EC and contesting political parties. Although, IPACs decisions are not binding, it has given room for political parties to interact with the EC and other parties toward consensus building and amicable solutions to disagreements. It also allows the EC to share with the parties, information which hitherto, they were not privy to.

Impartiality
The EC has democratically given equal platforms to political parties. Although, two parties always find themselves in the front seat of elections, the minor parties are not left out. Contesting parties are given copies of the voters register,[80] with their party agents granted access to polling stations and results.[81] In registering candidates, the commission has demonstrated fairness by emphasizing the registration rules and accordingly disqualifying candidates that do not meet the requirements.[82] However, the disqualified parties in the 2016 elections raised concerns about partiality toward the two main parties indicating that the conditions that were used to disqualify some parties were not applied to the two main parties.[83]

As an independent commission, the EC in announcing results, has been firm and stood its grounds without partiality. Announcing the defeat of incumbent parties in 2000, 2008 and 2016 are examples that show the impartiality of the EC.[84] The 2012 election is another

[80] EC, "Voters Exhibition," *Electoral Commission of Ghana* (2012), www.ec.gov.gh/register/check-your-registration.html.

[81] African Union Commission, "Report of the African Union Elections Observation Mission to the 7 December 2012 General Election in the Republic of Ghana" (2012), 19.

[82] African Union Commission, "Reports of the African Union Election Observation" (2012).

[83] PPP, "Press Statement Issued by the Progressive Peoples Party at a Press Conference Organized to Address Matters Relating to the Alleged Disqualification of Dr. Papa Kwesi Nduom by the EC of Ghana," accessed October 24, 2016, http://pppghana.org/index.php/2016/10/14/press-statement-issued-by-the-progressive-peoples-party-at-a-press-conference-organised-to-address-matters-relating-to-the-alleged-disqualification-of-dr-papa-kwesi-nduom-by-the-electoral/.

[84] The fair and firmness with which the chairperson declared the 2000 and 2008 elections were unprecedented. At a time where there had never been constitutional change of government in the fourth Republic, it proved its impartiality and fairness in announcing results.

exemplary show of fairness from the commission. Due to tensions surrounding the elections, many perceived that it would follow the trend of its neighboring countries which were in turmoil. However, the chairperson took control of the situation and declared the election results in a timely manner, with figures presented being in line with what the media, CSOs and observers were reporting, thereby maintaining its credibility.

Transparency
Transparency is one of the hallmarks of the EC. After being accused of not running a transparent process in the 1992 elections, it put in place measures that have ensured transparency. The EC involves political parties in the printing of ballot papers, allow agents of parties to observe and report on the registration of voters and polls.[85] There are portions for party agents to sign and confirm the polls and its processes.[86] The parties are also given copies of the voters register to know the details of the register.

After the introduction of the Biometric Voters' Registration (BVR) system, the EC was lauded by stakeholders, observers and citizens. The African Union Election Observation Mission (AUEOM) commended the EC on how participatory and inclusive the registration exercise was conducted.[87] In procuring the devices, the EC, in line with the rules of procurement, advertised for bidding from interested companies.[88] In examining companies, results were handed to the Procurement Board for confirmation of choice as an accountability and transparency measure.[89] In a further show of transparency, the political parties after partaking in assessing and experimenting samples, they also observed the registration process.[90]

---

[85] Gyimah-Boadi, *Modeling Success* (2007), 15.

[86] Ibid.

[87] African Union, "Report of the AUEOM to the 7 December 2012 General Election in the Republic of Ghana" (2012), 19.

[88] African Union, "Report of the AUEOM to the 7 December 2012 General Election in the Republic of Ghana" (2012), 11.

[89] African Union, "Report of the African Union Elections Observation Mission to the 7 December 2012 General Election in the Republic of Ghana" (2012), 11.

[90] African Union, "Report of the AUEOM to the 7 December 2012 General Election in the Republic of Ghana" (2012), 12.

Professionalism

Noting its independence, the EC has since 1993 conducted its activities in a very professional manner. Its professional reputation has been enshrined in its activities such as candidates and voters registration, voting activities, declaring electoral results and making itself available for settling court cases.[91] Its autonomy and manner of conducting elections could be argued as the reason why opposition parties accept its declarations of results. The commission's staff are also known to be committed to their tasks with set out rules and regulations for the conduct of their activities.[92] However, professionalism on the part of the temporal staff is sometimes brought into question. Instances such as unsigned declaration forms and unindicated polling stations on declaration sheets are some of the reasons the EC was dragged to court in 2013.[93]

4.3   *The Democracy Enhancing Roles Played by the Electoral Commission of Ghana*

Electoral Reforms

The EC can formulate regulations to enhance the performance of its functions. This is done through Constitutional Instruments (CI) for their mandated activities.[94] This paper argues that the independence enjoyed by the EC is grounded in the CIs which build mechanisms for conducting trustworthy elections. For example, at the period the EC established the necessity for reforming the electoral process, it drew the Public Elections (Registration of Voters) Regulation, 1995 (CI 12) for defining the basis for the registration of the 1996 electorates.[95]

---

[91] Darsheenee Raumnauth and Roopanand Mahadew, "A Comparative Analysis of Multi-Party Politics in Ghana and Mauritius," in *Ghana @ 60: Governance and Human Rights in Twenty First Century Africa*, ed. Michael Addaney and Michale Gyan Nyarko (Pretoria: Pretoria University Law Press, 2017).

[92] African Union, "Report of the AUEOM to the 7 December 2012 General Election in the Republic of Ghana" (2012), 12.

[93] The 2013 election petition will forever stand out as the forum which brought out minor short falls of the commission's work which is always observed as 'generally free and fair'. The extent of generally free and fair always cover these shortfalls which could heavily and negatively taint the commission's work.

[94] Article 55 of the 1992 Constitution of Ghana.

[95] Gyimah-Boadi, *Modeling Success* (2007), 16.

Before the 2012 elections, it was reformed into CI 72.[96] In addition, it designed guidelines for conducting the 1996 elections by drafting the Public Elections Regulations, 1995 (CI 15) now reformed to CI 75.[97]

Further, after the 2013 Supreme Court hearing, the EC requested for electoral reform proposals from all political parties and CSOs to be considered for reforms.[98] The EC then announced 27 reforms it had undertaken in a bid to meet the recommendations of the Supreme Court.[99] These include mounting large screens in communities for projecting results for people to see and understand the transparency of the electoral process, logistic improvements and training activities for staff.[100] The abovementioned reforms are voices of the electorates representing democracy and good governance. Nevertheless, no record exists evidencing communication from the EC to the general public on the steps taken toward implementing the reforms. The EC should have sorted to IPAC in communicating with stakeholders of the election on how these reforms will be implemented. In addition, the EC should have coordinated with the NCCE and other civil societies with election mandates to inform and educate the general public on plans they have put in place to implement these reforms.

As the discussion above denotes, the EC announced about 27 reforms for improving Ghana's democracy. These reforms stood to democratically address the shortfalls of previous electoral exercises and also presented the best practices for enhancing future democratic elections. However, the timing between the electoral reforms and elections should be critically looked at. This chapter found that the promulgation of CI 75 was in September 2012, three months before the general elections, when the usual political atmosphere of rivalry and suspicion was tense. If electoral reforms are done within two or three months before elections, it does not allow enough time for parties, stakeholders and the general

---

[96] T. Dowetin, "Ghana: The Role of EMB in Electoral Reform," para. 4, http://aceproject.org/ace-en/topics/lf/lfc/ghana-the-role-of-the-emb-in-electoral-reform.

[97] Gyimah-Boadi, *Modeling Success* (2007), 16.

[98] AU (n. 78 above) 12.

[99] Electoral Commission of Ghana, "EC Implements 27 Reforms for Better Elections," *Electoral Commission of Ghana* (2016), http://www.ec.gov.gh/medias/news/89-ec-implements-27-reforms-for-better-elections.html.

[100] EC, "EC Implements 27 Reforms for Better Elections" (2016).

public to familiarize themselves with new laws and could be one of the reasons for these minor mistakes.

The Conduct of Elections

With the mandate of conducting elections, the EC is tasked with the duty to register eligible voters and periodically maintain the voters' register. Constitutionally, every eligible Ghanaian has the right to be registered and to vote.[101] The EC progressively registered eligible voters. In the 1992, 1996, 2000, 2008, 2012 and 2016 elections, the EC either created a new register or periodically opened registration for eligible voters to partake in the electoral process.[102] Details of who is eligible to vote, demarcated areas for registration, complaint mechanisms on registration, objections and claims as well as offenses relating to the registration process are provided for.[103] For progress, sustainability and a clean register, between 4 March and 5 May 2012, the Biometric Voters Registration (BVR) was introduced for the 2012 elections, ensuring a decrease in associated problems, importantly multiple registrations which had persisted with the manual register.[104] Through this process, the EC, within its mandate ensured a clean compilation of a new voters register.

The EC has also been very firm with the registration of candidates in accordance with the Political Parties Laws Act 574 of 2000 and the CI 94. Based on these instruments, some candidates were rejected in the 2012 election on breaching regulations such as regulation 7(4) of CI 94 and regulation 7(2)(b) of CI 94.[105] In registering for the 2016 elections, 13 candidates were rejected based on the same instrument for failing to meet the requirements of the provisions.[106] Although the EC raised

---

[101] Article 42 of the 1992 Constitution of Ghana.

[102] Creating a new register is one of the key aspects that enhance the democratic elections. From the creation of a register to the following election, some people may have passed on, younger ones may have attained 18 and others, migration playing a part. The BVR machine in 2012 helped in this regard as it decreased such problems.

[103] The necessities, details and processes of registration are further provided for in the Regulations and Registration of Voters Regulations of 1995.

[104] African Union Commission, "AUEOM Report," 13.

[105] The NDP candidate Mrs. Rawlings was rejected on the grounds of breaching some of the provisions of the Political Parties Act 574 of 2000.

[106] GBN, "EC Gives Reasons for Disqualifying Candidates for 2016 Elections," *Ghana Business News* (2016), https://www.ghanabusinessnews.com/2016/10/11/ec-gives-reasons-for-disqualifying-candidates-for-2016-elections/.

legitimate points for rejecting the candidates, the EC failed to apply the same instruments to the two main parties. For instance, the 1992 Constitution and the Political Parties Law Act 574 of 2000 calls for declaration of assets before a candidate is registered. However, besides Dr. Papa Kwasi Nduom of the PPP,[107] no record exists of any candidate declaring his or her assets or source of party funding. The EC rather focused on clerical errors to sideline the minor political parties. The EC as an autonomous body with higher integrity is expected to apply the laws fairly to all the political parties but failed to apply the provisions of the law.

Women's Political Participation

For a country to develop as it should it does not only need adequate use of its mineral resources but also needs to harness this human resources. A higher percentage of Ghana's population (51.2%)[108] are women implying without women's involvement in 'public dialogues or in the decision making process', the achievement of sustainable development and good governance will be more challenging.

The Constitution bars discrimination against anyone based on gender or sex and provides for gender equality.[109] In addition, the international, regional and subregional instruments ratified by the country, such as Convention on the Elimination of All Forms of Discrimination Against Women (CEDAW), the Beijing Platform for Action (BPfA), The African Charter on Human and Peoples Rights,[110] the Protocol to the African Charter on Human and Peoples Rights on the Rights of Women in Africa (Maputo Protocol),[111] among others, underscores the government's willingness to ensure gender equality in the country.[112]

---

[107] GNA Politics, "Nduom Declares Assets Campaign Funds Deepens Frontiers of Transparency," Ghana News Agency (2018), http://www.Ghananewsagency.org/politics/nduom-declares-assets-campaignfunds-deepens frontiers-of-transparency-53401.

[108] Ghana Statistical Service, "2010 Population and Housing Report" (2013), xi.

[109] The 10% women representation in parliament is woeful. It falls far behind the expected MDG expectation of 30% minimum women representatives in Parliament.

[110] Article 2 of the African Charter.

[111] Article 9(1 and 2) of the Maputo Protocol.

[112] Ratifying such instruments is a clear intent of upholding right and freedom enshrined in that instrument. However, ratifying is one thing whereas grounds implementation is another.

However, the situation on ground is not encouraging. Although, five of the seven commissioners, including the chairperson, are women, the 2016 elections recorded 35 women (12.75%) of the 275 seat parliament, a minimal rise from the 10.7% and 10.1% recorded from the 2008 and 2012 elections, respectively.[113] Since independence, only one woman has contested for presidency in the country, which happened in the 2016 elections.

The Constitution further provides for equal participation in the process of decision making at all levels.[114] Nevertheless, the situation is the same at the local assembly level. 7% of people elected into local assemblies during the 2015 elections were women, representing a fall from 10.10% in the previous election.[115] This is as a result of the EC not having clear affirmative action plans in place to promote gender equality. As a democratic enhancing institution with the power to make legal and other reforms, the EC is perfectly placed to help harness the highly untapped human resource from women for democratic involvement. The commission can advocate for quota systems from the parties and can also front constitutional and electoral reforms for quota system for women. Kenya provides an example. Although, majority of Senate seats (47) are filled through universal election where both females and males compete, 16 seats are reserved for women whose nomination comes from political parties on the basis of the parties percentage of elected representatives in the Senate and from an entirely female party list presented to Kenya's Electoral Commission, within 45 days before the election day.[116] An additional two (2) women to be members of the Senate are nominated by the contesting parties on the basis of proportional representation to represent PWDs and the youth.[117]

---

[113]UNDP, "Consolidating Representation and Participation in Ghana: 2015–2016 Work Plan" (2015), 5.

[114]The two women who were disqualified in the 2012 elections have again been disqualified in the 2016 elections and are currently seeking redress in court to contest.

[115]EC, "Research and Monitoring the 2012 Elections" (2014).

[116]Article 98(1)(b) of the Constitution of Kenya 2010; section 35 of the Election Act 24.

[117]Articles 98(1)(c) and (d) of the Constitution of Kenya 2010.

The Involvement of Civil Society Organizations
International and local CSOs, Community Based Organizations (CBO) and Faith Based Organizations (FBO) have been very fundamental in Ghanaian Elections. From funding the EC, offering trainings to staff of the EC to training other NGOs for elections, these organizations promote the quality of the elections thereby enhancing the EC's democratic role. They have served as an observatory mechanism for the EC in training, financing and disseminating information to the general public. They also coordinate outreach programs to areas where the media is not able to reach and sensitize voters on the electoral process.[118] CBOs and FBOs have closer contact with electorates as they are based in communities. Through trainings, CSOs supported the Commission to register over 14 million voters in 2012.[119] CSOs also have seats at IPAC meetings as observers to monitor democratic dialogues. Coffey International trained over 650 workers of the EC on the use of the biometric device.[120] The EC is aware of how democratically influential CSOs are and has kept them close in its activities.

Election Observation
Election observation is one of the main areas that has promoted Ghana's democracy. These have been from intergovernmental organizations as well as other international and local CSOs. The Coalition of Domestic Election Observers (CODEO)[121] helps organize CSOs in the country for electoral observation. Of the 138 electoral constituencies, CODEO has positioned representatives in 134 of the constituents who periodically report on the EC's activities.[122] They are also represented at IPAC meetings. Further, international bodies such as the ECOWAS Observer Mission under the leadership of General Obasanjo, the African Union observer Mission, the European Union, the Commonwealth

---

[118] African Union Commission, "AUEOM to 2012 Elections, Ghana" (2012), 12.

[119] Ibid.

[120] Coffey is an NGO that collaborates with governments and governance institutions for the improvement of governance focused challenges.

[121] CODEO is a platform for domestic election observers with the aim of enhancing electoral credibility, preventing electoral fraud and advancing free and fair elections.

[122] CODEO, "CODEOs Pre-election Environment Observation Statement—September" (2016), para. 1.

Observatory Mission and the Carter Center Observation mission[123] have all been invited by the commission to observe Ghana's elections. Election observers and the media serve as a mirror that reflects the electoral process to the electorate. In partnering and inviting Election Observation Missions (EOMs), the EC has stood to reinforce the respect of basic freedoms and political rights. Comprehensively, it has also enhanced the broad assessment of the process of elections, boosted the confidence of electorates in the electoral process and provided international instruments which include dissuasion from electoral fraud, as well as contributing to conflict resolution and prevention.[124]

The political parties also observe the proceedings of the voting process on the voting day through party agents. These agents are expected to observe proceedings and report to their political parties. The difference between the political parties' agents and the organizations who observe is that the party agents are given closer access to the start of the day and end of day proceedings. They also have to sign the results sheet (pink sheet) after the announcement of the votes cast. Although, party agents are relatively closer to the ECs activities during the voting process, many things happen on their blind side which turn out to be the reason for electoral disputes. Some parties present half-baked agents and representatives whereas observers as their name implies should stand afar, observe and report impartially on what they see. Their presence is seen at the polling stations but they often fail to detect many mistakes made by the staff of the EC.

This finding, among others, affected the credibility of the EC. Interestingly, a 2014 survey conducted by Governance and Peace Polls (GaP) discovered that only 57% of the population, a slender majority, still trust the ECs electoral process.[125] The poor management of the voters register, the low quality of temporal staff and inadequacy in communicating with electoral stakeholders played a major role in this. The EC must reflect on its electoral mandate and improve on them as they are key to improving democracy in the country.

---

[123] All Africa, "West Africa: Obasanjo Leads ECOWAS Observer Mission for Ghana's Elections" (2016), http://allafrica.com/stories/201211300632.html.

[124] EU, *Handbook for European Union Election Observation* (Luxembourg: Publication Office of the European Union, 2016), 16.

[125] UNDP, "Governance and Peace Polls in Ghana" (2014), www.gh.undp.org/.../ UNDP_GH_GAP%20Poll%20Findings-Final%20R.

5 Conclusion and Recommendations

This chapter has highlighted the importance and integral position of EMBs in promoting democracy in Africa. The discussion established that although EMBs do not equate to democracy, elections are at the core of democracy and democratic governance. The quality of democracy practiced can be assessed with the elections the country hold. The EC has been ushered with praises for successfully conducting seven (7) uninterrupted elections with only the 2012 election results being contested at the Supreme Court of Ghana. It has positively worked with international and local civil societies and Election Observers alike. However, upon being assessed against the democracy enhancing qualities of EMBs as postulated by International Institute for Democracy and Electoral Assistance, such as independence, impartiality, integrity, transparency, service mindedness, and professionalism as well as democracy enhancing roles such as electoral reforms, the conduct of elections, women's political participation, involvement of civil societies, and election observations, it was evident that the Commission can do more than conducting elections and delivering a president of choice for Ghanaians. Appointment of Commissioners makes the impartiality tag of the Commission questionable. The quality of the short term staff the Commission employs during election periods also throws the Commission's service mindedness and professionalism tag in the balance.

The Commission again has not done enough in supporting and pushing women into political and decision-making organs of the country considering the strategic position the Commission finds itself. Although it can boast of five of its seven Commissioners being women, they are political appointments from the Executive. Therefore, the Commission can do more than it has done in promoting gender equality in Ghana. The Commission has failed to apply the electoral laws fairly to all contesting political parties in most of the elections it conducted. In light of the above, this chapter recommends the following:

Firstly, the ECs legal and structural reforms must not be embarked on close to the election period when stakes and tensions are very high. This does not give room for deliberations to build enough consensuses between stakeholders and the EC. Considering the complexities of elections, enough time is needed for familiarizing with machines and process for elections and as such the time frame should be considered.

Failure to properly operate these devices can disenfranchise electorates. For such reasons, the EC must have comprehensive plans for electoral reforms and its implementations in a timely manner.

Secondly, there should be changes in the process of choosing Commissioners. The Commissioners being appointed by presidents subsequent to consulting his selected council breeds partiality concerns. Selection must therefore be open to the general public and handled by a selected competent committee with public scrutiny as practiced in countries such as Namibia.

Thirdly, there should be an affirmative action for bridging the gender gap. The EC has had several law reforms but has never considered provisions for improving women's political participation. As a body for selecting people to fill positions, an electoral law binding the state and political parties to be gender-sensitive will serve as a good platform for improving gender equality. The EC must use platforms such as IPAC for engaging with political parties on women's involvement in politics. This does not auger well for a highly acclaimed democratic country such as Ghana to have had only one woman presidential aspirant. The EC can therefore make use of such platforms to promote gender balance.

Further, the EC in collaboration with the NCCE has to also set up gender balance activities. The NCCE as an information tool informs the general public on electoral reforms and electoral processes. The NCCE is therefore in a position to reach the general public. In this regard the EC can use them as a medium to reach the general public on the importance of involving the higher percentage of Ghana's population (women) in the political discourse.

Finally, in hiring temporal staff to support the ECs work, stringent measures must be put in place to hire quality personnel. The EC should be aware that electoral rights are human rights and so administrative and other errors by staff could disenfranchise electorates and violate their right to participate in governance. For such reasons hiring competent staff should be a priority. The EC must put in place necessary measures for the hiring of competent temporary staff.

REFERENCES

LIST OF LAWS

International Law
African Charter on Human and Peoples' Rights
Beijing Platform for Action
Convention on the Elimination of All forms of Discrimination Against Women
International Covenant on Civil and Political Rights
Protocol to the African Charter on Human and Peoples Rights on the Rights of Women in Africa
The UNDP Policy Paper for EMBs in the Promotion of Gender Equality and Women's Participation
United Nations Declaration on the Principles of International Election Observation and Code of Conduct for International Election Observation

Constitution
The Constitution of the Republic of Ghana, 1992
The Constitution of the Republic of Kenya, 2010

Ghanaian Legislation
Electoral Commissions Act 451, 1993
Political Parties Law Act 574, 2000
Public Elections Regulation of 1999

Other Legislation
The Namibian Electoral Act 5, 20014

List of Cases
Maletsky v The Electoral Commission of Namibia 2014 (326) NAHCMD 365
Rally for Democracy and Progress and Others v Electoral Commission of Namibia and Others 2011 (12) SA NASC 21

BIBLIOGRAPHY

Books
Das, Ravindra. *Adopting Biometric Technology: Challenges and Solutions.* Boca Raton, US: CRC Press, 2016.
Dundas, Carl W. *Close Elections and Political Succession in the African Union.* Bloomington, USA: Author House, 2012.
Dundas, Carl W. *Electoral Essays and Discourses.* Bloomington, UK: Author House, 2014.
Dundas, Carl W. *The Lag of 21st Century Democratic Elections: In Africa Union Member States.* Bloomington, USA: Author House, 2011.

European Union. *Handbook for European Union Election Observation.* Brussels, Belgium: Publication Office of the European Union, 2016.

Ilo, Stan Chu. *The Face of Africa: Looking Beyond the Shadows.* Eugene, OR, US: Author House, 2006.

International IDEA. *Electoral Law Reforms in Africa: Insight into the Role of EMBs and Approaches to Engagement.* Stockholm, Sweden: Bulls Graphic, 2014.

LeDuc, Lawrence, et al. *Comparing Democracies 3: Election and Voting in the 21st Century.* London, UK: Sage, 2010.

Ndletyana, Mcebisi. *Institutionalizing Democracy: The Story of the Electoral Commission of South Africa 1993–2014.* Pretoria, South Africa: Africa Institute of South Africa, 2015.

Nohlen, Dieter, et al. *Elections in Africa: A Data Handbook.* New York, US: Oxford University Press, 1999.

Norris, Pippa. *Why Elections Fail.* New York, US: Cambridge University Press, 2015.

UNDP, and UN Women. *Inclusive Electoral Process: A Guide for Electoral Management Bodies on Promoting Gender Equality and Women's Participation.* UN: UNDP and UN Women, 2015.

Chapter of Books

Aubynn, Anthony Kwesi. "Behind the Transparent Ballot Box: The Significance of the 1990s Elections." In *Multi-Party Elections in Africa*, edited by Michael Cowen and Lisa Laakso. New York, US: Palgrave, 2012.

Keating, Michael. "Can Democratization Undermine Democracy? Economic and Political Reform in Uganda?" In *Democratization in Africa: Challenges and Prospects*, edited by Gordon Crowford and Gabrielle Lynch. New York, USA: Routledge, 2012.

Olaniyi, Johnson. "Enhancing Democracy and Surmounting the Challenges of Election Management in Africa: Insights from Nigeria." In *Myths of Peace and Democracy? Towards Building Pillars of Hope, Unity and Transformation in Africa*, edited by Munyaradzi Mawere and Ngonidzashe Marongwe, 123–166. Bamenda, Cameroon: African Books Collective, 2016.

Raumnauth, Darsheenee, and Roopanand Mahadew. "A Comparative Analysis of Multi-Party Politics in Ghana and Mauritius." In *Ghana @ 60: Governance and Human Rights in Twenty First Century Africa*, edited by Michael Addaney and Michael Gyan Nyarko, 172–190. Pretoria, South Africa: Pretoria University Law Press, 2017.

Sefah, Bright Joe, and Kennedy Kariseb. "Women's Political Participation in Decision Making Processes and Organs: Trends, Practices and Social Realities." In *Ghana @ 60: Governance and Human Rights in Twenty First Century Africa*, edited by Michael Addaney and Michael Gyan Nyarko, 101–120. Pretoria, South Africa: Pretoria University Law Press, 2017.

Journal Articles

Mapuva, Jephias. "Elections and Electoral Processes in Africa: A Gimmick or a Curse?" *African Journal of History and Culture* 5, no. 5 (2013): 92.

Omotola, Shola. "The Electoral Commission of Ghana and the Administration of the 2012 Elections." *Journal of African Elections* 2 (2014): 12–55.

Tostensen, Arne. "Elections Observation as an Informal Means of Enforcing Political Rights." *Nordsk Tidsskrift for Menneskerettigheter* 22 (2004): 330–344.

Articles

Dowetin, T. "Ghana: The Role of EMB in Electoral Reform." Para. 4. http://aceproject.org/ace-en/topics/lf/lfc/ghana-the-role-of the-emb-in-electoral-reform.

EC. "Research and Monitoring the 2012 Elections" (2014).

International IDEA. "Electoral Management Design" (2014).

Lasham, Charles. "Transparency and Impartiality of the Electoral Administration on Election Day: The Importance of the Management of the Elections and the Role of the Electoral Administrator" (2005).

UNDP. "Consolidating Representation and Participation in Ghana: 2015–2016 Work Plan" (2015).

News Articles

All Africa. "West Africa: Obasanjo Leads ECOWAS Observer Mission for Ghana's Elections." Accessed October 25, 2016. http://allafrica.com/stories/201211300632.html.

Alonge, Sede. "'My Wife Belongs to the Kitchen'? President Buhari Isn't Helping Nigeria." *The Guardian*, October 2016. https://www.theguardian.com/commentisfree/2016/oct/17/wife-job-look-after-me-buhari-nigerian-girls.

GBN. "EC Gives Reasons for Disqualifying Candidates for 2016 Elections." Accessed October 25, 2016. https://www.ghanabusinessnews.com/2016/10/11/ec-gives-reasons-for-disqualifying-candidates-for-2016-elections/.

GNA Politics. "Nduom Declares Assets Campaign Funds Deepens Frontiers of Transparency." Ghana News Agency (2018). http://www.Ghananewsagency.org/politics/nduom-declares-assets-campaignfunds-deepens-frontiers-of-transparency-53401.

Thesis

Amedeker, Alfred. "An Assessment of Ghana's Democratic Consolidation Since 1992 and the Implications for International Relations." MA dissertation, University of Ghana, 2013.

Reports and Policy Briefing

African Union Commission. "Report of the African Union Elections Observation Mission to the 7 December 2012 General Election in the Republic of Ghana" (2012).

Citifmonline. "NDC Appointed Charlotte Osei to Rig Elections-Martin Amidu." August 2017. http://citifmonline.com/2017/08/07/ndc-appointed-charlotte-osei-to-rig-election-martin-amidu/.

CODEO. "CODEO's Pre-election Environment Observation Statement—September" (2016).

Electoral Institute for Sustainable Democracy in Africa. "Ghana: Electoral Commission of Ghana" (2012). Para 7. https://www.eisa.org.za/wep/gha3.htm.

Ghana Statistical Service. "2010 Population and Housing Report" (2013).

Government of Ghana. "Charlotte Osei Appointed New EC Chairperson." June 2015. http://www.ghana.gov.gh/index.php/news/1523-charlotte-osei-appointed-new-ec-chairperson.

Government of Ghana. "New EC Chairperson, Two Deputies and Executive Member Sworn into Office." August 2018. http://www.ghana.gov.gh/index.php/news/4900-new-ec-chairperson-two-deputies-and-executive-member-sworn-into-office.

The Economist Intelligence Unit's Democracy Index 2015. "Democracy in an Age of Anxiety" (2016), 1.

UN Economic Commission for Africa. "African Governance Report III: Elections and the Management of Diversity" (2013).

Websites

Cincotta, E. "What Is Democracy" (1998). Para. 1. http://www.ait.tw/infousa/zhtw/DOCS/whatsdem/homepage.htm.

EC. "EC Implements 27 Reforms for Better Elections." http://www.ec.gov.gh/medias/news/89-ec-implements-27-reforms-for-better-elections.html.

EC. "Online Recruitment System" (2016). www.ec.gov.gh/…/115-recruitment-temporary-election-officials.html.

EC. "Voters Exhibition." October 2012. www.ec.gov.gh/register/check-your-registration.html.

Mohammed, Omar. "The Six African Elections to Watch Out for in 2016" (2016). Para. 5. http://qz.com/585357/the-six-africans-elections-to-watch-out-for-in-2016-and-why/.

PPP. "Press Statement Issued by the Progressive Peoples Party at a Press Conference Organized to Address Matters Relating to the Alleged Disqualification of Dr. Papa Kwesi Nduom by the EC of Ghana" (2016). http://pppghana.org/index.php/2016/10/14/press-statement-issued-by-the-progressive-peoples-party-at-a-press-conference-organised-to-address-matters-relating-to-the-alleged-disqualification-of-dr-papa-kwesi-nduom-by-the-electoral/.

UNDP. "Governance and Peace Polls in Ghana" (2014). www.gh.undp.org/…/UNDP_GH_GAP%20Poll%20Findings-Final%20R.

PART IV

Emerging Challenges in Governance and Human Rights In Africa

Balancing National Security and Human Rights in the Fight Against Boko Haram in Nigeria

Chairman Okoloise

1 INTRODUCTION

The tendency to use security as a pretext for justifying the extreme responses of states to perceived existential threats often raises questions about states' commitment to national and international human rights norms and values.[1] Even before the 11 September 2001 bombing of the twin towers of the World Trade Centre and the Pentagon in the United States, state security has long been a "sexy" phrase used by governments to "reconstitute" human rights,[2] and evade accountability for human

[1] Martin Scheinin and Mathias Vermeulen, "Unilateral Exceptions to International Law: Systematic Legal Analysis and Critique of Doctrines That Seek to Deny or Reduce the Applicability of Human Rights Norms in the Fight Against Terrorism." *Essex Human Rights Review* 8, no. 1 (2011): 20.

[2] Andrew Ashworth, "Security, Terrorism and the Value of Human Rights," in *Security and Human Rights*, ed. Benjamin J. Goold and Liora Lazarus (Oxford: Hart Publishing, 2007), 203, 209 ("governments make great play of the extra security allegedly provided by

C. Okoloise (✉)
University of Pretoria, Pretoria, South Africa

© The Author(s) 2020
M. Addaney et al. (eds.), *Governance, Human Rights, and Political Transformation in Africa*,
https://doi.org/10.1007/978-3-030-27049-0_12

309

rights violations committed during counter-terrorism operations. The inclination to prioritise security over fundamental human rights creates potential conflict between state and citizen, on the one hand, and security and human rights, on the other.

The preference of states for administering security over human rights frequently stokes concerns about the extent to which suppressing human rights may be reasonably justified. This precipitates the context for striking a delicate balance between the two contending priorities.[3] The dangers of encroaching on human dignity, of invalidating the security of the human person, and of exposing vulnerable individuals to potential abuse bring to the fore pressing questions about the future of human rights in states where counter-terrorism measures are aggressively pursued. Since the value of an end is only as good as the means by which it is achieved, this study makes a conscious assessment of the intrinsic issues that arise whenever state security and human rights are in discourse and their impact on the future of human rights protection.

For the purpose of laying out a vivid context and achieving specificity, the dialectic of state security and human rights is evaluated against the backdrop of the fight against the *Boko Haram* sect (the second deadliest terror group in the world)[4] in Nigeria and its consequences for human rights. By embellishing legal and security perspectives in the analysis, the chapter essentially articulates from the outset that human rights should never be sacrificed on the altar of political, social or legal expediency. Limitations of or derogations from human rights are generally inconsistent with the inherent right to security of the individual. Hence, unilateral

---

new measures, without providing the necessary evidence"); Lucia Zedner, "Seeking Security by Eroding Rights: The Side-Stepping of Due Process," in *Security and Human Rights*, ed. Benjamin J. Gould and Liora Lazarus (Oxford: Hart Publishing, 2007), 257–276; Trevor C.W. Farrow, "Security and Rights," *Review of Constitutional Studies* 10, nos. 1 and 2 (2005): 94; and Philip B. Heymann, "Civil Liberties and Human Rights in the Aftermath of September 11," *Harvard Journal of Law & Public Policy* 25, no. 2 (2002): 441.

[3] Karl Maier, *This House Has Fallen: Nigeria in Crisis* (New York: Basic Books, 2002), 68; Itzhak Zamir, "Human Rights and National Security," *Israeli Law Review* 23, nos. 2 and 3 (1989): 375; and Adda B. Bozeman, "Human Rights and National Security," *Yale Journal of World Public Order* 9, no. 1 (1982): 40, 41.

[4] Andrea Booth, "Nigeria's Boko Haram: Inside the World's Second Deadliest Terrorist Organisation," SBS News, August 24, 2017, accessed February 8, 2018, https://www. sbs.com.au/news/nigeria-s-boko-haram-inside-the-world-s-second-deadliest-terrorist-organisation.

exceptions to human rights on the ground of security must never be of a nature that contravenes the core of a right or completely overshadow a right in such a way as to make it illusory.[5] If at all necessary, restrictions on rights may only be permissible to the extent that they fulfil the solemn aspirations of international human rights standards.

In making this assessment, I have chosen to do so with a doctrinal methodology in mind. While the war against Boko Haram and its impacts on human rights make a compelling case for field visits and the generation of raw data to buttress the impacts of counter-terrorism measures on human rights in Nigeria, time constraints and distance are two immediately scarce and limiting factors. Hence, doctrinal analysis is utilised to not only assess the basis of state violations during counter-insurgency operations, but also to weigh them against the fundamental human interests of society. The research is essentially desk-based and, even though more oriented in the realm of black letter law, it aims nevertheless to justify its outcome on the basis of multidisciplinary perspectives to human rights and security.

2   SECURITY AND HUMAN RIGHTS IN NIGERIA

"Security," as a concept, has no precise definition. According to Anyadike, "security is a situation where a person or thing is not exposed to any form of danger or risk of physical or moral aggression, accident, theft or deterioration."[6] In this context, one can speak of human security, food security, social security or state security. It is a multidimensional and crosscutting concept. As a social phenomenon, it is an elusive objective and as such approached from several perspectives.[7] Since security is a "first order value" worthy of preservation, it is often connected with

---

[5] *Constitutional Rights Project and Others v Nigeria* (2000) AHRLR 227 (ACHPR 1999), para. 42 (where the African Commission on Human and Peoples' Rights held that "a limitation may not erode a right such that the right itself becomes illusory"). Also see *Media Rights Agenda & Others v Nigeria* (2000) AHRLR 200 (ACHPR 1998), para. 70, equally decided by the African Commission.

[6] Nkechi O. Anyadike, "Boko Haram and National Security Challenges in Nigeria: Causes and Solutions," *Journal of Economics and Sustainable Development* 4, no. 5 (2013): 12, 13.

[7] Bozeman, "Human Rights," 2.

the wellbeing of the individual and the survival of the state.[8] Although normatively attractive, "state security" as an idea is an analytically weak concept,[9] associated with an individual, a thing or the general welfare of society. This chapter, therefore, operationalises the concept of security within the context of the Nigerian state hence the notion of "state security" or "national security."

Relatedly, human rights are the entitlements that every individual may claim by virtue of being a human being.[10] Personal liberty and security are important components of the human rights of every individual. For this reason, the state has a duty to guarantee and protect the fundamental freedoms of every person within its territory. In Nigeria, as will be shown shortly, there is often a conflict between the state's obligation to protect human rights and at the same time ensure the security of the general population; thereby raising queries about Nigeria's unilateral exceptions to human rights principles in the war against terror. This section, consequently, evaluates Nigeria's approach to national security and counter-terrorism operations in light of its domestic and international human rights commitments.

2.1   Antecedents of Nigeria's Approach to Security and Counter-Terrorism

A security state, according to Zoglin, exists where there is constant deployment of extraordinary security measures in response to a perceived internal threat to the existence of the state.[11] Going by this definition, it would seem that Nigeria has been in an endless state of perceived internal destabilisation either arising from colonial resistance, ethno-religious clashes, military coups and counter-coups, the 1967–1970 Civil War, militancy in its oil-rich Niger Delta region or terrorism. Following years of security resistance, the Nigerian security apparatus has a history as well

---

[8] As above, 12.

[9] Edward Newman, "A Normatively Attractive but Analytically Weak Concept," *Security Dialogue* 35 (2004): 358.

[10] United for Human Rights, "Human Rights Defined," accessed June 19, 2017, http://www.humanrights.com/what-are-human-rights/.

[11] Kathryn J. Zoglin, "The National Security Doctrine and the State of Siege in Argentina: Human Rights Denied." *Suffolk Transnational Law Journal* 12, no. 2 (1989): 265, 266.

as a heritage of violence and brutalisation.[12] Since the eras of colonialism, military dictatorship and, now, civilian rule, it has hardly shed its skin of oppression. Like Zamir considers about Isreal's default institutional preference for national security over human rights, Nigeria's approach to security is similarly such that prioritises security over all other interests.[13]

For over a decade, Nigeria has been bogged down by the emergence of the deadly terror group, *Jama'atuAhlis Sunna Lidda'awatiwal-Jihad* (popularly known as *Boko Haram*, meaning "Western education is forbidden"). The group was founded in 2003,[14] and has declared its intent to enforce strict adherence to Islamic law in Northern Nigeria.[15] While it is not entirely certain what the core drivers of the group are, it is clear that the group feels disenchanted with Nigeria's trajectory of extreme poverty (especially in the North), large-scale corruption, lack of employment and basic infrastructure. Former United States Ambassador to Nigeria writes that "Boko Haram is a recent manifestation of a decades-long civil war within Islam" and a response to the brutality of the secular state it has rejected.[16]

Government's efforts to address the challenge of insecurity has, unfortunately, been caught between two extremes—one of weak political will or brutal military violence.[17] In a bid to suppress the group, its founder, Ustaz Mohammed Yusuf and dozens of followers, were extra-judicially executed in 2009 by the Nigerian security forces on account of national security.[18] Since then, the terror group has become more murderous and daring in its activities, first targeting officials of the Nigerian Police, the Army and state officials, and subsequently soft targets—churches,

---

[12]Jacob A. Dada, "Impediments to Human Rights Protection in Nigeria," *Annual Survey of International & Comparative Law* 18, no. 1 (2012): 67, 77; Olusegun Fakoya, "Nigeria Police Force—A Legacy of Brutality," last modified August 1, 2008, accessed February 10, 2018, www.nigeriavillagesquare.com/articles/nigeria-police-force-—-a-legacy-of-brutality.html.

[13]Zamir, "Human Rights," 376.

[14]Human Rights Watch, "Spiraling Violence: Boko Haram Attacks and Security Force Abuses in Nigeria," 30, accessed December 17, 2017, https://www.hrw.org/sites/default/files/reports/nigeria1012webwcover_0.pdf.

[15]As above, 10.

[16]John Campbell, "Boko Haram: Origins, Challenges and Responses," *NOREF Policy Brief* (2014): 1.

[17]John Campbell, "U.S. Policy to Counter Nigeria's Boko Haram," *Council of Foreign Relations Report*, no. 70 (November 1, 2014): 16.

[18]Human Rights Watch, "Spiraling Violence," 10.

mosques, political rallies and prisons, as well as perceived critics. On 14 April 2014, it kidnapped 276 school girls in Chibok, Borno State many of whom are yet to be returned to their parents.[19] The group is known to have turned the young among those it has kidnapped into terrorists and married off female victims to its fighters or subjected them to excruciating sexual violence.[20] It is estimated that between 2009 and 2019 no less than 15,000 people have been killed and at least 2.6 million people displaced in Nigeria's North-eastern zone due to the terrorist activities of the group.[21]

[19] Morgan Winsor, "Nigeria Marks 3 Years Since 276 Chibok Schoolgirls Abducted by Boko Haram," ABC News, last modified April 14, 2017, accessed February 10, 2018, http://abcnews.go.com/International/nigeria-marks-years-276-chibok-schoolgirls-abducted-boko/story?id=46774809; Kevin Sieff, "Boko Haram Kidnapped 276 Girls Two Years Ago: What Happened to Them?" *Washington Post*, April 14, 2016, accessed February 10, 2018, https://www.washingtonpost.com/news/worldviews/wp/2016/04/14/boko-haram-kidnapped-276-girls-two-years-ago-what-happened-to-them/?utm_term=.fe68fd4820b5.

[20] Amnesty International, "Nigeria: Deadliest Boko Haram Attack on Rann Leaves at Least 60 People Murdered," February 1, 2019, accessed June 12, 2019, https://www.amnesty.org/en/latest/news/2019/02/nigeria-deadliest-boko-haram-attack-on-rann-leaves-at-least-60-people-murdered/; Brent Swails and David McKenzie, "Kidnapped to Kill: How Boko Haram Is Turning Girls into Weapons," CNN, April 13, 2016, accessed June 12, 2019, https://edition.cnn.com/2016/04/12/africa/cameroon-boko-haram-child-bombers/index.html; Dionne Searcey, "Boko Haram Turns Female Captives into Terrorists," *New York Times*, April 7, 2016, accessed June 12, 2019, https://www.nytimes.com/2016/04/08/world/africa/boko-haram-suicide-bombers.html; and Mia Bloom and Hilary Matfess, "Women as Symbols and Swords in Boko Haram's Terror," *PRISM* 6, no. 1 (March 1, 2016), accessed June 12, 2019, https://cco.ndu.edu/PRISM/PRISM-volume-6-no1/Article/685093/women-as-symbols-and-swords-in-boko-harams-terror/.

[21] Amnesty International, "Nigeria: Satellite Imagery Shows Charred Remains of Rann After Boko Haram Attack," January 18, 2019, accessed June 12, 2019, https://www.amnesty.org/en/latest/news/2019/01/nigeria-satellite-imagery-shows-charred-remains-of-rann-after-boko-haram-attack/; Amnesty International, "'Our Job Is to Shoot, Slaughter and Kill': Boko Haram's Reign of Terror in North-East Nigeria," April 2015, accessed June 12, 2019, https://www.amnesty.org/download/Documents/AFR4413602015ENGLISH.PDF; and Kevin Uhrmacher and Mary B. Sheridan, "The Brutal Toll of Boko Haram's Attacks on Civilians," *Washington Post*, April 3, 2016, accessed December 17, 2017, https://www.washingtonpost.com/graphics/world/nigeria-boko-haram/.

In the quest for upholding state security, human rights abuses are seen as "a necessary outcome for the imperative of the state."[22] In the fight against Boko Haram, Nigeria's security forces are reported to have been involved in countless human rights indignities. Apart from the hundreds of security agents who have lost their lives in the process of restoring national security, several Boko Haram *suspects* and other innocents caught up in the war have also died from the high-handedness of Nigeria's security forces. Since 2011, there have been reports of extrajudicial killings, summary execution, prolonged detention, torture and deadly reprisals by the Nigerian security forces. In 2011, for example, the killing of a Nigerian soldier instigated a lethal retaliation by enraged security forces that resulted in the deaths of 30 civilians and the lynching of 50 homes and shops.[23]

Human Rights Watch reports that not only have the security forces been implicated in serious human rights infractions, "[t]he authorities have also brushed aside due process rights of detainees in the name of ending the group's threat to Nigeria's citizens."[24] It was also reported in 2014 that "uncontrolled reprisals" by Nigerian security agents resulted in the death of hundreds. Amnesty International reports that it had credible evidence that the military extra-judicially executed more than 600 detainees.[25]

[22] Basil Ugochukwu, "The State Security Service and Human Rights in Nigeria," *Third World Legal Studies* 1996 (1996–1997): 71, 86.

[23] Adam Nossiter, "Nigerian Forces Kill Dozens in Night Assault, Fuelling Long Battle with Sect," last modified November 2, 2012, accessed December 17, 2017, www.nytimes.com/2012/11/03/world/africa/nigeria-forces-kill-dozens-in-night-assault.html. Also see Daniel Agbiboa, "The Ongoing Campaign of Terror in Nigeria: Boko Haram Versus the State," *Stability: International Journal of Security and Development* 2, no. 3 (2013): 111–113.

[24] Human Rights Watch, "Spiraling Violence," 58; Daniel E. Agbiboa, "Peace at Daggers Drawn? Boko Haram and the State of Emergency in Nigeria," *Studies In Conflict & Terrorism* 37, no. 1 (2014): 41–67.

[25] Amnesty International, "Nigeria: War Crimes and Crimes Against Humanity as Violence Escalates in North-East," last modified March 31, 2014, accessed December 17, 2017, https://www.amnesty.org/en/latest/news/2014/03/nigeria-war-crimes-and-crimes-against-humanity-violence-escalates-north-east/; British Broadcasting Corporation, "Boko Haram Giwa Barracks Attack: Nigerian Army 'Killed Hundreds,'" last modified March 31, 2014, accessed December 17, 2017, www.bbc.com/news/world-africa-26819965.

Also, in June 2015, the *New York Times* similarly relying on an official report by Amnesty International, reported that[26]

> at least 7,000 people have died in government detention because of brutal conditions, an additional 1,200 have been "extra-judicially executed" by Nigerian security forces, and at least 20,000 have been "arbitrarily arrested" by the authorities.

Apart from its vicious and violent approach to keeping the peace, Nigeria's security agencies have also been criticised for other forms of misconduct—abuse of power, torture, rape, corruption and other irresponsible conducts.[27] In many police stations, torture chambers are alleged to be maintained and it has been reported that in each of such police stations, there is an officer-in-charge of torture.[28] In a report published in 2014, Nigerian detention centres were equated with "hell fire."[29] Human Right Watch reports that dozens of brutal acts of torture have resulted in deaths.[30] There have also been allegations of secret trial

---

[26] Adam Nossiter, "Abuses by Nigeria's Military Found to Be Rampant in War Against Boko Haram," *New York Times*, last modified June 3, 2015, accessed December 17, 2017, https://www.nytimes.com/2015/06/04/world/africa/abuses-nigeria-military-boko-haram-war-report.html. Also see Human Rights Council, "Violations and Abuses Committed by Boko Haram and the Impact on Human Rights in the Countries Affected: Report of the United Nations High Commissioner for Human Rights," UN Doc. A/HRC/30/67, December 9, 2015, accessed January 7, 2019, https://digitallibrary.un.org/record/819031/files/A_HRC_30_67-EN.pdf.

[27] Charles Mwalimu, "Police, State Security Forces and Human Rights in Nigeria and Zambia: Dynamic Perspectives in Comparative Constitutionalism," *Third World Legal Studies* 1990 (1990): 85, 95.

[28] Amnesty International, "Torture, the Way of Life for the Nigerian Security Forces," accessed December 17, 2017, https://www.amnestyusa.org/torture-the-way-of-life-for-the-nigerian-security-forces/; Amnesty International, "Torture, Cruel Inhuman and Degrading Treatment of Detainees by Nigerian Security Forces: Amnesty International's Written Statement to the 25th Session of the UN Human Rights Council (March 3–28, 2014)," 1–3, February 20, 2014, accessed December 17, 2017, https://www.amnesty.org/download/Documents/4000/afr440012014en.pdf.

[29] Amnesty International, *"Welcome to Hell Fire": Torture and Other Ill-Treatment in Nigeria* (London, UK: Amnesty International Publications, 2014), 24.

[30] Human Rights Watch, "'Rest in Pieces': Police Torture and Deaths in Custody in Nigeria," *Human Rights Watch* 10, no. 11A (2005): 1.

of terror suspects and trials *in camera*. In the name of the anti-terrorism war, telecommunications have been shut down, and movement significantly restricted.

Recently, Amnesty International voiced concerns that the military and the paramilitary organisation known as Civilian Joint Task Force have been involved in what may amount to war crimes and crimes against humanity.[31] They have been cited for not just emptying rural villages, separating families and orchestrating forced displacement, but also for committing arbitrary detention, torture and sexual violence against female refugees in safety camps. Amnesty International reports that thousands of refugees in satellite camps have died from hunger and those in need of food are exploited through organised systems of sexual violence, rape and abuses.[32] Besides the arbitrary detention of terror victims, especially women fleeing theatres of violence without their husbands, the relatives of Boko Haram fighters have been subjected to torture, inhuman and degrading treatment or even death in military facilities. These continue to occur without adequate government oversight and accountability.

In 2016, an interagency fact-finding committee set up by the Federal Government to investigate allegations of trafficking and sexual violence in the satellite camps found that there was a "high likelihood" that aid and protection officers took advantage of the vulnerable situation of

[31] Amnesty International, "'They Betrayed Us': Women Who Survived Boko Haram Raped, Starved and Detained in Nigeria" (2018), accessed June 12, 2019, https://www.amnesty.org/download/Documents/AFR4484152018ENGLISH. PDF; Amnesty International, "Nigeria: Boko Haram Killing of Aid Worker Hauwa Liman Is a War Crime," October 16, 2018, accessed June 12, 2019, https://www.amnesty.org/en/latest/news/2018/10/nigeria-boko-haram-killing-of-aid-worker-hauwa-liman-is-a-war-crime/; and International Committee of the Red Cross, "Nigeria: Health Worker Hauwa Mohammed Liman Executed in Captivity," October 16, 2018, accessed June 12, 2019, https://www.icrc.org/en/document/nigeria-health-worker-hauwa-mohammed-liman-executed-captivity.

[32] Amnesty International, "They Took Our Husbands and Forced Us to Be Their Girlfriends: Women in North-East Nigeria Starved and Raped by Those Claiming to Rescue Them," September 2018, accessed June 12, 2019, https://www.amnesty.org/download/Documents/AFR4491222018ENGLISH.PDF; Amnesty International, "Boko Haram Survivors Have Been Starved and Raped by Nigeria's Military," May 24, 2018, accessed June 12, 2019, https://www.amnesty.org/en/latest/news/2018/05/boko-haram-survivors-have-been-starved-and-raped-by-nigerias-military/.

women and girls to seek sexual gratification.[33] However, the report of the committee was not made public and no follow-up mechanisms or actions were taken to prosecute and punish those found culpable or to prevent future occurrence. Moreover, the deployment of female police officers at the instance of the President, although a positive step, has not been an effective measure either against sexual violence and rape in the satellite camps or towards accountability. More so, commitments by Chief of Army Staff to investigate such allegations have not been fulfilled as none of the victims have been invited to testify before any military investigative panel.[34]

The horrifying incidents emanating from the war on terror signal that Nigeria's domestic approach to security is fundamentally faulty in several ways. Firstly, the indignities of Nigeria's security personnel go against the grain of protecting the human dignity of victims brutalised by the violent Boko Haram terrorist group and further worsen the trauma of women and girls who have fallen prey to sexual violence and rape. Considering that the responsibility to restore Nigeria's territorial integrity requires a careful and well-coordinated response to the Boko Haram insurgency, security personnel have a duty to preserve the rights and dignity of those vanquished by violence fomented by terrorists. The failure to protect terror victims, especially women and girls, is a bloat on the image of the Nigerian military and a violation of international law. Second, the lack of an adequate response by the government to the allegations of blatant abuses entrenches a culture of impunity. These necessitate a careful reassessment of Nigeria's human rights and security frameworks in the lights of the high-handedness of its military and paramilitary services in anti-terrorism operations.

2.2   Nigeria's Human Rights Framework

Despite the intrusive and violent history of its security services, Nigeria has a relatively comprehensive human rights framework that firmly affirms the individual's security. In Chapter IV of the Constitution of the Federal Republic of Nigeria 1999 (as amended) ("Constitution"), a Bill

---

[33] Report of fact-finding committee on the allegation of 'rape and child trafficking' in internally displaced persons (IDPs) camps in the North-East of Nigeria, February 2015 cited in Amnesty International, "They Betrayed Us," 61.

[34] Amnesty International, "They Betrayed Us," 61–62.

of Rights is enshrined as "fundamental rights." The Bill of Rights guarantees civil and political rights such as the rights to life, human dignity, fair hearing, privacy, and freedoms of conscience, thought and belief, expression and the press, association and assembly, movement, protection from discrimination and prejudices and property.[35] While these rights are clearly enshrined in the Constitution, they are neither absolute nor non-derogable. They may be lawfully restricted or derogated from within the tenor of the Constitution, especially in times of emergency.

In addition to its constitutional guarantees, Nigeria is also party to international human rights treaties adopted under the auspices of the United Nation (UN).[36] It has ratified the International Covenant on Civil and Political Rights 1966, the Covenant against Torture and Other Cruel, Inhuman or Degrading Treatment 1984,[37] and the Four Geneva Conventions applicable to non-combatants in times of armed conflicts. As a member state of the UN, Nigeria is also obliged to be guided by UN model standards. For example, Standard Minimum Rules for the Treatment of Prisoners 1955, Code of Conduct for Law Enforcement Officials 1979, UN Body of Principles for the Protection of All Persons under Any Form of Detention or Imprisonment 1988 (UN Body of Principles) and Basic Principles on the Use of Force and Firearms by Law Enforcement Officials 1990. Specifically, the UN Body of Principles not only prohibits the torture or cruel, inhuman and degrading treatment of persons under any form of detention or imprisonment, it also categorically provides that "[n]o circumstance whatever may be invoked as a justification for torture or other cruel, inhuman or degrading treatment or punishment."[38]

---

[35] Constitution, §33–44.

[36] Christopher C. Joyner, "The United Nations and Terrorism: Rethinking Legal Tensions Between National Security, Human Rights, and Civil Liberties," *International Studies Perspectives* 5, no. 3 (2004): 240–257.

[37] African Commission on Human and Peoples' Rights, "Ratification Table: United Nations Convention Against Torture and Other Cruel, Inhuman or Degrading Treatment or Punishment," accessed December 17, 2017, http://www.achpr.org/instruments/uncat/ratification/.

[38] UN Body of Principles for the Protection of All Persons under Any Form of Detention or Imprisonment 1988 principles 1 and 6. Also see *Ouko v. Kenya* (2000) AHRLR 135 (ACHPR 2000), para. 23–25; *Huri-Laws v. Nigeria* (2000) AHRLR 273 (ACHPR 2000), para. 40.

At the regional level, Nigeria is also a member of the African Union (AU) and state party to African human rights treaties like the African Charter on Human and Peoples' Rights 1981 (African Charter).[39] To give domestic effect to the Charter, it has adopted the African Charter on Human and Peoples' Rights (Ratification and Enforcement) Act,[40] which essentially domesticates the Charter in its entirety. As a member state of the AU, Nigeria is also obligated to comply with human rights standards enunciated in the form of resolutions, guidelines and general comments by AU bodies such as the African Commission on Human and Peoples' Rights (African Commission). As such, it is obliged to comply in its anti-terrorism fight with the following: the Resolution on Guidelines and Measures for the Prohibition and Prevention of Torture, Cruel, Inhuman or Degrading Treatment or Punishment in Africa 2002 ("Robben Island Guidelines on Torture"), Principles and Guidelines on the Right to a Fair Trial and Legal Assistance in Africa 2003 ("Right to Fair Trial principles"), and General Comment No. 3 on the African Charter on Human and Peoples' Rights: The Right to Life (article 4).

The Right to Fair Trial principles, in particular, provide that[41]:

> No circumstances whatsoever, whether a threat of war, a state of international or internal armed conflict, internal political instability or any other public emergency, may be invoked to justify derogations from the right to a fair trial.

However, the limitation and derogation provisions in Nigeria's Constitution and the treaties it has ratified contain 'claw-back' clauses that allow for unilateral exceptions to human rights, where its national security interests are involved.

---

[39] Nigeria ratified the African Charter on 22 June 1983. Nigeria is also state party to the Protocol to the African Charter on Human and Peoples' Rights on the Rights of Women in Africa 2003, ratified on 28 April 2002; the African Youth Charter 2006, ratified on 21 April 2009.

[40] Cap A9 Laws of the Federation of Nigeria 2004.

[41] Principles and Guidelines on the Right to a Fair Trial and Legal Assistance in Africa 2003 clause R.

2.3   The Nigerian Security and Anti-terrorism Framework

It would seem that the brutal approach to upholding the normatively attractive but analytically weak concept of state security is not only tolerated by Nigeria's human rights framework, it is also fortified by its counter-terrorism and security framework. Importantly, the current legal regime of Nigeria's security forces consists of the Constitution, and the laws and regulations pertaining to the Nigeria Police Force,[42] Nigerian Security and Civil Defence Corps,[43] Nigerian Armed Forces (consisting of the Army, Navy and Air force),[44] and the National Security Agencies (comprising the Department of Security Services, National Intelligence Agency and Defence Intelligence Agency).[45]

Under the Constitution, the security and welfare of the people is the primary responsibility of government.[46] In fulfilment of this obligation, the state acts through its security agencies to prevent and detect crime, apprehend offenders, preserve public security and order, and protect lives and property.[47] Of particular relevance to the war on terror in Nigeria's North-East zone are the Terrorism (Prevention) Act of 2011 and the Terrorism (Prevention) (Amendment) Act of 2013 ("Act"). The Act contains a generalised definition of "act of terrorism" and includes the disruption of a service in pursuance of a protest.[48] Although the Act clarifies that striking workers and demonstrators do not fall under this definition, it is difficult to see how security forces will apply this in reality. Secondly, the Act confers unusually wide powers on the President in terms of declaring a person an international terrorist where the President "reasonably suspects" or "reasonably believes that the person is a risk to national security."[49] The wide margin of discretion granted the President

---

[42] Nigeria Police Act P19, Laws of the Federation of Nigeria 2004 and the Nigeria Police (Amendment) Act 2012; also see the Nigerian Police Regulations 53 of 1968; Code of Conduct for the Nigerian Police 2013.

[43] Nigerian Security and Civil Defence (Amendment) Act 6 of 2007.

[44] Nigerian Armed Forces Act A20, Laws of the Federation of Nigeria 2004.

[45] National Security Agencies Act 19 of 1986.

[46] Constitution, §14(2)(b).

[47] Police Act, §4.

[48] Terrorism (Prevention) Act 2011, §1(3).

[49] Terrorism (Prevention) Act 2011, §9(1)(i) and (iii).

is prone to abuse as the Act does not specify the criteria for the President's suspicion or belief. Lastly, the Act permits the detention of a person until the completion of a search. The vagueness in this provision is in the non-provision of a threshold for completing a search: what happens to a detained terror suspect, where the security agencies certify that a search is incomplete?

3   A CLASH: NATIONAL SECURITY VS HUMAN RIGHTS

Where domestic and international law provide permissible circumstances under which derogations or limitation of human rights may be allowed, the goal of securing the state in times of terror will certainly take priority over human rights concerns. Yet, as Scheinin and Vermeulen have firmly stated, even though governments may have elaborate discretion to justify restrictions on human rights, there is no justification for states to remove terror suspects from the protective cover of international humanitarian law where they have been captured and disarmed.[50] Luban argues that the "war model" of addressing terror threats is problematic because it poses a significant challenge to international human rights law and states are "willing to tolerate torture for security reasons."[51]

The state's duty to ensure the security of every individual within its domain is only validated and discharged to the extent that the right to the security of the human person is itself guaranteed to everyone by the state. The right to the human security of every individual is intertwined with the state's duty to protect the public.[52] As such, the safety of the collective or of a multitude of individuals cannot be weighed as greater than the human rights of a single individual. As Scheinin poignantly asserts, it is quite possible to effectively confront the challenges associated with countering terrorism while equally complying with international human rights standards. There is really no necessity to strike a balance between human rights and security, "as the proper balance can and must be found within human rights law itself. Law is the balance,

---

[50] Scheinin and Vermeulen, fn. 1 above, 56.

[51] David Luban, "The War on Terrorism and the End of Human Rights," *Philosophy and Public Policy Quarterly* 22 (2002): 9, 13.

[52] Helsinki Accords of 1975; Rhoda E. Howard-Hassmann, "Human Security: Understanding Human Rights," *Human Rights Quarterly* 34, no. 1 (2012): 88, 89.

not a weight to be measured."[53] For this reason, Scheinin describes "unilateral exceptions" by states as an effort to justify an otherwise internationally wrongful act or abandon the substantive primary norms that express the normative contents of international law.[54] Fitzpatrick similarly states that:

> The human rights framework is not inflexible in the face of extraordinary dangers, and a complex derogation jurisprudence has developed to balance rights against the imperative needs of security.[55]

In the case of Nigeria, it appears that state security interests preponderate over human rights where lawful restrictions are considered to be "reasonably justifiable in a democratic society."[56] The right to life, for example, is subject to constitutional restrictions so much so that extrajudicial executions may be justified in order to effect a lawful arrest, prevent a person's escape from prison or for the purpose of suppressing a riot or insurrection or mutiny.[57] The right to personal liberty is equally subject to the permissible limits of the law.[58] In fact, the Constitution allows detention for up to three months where it is impossible to produce a person before a court of law within a reasonable time.[59] The right to fair hearing may similarly be restricted where a law duly "confers on any government or authority power to determine questions arising in the administration of a law that affects or may affect the civil rights and obligations of any person."

That is not to say that lawful restrictions may be used as a pretext for the disproportionate use of lethal force in circumstances that do not require it. The accounts of Amnesty International and Human Rights

[53] Martin Schienin, "Document No. 18: Report of the Special Rapporteur on the Promotion and Protection of Human Rights and Fundamental Freedoms While Countering Terrorism 16 August 2006," in *Terrorism: Commentary on Security Documents Volume 122: U. N. Response to Al Qaeda—Developments Through 2011*, ed. Kristen E. Boon et al. (Oxford: Oxford University Press, 2012), 435.

[54] Schienin and Vermeulen, "Unilateral Exceptions," 28.

[55] Joan Fitzpatrick, "Speaking Law to Power: The War Against Terrorism and Human Rights," *European Journal of International Law* 14, no. 2 (2003): 241, 243.

[56] Constitution, §39; Zamir, "Human Rights," 376.

[57] Constitution, §33(1) and (2).

[58] Constitution, § 35(1)(a)–(e).

[59] Constitution, §35(4)(a)(b) and (5).

Watch on the deadly reprisal attacks by Nigeria's security forces show the worst forms of security interventions in circumstances that clearly demand a decent application of the rules of armed engagement and the cautious use of lethal force. The arbitrary arrest of civilians and the killing of unarmed detainees or their subjection to degrading conditions in prison are indicative of a clear abandonment of human rights principles during counter-terrorism operations. One of the reasons for this is the retention of old rules of engagement by Nigeria's security establishment such as the Force Order 237,[60] used by the Nigeria Police. Araromi and Oke state that the provisions of the Order have "resulted in numerous unlawful killings and facilitated extrajudicial executions, while police officers go largely unpunished."[61]

It must be emphasised that Nigeria's prioritisation of security over human rights does not, nonetheless, suspend its international human rights obligations under the ICCPR, CAT and the African Charter. In the case of *Media Rights Agenda and Others v. Nigeria*,[62] the African Commission on Human and Peoples' Rights held that "the African Charter does not contain a derogation clause. Therefore, limitations on the rights and freedoms contained in the Charter cannot be justified by emergencies or special circumstances."[63]

Comparatively, in the case of *Lawless v. Ireland*,[64] the European Court for Human Rights similarly held that states retain the obligation to reconcile their counter-terrorism actions with their obligations to observe human rights. Also, the International Court of Justice, in its Advisory

---

[60] Rules for guidance in the use of firearms by the police.

[61] Marcus A. Araromi and Sunday A. Oke, "A Critical Review of the Regulatory Frameworks for Police Accountability in the Nigeria's Justice System," *Nigerian Law Journal* 17 (2014): 187, 205.

[62] *Media Rights Agenda* case, fn. 5 above, para. 67.

[63] Also see *Constitutional Rights Project and Others v. Nigeria* (2000) AHRLR 227 (ACHPR 1999), para. 38; *Constitutional Rights Project and Others v. Nigeria* (2000) AHRLR 227 (ACHPR 1999), para. 41. On findings of violations of the provisions of the African Charter pertaining to the life, dignity and security of individuals in the brutal preservation of state security, see *Article 19 v. Eritrea* (2007) AHRLR 73 (ACHPR 2007), paras. 98–101; *Doebbler v. Sudan* (2003) AHRLR 153 (ACHPR 2003), para. 42; *Zegveld v. Eritrea* (2003) AHRLR 84 (ACHPR 2003), paras. 55–56; *International Pen & Others (on behalf of Saro-Wiwa) v. Nigeria* (2000) AHRLR 212 (ACHPR 1998), paras. 104, 111–113, 116; *Media Rights Agenda Case*, fn. 5 above, paras. 83–88.

[64] 332/57, 14 November 1960.

Opinion on the *Legality of the Threat or Use of Nuclear Weapons*,[65] has held that "the protection of the International Covenant of Civil and Political Rights [ICCPR] does not cease in times of war…. In principle, the right not arbitrarily to be deprived of one's life applies also in hostilities."

4 CONCLUSION

It therefore follows that while states like Nigeria are at liberty to pursue counter-terrorism measures that are best suited to their national security interests and context, where they have subscribed to international human rights law via treaty or customary practice accepted as binding, they lack the freedom to unilaterally depart from those obligations. They cannot also rely on the provisions of their constitutions as seen above as justification for evading an international human rights obligation.[66] While years of high-handedness and excessive use of force by Nigeria's security forces may have resulted in thousands of deaths in the fight against Boko Haram, neither the Nigerian Constitution nor the provisions of its security or counter-terrorism legislation absolves Nigeria of its human rights responsibilities under international law. The future of human rights in Nigeria therefore lies in the state's ability to confront the challenges of fighting terrorism while at the same time complying with its human rights obligations. It can do this by adopting a counter-terrorism strategy that addresses the excessive use of force by its security personnel and other indignities like rape, corruption and other forms of misconduct. Also, it can establish, fund and strengthen independent oversight mechanisms to investigate and punish irresponsible security personnel at all levels, as well as ensure access to effective remedies by victims and their beneficiaries.

Acknowledgements LLD Candidate & DAAD Scholar, Centre for Human Rights, University of Pretoria, South Africa. This chapter was developed from a paper submitted for a postgraduate diploma received from the Institute for Human Rights, Åbo Akademi University, Turku, Finland in 2017. Due

---

[65]ICJ (July 8, 1996), paras. 24–25; *Advisory Opinion on Legal Consequences of the Construction of a Wall in the Occupied Palestinian Territory* ICJ (July 9, 2004), paras. 102, 105.

[66]Vienna Convention on the Law of Treaties 1969, art. 27.

acknowledgment is, therefore, given to the Finnish Ministry of Foreign Affairs which sponsored the author's participation in the Intensive Course on Contemporary Challenges to International Human Rights Law in Finland.

REFERENCES

Books

Amnesty International. *"Welcome to Hell Fire": Torture and Other Ill-Treatment in Nigeria*. London, UK: Amnesty International Publications, 2014.

Ashworth, Andrew. "Security, Terrorism and the Value of Human Rights." In *Security and Human Rights*, edited by Benjamin J. Goold and Liora Lazarus, 203–226. Oxford: Hart Publishing, 2007.

Maier, Karl. *This House Has Fallen: Nigeria in Crisis*. Boulder, CO: Westview Press, 2002.

Schienin, Martin. "Document No 18: Report of the Special Rapporteur on the Promotion and Protection of Human Rights and Fundamental Freedoms While Countering Terrorism 16 August 2006." In *Terrorism: Commentary on Security Documents Volume 122: U.N. Response to Al Qaeda—Developments Through 2011*, edited by Kristen E. Boon et al. Oxford: Oxford University Press, 2012.

Zedner, Lucia. "Seeking Security by Eroding Rights: The Side-Stepping of Due Process." In *Security and Human Rights*, edited by Benjamin J. Goold and Liora Lazarus, 257–276. Oxford: Hart Publishing, 2007.

Journal Articles

Agbiboa, Daniel E. "Peace at Daggers Drawn? Boko Haram and the State of Emergency in Nigeria." *Studies in Conflict & Terrorism* 37, no. 1 (2014): 41–67.

Agbiboa, Daniel. "The Ongoing Campaign of Terror in Nigeria: Boko Haram Versus the State." *Stability: International Journal of Security and Development* 2, no. 3 (2013): 1–18.

Anyadike, Nkechi O. "Boko Haram and National Security Challenges in Nigeria: Causes and Solutions." *Journal of Economics and Sustainable Development* 4, no. 5 (2013): 12.

Araromi, Marcus A., and Sunday A. Oke. "A Critical Review of the Regulatory Frameworks for Police Accountability in the Nigeria's Justice System." *Nigerian Law Journal* 17 (2014): 187, 205.

Bloom, Mia, and Hilary Matfess. "Women as Symbols and Swords in Boko Haram's Terror." *PRISM* 6, no. 1 (2016, March 1). Accessed June 12, 2019.

https://cco.ndu.edu/PRISM/PRISM-volume-6-no1/Article/685093/women-as-symbols-and-swords-in-boko-harams-terror/.

Bozeman, Adda B. "Human Rights and National Security." *Yale Journal of World Public Order* 9, no. 1 (1982): 40, 41.

Campbell, John. "Boko Haram: Origins, Challenges and Responses." *NOREF Policy Brief* (2014): 1.

Campbell, John. "U.S. Policy to Counter Nigeria's Boko Haram." *Council of Foreign Relations Report*, no. 70 (November 1, 2014): 16.

Dada, Jacob A. "Impediments to Human Rights Protection in Nigeria." *Annual Survey of International & Comparative Law* 18, no. 1 (2012): 67

Farrow, Trevor C.W. "Security and Rights." *Review of Constitutional Studies* 10, nos. 1 and 2 (2005): 94.

Fitzpatrick, Joan. "Speaking Law to Power: The War Against Terrorism and Human Rights." *European Journal of International Law* 14, no. 2 (2003): 241, 243.

Heymann, Philip B. "Civil Liberties and Human Rights in the Aftermath of September 11." *Harvard Journal of Law & Public Policy* 25, no. 2 (2002): 441.

Howard-Hassmann, Rhoda E. "Human Security: Understanding Human Rights." *Human Rights Quarterly* 34, no. 1 (2012): 88.

Human Rights Watch. "'Rest in Pieces': Police Torture and Deaths in Custody in Nigeria." *Human Rights Watch* 10, no. 11A (2005): 1.

Joyner, Christopher C. "The United Nations and Terrorism: Rethinking Legal Tensions Between National Security, Human Rights, and Civil Liberties." *International Studies Perspectives* 5, no. 3 (2004): 240–257.

Luban, David. "The War on Terrorism and the End of Human Rights." *Philosophy and Public Policy Quarterly* 22 (2002): 9.

Mwalimu, Charles. "Police, State Security Forces and Human Rights in Nigeria and Zambia: Dynamic Perspectives in Comparative Constitutionalism." *Third World Legal Studies* 1990 (1990): 85, 95.

Newman, Edward. "A Normatively Attractive but Analytically Weak Concept." *Security Dialogue* 35 (2004): 358.

Scheinin, Martin, and Mathias Vermeulen. "Unilateral Exceptions to International Law: Systematic Legal Analysis and Critique of Doctrines That Seek to Deny or Reduce the Applicability of Human Rights Norms in the Fight Against Terrorism." *Essex Human Rights Review* 8, no. 1 (2011): 20.

Ugochukwu, Basil. "The State Security Service and Human Rights in Nigeria." *Third World Legal Studies* 1996 (1996–1997): 71, 86.

Zamir, Itzhak. "Human Rights and National Security." *Israeli Law Review* 23, nos. 2 and 3 (1989): 375.

Zoglin, Kathryn J. "The National Security Doctrine and the State of Siege in Argentina: Human Rights Denied." *Suffolk Transnational Law Journal* 12, no. 2 (1989): 265.

Website References

African Commission on Human and Peoples' Rights. "Ratification Table: United Nations Convention Against Torture and Other Cruel, Inhuman or Degrading Treatment or Punishment." Accessed December 17, 2017. http://www.achpr.org/instruments/uncat/ratification/.

Amnesty International. "Boko Haram Survivors have been Starved and Raped by Nigeria's military," May 24, 2018. Accessed June 12, 2019. https://www.amnesty.org/en/latest/news/2018/05/boko-haram-survivors-have-been-starved-and-raped-by-nigerias-military/.

Amnesty International. "Nigeria: Boko Haram Killing of Aid Worker Hauwa Liman is a War Crime," October 16, 2018. Accessed June 12, 2019. https://www.amnesty.org/en/latest/news/2018/10/nigeria-boko-haram-killing-of-aid-worker-hauwa-liman-is-a-war-crime/.

Amnesty International. "Nigeria: Deadliest Boko Haram Attack on Rann Leaves at Least 60 People Murdered," February 1, 2019. Accessed June 12, 2019. https://www.amnesty.org/en/latest/news/2019/02/nigeria-deadliest-boko-haram-attack-on-rann-leaves-at-least-60-people-murdered/.

Amnesty International. "Nigeria: Satellite Imagery Shows Charred Remains of Rann after Boko Haram Attack," January 18, 2019. Accessed June 12, 2019. https://www.amnesty.org/en/latest/news/2019/01/nigeria-satellite-imagery-shows-charred-remains-of-rann-after-boko-haram-attack/.

Amnesty International. "Nigeria: War Crimes and Crimes Against Humanity as Violence Escalates in North-East." Last modified March 31, 2014. Accessed December 17, 2017. https://www.amnesty.org/en/latest/news/2014/03/nigeria-war-crimes-and-crimes-against-humanity-violence-escalates-north-east/

Amnesty International. "'Our Job is to Shoot, Slaughter and Kill': Boko Haram's Reign of Terror in North-East Nigeria," April 2015. Accessed June 12, 2019. https://www.amnesty.org/download/Documents/AFR4413602015ENGLISH.PDF.

Amnesty International. "'They Betrayed us': Women Who Survived Boko Haram Raped, Starved and Detained in Nigeria," 2018. Accessed June 12, 2019. https://www.amnesty.org/download/Documents/AFR4484152018ENGLISH.PDF.

Amnesty International. "They Took Our Husbands and Forced Us to Be Their Girlfriends: Women in North-east Nigeria Starved and Raped by Those Claiming to Rescue Them," September, 2018. Accessed June 12, 2019. https://www.amnesty.org/download/Documents/AFR4491222018ENGLISH.PDF.

Amnesty International. "Torture, Cruel Inhuman and Degrading Treatment of Detainees by Nigerian Security Forces: Amnesty International's Written Statement to the 25th Session of the UN Human Rights Council (3–28 March 2014)." 1–3. Last modified February 20, 2014. Accessed December 17, 2017. https://www.amnesty.org/download/Documents/4000/afr440012014en.pdf.

Amnesty International. "Torture, the Way of Life for the Nigerian Security Forces." Accessed December 17, 2017. https://www.amnestyusa.org/torture-the-way-of-life-for-the-nigerian-security-forces/.

"Boko Haram Giwa Barracks Attack: Nigerian Army 'Killed Hundreds.'" British Broadcasting Corporation, March 31, 2014. Accessed December 17, 2017. www.bbc.com/news/world-africa-26819965.

Booth, Andrea. "Nigeria's Boko Haram: Inside the World's Second Deadliest Terrorist Organisation." SBS News, August 24, 2017. Accessed February 8, 2018. https://www.sbs.com.au/news/nigeria-s-boko-haram-inside-the-worlds-second-deadliest-terrorist-organisation.

Fakoya, Olusegun. "Nigeria Police Force—A Legacy of Brutality." Last modified August 1, 2008. Accessed February 10, 2018. www.nigeriavillagesquare.com/articles/nigeria-police-force---a-legacy-of-brutality.html.

Human Rights Council. "Violations and Abuses Committed by Boko Haram and the Impact on Human Rights in the Countries Affected: Report of the United Nations High Commissioner for Human Rights." UN Doc. A/HRC/30/67, December 9, 2015. Accessed January 7, 2019. https://digital-library.un.org/record/819031/files/A_HRC_30_67-EN.pdf.

Human Rights Watch. "Spiraling Violence: Boko Haram Attacks and Security Force Abuses in Nigeria." 30. Accessed December 17, 2017. https://www.hrw.org/sites/default/files/reports/nigeria1012webwcover_0.pdf.

International Committee of the Red Cross. "Nigeria: Health Worker Hauwa Mohammed Liman Executed in Captivity," October 16, 2018. Accessed June 12, 2019. https://www.icrc.org/en/document/nigeria-health-worker-hauwa-mohammed-liman-executed-captivity.

Nossiter, Adam. "Abuses by Nigeria's Military Found to Be Rampant in War Against Boko Haram." *New York Times*, June 3, 2015. Accessed December 17, 2017. https://www.nytimes.com/2015/06/04/world/africa/abuses-nigeria-military-boko-haram-war-report.html.

Nossiter, Adam. "Nigerian Forces Kill Dozens in Night Assault, Fuelling Long Battle with Sect." Last modified November 2, 2012. Accessed December 17, 2017. www.nytimes.com/2012/11/03/world/africa/nigeria-forces-kill-dozens-in-night-assault.html.

Searcey, Dionne. "Boko Haram Turns Female Captives Into Terrorists." *New York Times*, April 7, 2016. Accessed June 12, 2019. https://www.nytimes.com/2016/04/08/world/africa/boko-haram-suicide-bombers.html.

Sieff, Kevin. "Boko Haram Kidnapped 276 Girls Two Years Ago: What Happened to Them?" *Washington Post*, April 14, 2016. Accessed February 10, 2018. https://www.washingtonpost.com/news/worldviews/wp/2016/04/14/boko-haram-kidnapped-276-girls-two-years-ago-what-happened-to-them/?utm_term=.fe68fd4820b5.

Swails, Brent, and David McKenzie. "Kidnapped to Kill: How Boko Haram is Turning Girls Into Weapons." *CNN*, April 13, 2016. Accessed June 12, 2019. https://edition.cnn.com/2016/04/12/africa/cameroon-boko-haram-child-bombers/index.html.

Uhrmacher, Kevin, and Mary B. Sheridan. "The Brutal Toll of Boko Haram's Attacks on Civilians." *Washington Post*, April 3, 2016. Accessed December 17, 2017. https://www.washingtonpost.com/graphics/world/nigeria-boko-haram/.

United for Human Rights. "Human Rights Defined." Accessed June 19, 2017. http://www.humanrights.com/what-are-human-rights/.

Winsor, Morgan. "Nigeria Marks 3 Years Since 276 Chibok Schoolgirls Abducted by Boko Haram." ABC News, April 14, 2017. Accessed February 10, 2018. http://abcnews.go.com/International/nigeria-marks-years-276-chibok-schoolgirls-abducted-boko/story?id=46774809.

Treaties

African Charter on Human and Peoples' Rights 1981.

African Youth Charter 2006.

Helsinki Accords of 1975.

Principles and Guidelines on the Right to a Fair Trial and Legal Assistance in Africa 2003 clause R.

Protocol to the African Charter on Human and Peoples' Rights on the Rights of Women in Africa 2003.

UN Body of Principles for the Protection of All Persons under Any Form of Detention or Imprisonment 1988.

Vienna Convention on the Law of Treaties 1969.

International Cases

Advisory Opinion on Legal Consequences of the Construction of a Wall in the Occupied Palestinian Territory ICJ (9 July 2004).

Lawless v. Ireland 332/57, 14 November 1960.

Legality of the Threat or Use of Nuclear Weapons ICJ (8 July 1996).

Regional Cases

Article 19 v. Eritrea (2007) AHRLR 73 (ACHPR 2007).

Constitutional Rights Project and Others v Nigeria (2000) AHRLR 227 (ACHPR 1999).

Doebbler v. Sudan (2003) AHRLR 153 (ACHPR 2003).

Huri-Laws v. Nigeria (2000) AHRLR 273 (ACHPR 2000).
International Pen & Others (on behalf of Saro-Wiwa) v. Nigeria (2000) AHRLR 212 (ACHPR 1998).
Media Rights Agenda & Others v Nigeria (2000) AHRLR 200 (ACHPR 1998).
Ouko v. Kenya (2000) AHRLR 135 (ACHPR 2000).
Zegveld v. Eritrea (2003) AHRLR 84 (ACHPR 2003).

Constitution and Statutes

African Charter on Human and Peoples' Rights (Ratification and Enforcement) Act, Cap A9, Laws of the Federation of Nigeria 2004.
Code of Conduct for the Nigerian Police 2013.
Constitution of the Federal Republic of Nigeria 1999.
National Security Agencies Act 19 of 1986.
Nigeria Police (Amendment) Act 2012.
Nigerian Armed Forces Act A20, Laws of the Federation of Nigeria 2004.
Nigerian Police Regulations 53 of 1968.
Nigerian Security and Civil Defence (Amendment) Act 6 of 2007.
Police Act P19, Laws of the Federation of Nigeria 2004.
Rules for guidance in the use of firearms by the police.
Terrorism (Prevention) Act 2011.

CHAPTER 13

The Legal Challenges of Offering Protection to Climate Refugees in Africa

Michael Addaney

1 Introduction

The impacts of climate change[1] have increased in frequency and intensity globally[2] with disproportionate effects being felt on the African continent in particular.[3] The continent is facing deforestation, drought,

---

[1] Climate change is defined as 'a change of climate which is attributed directly or indirectly to human activity that alters the composition of the global atmosphere and which is in addition to other natural climate variability that has been observed over comparable time periods', see Article 1(2) UNFCCC. The Intergovernmental Panel on Climate Change (IPCC) has since expanded this definition as 'any change of climate over time as a result of human activity or due to natural variability.' See IPCC, *Climate Change 2007: Synthesis Report* (New York: Cambridge University Press, 2007), 30.

[2] Ottmar Edenhofer et al., *Climate Change 2014: Mitigation of Climate Change, Working Group III Contribution to the Fifth Assessment Report of the Intergovernmental Panel on Climate Change* (New York: Cambridge University Press, 2014).

[3] Christopher B. Field et al., eds., *Managing the Risks of Extreme Events and Disasters to Advance Climate Change Adaptation: Special Report of the Intergovernmental Panel on Climate Change* (SREX Report) (New York: Cambridge University Press, 2012), 16; Michael Addaney, Elsabé Boshoff, and Michael Gyan Nyarko, "Protection of

---

M. Addaney (✉)
Research Institute of Environmental Law, Wuhan University, Wuhan, China

© The Author(s) 2020
M. Addaney et al. (eds.), *Governance, Human Rights, and Political Transformation in Africa*,
https://doi.org/10.1007/978-3-030-27049-0_13

and desertification, owing to rising global temperatures and changing weather patterns.[4] The World Health Organization (WHO) estimates that a temperature increase of 2–3 °C could raise the rate of communicable disease transmission significantly and put millions of people at risk of contracting malaria and other diseases.[5] For example, McQue notes that twenty-five of the world's twenty-seven Ebola outbreaks over the past four decades have occurred in areas that experienced rapid environmental destruction.[6] Similarly, Olivero and others observe that deforestation in West Africa might have been the cause of the 2014 Ebola outbreak.[7] Moreover, in the drought-prone Lake Chad region that borders Cameroon, Chad, Nigeria, and Niger, pastoralist communities compete for shrinking natural resources in the face of desertification and water scarcity.[8] The Food and Agriculture Organization of the United Nations (FAO) estimates that about 319 million hectares of Africa is vulnerable

Environmental Assets in Urban Africa: Regional and Sub-regional Human Rights and Practical Environmental Protection Mechanisms," *Australian Journal of Human Rights* 24, no. 2 (2018): 182–200, https://doi.org/10.1080/1323238x.2018.1480235.

[4] John H. Knox, "Report of the Independent Expert on the Issue of Human Rights Obligations Relating to the Enjoyment of a Safe, Clean, Healthy and Sustainable Environment," A/HRC/22/43, 24 December 24, 2012; IPCC (2018). An IPCC Special Report on the Impacts of Global Warming of 1.5°C above Pre-industrial levels and related global greenhouse gas emission pathways, in the context of strengthening the global response to the threat of climate change, sustainable development and efforts to eradicate poverty: Summary for Policymakers (Geneva: IPCC, 2018), retrieved from http://ipcc.ch/report/sr15/.

[5] The World Health Organization, *Climate Change and Infectious Diseases* (2003), 16–17, https://www.who.int/globalchange/environment/en/chapter6.pdf.

[6] Katie McQue, "Did Deforestation Cause the Ebola Outbreak," *New Internationalist*, April 10, 2018, https://newint.org/features/web-exclusive/2018/04/10/deforestation-ebola-outbreak.

[7] Jesús Olivero et al., "Recent Loss of Closed Forests Is Associated with Ebola Virus Disease Outbreaks," *Scientific Reports* 7, no. 14291 (2017): 1–7.

[8] Michael Addaney, Elsabé Boshoff, and Bamisaye Oyetola, "The Climate Change and Human Rights Nexus in African," *Amsterdam Law Forum* 9, no. 3 (2017): 5–28; Stefano M. Torelli. "Climate-Driven Migration in Africa," *European Council of Foreign Relations*, December 20, 2017. https://www.ecfr.eu/article/commentary_climate_driven_migration_in_africa.

to desertification-related hazards due to sand movement.[9] The intensification of desertification could make most parts of the continent including entire countries uninhabitable. The UN reports that desertification in Africa could send about 50 million Sub-Saharan migrants elsewhere by 2020 with 700 million Africans being forced to leave the continent due to land degradation by 2050.[10] Additionally, the FAO reports that 26.4 million people were displaced in Africa by climate-related disasters on average every year between 2008 and 2015.[11] The combined effects of health-related risks and other extreme weather events are thus producing massive refugee[12] populations in Africa. This chapter argues that climate change is a major driver of mass migration in Africa. For purposes of this chapter, climate refugees are defined as 'persons or groups of persons who, for reasons of sudden or progressive climate-related change in the environment that adversely affects their lives or living conditions, are obliged to leave their habitual homes either temporarily or permanently, and who move either within their country or abroad'.[13]

While many people may have to move as a last resort, their ability to do so varies considerably.[14] McAdam observes that inhabitants in poorer regions and countries have a propensity to be affected more by climatic

[9] Food and Agriculture Organization (FAO), "The Magnitude of the Problem," http://www.fao.org/docrep/x5318e/x5318e02.htm.

[10] "Desertification: The People Whose Land Is Turning to Dust," BBC News, November 2, 2015, https://www.bbc.com/news/world-africa-34790661. IPBES Secretariat, "Media Release: Worsening Worldwide Land Degradation Now 'Critical', Undermining Well-Being of 3.2 Billion People," March 23, 2018, https://www.ipbes.net/news/media-release-worsening-worldwide-land-degradation-now-%E2%80%98critical%E2%80%99-undermining-well-being-32.

[11] FAO, "The Magnitude of the Problem."

[12] The term 'refugee' offers legal protection based on a defined conceptualization under the 1951 Geneva Refugee Convention. However, there is no agreement over the definition and the legal treatment of persons forcibly displaced by climate change. Currently, they are treated as economic migrants, resulting in barriers to entering crossing international borders legally. See Torelli, "Climate-Driven Migration in Africa."

[13] See Environmental Justice Foundation, "Protecting Climate Refugees: Securing International Protection for Climate Refugees," https://ejfoundation.org/what-we-do/climate/protecting-climate-refugees.

[14] Graeme Hugo, "Climate Change—Induced Mobility and the Existing Migration Regime in Asia and the Pacific," in *Climate Change and Displacement: Multidisciplinary Perspectives*, ed. Jane McAdam (Oxford: Hart Publishing, 2010), 13.

changes than people from developed countries.[15] This is largely attributed to their poor adaptive capacity to respond to the adverse effects of climate change. Despite their predicament, climate refugees are not legally recognized and protected by international law.[16] The legal protection of climate refugees at the international level and in Africa particularly is therefore not clear. This raises the question of whether the existing international and regional refugee protection frameworks may possibly be applied to or interpreted in order to protect climate refugees in Africa. This chapter, consequently, assesses whether, given the expansive definition of refugee in the 1969 OAU Convention Governing the Specific Aspects of Refugee Problems in Africa (1969 OAU Convention), legal recognition and protection of climate refugees is feasible.[17] This chapter joins the ongoing argument for reforms of existing regional laws and policies with the view of offering legal protection to climate change refugees.[18] It has been contended, inter alia, that such reforms will allow climate change refugees to access durable solutions and ultimately, to make them adaptable to the adverse effects of climate change.[19] Arguably, a regional approach also offers a better response to this challenge than an international one, because of commonalities between sending and host countries based on their specific regional capabilities and priorities. Following this introduction, Sect. 2 discusses the existing refugee protection framework focusing on the gaps in legal protection. Section 3 interrogates the provisions in the 1969 OAU Convention of the African Union (AU) that can shape the regional framework for addressing the specific aspects of Africa's refugee problems including climate refugees, followed by a conclusion in Sect. 4.

---

[15] Jane McAdam, *Climate Change, Forced Migration, and International Law* (New York: Oxford University Press 2012), 1–2.

[16] Convention Relating to the Status of Refugees (adopted July 28, 1951, entered into force April 22, 1954) 189 U.N.T.S. 137, Art 1A(2).

[17] Organization of African Unity (now African Union) Convention Governing the Specific Aspects of Refugee Problems in Africa (adopted 10 September 1969, entered into force June 20, 1974) 1001 U.N.T.S. 45, Art 1(2).

[18] Kelsey Moe, "Climate Change Refugees: Regional Agreements Can Better Fill the Gap in Legal Protection," *Hastings Environmental Law Journal Blog Post*, January 13, 2018, http://sites.uchastings.edu/helj/2018/01/13/climate-change-refugees-regional-agreements-can-better-fill-the-gap-in-legal-protection/.

[19] Ibid.

2 CLIMATE CHANGE REFUGEES: INTERNATIONAL LAW AND GAPS IN LEGAL PROTECTION

The contemporary refugee protection system is a product of the twentieth century.[20] Its codification by the UN took place just after the adoption of the Universal Declaration of Human Rights (Universal Declaration), and was greatly influenced by the Declaration's normative content and structure. The refugee protection regime does not exist as an alternative to, or in competition with, general human rights law or climate change law. For instance, Hathaway observes that the refugee protection regime should be understood as a mechanism by which situation-specific vulnerabilities that would otherwise deny refugees meaningful benefit of the more general system of human rights protection are addressed.[21] Climate refugees do not explicitly enjoy any rights under international law, apart from the basic human rights that are accorded to all human beings. They cannot seek asylum under international refugee law because they do not fall within the definition of a refugee. The recognition and protection of the rights of climate refugees have, however, always been, and continues to be subject to varied contestations.[22]

Article 14(1) of the Universal Declaration provides that 'everyone has the right to seek and to enjoy in other countries asylum from persecution'.[23] Climate refugees are also generally covered by article 13(2) of the Universal Declaration which provides that everyone has the right to leave any country including his or her own.[24] The International Covenant on Civil and Political Rights reaffirms this

[20] Michael Addaney, "A Step Forward in the Protection of Urban Refugees: The Legal Protection of the Rights of Urban Refugees in Uganda," *African Human Rights Law Journal* 17, no. 1 (2017): 218–243.

[21] James C. Hathaway, *The Rights of Refugees Under International Law* (Cambridge: Cambridge University Press, 2005), 75.

[22] Elizabeth Ferris and Jonas Bergmann, "Soft Law, Migration and Climate Change Governance," *Journal of Human Rights and the Environment* 8, no. 1 (2017): 6–29; Benoit Mayer, "Climate Change and International Law in the Grim Days," *European Journal of International Law* 24, no. 3 (2013): 949; Frank Biermann and Ingrid Boas, "Preparing for a Warmer World: Towards a Global Governance System to Protect Climate Refugees," *Global Environmental Politics* 10, no. 1 (2010): 60–88.

[23] Universal Declaration, art. 14(1) and (2).

[24] Universal Declaration, art. 13(2).

provision in article 12(2).[25] Persons from states that are particularly vulnerable or affected by the adverse effects of climate change cannot therefore be prevented from leaving their country. There are however some permissible restrictions on the right to leave one's country.[26] In practice, it is mostly the absence of the right to access a third country which restricts the right to leave one's country and this has a negative impact on climate refugees, particularly as climate refugees are not covered by the conventional definition provided in the 1951 Refugee Convention.[27]

The cornerstone of the international refugee protection system, the 1951 Convention relating to the Status of Refugees (1951 Convention),[28] defines a refugee as a person who:

> owing to a well-founded fear of being persecuted for reasons of race, religion, nationality, membership of a particular social group or political opinion, is outside the country of his nationality and is unable, or owing to such fear, is unwilling to avail himself of the protection of that country; or who, not having a nationality and being outside the country of his former habitual residence as a result of such events, is unable or, owing to such fear, is unwilling to return to it.[29]

The 1951 Refugee Convention arose from a desire to structure State cooperation in solving the enormous tragedy of persons displaced in Europe by the Second World War.[30] The 1951 Convention and the 1969 Optional Protocol therefore enjoy widespread adherence, with

---

[25] International Covenant on Civil and Political Rights (ICCPR), December 19, 1966, 999 UNTS 14668, art. 12(2).

[26] Ibid., art. 12(3).

[27] Benoît Mayer, "The International Legal Challenges of Climate-Induced Migration: Proposal for an International Legal Framework," *Colorado Journal of International Environmental Law and Policy* 22, no. 3 (2011): 357.

[28] The 1967 Protocol removes the geographic and temporal limitations included in the 1951 Convention, making it a truly universal and inclusive system of protection for those fleeing persecution. The 1967 Protocol also incorporates all the substantive provisions of the 1951 Convention, so while many States have chosen to ratify both instruments it is actually necessary to ratify only the 1967 Protocol.

[29] 1951 Refugee Convention, at art. 1.

[30] António Guterres, UN Refugee Agency, 1951 Convention Relating to the Status of Refugees and Its 1967 Protocol (2011), 1.

147 States party to one or both instruments, including more than fifty African states. However, it is clear that a person fleeing his or her home or country due to climate-related events does not satisfy the conditions necessary to be considered a 'conventional refugee' under the above definition because it would be impossible for him or her to establish a well-founded fear of persecution based on any of the grounds enumerated in the 1951 Refugee Convention. Yet, in the nearly sixty-seven years since its adoption, it has become evident that the Convention's definition must be interpreted in a manner responsive to broader developments in international law, particularly the growth of international human rights law. For instance, there is an example of evolving interpretations of the term 'refugee' by many States to include various forms of gender-based violence, such as female genital mutilation, and forced sterilization, as such acts properly fall within the notion of persecution.[31] McAdam also argues that 'membership of a particular social group' may be extended to include climate refugees.[32] Conversely, Hodgkinson and colleagues argue that including climate refugees within the refugee convention would risk devaluing the current protection for refugees.[33] This position flows from the fear that expanding the conventional definition of 'refugee' to include both climate refugees and traditional refugees obscures elemental differences of experience between the two groups especially as the nexus between climate refugees and their states has not been cut off through persecution. Further, it has been contended that attempts to extend the definition of a refugee to climate migrants would lead to an enormous increase in the number of refugees.[34]

Since the origin of the 1951 Refugee Convention, the cause of forced migration has been understood as 'deriving from the relations between

[31] Efrat Arbel, Catherine Dauvergne, and Jenni Millbank, eds., *Gender in Refugee Law: From the Margins to the Centre* (London and New York: Routledge, 2014).

[32] Alex Aleinikoff, "Protected Characteristics and Social Perceptions: An Analysis of the Meaning of 'Membership of a Particular Social Group,'" In *Refugee Protection in International Law: UNHCR's Global Consultations on International Protection*, ed. Erika Feller, Volker Türk, and Frances Nicholson (Cambridge: Cambridge University Press, 2003), 263.

[33] Heather Anderson, Tess Burton, David Hodgkinson, and Lucy Young, "The Hour When the Ship Comes In: A Convention for Persons Displaced by Climate Change," *Monash University Law Review* 36, no. 1 (2010): 76.

[34] Angela Williams, "Turning the Tide: Recognizing Climate Change in International Law," *Law and Policy* 30, no. 4 (2008): 509.

the State and its nationals'.[35] The UNHCR confirms that 'persecution is normally related to action by the authorities of a country',[36] either because national authorities persecute someone or because they allow persecution. The requirement that a person be deprived of their fundamental rights because of national authorities excludes climate refugees from the protective status of conventional refugees.[37] Hong argues that 'the development of refugee law, as evidenced by legislative history and interpretative guides, indicates that the drafters recognized natural calamities as major causes of human migration and purposefully declined to extend refugee status to the victims of such events'.[38] Climate-related events that cause movements across international borders are not, thus, grounds in and of themselves for the granting of refugee status under international law.[39] The indication of persecution as a specific object by the UNHCR Handbook implies that the 1951 Refugee Convention 'automatically makes all other reasons for escape irrelevant to the definition' and 'rules out such persons as victims of famine or natural disaster, unless they also have well-founded fear of persecution'.[40] Mayer argues that the 'source-of-persecution' requirement could be fulfilled if a government has not been willing to reduce the known vulnerability of a particular group to climatic phenomena.[41] He explains that, for instance, a national policy that prevents any internal displacement of vulnerable populations who move from an endangered location could be qualified as 'persecution', entitling some climate refugees to legal protection.[42] This would also be the case if a government excluded a minority from any protection in face of a natural catastrophe, as the minority members who

---

[35] Jeanhee Hong, "Refugees of the 21st Century: Environmental Injustice," *Cornell Journal of Law and Public Policy* 10, no. 2 (2001): 331.

[36] UNHCR, *Handbook on Procedures and Criteria for Determining Refugee Status Under the 1951 Convention and the 1967 Protocol Relating to the Status of Refugees* (Geneva: UNHCR, 1979), 39.

[37] Mayer, "The International Legal Challenges of Climate-Induced Migration," 357.

[38] Hong, "Refugees of the 21st Century," 331.

[39] Inter-Agency Standing Committee (IASC), "Climate Change, Migration and Displacement: Who Will Be Affected?" (2008) 4, http://unfccc.int/resource/docs/2008/smsn/igo/022.pdf.

[40] UNHCR, *Handbook on Procedures and Criteria for Determining Refugee Status*, 39.

[41] Mayer, "The International Legal Challenges of Climate-Induced Migration," 357.

[42] Ibid.

would be discriminated against might be considered to be suffering from persecution by the government.

Alternatively, preventing the provision of international humanitarian assistance to the victims of a climate-related events may be considered a form of persecution. Thus, when a state is unwilling to protect any part of its population against the consequences of climate change, people 'seeking refuge from the resulting climatic events are effectively seeking refuge from their government as well'.[43] Though most climate refugees would have no difficulty proving that they could suffer a sufficient level of harm, a generally insuperable difficulty stems from the 'source-of-persecution' requirement that 'the cause of the harm be either the government or a person or group of persons that the government is unwilling or unable to prevent from continuing the persecution'.[44] For example, Jastram argues that even if one argued that the results of climate change amount to persecution, it would be nearly impossible to show that the actions that resulted in climate change were undertaken with the motivation of causing harm to a person or group because of their protected characteristic.[45]

In relation to the promotion and protection of the human rights of climate refugees, in simple and general terms, climate refugees flee depravation of their core fundamental rights, in particular their right to life, more than they pursue a better standard of life in a more prosperous country. As a result, climate refugees and political refugees have some similar needs in terms of legal protection. In particular, the non-refoulement principle, which is at the core of the international protection of political refugees, is equally a moral requirement for climate refugees.[46] Given the large number of people that are already displaced and the projections made of the number of people to be displaced as a result of climate-induced consequences, it is only a matter of time before the international community will be compelled to deal with the lacuna in the law relating to this category of displaced persons, particularly where

[43] Jessica B. Cooper, "Environmental Refugees: Meeting the Requirements of the Refugee Definition," *New York University Environmental Law Journal* 6 (1998): 502.

[44] Kara K. Moberg, "Extending Refugee Definitions to Cover Environmentally Displaced Persons Displaces Necessary Protection," *Iowa Law Review* 94 (2009): 1121.

[45] Kate Jastram, "Warm World, Cold Reception: Climate Change, National Security and Forced Migration," *Vermont Journal of Environmental Law* 15, no. 4 (2014): 751–765.

[46] Mayer, "The International Legal Challenges of Climate-Induced Migration," 357.

they cross international borders.[47] One can argue that the basic human rights accorded by international human rights law should be applicable regardless of displaced persons' categorization and regardless of whether they have crossed an international border. As long as the displacement is temporary, this argument can be made. However, problems arise when the displacement is not temporary. An international framework would be necessary to recognize this category of people as a group that requires special protection.

On the other hand, the relatively small body of international law on climate change comprising the United Nations Framework Convention on Climate Change (UNFCCC), the Kyoto Protocol, and the 2015 Paris Agreement does not guarantee any protection to climate refugees.[48] The effectiveness of the UNFCCC lies in its accompanying instruments, widely attended annual COPs and its virtually universal membership of 197 parties, including the AU as a regional organization.[49] Promisingly, the UNFCCC incorporated climate-induced migration into its agenda in 2010 under the Cancun Adaptation Framework. Article 14(f) of the Cancun Framework calls for parties to take 'measures to enhance understanding, coordination and cooperation with regard to climate-induced displacement, migration, and planned relocation'.[50] By bringing climate-induced displacement under adaptation, the paragraph theoretically rendered migration a possible form of adaptation. Kälin argues that the significance of this provision lies first in its explicit recognition of the humanitarian consequences of forced migration due to climate change; second, in its expectation that displacement issues will become part of national adaptation plans; and third, in its inclusion of cross-border and not just internal displacement

---

[47] Jastram, "Warm World, Cold Reception," 751.

[48] Rina Kuusipalo, "Exiled by Emissions—Climate Change Related Displacement and Migration in International Law: Gaps in Global Governance and the Role of the UN Climate Convention," *Vermont Journal of Environmental Law* 18, no. 4. (2017): 615–647.

[49] Status of Ratification of the Convention of the United Nations Framework Convention on Climate Change, http://unfccc.int/essential_background/convention/status_of_ratification/items/2631.php.

[50] Conference of the Parties to the Framework Convention on Climate Change, *Report of the Conference of the Parties on Its Sixteenth Session*, 14, 14(f), UN Doc. FCCC/CP/2010/7/Add.1 March 15, 2011, https://unfccc.int/resource/docs/2010/cop16/eng/07a01.pdf.

on the international agenda.[51] Consequently, the **2012 UNFCCC** Doha Decision recognized climate-induced migration but located it under the loss and damage mechanism, encouraging 'understanding of and expertise on loss and damage' and including 'how impacts of climate change are affecting patterns of migration, displacement and human mobility'.[52] The Paris Agreement strengthens the UNFCCC mandate to tackle the issue under loss and damage—paragraph 50 of the Paris Decision requests the Executive Committee of the Warsaw International Mechanism on Loss and Damage 'to establish ... a task force ... to develop recommendations for integrated approaches to avert, minimize and address displacement related to the adverse impacts of climate change'.[53] These recent developments indicate the high probability of the adoption of international and regional instruments to offer some form of protection to climate refugees.

From the discussion above, it is obvious that individuals displaced by climate change are not protected by international law, leaving a gap in the legal protection for climate refugees. Several options have been advanced to fill this gap including the development of a new international treaty specifically to address climate refugees.[54] Giannini and Docherty argue that existing legal instruments do not offer any form of protection for climate change refugees and that a new international treaty is the only feasible solution.[55] Williams agrees with Giannini and Docherty, but she argues that the development of a new global agreement would be problematic, opting instead for a solution based on the development and adoption of regional agreements to protect climate refugees.[56] She concludes that such regional efforts could be effectively coordinated under the UNFCCC.[57] Grounding her argument in the

---

[51]Walter Kälin, "From the Nansen Principles to the Nansen Initiative," *Forced Migration Review* 41 (2012): 49.

[52]Conference of the Parties to the Framework Convention on Climate Change, *Report of the Conference of the Parties on Its Eighteenth Session*, 7(a)(iv), U.N. Doc. FCCC/CP/2012/8/Add.1, February 28, 2013, http://unfccc.int/resource/docs/2012/cop18/eng/08a01.pdf.

[53]Paris Agreement on Climate Change, 12 December 2015, T.I.A.S. No. 16-1104, art. 50.

[54]Tyler Giannini and Bonnie Docherty, "Confronting a Rise Tide: A Proposal for a Convention of Climate Change Refugees," *Harvard Environmental Law Review* 33 (2009): 349.

[55]Ibid.

[56]Williams, "Turning the Tide," 502.

[57]Ibid.

UNFCCC and Kyoto Protocol which call for regional cooperation in respect of adaptation action, she posits that there should be an unequivocal recognition of climate change refugees to allow for, and facilitate the adoption of regional agreements to address the problem.[58] McAdam argues that regional agreements can effectively fill the legal protection gaps for climate refugees due to similarities in cultural, geographical, and family ties within regions, adaptation capabilities of countries and the possibility of internal and migration to neighboring countries.[59] Arguably, cultural norms vary widely across countries, regions, and social groups; and regional agreements can help countries communicate how they want to be perceived both in terms of climate change and with migration and other forms of displacement. Ultimately, regional agreements focus attention on culturally sensitive outcomes for people in particular contexts, and respond to the nature, timing, and location of predicted movement within, from, and to particular countries, and their views on how they want to be perceived.

Arguably, the African and Latin American regional instruments on refugee law contain fairly broader definitions of refugees that potentially cover people fleeing natural disasters; their expansive application could at best cover people fleeing extreme climate events. More broadly, there is a common lack of enthusiasm at the policy level to bring climate refugees under these frameworks that protect traditional refugees to avoid creating confusion in agreements that took so much effort to simplify.[60] For instance, the UNHCR expressed strong reservation in its first report regarding the terminology. It emphasized that:

> The use of such terminology could potentially undermine the international legal regime for the protection of refugees whose rights and obligations are quite clearly defined and understood. It would also not be helpful to appear to imply a link and thus create confusion regarding the impact of climate change, environmental degradation and migration and persecution that is at the root of a refugee fleeing a country of origin and seeking international protection.

[58] Ibid.
[59] Jane McAdam, "Swimming Against the Tide: Why a Climate Change Displacement Treaty Is Not the Answer," *International Journal of Refugee Law* 23, no. 1 (2011): 2–27.
[60] Pierre-Marie Dupuy and Jorge E. Vinuales, *International Environmental Law* (Cambridge: Cambridge University Press, 2018), 369.

Due to the challenges of dealing with the predicament through international refugee law, the attention has shifted toward alternative legal frameworks such as international humanitarian law, international human rights law, and region-specific agreements.[61] Adopting the suggestion by William, this chapter makes a case for a regional agreement to offer protection for climate refugees in Africa. The next section explores the African regional refugee law and makes a case for a region-specific approach to recognizing and protecting climate refugees on the continent.

3 CREATING PATHWAYS TO OFFER PROTECTION TO CLIMATE REFUGEES IN AFRICA: PLUGGING IN THE HOLES

Most African states will not be able to cope with the consequences of climate change and many people will likely flee their countries.[62] Natural events such as massive floods or severe famine in the Sahel region might break the resilience of entire populations to climate change leading to a domino effect whereby millions of people suddenly decide to leave their habitual place of residence.[63] When combined with other economic, social, and political instabilities prevailing in Africa, climate change as 'a threat multiplier' will exacerbate preexisting vulnerabilities in areas already affected by poverty or conflict. For instance, it has been argued that the conflict in South Sudan and Somalia were partly sparked by the worst drought in those countries.[64] Thus, climate change could, if displacement resulting from it is poorly managed, lead to regional instability on the already vulnerable continent.[65] This is especially dire for the current era, which is characterized by high population density in many

---

[61] Ibid., 370.

[62] Ademola Oluborode Jegede, "Indigenous Peoples, Climate Migration and International Human Rights Law in Africa, with Reflections on the Relevance of the Kampala Convention," in *Research Handbook on Climate Change, Migration and the Law*, ed. Benoît Mayer and François Crépeau (Cheltenham: Edward Elgar Publishing, 2017), 169–189.

[63] Ibid.

[64] Addaney, Boshoff, and Olutola, "The Climate Change and Human Rights Nexus in Africa," 5.

[65] McAdam, *Climate Change, Forced Migration, and International Law*, 267.

subregions on the continent. The AU and its member states therefore cannot ignore the challenges arising from climate-induced displacement. The adoption of the 1969 Convention was a watershed event for the refugee protection system in Africa. Owing to the opportunities it opens for new developments, the 1969 AU Convention, when read with the African Charter on Human and Peoples' Rights (African Charter),[66] serves as an important regional bridge over the weakness in international refugee law instruments in addressing the plight of climate refugees.[67] Article 2(1) of the 1969 Convention obliges[68] member states to use their best endeavors consistent with their respective legislation to receive refugees and to secure the settlement of those who, for well-founded reasons, are unable or unwilling to return to their country of origin or nationality. Additionally, the Convention provides that 'granting asylum to refugees is a peaceful and humanitarian act which shall not be treated as an unfriendly act by any member state'.[69] It has been observed that article 2(1) of the 1969 Convention is one of the most significant contributions to refugee jurisprudence in general.[70] Rwelamira states that 'although the legal purposes of the Convention are essentially limited … it is a landmark event for refugee law and policy'.[71] Okoth-Obbo, however, contends that the central role assigned to national legislation in granting asylum under the Convention implies that if a state adopts a stringent refugee policy, it can effectively undermine the realization of the provisions in the Convention.[72] The central role of national legislation, however, can play a positive facilitative role in legally recognizing and protecting climate refugees through the principle of solidarity and humanitarianism as demonstrated during the liberation struggle.

[66] African Charter on Human and Peoples' Rights, June 27, 1981, OAU Doc. CAB/LEG/67/3 rev. 5.

[67] Jegede, "Indigenous Peoples, Climate Migration and International Human Rights Law in Africa," 169.

[68] 1969 OAU Convention, art. 2(1).

[69] 1969 OAU Convention, art. 2(2).

[70] Addaney, "The Legal Protection of the Rights of Urban Refugees in Uganda," 218.

[71] R.K. Medard, *Rwelamira*, "Two Decades of the Convention Governing the Specific Aspects of Refugee Problems in Africa," *International Journal of Refugee Law* 1, no. 4 (1989): 557.

[72] George Okoth-Obbo, "Thirty Years On: A Legal Review of the 1969 OAU Refugee Convention Governing the Specific Aspects of Refugee Problems in Africa," *Refugee Survey Quarterly* 20, no. 1 (2001): 79.

Burgeoning regional solidarity may be invoked to justify a moral, if not legal, obligation of states to somehow intervene to offer assistance to other states facing climate-related crises including admitting their citizens into their territories on humanitarian grounds.[73]

As stated before, the 1951 Convention defines a refugee as someone with 'a well-founded fear of persecution on the basis of his or her race, religion, nationality, membership of a particular social group, or political opinion'.[74] In contrast, the 1969 Convention incorporates the same definition[75] but expands the scope. Article I(2) of the 1969 Convention provides that:

> the term "refugee" shall also apply to every person who, owing to external aggression, occupation, foreign domination or *events seriously disturbing public order in either part [or] the whole of his country of origin or nationality*, is compelled to leave his place of habitual residence in order to seek refuge in another place outside his country of origin or nationality. (Emphasize by author)

The 1969 Convention thus seeks to expand the definition of refugees to include those fleeing 'events seriously disturbing public order'.[76] It is likely that those who flee natural disasters such as a drought, famine, tsunami or an earthquake would fall within this definition. It recognizes that international protection might be needed for events that gravely disturb public order and consequently potentially offer protection for people displaced by circumstances accompanying such events. For instance, the Brazil Plan of Action which was adopted in 2014 by 28 countries also unequivocally declares climate change as a challenge to the region and calls on UNHCR to support the development of regional and national policies to respond to the protection needs of those forced to move

---

[73] Mayer, "The International Legal Challenges of Climate-Induced Migration," 357.

[74] 1951 Convention, art. 1A provides: The term "refugee" shall apply to any person who: … (2) who owing to well-founded fear of being persecuted for reasons of race, religion, nationality, membership of a particular social group or political opinion is outside the country of his nationality and is unable or owing to such fear is unwilling to avail himself of the protection of that country or who not having a nationality and being outside the country of his former habitual residence as a result of such events is unable or owing to such fear is unwilling to return to it.

[75] 1969 OAU Convention, art. I(1).

[76] 1969 OAU Convention, art. 1(2).

because of climate-induced disasters.[77] The Declaration notes that because of previous massive refugee flows in Central America, it is necessary to consider enlarging the concept of refugees to include 'persons who have fled their country because their lives, safety or freedom have been threatened by generalized violence, foreign aggression, internal conflicts, massive violation of human rights or other circumstances which have seriously disturbed public order'.[78] The AU can therefore adopt a similar approach as it was used by some states in the Horn of Africa during the 2011–2012 droughts to admit people displaced from Somalia, and by others in Latin America to grant asylum to Haitians displaced by the 2010 earthquake.[79] The UNHCR has been using both definitions in its operations in Africa[80] notwithstanding the comparative ease of applying article I(2) of the 1969 Convention in the case of mass influxes which is a usual feature of refugee movements in Africa.[81] Practically, it has been observed that states and the UNHCR regularly rely only on article I(2) to recognize refugees in Africa. Article I(2) of the 1969 Convention unambiguously establishes objective principles which are based on the prevailing conditions in the country of origin to determine refugee status.[82] Mandal observes that these objective principles 'entail neither the elements of deliberateness nor discrimination inherent in the definition of the 1951 Convention'.[83]

[77] "Brazil Declaration: A Framework for Cooperation and Regional Solidarity to Strengthen the International Protection of Refugees, Displaced and Stateless Persons in Latin America and the Caribbean," December 3, 2014, http://www.acnur.org/t3/fileadmin/scripts/doc.php?file=t3/fileadmin/Documentos/BDL/2014/9865.

[78] Organization of American States, "Cartagena Declaration on Refugees, Colloquium on the International Protection of Refugees in Central America, Mexico and Panama," November 22, 1984.

[79] Elizabeth Ferris and Jonas Bergmann, "Soft Law, Migration and Climate Change Governance," *Journal of Human Rights and the Environment* 8, no. 1 (2017): 6–29.

[80] EO Awuku, "Refugee Movements in Africa and the OAU Convention on Refugees," *Journal of African Law* 39 (1995): 81; UNHCR, Executive Committee of the High Commissioner's Programme, Note on International Protection, 45th Session, UN Doc. A/AC.96/830, September 7, 1994, at para. 32.

[81] Ibid., Part II.C.

[82] Paul Weis, "The Convention of the Organisation of African Unity Governing the Specific Aspects of Refugee Problems in Africa," *Revue des droits de l'homme* 3 (1970): 455.

[83] Ruma Mandal, "Protection Mechanisms Outside of the 1951 Convention ('Complementary Protection'), Legal and Protection Policy Research Series" (Geneva: UNHCR Department of Internal Protection, 2005), 13, http://www.unhcr.org/435df0aa2.pdf.

The 2009 Convention for the Protection and Assistance of Internally Displaced Persons in Africa (Kampala Convention) is another regional instrument, which expressly protects and assists internally displaced persons (IDPs) in Africa. Although largely devoted to displacement within national borders, when read together with the 1969 OAU Convention and the African Charter on Human and Peoples' Rights (African Charter),[84] a number of its provisions may connote pioneering possibilities for the protection of the collective rights of climate refugees in Africa. This development represents a move from the normative status quo under international law. Due to the opportunities it opens for novel improvements in the protection of IDPs, the Kampala Convention serves as a significant regional conduit over the flaws in international human rights and refugee protection instruments in addressing the plight of climate-induced displaced persons.[85] The Kampala Convention plainly recognizes the link between climate change and migration. For instance, it defines IDPs as:

[p]ersons or groups of persons who have been forced or obliged to flee or to leave their homes or places of habitual residence, in particular as a result of or in order to avoid the effects of ... natural or human-made disasters, and who have not crossed an internationally recognized State border.[86]

This definition implies that the Kampala Convention leaves no one in uncertainty as to whether climate change is contained under 'natural or human-made disasters'.[87] In addition, article 5(4) of the Kampala Convention requires States to 'take measures to protect and assist persons who have been internally displaced due to natural or human-made disasters, including climate change'. Although climate refugees fall outside the protection afforded in the Kampala Convention because the Convention applies only to IDPs, that the instrument however anticipates that the IDPs may include persons adversely affected by climate change is not difficult to conclude from its provisions. Therefore, when

---

[84] African (Banjul) Charter on Human and Peoples' Rights, June 27, 1981, OAU Doc. CAB/LEG/67/3 rev. 5 (African Charter).

[85] Jegede, op. cit., note 53.

[86] African Union Convention for the Protection and Assistance of Internally Displaced Persons in Africa (Kampala Convention), October 23, 2009, 7796-treaty-0039, article 1(k).

[87] Jegede, "Indigenous Peoples, Climate Migration and International Human Rights Law in Africa," 169.

article 1(2) of the 1969 OAU Convention[88] is read together with article 5(4) of the Kampala Convention, a case can be made for the former to offer legal protection to climate refugees.

Furthermore, from a political perspective, the principle of solidarity and mutual assistance that underlined the formation of the OAU and now the African Union is being tested in the era of climate change that requires cooperation in managing its adverse impacts. The preamble to the AU Constitutive Act[89] was inspired by the noble ideals which guided the founding fathers of the Organization of African Unity and generations of Pan-Africanists in their determination to promote unity, solidarity, cohesion, and cooperation among the peoples of Africa and African States. Consequently, Article 3(a) of the objectives of the AU seeks to 'achieve greater unity and solidarity between the African countries and the peoples of Africa'.[90] This is particularly significant in the quest to offer protection to climate refugees in Africa in an era when states are closing their borders to refugees. For instance, in most African countries plagued by economic crises and social problems, 'governments and the local population accuse refugees of being responsible for higher rents, intermittent shortages of basic necessities, overcrowded schools and inadequate healthcare facilities, increasing crime rates and other urban ills'.[91] In particular, countries such as Egypt, Ethiopia, and Nigeria are already facing high demographic pressure and are technically unable to cope with the foreseeable loss of inhabitable territory resulting from climate change, thus making it harder for them to accommodate refugees.[92] There is also a misconception among governments that refugees

---

[88] Article 1(2) provides that the term "refugee" shall also apply to every person who, owing to external aggression, occupation, foreign domination or *events seriously disturbing public order in either part [or] the whole of his country of origin or nationality*, is compelled to leave his place of habitual residence in order to seek refuge in another place outside his country of origin or nationality.

[89] Constitutive Act of the African Union, Adopted on November 7, 2000 and entered into force on May 26, 2001, https://au.int/sites/default/files/pages/32020-file-constitutiveact_en.pdf.

[90] Ibid., at art. 3(a).

[91] Addaney, "The Legal Protection of the Rights of Urban Refugees in Uganda," 218.

[92] Ulrike Grote and Koko Warner, "Environmental Change and Migration in Sub-Saharan Africa," *International Journal of Global Warming* 2, no. 1 (2010): 36; Jamila Abdullahi et al., *Rural–Urban Migration of the Nigerian Work Populace and Climate Change Effects on Food Supply: A Case Study of Kaduna City in Northern Nigeria*, June

cause an increase in crime rates in the cities.[93] As a result, most African governments are hostile toward refugees in general.[94] Particularly, the experiences of refugees in cities such as Cairo, Johannesburg, Kampala, and Khartoum are typified by a high level of helplessness due to the subjective enforcement of international and national protection regimes.[95] These developments reinforce the hesitation of the AU to adopt a policy response to protect climate refugees on the continent.

Nonetheless, the UN Secretary-General's 2009 Report on climate change and its possible security implications highlighted that 'multilateral comprehensive agreements would be the ideal preventive mechanism, providing where, and on what legal basis, affected populations would be permitted to move elsewhere, as well as their status'.[96] Regional agreements in Africa may therefore be easier to make than global ones, as few developed states are likely to welcome a significant number of climate refugees. Consequently, it is likely that regional negotiations will result in more ambitious decisions than in universal ones.[97] On this premise, it can be argued that through cooperation underpinned by the principle of African solidarity, the AU can adopt regional policy to legally recognize and protect climate refugees based on the rich development of mechanisms for protecting refugees in Africa. By encouraging regional efforts to host refugees, the AU's efforts would be cost-effective and, particularly at times when there are similarities in local languages and customs

28–30, 2009, http://siteresources.worldbank.org/INTURBANDEVELOPMENT/Resources/336387-1256566800920/6505269-1268260567624/Abdullahi.pdf.

[93] Gerhard Hoffstaedter, "Between a Rock and a Hard Place: Urban Refugees in a Global Context," in *Urban Refugees: Challenges in Protection, Services and Policy*, ed. Koichi Koizumi and Gerhard Hoffstaedter (New York and London: Routledge, 2016), 1–10.

[94] Michael Addaney, "Toward Promoting Protection: Refugee Protection and Local Integration in Sub-Saharan Africa," *Studia Migracyjne – Przegląd Polonijny* 165, no. 3 (2017): 71–87.

[95] Anita Fábos and Gaime Kibreab, "Urban Refugees: Introduction," *Refuge* 24, no. 1 (2007): 3–8.

[96] UN Secretary-General, *Climate Change and Its Possible Security Implications: Report of the Secretary-General*, 54, UN Doc. A/64/350, September 11, 2009, http://www.unhcr.org/refworld/pdfid/4ad5e6380.pdf.

[97] Aurélie Sgro, *Towards Recognition of Environmental Refugees by the European Union*, ASYLON(S) (2008) 6, http://wwwreseau-terra.eu/article844html.

across neighboring states, socioculturally appropriate.[98] This approach also has the potential to help preempt refugee flows and manage displacement which might cost far less than dealing with regional conflicts or supporting individuals who arrive in a country *en masse* because of climate-induced conflict.[99] In the end, the effectiveness of the legal protection of climate refugees in Africa would essentially depend on states' commitment to and involvement in regional negotiations in this regard. It is the fate of any regional legal scheme that the beginning and the end of the story lie in the hands of states. If AU cannot do anything without the consent of states, it should do everything possible to encourage states to cooperate especially through the spirit of solidarity and regional cooperation to lessen the human suffering arising from the adverse effects of climate change.

4   Conclusion

Many populations in the African region have already or will experience forced migration as a result of the adverse effects of climate change. Some of the notable examples of these adverse effects of climate change include extreme climatic events (flooding and drought), nonviable lands, famine, loss of livelihoods, and other development-induced displacement associated with the implementation of the Reducing Emissions from Deforestation and Forest Degradation (REDD+) and Clean Development Mechanism projects. The discussions in this chapter highlight that unlike the international instruments developed under the auspices of the UN, the 1969 OAU Convention has promising provisions which address the identifiable gaps in the international framework. These gaps are primarily related to a lack of an explicit confirmation of the link between climate change and forced migration and corresponding obligations of international humanitarian institutions. The Kampala Convention clearly links migration to the adverse effects of climate change through the combined reading of its provisions, particularly,

---

[98] Vikram Odedra Kolmannskog, *Norwegian Refugee Council, Future Floods of Refugees: A Comment on Climate Change, Conflict and Forced Migration* (2008), 19–21, http://www.nrc.no/arch/_img/9268480.pdf.

[99] Hans Joachim Schellnhuber, *Climate Change as a Security Risk* (Berlin: German Advisory Council on Global Change, 2008), 204–207, http://www.wbgu.de/wbgu_jg2007_engl.pdf.

articles 1(c), 1(k), 5(4), and 9(2)(e). Article 1(2) of the 1969 OAU Convention underscores that the term 'refugee' is also applicable to every person who, owing to external aggression, occupation, foreign domination, or *events seriously disturbing public order in either part or the whole of his country of origin or nationality*, and is compelled to leave his place of habitual residence in order to seek refuge in another place outside his country of origin or nationality.[100] These provisions read together lay concrete foundations and obligations for the AU and the member states who are States Parties to both Conventions. The AU Constitutive Act specifically through using the principle of cooperation between African states to address continental problems, 1969 OAU Convention and the 2009 Kampala Convention thus contain valuable provisions that can serve as significant normative lessons to the development of regional framework for the protection of climate refugees in Africa.

REFERENCES

Abdullahi, Jamila et al. *Rural—Urban Migration of the Nigerian Work Populace and Climate Change Effects on Food Supply: A Case Study of Kaduna City in Northern Nigeria*, June 28–30, 2009. http://siteresources.worldbank.org/INTURBANDEVELOPMENT/Resources/336387–1256566800920/6505269-1268260567624/Abdullahi.pdf.

Addaney, Michael. "A Step Forward in the Protection of Urban Refugees: The Legal Protection of the Rights of Urban Refugees in Uganda." *African Human Rights Law Journal* 17, no. 1 (2017): 218–243.

Addaney, Michael. "Toward Promoting Protection: Refugee Protection and Local Integration in Sub-Saharan Africa." *Studia Migracyjne – Przegląd Polonijny* 165, no. 3 (2017): 71–87.

Addaney, Michael, Elsabé Boshoff, and Michael Gyan Nyarko. "Protection of Environmental Assets in Urban Africa: Regional and Sub-regional Human Rights and Practical Environmental Protection Mechanisms." *Australian Journal of Human Rights* 24, no. 2 (2018): 182–200.

Addaney, Michael, Elsabé Boshoff, and Bamisaye Oyetola. "The Climate Change and Human Rights Nexus in African." *Amsterdam Law Forum* 9, no. 3 (2017): 5–28.

African Charter on Human and Peoples' Rights, June 27, 1981, OAU Doc. CAB/LEG/67/3 rev. 5.

---

[100] 1969 OAU Convention, art. 1(2).

African Union Convention for the Protection and Assistance of Internally Displaced Persons in Africa (Kampala Convention), October 23, 2009, 7796-treaty-0039.

Aleinikoff, Alex. "Protected Characteristics and Social Perceptions: An Analysis of the Meaning of 'Membership of a Particular Social Group.'" In *Refugee Protection in International Law: UNHCR's Global Consultations on International Protection*, edited by Erika Feller, Volker Türk, and Frances Nicholson. Cambridge: Cambridge University Press, 2003.

Anderson, Heather, Tess Burton, David Hodgkinson, and Lucy Young. "The Hour When the Ship Comes In: A Convention for Persons Displaced by Climate Change." *Monash University Law Review* 36, no. 1 (2010): 76.

Arbel, Efrat, Catherine Dauvergne, and Jenni Millbank, eds. *Gender in Refugee Law: From the Margins to the Centre*. London and New York: Routledge, 2014.

Awuku, E.O. "Refugee Movements in Africa and the OAU Convention on Refugees." *Journal of African Law* 39 (1995): 81.

Biermann, Frank, and Ingrid Boas. "Preparing for a Warmer World: Towards a Global Governance System to Protect Climate Refugees." *Global Environmental Politics* 10, no. 1 (2010): 60–88.

"Brazil Declaration: A Framework for Cooperation and Regional Solidarity to Strengthen the International Protection of Refugees, Displaced and Stateless Persons in Latin America and the Caribbean," December 3, 2014. http://www.acnur.org/t3/fileadmin/scripts/doc.php?file=t3/fileadmin/Documentos/BDL/2014/9865.

Conference of the Parties to the Framework Convention on Climate Change. *Report of the Conference of the Parties on Its Sixteenth Session*, 14, 14(f), UN Doc. FCCC/CP/2010/7/Add.1, March 15, 2011. https://unfccc.int/resource/docs/2010/cop16/eng/07a01.pdf.

Conference of the Parties to the Framework Convention on Climate Change. *Rep. of the Conference of the Parties on Its Eighteenth Session*, 7(a)(iv), U.N. Doc. FCCC/CP/2012/8/Add.1, February 28, 2013. http://unfccc.int/resource/docs/2012/cop18/eng/08a01.pdf.

Constitutive Act of the African Union, Adopted on November 7, 2000 and entered into force on May 26, 2001. https://au.int/sites/default/files/pages/32020-file-constitutiveact_en.pdf.

Convention relating to the Status of Refugees (adopted July 28, 1951, entered into force April 22, 1954, 189 U.N.T.S. 137.

Cooper, Jessica B. "Environmental Refugees: Meeting the Requirements of the Refugee Definition." *New York University Environmental Law Journal* 6 (1998): 502.

"Desertification: The People Whose Land Is Turning to Dust." BBC News, November 2, 2015. https://www.bbc.com/news/world-africa-34790661.

Dupuy, Pierre-Marie, and Jorge E. Vinuales. *International Environmental Law*. Cambridge: Cambridge University Press, 2018.

Edenhofer, Ottmar et al. "Climate Change 2014: Mitigation of Climate Change, Working Group III Contribution to the Fifth Assessment Report of the Intergovernmental Panel on Climate Change." New York: Cambridge University Press, 2014.

Environmental Justice Foundation. "Protecting Climate Refugees: Securing International Protection for Climate Refugees." https://ejfoundation.org/what-we-do/climate/protecting-climate-refugees.

Fábos, Anita, and Gaime Kibreab. "Urban Refugees: Introduction." *Refuge* 24, no. 1 (2007): 3–8.

Ferris, Elizabeth, and Jonas Bergmann. "Soft Law, Migration and Climate Change Governance." *Journal of Human Rights and the Environment* 8, no. 1 (2017): 6–29.

Field, B. Christopher et al., eds. *Managing the Risks of Extreme Events and Disasters to Advance Climate Change Adaptation: Special Report of the Intergovernmental Panel on Climate Change* (SREX Report). New York: Cambridge University Press, 2012.

Food and Agriculture Organization (FAO). "The Magnitude of the Problem." http://www.fao.org/docrep/x5318e/x5318e02.htm.

Giannini, Tyler, and Bonnie Docherty. "Confronting a Rise Tide: A Proposal for a Convention of Climate Change Refugees." *Harvard Environmental Law Review* 33 (2009): 349.

Grote, Ulrike, and Koko Warner. "Environmental Change and Migration in Sub-Saharan Africa." *International Journal of Global Warming* 2, no. 1 (2010): 36.

Guterres, António. UN Refugee Agency, 1951 Convention Relating to the Status of Refugees and Its 1967 Protocol, 2011.

Hathaway, James C. *The Rights of Refugees Under International Law*. Cambridge: Cambridge University Press, 2005.

Hoffstaedter, Gerhard. "Between a Rock and a Hard Place: Urban Refugees in a Global Context." In *Urban Refugees: Challenges in Protection, Services and Policy*, edited by Koichi Koizumi and Gerhard Hoffstaedter, 1–10. New York and London: Routledge, 2016.

Hong, Jeanhee. "Refugees of the 21st Century: Environmental Injustice." *Cornell Journal of Law and Public Policy* 10, no. 2 (2001): 331.

Hugo, Graeme. "Climate Change—Induced Mobility and the Existing Migration Regime in Asia and the Pacific," in *Climate Change and Displacement: Multidisciplinary Perspectives*, edited by Jane McAdam. Oxford: Hart Publishing, 2010.

Inter-Agency Standing Committee (IASC). "Climate Change, Migration and Displacement: Who Will Be Affected?" (2008). http://unfccc.int/resource/docs/2008/smsn/igo/022.pdf.

Intergovernmental Panel on Climate Change (IPCC). *Climate Change 2007: Synthesis Report*. New York: Cambridge University Press, 2007.

International Covenant on Civil and Political Rights (ICCPR), December 19, 1966, 999 UNTS 14668.

IPBES Secretariat. "Media Release: Worsening Worldwide Land Degradation Now 'Critical', Undermining Well-Being of 3.2 Billion People." March 23, 2018. https://www.ipbes.net/news/media-release-worsening-world-wide-land-degradation-now-%E2%80%98critical%E2%80%99-undermin-ing-well-being-32.

IPCC. "An IPCC Special Report on the Impacts of Global Warming of 1.5°C Above Pre-industrial Levels and Related Global Greenhouse Gas Emission Pathways, in the Context of Strengthening the Global Response to the Threat of Climate Change, Sustainable Development and Efforts to Eradicate Poverty: Summary for Policymakers." Geneva: IPCC, 2018. http://ipcc.ch/report/sr15/.

Jastram, Kate. "Warm World, Cold Reception: Climate Change, National Security and Forced Migration." *Vermont Journal of Environmental Law* 15, no. 4 (2014): 751–765.

Jegede, Ademola Oluborode. "Indigenous Peoples, Climate Migration and International Human Rights Law in Africa, with Reflections on the Relevance of the Kampala Convention." In *Research Handbook on Climate Change, Migration and the Law*, edited by Benoît Mayer and François Crépeau, 169–189. Cheltenham: Edward Elgar, 2017.

Kälin, Walter. "From the Nansen Principles to the Nansen Initiative." *Forced Migration Review* 41 (2012): 49.

Knox, John Henry. "Report of the Independent Expert on the Issue of Human Rights Obligations Relating to the Enjoyment of a Safe, Clean, Healthy and Sustainable Environment." A/HRC/22/43, December 24, 2012.

Kolmannskog, Vikram Odedra. *Norwegian Refugee Council, Future Floods of Refugees: A Comment on Climate Change, Conflict and Forced Migration*. Oslo: Norwegian Refugee Council, 2008. http://www.nrc.no/arch/_img/9268480.pdf.

Kuusipalo, Rina. "Exiled by Emissions—Climate Change Related Displacement and Migration in International Law: Gaps in Global Governance and the Role of the UN Climate Convention." *Vermont Journal of Environmental Law* 18, no. 4 (2017): 615–647.

Mandal, Ruma. "Protection Mechanisms Outside of the 1951 Convention ('Complementary Protection'), Legal and Protection Policy Research Series." Geneva: UNHCR Department of Internal Protection, 2005. http://www.unhcr.org/435df0aa2.pdf.

Mayer, Benoit. "Climate Change and International Law in the Grim Days." *European Journal of International Law* 24, no. 3 (2013): 949.

Mayer, Benoît. "The International Legal Challenges of Climate-Induced Migration: Proposal for an International Legal Framework." *Colorado Journal of International Environmental Law and Policy* 22, no. 3 (2011): 357.

McAdam, Jane. *Climate Change, Forced Migration, and International Law.* New York: Oxford University Press, 2012.

McAdam, Jane. "Swimming Against the Tide: Why a Climate Change Displacement Treaty Is Not the Answer." *International Journal of Refugee Law* 23, no. 1 (2011): 2–27.

McQue, Katie. "Did Deforestation Cause the Ebola Outbreak." *New Internationalist,* April 10, 2018. https://newint.org/features/web-exclusive/2018/04/10/deforestation-ebola-outbreak.

Moberg, Kara K. "Extending Refugee Definitions to Cover Environmentally Displaced Persons Displaces Necessary Protection." *Iowa Law Review* 94 (2009): 1121.

Moe, Kelsey. "Climate Change Refugees: Regional Agreements Can Better Fill the Gap in Legal Protection." *Hastings Environmental Law Journal Blog Post,* January 13, 2018. http://sites.uchastings.edu/helj/2018/01/13/climate-change-refugees-regional-agreements-can-better-fill-the-gap-in-legal-protection/.

Okoth-Obbo, George. "Thirty Years On: A Legal Review of the 1969 OAU Refugee Convention Governing the Specific Aspects of Refugee Problems in Africa." *Refugee Survey Quarterly* 20, no. 1 (2001): 79.

Olivero, Jesus et al. "Recent Loss of Closed Forests Is Associated with Ebola Virus Disease Outbreaks." *Scientific Reports* 7, no. 14291 (2017): 1–7.

Organization of African Unity (Now African Union) Convention Governing the Specific Aspects of Refugee Problems in Africa (adopted 10 September 1969, entered into force June 20, 1974), 1001 U.N.T.S. 45.

Organization of American States. "Cartagena Declaration on Refugees, Colloquium on the International Protection of Refugees in Central America, Mexico and Panama." November 22, 1984.

Paris Agreement on Climate Change, 12 December 2015, T.I.A.S. No. 16-1104.

Rwelamira, Medard R.K. "Two Decades of the Convention Governing the Specific Aspects of Refugee Problems in Africa." *International Journal of Refugee Law* 1, no. 4 (1989): 557.

Schellnhuber, Hans Joachim. *Climate Change as a Security Risk.* Berlin: German Advisory Council on Global Change, 2008. http://www.wbgu.de/wbgu_jg2007_engl.pdf.

Sgro, Aurélie. *Towards Recognition of Environmental Refugees by the European Union,* ASYLON(S) (2008), 6. http://wwwreseau-terra.eu/article844html.

Status of Ratification of the Convention of the United Nations Framework Convention on Climate Change. http://unfccc.int/essential_background/convention/status_of_ratification/items/2631.php.

Stefano M. Torelli. "Climate-Driven Migration in Africa." *European Council of Foreign Relations,* December 20, 2017. https://www.ecfr.eu/article/commentary_climate_driven_migration_in_africa.

UNHCR. Executive Committee of the High Commissioner's Programme, Note on International Protection, 45th Session, UN Doc. A/ AC.96/830, September 7, 1994, at para. 32.

UNHCR. *Handbook on Procedures and Criteria for Determining Refugee Status Under the 1951 Convention and the 1967 Protocol Relating to the Status of Refugees.* Geneva: UNHCR, 1979.

UN Secretary-General. *Climate Change and Its Possible Security Implications: Report of the Secretary-General,* 54, UN Doc. A/64/350, September 11, 2009. http://www.unhcr.org/refworld/pdfid/4ad5e6380.pdf.

Weis, Paul. "The Convention of the Organisation of African Unity Governing the Specific Aspects of Refugee Problems in Africa." *Revue des droits de l'homme* 3 (1970): 455.

Williams, Angela. "Turning the Tide: Recognizing Climate Change in International Law." *Law and Policy* 30, no. 4 (2008): 509.

World Health Organization. *Climate Change and Infectious Diseases,* 2003, 16–17. https://www.who.int/globalchange/environment/en/chapter6.pdf.

CHAPTER 14

The Best Interest of the Child and Climate Change Adaptation in Sub-Saharan Africa

Elsabé Boshoff

1   INTRODUCTION

The far-reaching impacts of climate change are being felt in all parts of the world.[1] Africa is particularly vulnerable to the adverse effects of climate change such as flooding, drought, sea-level rise and spread of disease.[2] Africa furthermore contributes very little of the greenhouse gas (GHG) emissions that cause climate change, but suffers some of the worst consequences, and for this reason, adaptation "is an overriding priority for the

---

[1] African Union (AU), "Draft African Union Strategy on Climate Change" (2014), at 1, 8; Climate and Development Knowledge Network (CDKN), "The IPCC's Fifth Assessment Report: What's in It for Africa?" (2014), at 1, 11, available at http://cdkn.org/resource/highlights-africa-ar5/?loclang=en_gb, accessed October 10, 2016.

[2] Paul Collier et al., "Climate Change and Africa," *Oxford Review of Economic Policy* 24 (2008), at 337; J.J. Romm, "Present and Future Climate Realities for Children," in *The Challenge of Climate Change: Children on the Front Line*, ed. UNICEF (2014), at 6; Rema Hanna and Paulina Oliva, "Implications of Climate Change for Children in Developing Countries," in *Children and Climate Change*, ed. The Future of Children (2016), available at http://www.futureofchildren.org/publications/journals/journal_details/index.xml?

E. Boshoff (✉)
Technical Assistant, African Commission on Human and Peoples' Rights, Banjul, The Gambia

© The Author(s) 2020
M. Addaney et al. (eds.), *Governance, Human Rights, and Political Transformation in Africa*,
https://doi.org/10.1007/978-3-030-27049-0_14

359

continent".[3] It is thus imperative that African governments take steps in the form of policies, legislation and programmes to address the negative impacts of climate change through adapting to this change and strengthening the continent's adaptive capacity and its resilience to future shocks. Yet, in the formulation of such policies, the most vulnerable groups are often overlooked, with the result that adaptation can lead to uneven allocations of benefits and costs to citizens, with potentially devastating social consequences.[4] One vulnerable group which has not received sufficient attention in climate change policy is children.[5] This is while according to UNICEF "those who have contributed the least to climate change [such as] the youngest and most disadvantaged should receive the strongest protections [from climate change impacts]".[6]

Children are the most vulnerable to negative impacts of climate change such as more widespread diseases, climate-induced migration, and lack of access to water and food, since these directly threaten their survival and development.[7] When disaster strikes they may be taken from school and required to work to support their families.[8] Climate change, thus, in "many ways [...] threatens children's physical and mental

---

journalid=86, accessed September 25, 2016, at 115; and Isabelle Niang et al., "Africa," in *Impacts, Adaptation, and Vulnerability. Part B: Regional Aspects. Contribution of Working Group II to the Fifth Assessment Report of the Intergovernmental Panel on Climate Change*, ed. IPCC Working Group II (2014), at 1237–1238.

[3] AU, *Draft Strategy*, 20–21.

[4] Niang et al., *Africa*, 1227; Edward R. Carr, "Between Structure and Agency: Livelihoods and Adaptation in Ghana's Central Region," *Global Environmental Change* 18 (2008), at 690; J. Guillemot and J. Burgess, "Children Rights at Risk," in *Children on the Front Line*, ed. UNICEF (2014), at 50; and AU, *Draft Strategy*, 54.

[5] Children in a changing climate coalition (CCCC), "Child-Centred Adaptation: Realising Children's Rights in a Changing Climate" (2015), at 2; See also Report of the Special Rapporteur on the issue of human rights obligations relating to the enjoyment of a safe, clean, healthy and sustainable environment to the General Assembly on 24 January 2018, which related specifically to the rights of children.

[6] UNICEF, "Unless We Act Now: The Impact of Climate Change on Children" (2015), at 66; CCCC, *Child-Centred Adaptation*, 2, 6.

[7] Courtenay Cabot Venton "Why We Need a Child-Centred Approach to Adaptation," in UNICEF, *The Challenge of Climate Change*, above at note 2 at 32; Guillemot and Burgess, *Children Rights at Risk*, 47–48; Janet Currie and Olivier Deschênes, "Children and Climate Change: Introducing the Issue," in *Children and Climate Change*, 3–4.

[8] Venton, *Child-Centred Approach*, 32.

well-being".[9] In addition, children make up almost half of the population in the majority of African countries, and as such is a significant percentage whose specific needs should not be overlooked.[10]

To date, policies on climate change responses and adaptation have not paid sufficient attention to how such measures can include children.[11] There is no clear international normative framework for the best interest of the child in the context of climate change adaptation and, it will be argued below, insufficient recognition of children's interests in national climate change adaptation policies in Africa.[12] What is available is the wide concept of "the best interest of the child", which, according to the Convention on the Rights of the Child (CRC) must be "the primary concern in all decisions affecting children". The best interest principle may thus provide a mechanism through which the specific needs and concerns of children with regard to climate change could be given legal protection.

Following this introduction, Sect. 2 of this chapter provides clarification of the core concepts of climate change adaptation and the best interest of the child. Part three looks in more depth at the best interest of the child and principles which have been developed as to how it should be applied in a human rights/climate change context. Part four discusses national adaptation policies in relation to children and parts five extracts from the previous discussions the main elements which constitute the best interest of the child in the context of adaptation in Africa. Part six concludes the discussion. The objective of this chapter is to explore the potential of the best interest principle as a standard to (a) measure existing national climate change policies; and (b) serve as a guideline when formulating national and local level policies to ensure that the concerns of this particularly vulnerable group are not left out of when planning for adaptation futures.

---

[9] Currie and Deschênes, *Children and Climate Change*, 3.

[10] UNICEF, *The Challenge of Climate Change*, 1.

[11] Mounkaila Goumandakoyc and Richard Munang, "Engaging Children in the African Climate Change Discourse," in UNICEF, *The Challenge of Climate Change: Children on the Front Line* (2014), at 73; UNICEF, "Children's Vulnerability to Climate Change and Disaster Impacts in East Asia and the Pacific" (2009), at 18.

[12] UNICEF, *The Challenge of Climate Change*, 3.

2 DEFINING THE CONCEPTS: CLIMATE CHANGE ADAPTATION AND THE 'BEST INTEREST OF THE CHILD'

2.1   Climate Change Adaptation

Adaptation refers to "adjustments in ecological, social or economic systems in response to actual or expected climatic stimuli".[13] In simple terms, adaptation refers to the ways in which people adjust their lives to survive in a changing climate. Local-level adaptation is often the most effective, since it takes account of the specific local circumstances and knowledge within a community.[14] However, there is also a danger that such a piecemeal approach may result in "unsustainable coping mechanisms", which could "compromise children's long-term prospects".[15] Therefore it is necessary that coordinated and integrated state policies be formulated which have a long-term sustainable focus and take into account all the consequences of climate change.[16]

One may distinguish three ways in which adaptation can be implemented based on its political point of departure: adaptation can take the form of resilience, transition or transformation.[17] Resilience involves incremental adjustments to ensure that existing systems can withstand environmental onslaughts—thus largely maintaining the status quo, together with the current injustices and inequalities, and vested interests. The other two approaches arguably display a political commitment to socio-economic change in line with human rights and sustainable development.[18] While transition does so gradually, transformation has drastic implications for the status quo and aims to eradicate inequality,

---

[13] Collier et al., *Climate Change and Africa*, 337.

[14] Emily Polack, "Child Rights and Climate Change Adaptation: Voices from Kenya and Cambodia," *Children in a Changing Climate* (2010), at 37; Mark Pelling, *Adaptation to Climate Change: From Resilience to Transformation* (2012), at 7.

[15] UNICEF, *Unless We Act Now*, 54; Government of Kenya, "National Climate Change Action Plan 2013–2017" (NCCAP) (2013), at 4; Thea Dickenson and Ian Burton, "Palliative Climate Change Planning and Its Consequences for Youth," in UNICEF, *The Challenge of Climate Change*, at 40.

[16] United Nations Environmental Programme (UNEP), "Guidebook on National Legislation for Adaptation to Climate Change" (2011), at vi.

[17] Pelling, *Adaptation to Climate Change*, 23.

[18] Id., 24.

exploitation and unsustainable consumption.[19] The general consensus, particularly among developing countries, is that adaptation should go hand-in-hand with sustainable development, and should benefit those who are most vulnerable through improved standards of living.[20] The developing world, not surprisingly, thus largely tends to favour a transformational approach to climate change adaptation.

2.2   The Best Interest of the Child

The best interest of the child principle was introduced into international law with the first Declaration on the Rights of the Child, 1959.[21] It has since been taken up in the CRC,[22] The African Charter on the Rights and Welfare of the Child (ACRWC)[23] and also in most national laws concerning children.[24] However, there is no attempt in either the CRC or the other international instruments to define what is meant by the "best interests of the child". Attempts at providing a generic definition of the best interest principle include that it means that a child must be considered "before a decision affecting his/her life is made", or that all policies and distribution of resources must "be used in a progressive way" to fulfil the best interest of the child "to the maximum extent possible".[25] Freeman, one of the most prolific authors on the topic

[19] Ibid.

[20] AU, "Agenda 2063" ed 2 (2014), at 3; AU, *Draft Strategy*, 16, 36; NCCAP at 21, 27; Michal Nachmany et al., "The GLOBE Climate Legislation Study: A Review of Climate Change Legislation in 66 Countries," 4th ed. (2014), at 418; and Nachmany et al., "The 2015 Global Climate Legislation Study: A Review of Climate Change Legislation in 99 Countries," Grantham Institute (2015), at 3.

[21] Michael Freeman, "Article 3: The Best Interest of the Child," in *A Commentary on the United Nations Convention on the Rights of the Child*, ed. Andre Alen et al. (2007), at 15.

[22] Art 3(1) of the CRC. The best interest principle is also mentioned elsewhere in the CRC, but these are concerned with specific contexts which are not presently relevant

[23] Art 4(1) of the ACRWC.

[24] Marta Mauras, "Public Policies and Child Rights: Entering the Third Decade of the Convention on the Rights of the Child," *Annals* 633 (2011), at 54; United Nations Committee on the Rights of the Child (CRC) General Comment 14, "On the Right of the Child to Have His or Her Best Interests Taken as a Primary Consideration," adopted on 29 May 2013 at the 62nd session of the CRC (GC14), para. 2.

[25] Yvonne Dausab, "The Best Interest of the Child," in *Children's Rights in Namibia*, ed. Oliver C. Ruppel (2009), at 147; Mauras, *Public Policies*, 53.

views the best interest principle as indeterminate and able to reflect the "dominant meanings" given to "best interest" in a certain time or culture.[26] The main characteristic of the best interest of the child and the way it has been treated is thus that it is flexible and should be defined on a case-by-case basis.[27] This makes it difficult to define the best interest of the child in the abstract and means that there is indeterminacy as to its exact meaning, which has led to many criticisms.[28] One of the main criticisms is that it is a "colourless meta-value" or "hollow theory", which adds very little and can be used to justify any number of contradictory decisions, and is open to abuse and inconsistent application.[29] Another criticism is that it is paternalistic in that it is a way for adults to determine what they consider to be in the best interest of the child.[30] The adoption of General Comment 14 on the right of the child to have his or her best interests taken as a primary consideration (GC14) in 2013 has thus brought much-needed clarity on how the principle should be understood.[31]

2.3   The Elements of the Best Interest of the Child in General Comment 14

The GC14 sets out concrete elements to be considered when determining the best interest of the child, thereby providing a more substantive

---

[26] Freeman, "Article 3," 2.

[27] GC14, para. 32.

[28] Julia Sloth-Nielson, "Book Review of M. Freeman, 'Article 3: The Best Interests of the Child,'" in *A Commentary on the United Nations Convention on the Rights of the Child*, ed. A. Alen, J. Van de Lanotte, E. Verhellen, F. Ang, E. Berghmans, and M. Verheyde, *International Journal of Children's Rights* 16 (2008), at 153; Dausab, *Best Interest*, 147; Mark Henaghan, "Above and Beyond the Best Interests of the Child," in *Perspectives on Fathering*, S. Birks and P. Callister (1999), at 121; Erica K. Salter, "Deciding for a Child: A Comprehensive Analysis of the Best Interest Standard," *Theoretical Medicine and Bioethics* 33 (2012), at 190–191; *S v M* 2008 (3) SA 232 (CC), para. 23.

[29] Salter, *Deciding for a Child*, 182, 190–191; Henaghan, *Above and Beyond*, 114–116; John Eekelaar, "Decisions Affecting Children and Decisions About Children," *International Journal of Children's Rights* 23 (2015): 25; Joan B. Kelly, "The Best Interests of the Child a Concept in Search of Meaning," *Family and Conciliation Courts Review* 35 (1997): 377.

[30] Freeman, "Article 3," above at note 44 at 50.

[31] GC14, paras. 4, 16, 34.

and objective understanding of the principle.[32] For example, GC14 states that the best interest of the child must be understood in the context of the rest of the CRC.[33] This means that the best interest principle should be contextualised as one of four interpretative principles in the CRC, the other three being non-discrimination, the right to life, survival and development and the right to be heard.[34] Taken from this contextualised view, the best interest in the context of, say, the right to be heard is saved from the paternalistic criticism through the incorporation of a right for the child to have a say.[35]

In addition, the GC14 states that the best interest of the child must be understood as a substantive right of all children, as an interpretive principle when read together with other rights and finally as a rule of procedure. The consequence of the best interest being a substantive right is that a child can rely on this right to claim fulfilment of its obligations from the state. In terms of the best interest being an interpretive principle, if more than one interpretation of a right is possible, the one that best serves the interest of the child should be followed.[36] As a rule of procedure, any action must be assessed for the potential impacts on children and the end decision must be justifiable in terms of the best interest of the child.[37]

Section V of the GC14 puts some flesh on the bones of the best interest principle. In order to give effect to the child's best interest, the first requirement is that its relevant elements must be identified. Thereafter these elements must be given specific weight and content. The GC14 provides a non-exhaustive list of possible elements of the child's interest to be

[32] Jason M. Pobjoy, "The Best Interests of the Child Principle as an Independent Source of International Protection," *International and Comparative Law Quarterly* 64 (2015), at 350.

[33] GC14, para. 1.

[34] Id., paras. 41–43.

[35] Kirsten Sandberg, "The Genesis and Spirit of the Convention on the Rights of the Child," in *25 Years of the Convention on the Rights of the Child*, ed. UNICEF (2014), at 64; Freeman, "Article 3," above at note 44 at 51.

[36] GC14, para. 6(b).

[37] 'In this regard, States parties shall explain how the right has been respected in the decision, that is, what has been considered to be in the child's best interests; what criteria it is based on; and how the child's interests have been weighed against other considerations [...],' GC14, para. 6(c).

considered: (1) the child's views,[38] (2) the identity of the child,[39] (3) preservation of the family environment and relations, (4) care, protection and safety of the child,[40] (5) situation of vulnerability,[41] (6) right to health,[42] and (7) the right to education. Because it is a non-exhaustive list, in a specific context other elements may also be relevant and some of the stipulated elements may be given more or less weight.[43]

The second requirement is that there must be procedures in place to ensure that the implementation of the best interest of the child is guaranteed. Vital to the process of determining the best interest of the child is that "the child must be given an opportunity to express his or her views and to have such views taken into account".[44] Thirdly, children have a perception of time which differs from that of adults, with the implication that decisions affecting them should be "prioritised and completed in the shortest possible time".[45] Three further procedural mechanisms are prescribed by GC14 to ensure that the child's best interest is served by a decision: (1) decisions concerning children must be "motivated, justified and explained"; (2) decisions should allow for a process of review; and (3) a child rights impact assessment should be carried out before any policy is adopted.

Article 3 of the CRC requires of "[e]very legislative, administrative and judicial body or institution [...] to apply the best interest's principle by systematically considering how children's rights and interests are or will be affected by their decisions or actions". This means that states have to review laws for their compliance with the best interest principle, must uphold the principle in budgetary allocations and provide children

---

[38] Art 12 of the CRC.

[39] The expression of the basic needs of the child differs based on national, religious, cultural and personality characteristics as well as other differences.

[40] This must be understood in terms of the general well-being and development of the child and includes "basic material, physical, educational, and emotional needs, as well as needs for affection and safety", GC14, para. 71.

[41] Situations of vulnerability include disability, belonging to a minority group, being a refugee or asylum seeker, victim of abuse, living in a street situation. GC14, para. 75.

[42] Article 24 of the CRC.

[43] GC14, para. 50.

[44] Id., para. 89. By including this in GC14, the Committee brought back the views of the child into the understanding of the best interest of the child, from where it had been removed during the drafting of the Charter, Freeman, "Article 3," 51.

[45] GC14, para. 93.

with the opportunity to express their views in the public space.[46] In determining the obligations of states, it is useful to consider the state's duty to respect, protect and promote rights.[47] Thus the best interest of the child must be respected (the state cannot do anything which infringes this right or a related right), the state must protect the right of all children to have their best interest respected by third parties and the state must take positive steps to promote the best interest of the child. These state obligations apply in decisions which directly concern children, but also decisions where children are not the direct object of the decision but will be affected by it in some way.[48]

3   THE BEST INTEREST OF THE CHILD IN THE CONTEXT OF HUMAN RIGHTS AND CLIMATE CHANGE

The analysis above applies to all situations affecting children. However, this discussion is particularly concerned with the way in which the best interest of the child should be understood where the child's (human) rights are violated or threatened in a climate change-related context. This section looks at principles which have crystallised at the international level this context.

3.1   UNHCR Guidelines

The UNHCR guidelines define the best interest as being "the well-being of a child" to be "determined by a variety of individual circumstances, such as the age, the level of maturity of the child, [...] the child's environment and experiences".[49] According to the Guidelines, the best interest of the child requires "consultation with children through participatory assessments that are systematic, age-appropriate and gender-sensitive; the collection of data by sex and age; giving primary consideration to the best interests of the child in resource

---

[46] Id., para. 15; Mauras, *Public Policies*, 64.

[47] GC14, para. 16; Mauras, *Public Policies*, 52.

[48] GC14, para. 19.

[49] United Nations High Commissioner for Refugees (UNHCR), "Guidelines on Determining the Best Interests of the Child" (2008), 14.

allocation; [and] the insertion of child-specific aspects in guidelines [and] policies".[50] In taking any decision related to a child, decision-makers must have relevant expertise and must balance "all relevant factors in order to assess the best option" which is child-centred and takes account of the future.[51] Importantly, the UNHCR determines that "[t]he best interests of the child is rarely determined by a single, overriding factor" and that the option that best secures "the attainment of the child's rights" is in the child's best interest.[52]

3.2   Interpretation of the Best Interest of the Child by the African Children's Committee

The first decision by the African Children's Committee on an individual complaint was in the case of *Institute for Human Rights and Development in Africa (IHRDA) and Open Society Justice Initiative on behalf of Children of Nubian Descent in Kenya v Kenya* (the Nubian case).[53] This decision is permeated by the best interest of the child principle, which is used both as an interpretive principle and a rule of procedure.[54] As a rule of procedure, the best interest principle is used to justify the admissibility of the case despite all local remedies not having been exhausted.[55] Specific consideration was given in this case to the differing time conception of children, in terms of which a delay in proceedings will have a greater, more detrimental impact on children than on adults. As an interpretive principle, the best interest of the child is used "in respect of almost all the cited provisions of the Charter," including the right to nationality[56] and socio-economic rights.[57] It also states that

---

[50] Id., at 20, 23.

[51] Id., at 23, 26, 27, 57.

[52] Id., at 67.

[53] Communication 002/2009 of the African Committee on the Rights and Welfare of the child, delivered on 22 March 2011.

[54] Frans Viljoen, *International Human Rights Law in Africa*, 2nd ed. (2012), at 403.

[55] Ebenezer Durojaye and Edmund A. Foley, "Making a First Impression: An Assessment of the Decision of the Committee of Experts of the African Children's Charter in the Nubian Children Communication." *African Human Rights Law Journal* 12 (2012), 565, 565.

[56] Nubian case, para. 42.

[57] Id., at para. 46.

discrimination against a group of children violates their dignity and best interests, thereby confirming the interrelated and indivisible nature of children's rights.[58] The African Children's Committee in a further case[59] held that the violations had "implications on the current and future best interests of children", thereby acknowledging the need to also take into account future interests where children are concerned.[60]

In the case on the plight of Talibés in Senegal,[61] in interpreting article 4 of the ACRWC, the Committee relied on GC14 when it states that "the best interest of the child aims at safeguarding the realisation of children's rights effectively and contributing to their holistic development".[62] The "realisation of children's rights" here relates to the function of the best interest of the child as an interpretive principle for other rights. The phrase "contributing to their holistic development" ties in the best interest of the child with article 6 of the CRC, the right to life, survival and development. The Committee also stresses the relationship between the best interest of the child and the state responsibilities to respect, protect and promote all rights.[63]

3.3 International Guidelines on How Climate Change Adaptation Policy Should Take Account of the Best Interest of the Child

International organisations such as UNICEF have provided guidelines as to how states should take account of children and their interests when formulating climate change adaptation policy. Firstly, in terms of procedure, the state must be able to justify its decisions with reference to the best interest of the child, which means that actors (a) have to consider the elements of the best interest in the given circumstances, and

---

[58] Id., at para. 57.

[59] *Michelo Hunsungule and Others (on behalf of children in Northern Uganda) v The Government of Uganda* decided at the Twenty first Ordinary Session, April 15–19, 2013 (the Ugandan case).

[60] Id., at para. 34.

[61] Decision on the communication submitted by the Centre for Human Rights (University of Pretoria) and La Recontre Africaine pour la defense des droits de l'homme (Senegal) v Government of Senegal Decision no. 003/Com/001/2012 on 15 April 2014 at the 23rd Ordinary Session of the African Committee of Experts on the Rights and Welfare of the Child (Senegal case).

[62] Id., at para. 34.

[63] Id., at para. 37.

(b) cannot claim that a policy is in the best interest of the child without giving clear reasons for why and how it complies.[64]

Secondly, the procedural element also requires that decisions should be based on high-quality data and because "children do not form one homogeneous group" such data must be disaggregated in terms of age, sex, dis/ability and other differentials, in order to address differing needs adequately.[65] States must furthermore provide children with adequate opportunity to express their views in the public space before adaptation policies are formulated, so that they can make meaningful contributions, taking into account that they are not only victims of climate change, but have an important role in addressing it.[66] Also, by giving children a chance to contribute, states are recognising "the child as a full human being with integrity and personality and the ability to participate freely in society" and provide children with the chance to participate on equal footing with adults.[67] Finally, in the allocation of the budget, states must uphold the best interest principle, thereby putting their money where their mouth is.[68]

With regard to the second aspect, namely the formulation of the content of adaptation actions, states can take account of children's interests in a number of ways. Central to enhancing the capacity of children to adapt to climate change is education, both on the effects of climate change and strategies to address it at a local level.[69] Adequate education on climate change is central to the ability of children to make informed

---

[64] John H. Knox and Ramin Pejan, "Human Rights Principles, Climate Change and the Rights of the Child," in UNICEF, *The Challenge of Climate Change*, above at note 7 at 55.

[65] Guillemot and Burgess, *Children Rights at Risk*, 2, 8.

[66] GC14, para. 15; Mauras, *Public Policies*, 60; Goumandakoye and Munang, *Engaging Children*, 74; UNICEF, "Children and the Changing Climate: Taking Action to Save Lives" (2015), at 2; CCCC, *Child-Centered Adaptation*, 2, 8; B.W. Edes, "Mitigating the Negative Impacts of Environmentally Driven Migration on Children and Other Vulnerable People," in UNICEF, *The Challenge of Climate Change*, above at note 7 at 30.

[67] Laura Lundy, "'Voice' Is Not Enough: Conceptualising Article 12 of the United Nations Convention on the Rights of the Child," *British Educational Research Journal* 33 (2007), at 928; and UNICEF, "Éducation au changementclimatique et à l'environnement" (2012), 27.

[68] Mauras, *Public Policies*, 47 at 62; Polack, *Child Rights*, 9, 37; UNICEF, *Unless We Act Now*, 9; Edes, *Mitigation the Negative Impacts*, 30; and Goumandakoye and Munang, *Engaging Children*, 74.

[69] Ibid.

contributions to adaptation discussions.[70] However, education by itself is insufficient.[71] UNICEF identifies that "[s]trengthening local institutions[72] and tackling gender inequality" are two further ways in which policymakers can ensure that adaptation policy is in children's best interest.[73] With regard to gender equality, for example, in a project in Ethiopia, women were empowered to start small businesses.[74] As a consequence, "family members of these groups eat three nutritious meals a day [and] all their children are sent to school".[75]

With regard to local institutions, children are often better able to participate at the local level and it ensures that the voice of all children is heard.[76] States must thus ensure that local governments have the resources and are equipped to deliver child-centred adaptation.[77] Intergenerational justice should be viewed as an integral part of the best interest of the child in the context of climate change adaptation legislation, since the interests of children may overlap more with those of future generations than those of adults and so "[p]olicy-makers [...] need to apply a cost-benefit analysis that values future quality of life".[78] Ecosystem-based adaptation through which the natural ecosystem is restored and taken into account in adaptation is recognised as a "long-term solution to reduce vulnerability".[79]

In terms of the third aspect of evaluating adaptation policies, UNICEF identifies an imperative on States to assess whether their policies have in practice been working in the best interest of the child. States also have to review all existing laws related to adaptation, for their

---

[70] Lundy, *Voice Is Not Enough*, 928.

[71] Ibid.

[72] See also Goumandakoye and Munang, *Engaging Children*, 74.

[73] Polack, *Child Rights*, 9.

[74] Venton, *Child-Centred Approach*, 36.

[75] Ibid.

[76] Polack, *Child Rights*, 37; Goumandakoye and Munang, *Engaging Children*, 74; and CCCC, *Child-Centered Adaptation*, 6.

[77] Ibid.

[78] Oliver C. Ruppel, "International Legal Climate Change Regimes and Climate Finance from a Southern African Perspective," in Ruppel and Ruppel-Schlichting, 300.

[79] M. Mumba "Ecosystem-Based Approaches to Adaptation and African Children," in UNICEF, *Children on the Front Line*, above at note 4 at 46.

compliance with the best interest principle.[80] One way of doing this is to have in place "[c]hild rights-based indicators for monitoring and evaluation" in national adaptation policies and programmes.[81] States must also be able to "quantify resources spent on children" and "demonstrate how priorities get set in resource allocation".[82] Finally, there should be adequate knowledge sharing between different levels of government so that approaches to adaptation which have proven to address children's needs, can be scaled-up.[83]

4   HOW DO NATIONAL CLIMATE CHANGE ADAPTATION POLICIES IN AFRICA TAKE ACCOUNT OF THE BEST INTEREST OF THE CHILD?

This section considers the climate change policies of three countries, Kenya, South Africa and Nigeria, each representing a region of Sub-Saharan Africa, for the extent to which they explicitly or indirectly protect children's rights, as well as to measure their policies against the elements of the best interest of the child already identified above. In order to limit the scope of this chapter, the focus will be on areas in which children in Africa are particularly vulnerable, namely access to water, nutrition and healthcare.[84]

5   SOUTH AFRICAN CLIMATE CHANGE FRAMEWORK AND THE BEST INTEREST OF THE CHILD

The South African flagship policy on climate change is the *National Climate Change Response Policy White Paper* (NCCRP), which was approved by Parliament in 2011.[85] The NCCRP provides for long-, medium- and short-term action in terms of adaptation and mitigation of

---

[80] GC14, para. 15; Mauras, *Public Policies*, 60.

[81] Polack, *Child Rights*, 9; Mauras, *Public Policies*, 62.

[82] Ibid.

[83] UNICEF, *Unless We Act Now*, 9; Pelling, *Adaptation to Climate Change*, 7.

[84] While the focus here is on adaptation policies related to nutrition, water and health, it must be noted that the best way for policymakers to express concern for the best interest of the child is through strong mitigation measures.

[85] Nachmany et al., *66 Countries*, 499.

climate change, and contains specific strategies for different sectors, thus providing a holistic approach.[86] The main objective as set out in the NCCRP is to reduce climate change vulnerability, by ensuring the "integration of climate change adaptation into existing and new policies", particularly those related to development. The objective is to be guided by, "special needs and circumstances", which specifically mentions "children, especially infants and child-headed families" as vulnerable groups that should receive special attention as well as "uplifting the poor and vulnerable".[87] This is a reference to the development aspect, whereby climate change measures should not only maintain the status quo, but should be aimed at transition or transformation to a more just and equal society.[88]

The third principle is "informed participation" through enhancing public understanding and awareness, and aims at "promoting participation and action at all levels".[89] This could be interpreted to mean that children should also be included in climate change discussions; however, while the NCCRP reaffirms the government's commitment to "substantive engagement and, where appropriate, partnerships with stakeholders from industry, business, labour and civil society", there is no specific mention of children in this regard.[90] In terms of the NCCRP, education is to be aimed at equipping "South African citizens to re-orient society towards social, economic and ecological sustainability".[91] Children are thus seen as people who should be educated in order to be able to make a contribution in the future, and there is thus no acknowledgement of the agency of children and the valuable contributions they can make as children. The fourth and final principle is that of "intra- and

---

[86] Id., at 500; Government of South Africa, "National Climate Change Response Policy White Paper" (NCCRP) (2011), at 16.

[87] Sibonelo Mbanjwa, "Toward National Climate Change Adaptation Strategy," Department of Environmental Affairs, *Climate Change Response Dialogue 2014*, November 10–14, 2014; NCCRP at 5, 8, 12.

[88] Pelling, *Adaptation to Climate Change*, 23–24.

[89] NCCRP at 8, 12.

[90] Id., at 38.

[91] Id., at 45.

inter-generational sustainability",[92] and the white paper recognises that "responding to climate change is a cross-generational challenge".[93]

The NCCRP also prescribes a prominent role for local government in climate change adaptation. Firstly it recognises that the local governments currently do not have the necessary power and funding to properly respond to climate change, and secondly provides for "[p]rogrammes to build capacity for local and provincial governments' climate response strategies".[94] This is a positive aspect of the NCCRP, because the closer government is to the people, the better they will know what the specific needs are, nevertheless, this should be maintained within a coordinated national framework to prevent piecemeal and uncoordinated adaptation.

In terms of the water sector, the NCCRP provides a broad outline of water-related adaptation, which is focussed largely on technological innovation and protecting industry, with the basic needs of people such as health and access to water relegated to a minor position, which does not reflect the seriousness of the impacts on the most vulnerable, particularly children, of water shortages caused by climate change.[95] It also follows a sectoral and technology focussed adaptation approach, not taking into account the potential of ecosystem-based adaptation.

The NCCRP recognises the health implications of climate change and provides for various emergency responses[96]; safe water and improved sanitation[97]; strengthening of "the awareness programme on malaria and cholera outbreaks"; food security and sound nutritional policies. It recognises that children are more vulnerable to "physical temperature stresses"[98] and recognises that the empowerment of women "who are often primary producers" can have a positive impact on children's nutrition.[99]

However, all of these laudable aims and ethical principles are disappointingly not reflected in the practical steps flowing from the

[92] Ibid.
[93] Id., at 49.
[94] Ibid.
[95] Id., at 17.
[96] Mbanjwa, *Adaptation Strategy*, NCCRP at 20.
[97] Ibid.
[98] NCCRP at 19.
[99] Id., at 23.

NCCRP, "leaving the impression that economic self-interest influenced [the state's] actual commitments", according to commentators.[100] One adaptation action to be taken in terms of the NCCRP is the setting up of an Inter-Ministerial Committee on Climate Change, chaired by the Minister of the Environment, "with the aim of implementing the National Climate Change Response Policy".[101] However, this ministry is traditionally weak, and may not have the clout to ensure cooperation between different departments. A National Climate Change Coordinating Committee was also put in place by the policy to provide "a forum for wide-ranging stakeholder input in the policy development process".[102] While the white paper aims to address adaptation in the short and long term,[103] the overall impression of the implementation process is of a process that is fragmented. Its consideration of children is also weak—where its provisions do take account of the interests of children, it is haphazard and incidental.

5.1   Kenya Climate Change Framework and the Best Interest of the Child

The flagship policy on climate change in Kenya is the 2013–2017 National Climate Change Action Plan (the Action Plan). The Action Plan recognises the fact that "climate change has a more severe effect on the poor, who are often women and children", and thus that climate change strategies have to take into account their developmental needs.

One of the "priority adaptation actions" identified in the Action Plan relates to the improvement of water management, including "enhanced irrigation and drainage [...], effective trans-boundary water resources management, and flood mitigation schemes" and recognises that water resource management is "directly linked to food security, health and

---

[100] Donald A. Brown and Prue Taylor, "Ethics and Climate Change: A Study of National Commitments," IUCN (World Commission on Environmental Law) *Environmental Policy and Law Paper No. 86* (2014): xxi.

[101] Id., at 37.

[102] Radhika Perrot, "South Africa's Consideration of Ethics and Justice Issues in Formulating Climate Change Policies," in D.A. Brown and P. Taylor, "Ethics and Climate Change: A Study of National Commitments" IUCN (World Commission on Environmental Law) *Environmental Policy and Law Paper No. 86* (2014), 28.

[103] Nachmany, *66 Countries*, 20.

GDP growth".[104] A second priority adaptation action identified in the Action Plan relates to health. It provides for "improved disease surveillance" and "improved community-level healthcare and dissemination of information on changing health risks", as well as "access to water and sanitation".[105] However, when it comes to the actions for which a budget is stipulated, there is no reference to disease-related adaptation, resulting in a lack of clarity as to how this would be implemented. The adaptation actions related to water have a specific sustainable development component and aim to address water-borne diseases through water supply and sewage services. However, the Kenyan adaptation policy could be improved by providing specifically for children's interests in the budget and providing a budget to improve healthcare, which provisions are currently absent.

The Action Plan also identifies ten indicators which the national government can take into account to determine whether their adaptation strategies are effective.[106] Two positive indicators in terms of the best interest of the child are the "number of urban slums with physical and social infrastructure installed annually" and the "number households in need of food aid".[107] "Physical infrastructure", if it includes water pipelines and access to healthcare clinics, would be very much in the best interest of some of the poorest children living in informal settlements, and the number of households in need of food aid is a good rough indicator of the number of children who may be suffering from malnutrition.

The Action Plan explicitly recognises the best interest of children and their right to access information, and recommends that climate education should be integrated into the "curricula for primary, secondary and tertiary institutions".[108] It profoundly states that climate change education should be introduced into "all primary school subjects".[109] This is recognition of the necessity of ensuring that children are equipped to contribute to discussions on climate change and to take the lead in future. The Action Plan is however silent on the involvement of

---

[104] Id., at 33.
[105] Id., at 39.
[106] NCCAP at 136.
[107] Ibid.
[108] Id., at 108.
[109] Id., at 112.

children in decision-making processes. A positive aspect is the provision in the Action Plan that doctors should be trained "to be aware of the effects of climate change on human health".[110] This is an indication of a forward-thinking approach by the Kenyan government which aims to ensure that climate change is taken seriously and pre-emptive steps are taken.

In conclusion, the Kenyan Action Plan sets out clearly defined measures on adaptation, with the funding that will be required, which is much more comprehensive than the policies of other African countries.[111] However, in this, it only takes account of the vulnerabilities of children, and does not provide for sufficient opportunities for children to engage in solutions.

5.2 Nigeria Climate Change Framework and the Best Interest of the Child

While Kenya and South Africa make passing references to children as a "vulnerable group", Nigeria has a specific focus on children's interests.[112] The Nigeria flagship policy is the National Policy on Climate Change which was adopted in 2013.[113] According to the National Policy on Climate Change, the principles which should guide climate change efforts in Nigeria include that the Policy must be "addressed within the framework of sustainable development" and requires an integrated response from different stakeholders.[114] Thus the main aim of the climate change policy is "high-growth economic development" while 'building a climate-resilient society'.[115] More than anything else, climate change is thus viewed as a threat to economic development.[116]

With regard to participation the policy recognises that adaptation requires the input and participation of all sectors of society, including the poor, women and children.[117] In this regard, it recognises the role

---

[110] Ibid.
[111] Nachmany et al., *66 Countries*, 15.
[112] Ibid.
[113] Id., at 419.
[114] Id., at 418; Nachmany et al., *99 Countries*, 3.
[115] Id., at 421.
[116] Ibid.
[117] Ibid.

of children as active participants in addressing climate change and does not frame them just in terms of their vulnerability. The Policy provides for climate change education in schools, with a sufficient focus on adaptation, "that will empower children to better respond to the threats of climate change".[118]

On the other hand, the policy also recognises that children are vulnerable to the negative impacts of climate change.[119] The policy sets out specific strategies through which to take account of the circumstances of vulnerable groups,[120] for example, there is provision for awareness-raising among government staff on how climate change affects vulnerable persons and training for government officials "on gender awareness tools", which, while critical, should be extended to also cover training on the needs of children. Positively, the policy does take account directly of the interests of children in terms of adapting schools to withstand environmental onslaughts, intensifying the immunisation of children and retraining healthcare workers "to appreciate emerging climate change challenges".[121]

Nigeria has set up a department of climate change within the Ministry for the Environment, to implement this Policy.[122] The most potent provision of the Nigerian policy framework for the recognition of the best interest of children is the section that provides for how the state should take account of the needs of vulnerable groups. All states would benefit from including such a provision in their adaptation framework. It also places more emphasis on the role of children as agents for addressing climate change and contributing to adaptation solutions.

It is clear from the discussion above that currently the best interest of children is not a central focus of climate change adaptation policies in Africa. Where children are considered, it is usually as part of undefined "vulnerable groups". While most policies provide for access to information and participation, children are not specifically included here, and thus tend to be overlooked, especially when it comes to consultation, searching for solutions, and participating in relevant processes.

[118]The Federal Government of Nigeria, "Nigeria's Intended Nationally Determined Contribution" (INDC) (2015), at 20.

[119]Nachmany et al., *99 Countries*, 2; Nigeria *INDC*, at 16.

[120]Nigeria *INDC*, 20.

[121]Ibid.

[122]Id., at 18.

This misses the opportunity of consulting with central stakeholders with a unique ability to contribute. Most policies, however, provide for some steps to address vulnerability. This is in line with the view of the CCCC that "[w]here children feature in adaptation strategy documents; it is connected with their vulnerability rather than their agency".[123] While there is a recognition that climate change is about more than the environment, and is a developmental and human rights issue which should be central to national developmental planning, ironically, in South Africa and in Nigeria, it is still the Ministry of Environment which is charged with climate change coordination. There are, thus, positive and negative lessons to be taken from these case studies. Given the importance of the best interest of the child principle, and the inconsistent way in which the climate change policies of African countries have given effect to it, the next section is aimed at consolidating the lessons from the discussion of the best interest of the child as well as the national policies as discussed above.

6   ELEMENTS OF THE BEST INTEREST OF THE CHILD IN THE CONTEXT OF ADAPTATION IN SUB-SAHARAN AFRICA

As identified before, the best interest of the child must be understood as a substantive right, an interpretive principle and a rule of procedure. As a substantive right, determining the best interest includes taking account of the child's views, the identity of the child, preservation of the family environment and relations, care, protection and safety of the child, a child's situation of vulnerability, the right to health and the right to education.[124] In the context of climate change adaptation, studies have shown that children are able to formulate views on adaptation, and thus, such views should be taken into account in policy formulation.[125] The identity of the child that the government must take account of in

---

[123]Polack, *Child Rights*, 10; Ivana Savic, "Partnering with and Catalysing Young Innovators," in UNICEF, *The Challenge of Climate Change*, above at note 7 at 63; UNICEF, *Children's Vulnerability*, above at note 7 at 15.

[124]GC14, para. 50.

[125]Polack, *Child Rights*, 9, 27.

formulating adaptation policies, is that of an African child, with limited ability to adapt[126] and specific vulnerabilities in terms of access to health-care, food and water.[127] The preservation of the family can be hard during migration associated with climate change, and a child's safety can be compromised by lack of access to food and having to collect water from far away.[128] Children's right to education can be affected by climate change when there is flooding which cuts off access from schools, or drought, which means that they have to collect water from further locations or have to work to ensure the sustenance of their families.[129] States also have a duty to fulfil the right to information of children through climate change education. Policymakers on climate change thus have to take all of these factors into account in ensuring that the best interest of the child as an independent right is addressed in adaptation policy.

As an interpretive principle, the rights affected by climate change must be interpreted in such a way that the best interest of the child is served. According to Guillemot and Burgess, "[c]hildren's vulnerability to climate change fundamentally threatens the realisation of many, if not all, of their rights".[130] The CRC specifically recognises the rights to clean drinking water and health, both of which require resource commitments by states as part of climate change adaptation policies.[131] The right to life, survival and development, along with the principles of the right to be heard and the right to non-discrimination are central to the best interest of the child in the context of climate change.[132] Given the interlinked nature of all of these rights, in decisions affecting any of these rights, states will have to weigh up all the different outcomes, to find the one that will best reflect the best interest of children. Some of the

---

[126] "The [African] continent is experiencing a number of demographic and economic constraints" which leads to "increased loss of livelihood and widespread poverty", impacting negatively on the adaptive capacity of all people, particularly the most vulnerable. Niang, "Africa", 1211.

[127] CCCC, *Child-Centered Adaptation*, 2.

[128] Polack, *Child Rights*, 36.

[129] Oliver C. Ruppel, "Climate Change and Human Vulnerability in Africa," in Ruppel and Ruppel-Schlichting, above at note 21 at 284.

[130] Guillemot and Burgess, *Children Rights at Risk*, 49.

[131] Article 24(2)(c) of the CRC; Polack, *Child Rights*, 11.

[132] GC14, paras. 41–43; Guillemot and Burgess, *Children Rights at Risk*, 47.

ways in which to ensure a holistic approach that reflects the indivisibility of children's rights include doing away with the approach that climate change can be dealt with in "silos" in favour of an integrated approach; following an ecosystem-based approach that recognises the interdependency of human and environmental health; and placing climate change issues under a ministry with enough clout to ensure compliance by other ministries.

As a rule of procedure the best interest of the child requires that the child's voice be taken into account; decisions must take into account the child's perception of time; decisions concerning children must be "motivated, justified and explained"; they should allow for a process of review and a child rights impact assessment should be carried out before any policy is adopted. The right of children to be heard has to be taken seriously in the context of climate change adaptation, and they have to be empowered to make an informed contribution on decisions that will affect them and future generations.[133] Up to now, commitments made by states in terms of climate change adaptation have not been very ambitious and in many cases do not set a definite timeline. This is not in the best interest of children which requires that decisions affecting them be "prioritised and completed in the shortest possible time" and that states systematically consider how its decisions will affect children.[134] The requirement that decisions affecting children must be motivated and justified may be a very powerful tool in ensuring that children's interests are never forgotten in the clamour of "causes" for the attention of legislatures and will increase the mainstreaming of children's concerns into policies in general. With regard to intergenerational justice, the extent to which the current generations "are allowed to impose risks on future generations"[135] should be the main consideration in the formulation of climate change adaptation policies, but up to now it has been neglected in favour of short-term economic considerations. This is clearly a violation of the best interest of children who will live in this future we are creating.

---

[133] Knox and Pejan, *Human Rights Principles*, 55; Polack, *Child Rights*, 12; Guillemot and Burgess, *Children Rights at Risk*, 48; and CCCC, *Child-Centered Adaptation*, 2.

[134] GC14, para. 93; CCCC, *Child-Centered Adaptation*, 2.

[135] Ibid.

7   CONCLUSION

Up to the present, state interventions in climate change have often been uncoordinated, have a "strong sectoral focus and a short-term investment horizon".[136] A shift to a focus on children will ensure that interventions are less focussed on the short-term thereby taking account of the needs of future generations and will provide the long-term view necessary to prevent short-term maladaptation.[137] Another reason why adaptation policies would benefit from a child-centred approach include that "children are capable of developing and implementing innovative solutions to complex problems", and thus, they should be provided with the necessary resources to contribute to adaptation "as well as to develop their own solutions to the specific local climate change impacts that affect them".[138] Obligations imposed by international and national climate change law to a large extent overlap with state obligations in terms of the CRC in other priority areas such as development and access to basic services, but viewing it through the climate change lens allows for a more holistic and urgent approach.[139] There are also moral arguments for a child-centred approach, namely that children have contributed the least to climate change and will suffer the most, and thus should receive the strongest protections.[140]

In attempting to formulate the principles which should underlie state adaptation policies to ensure that adaptation policies reflect the best interest of the child, the aim of this chapter is not to provide a definitive answer in this regard but rather to provide a starting point in assessing the compliance with the principle of the best interest of the child in climate change policy formulation. This is particularly pertinent at this point in time when many states are either adopting more sophisticated climate change policies, or moving in the direction of binding legislation. Thus, in order to give effect to the best interest of the child in the context of adaptation, states should be guided by the following principles:

---

[136] Venton, *Child-Centred Approach*, 35.

[137] Ibid.; UNICEF, *The Challenge of Climate Change*, 4.

[138] CCCC, *Child-Centered Adaptation*, 3.

[139] Venton, *Child-Centred Approach*, 35.

[140] UNICEF, *Unless We Act Now*, 66.

1. Adaptation policies must address the particular vulnerabilities of children.
2. The potential of children to contribute to policy formulation and problem-solving should be reflected in adaptation policies.
3. Children should be educated and empowered to make their contribution as meaningful as possible.
4. Policies must be focussed on long-term sustainable development.
5. Adaptation must be transformative and ensure greater equality and social reform rather than just maintaining the status quo.
6. Policies should be adopted as expeditiously as possible in line with the child's conception of time.
7. The best interest of the child should be regarded holistically, taking account of the indivisibility of rights.
8. All decisions should be underpinned by reliable, disaggregated data.

If states can ensure that policymakers keep these eight principles in mind when formulating policies or legislation, in recognition of the fact that the decisions being made today in the face of the worst environmental, social and economic threat of our time, will have consequences that extend far into the future, we may just be able to leave to our children a future in which they may not just survive, but thrive.

References

African Union (AU). "Draft African Union Strategy on Climate Change" (2014), at 1, 8; Climate and Development Knowledge Network (CDKN). "The IPCC's Fifth Assessment Report: What's in It for Africa?" (2014). Available at http://cdkn.org/resource/highlights-africa-ar5/?loclang=en_gb. Accessed 10 October 2016.

AU. "Agenda 2063" ed 2 (2014).

Brown, Donald A., and Prue Taylor. "Ethics and Climate Change: A Study of National Commitments." IUCN (World Commission on Environmental Law) *Environmental Policy and Law Paper No. 86* (2014).

Carr, Edward R. "Between Structure and Agency: Livelihoods and Adaptation in Ghana's Central Region." *Global Environmental Change* 18 (2008).

Children in a Changing Climate Coalition (CCCC). "Child-Centred Adaptation: Realising Children's Rights in a Changing Climate" (2015).

Collier, Paul et al. "Climate Change and Africa." *Oxford Review of Economic Policy* 24 (2008).

Communication 002/2009 of the African Committee on the Rights and Welfare of the Child, delivered on 22 March 2011.

Communication 003/Com/001/2012—Centre for Human Rights (University of Pretoria) and La Recontre Africaine pour la defense des droits de l'homme (Senegal) v Government of Senegal, April 15, 2014 at the 23rd Ordinary Session of the African Committee of Experts on the Rights and Welfare of the Child.

Currie, Janet, and Olivier Deschênes. "Children and Climate Change: Introducing the Issue." In *Children and Climate Change*.

Dausab, Yvonne. "The Best Interest of the Child." In *Children's Rights in Namibia*, edited by Oliver C. Ruppel (2009).

Dickenson, Thea, and Ian Burton. "Palliative Climate Change Planning and Its Consequences for Youth." In UNICEF, *The Challenge of Climate Change*.

Durojaye, Ebenezer, and Edmund A. Foley. "Making a First Impression: An Assessment of the Decision of the Committee of Experts of the African Children's Charter in the Nubian Children Communication." *African Human Rights Law Journal* 12 (2012).

Edes, B.W. "Mitigating the Negative Impacts of Environmentally Driven Migration on Children and Other Vulnerable People." In UNICEF, *The Challenge of Climate Change*.

Eekelaar, John. "Decisions Affecting Children and Decisions About Children." *International Journal of Children's Rights* 23 (2015).

Federal Government of Nigeria. "Nigeria's Intended Nationally Determined Contribution." (INDC) (2015).

Freeman, Michael. "Article 3: The Best Interest of the Child." In *A Commentary on the United Nations Convention on the Rights of the Child*, edited by Andre Alen et al. (2007).

Goumandakoye, Mounkaila, and Richard Munang. "Engaging Children in the African Climate Change Discourse." In UNICEF, *The Challenge of Climate Change: Children on the Front Line* (2014).

Government of Kenya. "National Climate Change Action Plan 2013–2017" (2013).

Government of South Africa. "National Climate Change Response Policy White Paper" (NCCRP) (2011).

Guillemot, J., and J. Burgess. "Children Rights at Risk." In *Children on the Front Line*, edited by UNICEF (2014).

Hanna, Rema, and Paulina Oliva. "Implications of Climate Change for Children in Developing Countries." In *Children and Climate Change*, edited by The Future of Children (2016). Available at http://www.futureofchildren.org/publications/journals/journal_details/index.xml?journalid=86. Accessed September 25, 2016.

Henaghan, Mark. "Above and Beyond the Best Interests of the Child." In *Perspectives on Fathering*, S. Birks and P. Callister (1999).

Kelly, Joan B. "The Best Interests of the Child a Concept in Search of Meaning." *Family and Conciliation Courts Review* 35 (1997).

Knox, John H., and Ramin Pejan. "Human Rights Principles, Climate Change and the Rights of the Child." In UNICEF, *The Challenge of Climate Change*.

Lundy, Laura. "'Voice' Is Not Enough: Conceptualising Article 12 of the United Nations Convention on the Rights of the Child." *British Educational Research Journal* 33 (2007).

Mauras, Marta. "Public Policies and Child Rights: Entering the Third Decade of the Convention on the Rights of the Child." *Annals* 633 (2011).

Mbanjwa, Sibonelo. "Toward National Climate Change Adaptation Strategy." Department of Environmental Affairs Climate Change Response Dialogue 2014, November 10–14, 2014.

Michelo Hunsungule and Others (on behalf of children in Northern Uganda) v The Government of Uganda decided at the Twenty first Ordinary Session, April 15–19, 2013.

Mumba, M. "Ecosystem-Based Approaches to Adaptation and African Children." In UNICEF, *Children on the Front Line*.

Nachmany, Michal et al. "The GLOBE Climate Legislation Study: A Review of Climate Change Legislation in 66 Countries." 4th ed. (2014).

Nachmany, Michal et al. "The 2015 Global Climate Legislation Study: A Review of Climate Change Legislation in 99 Countries." Grantham Institute, 2015.

Niang, Isabelle et al. "Africa." In *Impacts, Adaptation, and Vulnerability*, edited by IPCC Working Group II. Part B: Regional Aspects. Contribution of Working Group II to the Fifth Assessment Report of the Intergovernmental Panel on Climate Change (2014).

Pelling, Mark. *Adaptation to Climate Change: From Resilience to Transformation* (2012).

Pobjoy, Jason M. "The Best Interests of the Child Principle as an Independent Source of International Protection." *International and Comparative Law Quarterly* 64 (2015): 327–363.

Polack, Emily. "Child Rights and Climate Change Adaptation: Voices from Kenya and Cambodia." *Children in a Changing Climate* (2010).

Room, J.J. "Present and Future Climate Realities for Children." In *The Challenge of Climate Change: Children on the Front Line*, edited by UNICEF (2014).

Ruppel, Oliver C. "Climate Change and Human Vulnerability in Africa." In Ruppel and Ruppel-Schlichting.

Ruppel, Oliver C. "International Legal Climate Change Regimes and Climate Finance from a Southern African Perspective." In *Environmental Law and Policy in Namibia*, edited by Oliver C. Ruppel and K. Ruppel-Schlichting, 2nd ed. Windhoek: Orumbonde Press, 2013.

Salter, Erica K. "Deciding for a Child: A Comprehensive Analysis of the Best Interest Standard." *Theoretical Medicine and Bioethics* 33 (2012): 179–198.

Sandberg, Kirsten. "The Genesis and Spirit of the Convention on the Rights of the Child." In *25 Years of the Convention on the Rights of the Child*, edited by UNICEF (2014).

Savic, Ivana. "Partnering with and Catalysing Young Innovators." In UNICEF, *The Challenge of Climate Change*.

Sloth-Nielson, Julia. "Book Review of M. Freeman, 'Article 3: The Best Interests of the Child.'" Edited by A. Alen, J. Van de Lanotte, E. Verhellen, F. Ang, E. Berghmans, and M. Verheyde. In *"A Commentary on the United Nations Convention on the Rights of the Child." International Journal of Children's Rights* 16 (2008): 153–157.

S v M 2008 (3) SA 232 (CC).

United Nations Environmental Programme (UNEP). "Guidebook on National Legislation for Adaptation to Climate Change" (2011).

United Nations High Commissioner for Refugees (UNHCR). "Guidelines on Determining the Best Interests of the Child" (2008).

UNICEF. "Children and the Changing Climate: Taking Action to Save Lives" (2015).

UNICEF. "Children's Vulnerability to Climate Change and Disaster Impacts in East Asia and the Pacific" (2009).

UNICEF. "Éducation au changement climatique et à l'environnement" (2012).

UNICEF. "Unless We Act Now: The Impact of Climate Change on Children" (2015).

United Nations Committee on the Rights of the Child (CRC) General Comment 14. "On the Right of the Child to Have His or Her Best Interests Taken as a Primary Consideration." Adopted on 29 May 2013 at the 62nd session of the CRC (GC14).

Venton, Courtenay Cabot. "Why We Need a Child-Centred Approach to Adaptation." In UNICEF, *The Challenge of Climate Change*.

Viljoen, Frans. *International Human Rights Law in Africa*, 2nd ed. Oxford: Oxford University Press, 2012.

CHAPTER 15

Protecting Environmental Rights in the Context of Oil Extraction in Africa

Michael Addaney, Bamisaye Olutola and Charlotte Kabaseke

1 Introduction

There is a growing fragmentation of international tribunals, giving litigants several choices before which to litigate their context-specific disputes.[1] Although tribunals differ in their focus, they are all mandated to take into account the general principles of international law in their adjudication of cases. Questions have arisen as to whether human rights tribunals are legitimate for handling matters arising out of environmental

---

[1] Dinah Shelton, "Legitimate and Necessary: Adjudicating Human Rights Violations Related to Activities Causing Environmental Harm," *Journal of Human Rights and Environment* 6, no. 2 (2015): 139–155 at 140.

M. Addaney (✉) · C. Kabaseke
Research Institute of Environmental Law,
Wuhan University, Wuhan, China

B. Olutola
Faculty of Law, University of Pretoria, Pretoria, South Africa

© The Author(s) 2020   387
M. Addaney et al. (eds.), *Governance, Human Rights,
and Political Transformation in Africa*,
https://doi.org/10.1007/978-3-030-27049-0_15

disputes.[2] Their legitimacy has been justified through the absence of environmental-specific tribunals at international level, once the parties or litigants have exhausted the local remedies available to them.[3] Another reason which has been advanced for the non-existence of environment-specific tribunals is that non-state actors are usually the culprits in causing damage and harm to the environment. This only leaves states responsible for failure to take the necessary steps to prevent or remedy the harm caused by the non-state actors. States therefore rarely violate the domestic law. Shelton notes that:

> Most environmental protection treaties are not implemented through liability regimes or invocation of State responsibility, but rather through various incentives or trade-off mechanisms and State reporting. In contrast, human rights treaties not only rely upon State reporting procedures, but also inter-State complaints, and individual petitions or complaints, all of which directly or indirectly permit criticism of non-complying States.[4]

She adds that despite the fact that environmental law disputes are not ordinarily heard or determined by human rights bodies, those disputes related to environmental harm are rightly brought before the tribunals.[5] This makes up for the reluctance of state parties to put in place environment-specific tribunals. Voigt and Grant argue that although human rights bodies at the international and regional (Europe and America) levels in fact hear and determine environmental matters, they lack the jurisdiction to do so.[6] This is because the treaties that establish them lack provision on an environment-specific right. This however seems to be settled as these tribunals in fact entertain cases to do with human rights violations arising out of environmental harm, but do not entertain environmental matters.

---

[2] Ibid., at 141.

[3] Michael Addaney, Elsabé Boshoff, and Michael Gyan Nyarko, "Protection of Environmental Assets in Urban Africa: Regional and Sub-regional Human Rights and Practical Environmental Protection Mechanisms," *Australian Journal of Human Rights* 24, no. 2 (2018): 182–200.

[4] Shelton, "Legitimate and Necessary," 143.

[5] Ibid.

[6] Christina Voigt and Evadne Grant, "The Legitimacy of Human Rights Courts in Environmental Disputes," *Journal of Human Rights and the Environment* 6, no. 2 (2015): 131–138.

The African Commission and Court of Human rights have been noted to be the only regional tribunals that act within the mandate of the treaty establishing them because it enshrines a right to a satisfactory environment.[7] The need to adopt a context-specific human rights treaty suitable to the African continent could not be overemphasised as the various international human rights instruments were inadequate on some issues that are peculiar to the African region. Thus, in 1981, the African Charter on Human and Peoples' Rights (the African Charter) was adopted to supplement the relevant international human rights treaties and declarations providing protection and promotion of human rights and fundamental freedoms pertinent to African realities. These rights include social, economic and cultural rights—the right of all people to a general satisfactory environment favourable to their development,[8] the right of all people to freely dispose of their wealth and natural resources[9] and the right to the lawful recovery of its property as well as to an adequate compensation.[10] The African Charter further obliges state parties to eliminate all forms of foreign economic exploitation, particularly those practised by international monopolies to enable their peoples to fully benefit from the advantages derived from their national resources.[11] Similar to related regional human rights instruments, the African Charter established the African Commission on Human and Peoples' Rights (the Commission) as a treaty monitoring body with powers to receive individual communications, to enhance the promotion, protection, respect and realisation of and interpret as well as monitor the implementation of the African Charter.[12]

---

[7] Addaney, Boshoff, and Nyarko, "Protection of Environmental Assets in Urban Africa," 182.

[8] African Charter on Human and Peoples' Rights (the African Charter), adopted June 27, 1981, OAU Doc. CAB/LEG/67/3 rev. 5, 1520 U.N.T.S. 217, 245 (1982), Art. 24.

[9] Ibid., art. 21(10) states that, 'all peoples shall freely dispose of their wealth and natural resources. This right shall be exercised in the exclusive interest of the people. In no case shall a people be deprived of it.'

[10] Ibid., Art. 21(2).

[11] Ibid., Art. 21(4).

[12] Ibid., Art. 30; Frans Viljoen, *International Human Rights Law in Africa*, 2nd ed. (Oxford: Oxford University Press, 2012), 295.

The Commission, in undertaking this protective mandate, has so far delivered numerous decisions based on their merits including the *Social and Economic Rights Action Centre (SERAC) and Another v Nigeria* (the *SERAC v Nigeria* case),[13] making significant strides in the protection of the rights of the African peoples. This chapter examines the Commission's decision in the *SERAC v Nigeria* case, and highlights its approach to the exhaustion of domestic remedies, its interpretive approach to the provisions of the African Charter, as well as the gaps and the implications of the decision on the constitutional and legal protection of environmental rights in Africa in general and Nigeria in particular. Following this introduction, Sect. 2 discusses the historical overview and factual basis of the case. Section 3 discusses the approach adopted by the African Commission on the interpretation of Article 24 of the African Charter. Taking the discussion further, Sect. 4 draws the implications of the decision on the domestic protection of the right to general satisfactory environment in Africa. Section 5 concludes with recommendations.

2   THE GENESIS OF THE AGONIES OF THE OGONI PEOPLE: FACTS, ARGUMENTS AND OVERVIEWS

The *SERAC and Another v Nigeria* case was instituted by two non-governmental organisations (NGOs): the Social and Economic Rights Action Committee (SERAC) of Nigeria and the Centre for Economic and Social Rights (CESR), a New York based NGO on behalf of the people of Ogoniland in the Niger Delta area of Nigeria. The systematic violation of the environmental and other rights of the Ogoni people was well known. The *SERAC and Another v Nigeria* case was based on a communication submitted to the African Commission on 14 March 1996. The Ogoniland is located in the Niger Delta in the southern part of Nigeria; one of the most heavily populated areas in Africa.[14] The Niger Delta is recognized as one of the top ten significant marine ecosystems and wetlands internationally, hosting many rare species including numerous birds, ungulates and

---

[13] *Social and Economic Rights Action Centre (SERAC) and Another v Nigeria (SERAC case)* (2001) AHRLR 60 (ACHPR 2001).

[14] Barisere Rachel Konne, "Inadequate Monitoring and Enforcement in the Nigerian Oil Industry: The Case of Shell and Ogoniland," *Cornell International Law Journal* 47, no. 1 (2014): 181–204.

primates.[15] The area is home to an enormous mangrove ecosystem that serves as a vital habitat for the colossal fish population along the coastline of West Africa.[16] Majority of Nigeria's oil production takes place in the Niger Delta region.[17] Nigeria has been producing oil since 1958, when the Shell British Petroleum discovered crude oil (now Royal Dutch Shell [Shell]).[18] Nigeria has since then become the largest oil producer in Africa, producing an estimated 28.2 billion barrels of oil reserves as of May 2017.[19] As an emerging market, the economy of Nigerian depends heavily on the oil industry,[20] with oil production accounting for some 95% of export earnings and about 80% of the total government revenue.[21]

Shell serves as the largest oil company in Nigeria[22] and operates over an estimated 31,000 square kilometres including thousands of kilometres of pipelines, numerous of which are close to residential areas, farmlands and water resources.[23] The Niger Delta area is also home to several indigenous communities which include the people of Ogoniland.[24] The people of Ogoniland depend greatly on natural resources for livelihood

[15] Amnesty International (Amnesty), "Nigeria: Petroleum, Pollution and Poverty in the Niger Delta" (2009), 9. http://www.amnesty.eu/static/documents/2009/Nigeria0609 Report.pdf.

[16] Konne, "Inadequate Monitoring and Enforcement in the Nigerian Oil Industry," 181.

[17] "Report of an Independent Statistic and Analysis by the U.S. Energy Information Administration (EIA) on Nigeria, Country Analysis Brief," last updated on May 6, 2016, 2, https://www.eia.gov/beta/international/analysis_includes/countries_long/Nigeria/nigeria.pdf.

[18] Amnesty, Nigeria, 11.

[19] Nigerian National Petroleum Corporation, "Oil Production," http://nnpcgroup.com/ NNPCBusiness/UpstreamVentures/OilProduction.aspx.

[20] U.S. Energy Information Administration, Nigeria, Country Analysis Brief.

[21] Central Intelligence Agency (CIA), "The World Factbook: Nigeria" (2013), https:// www.cia.gov/library/publications/the-world-factbook/geos/ni.html.

[22] Amnesty, Nigeria, 12.

[23] Ibid.

[24] Richard Boele, Heike Fabig, and David Wheeler, "Shell, Nigeria and the Ogoni: A Case Study in Unsustainable Development: I. The Story of Shell, Nigeria and the Ogoni People—Environment, Economy, Relationships: Conflict and Prospects for Resolution," *Sustainable Development* 9, no. 2 (2001): 74–86, 74, 76.

and survival.[25] The oil industry has subjected people such as the Ogoni to gas flares, oil spills and significant environmental degradation and pollution that have damaged their farms, water bodies and fishing; the very key natural resources that serve as the livelihood and means of survival for these indigenous communities and people. The government of Nigeria failed to supervise the scale of the oil spillage and to implement existing environmental laws and policies that oblige oil producers to quickly react to oil spillage.[26] Pursuant to Article 55 of the African Charter, the complaint was filed against the Federal Republic of Nigeria (the Respondent State) claiming violations of the African Charter. The complainant alleged violations of the following: Article 2 on the enjoyment of the rights and freedoms recognised and guaranteed under the African Charter; Article 4, right to life and the integrity of the person; Article 14, the right to property; Article 16, right to enjoy the best attainable state of physical and mental health; Article 18(1), the right of families to be protected by the state (physical and moral health); Article 21, peoples' right to freely dispose of their wealth and natural resources; right to the lawful recovery of its property and adequate compensation; right to be protected against all forms of foreign economic exploitation particularly that practised by international monopolies and Article 24, on the right to a general satisfactory environment favourable to their development.

After a series of negotiations regarding the proceedings, the Respondent State became cooperative. It accepted the alleged violations and was open to the Commission's recommendations but submitted that it was already adopting measures to address the violations.[27] These measures included the establishment of the Federal Ministry of Environment (FME) which was resourced to tackle environment-related issues prevalent in Nigeria, prioritising the Niger Delta area. The FME took over from the Federal Environmental Protection Agency (FEPA)

---

[25] Boele et al. argues that, like other indigenous communities in the Niger Delta, the Ogoni people have never directly controlled any part of the petroleum earnings. See, Boele, Fabig, and Wheeler, "Shell, Nigeria and the Ogoni: A Case Study in Unsustainable Development," 74.

[26] CIA, "The World Factbook: Nigeria."

[27] *SERAC case*, para. 30.

which had been established through the FEPA Act.[28] This Act has since been repealed by the National Environmental Standards and Regulations Enforcement Agency (establishment) Act (NESREA Act).[29] This Act establishes the National Environmental Standards and Regulations Enforcement Agency (NESREA)[30] which replaced the FEPA and is charged with the enforcement of the regulatory framework governing environmental protection in Nigeria.[31] The FME is however challenged with the implementation of these laws because of corruption leading to wastage of resources.[32] The FME has also been noted to have overlapping duties and responsibilities with the State Ministries of Environment (SME). This causes confusion and delays in implementation of laws and policies.[33] The respondent state also mentioned/requested passing of a legislation setting up the Niger Delta Development Commission (NDDC) with sufficient financial resources to address the environmental and social problems prevalent in the Niger Delta and other oil producing areas of Nigeria. The Niger Delta Development Commission (Establishment) Act (NDDC Act)[34] provides that:

> the Commission shall ... tackle ecological and environmental problems that arise from the exploration of oil mineral in the Niger-Delta area and advise the Federal Government and the member States on the prevention and control of oil spillages, gas flaring and environmental pollution, liaise with the various oil mineral and gas prospecting and producing companies on all matters of pollution prevention and control.[35]

The NDDC has however been faulted for being corrupt and the government for being disinterested in issues relating to the environment.[36]

---

[28] Act no. 58 of 1988, Chapter 131, Laws of the Federation on Nigeria, which established the FEPA.

[29] Act no. 25 of 2007, Laws of the Federation of Nigeria.

[30] Ibid., Section 1(1).

[31] Ibid., Section 2(a) and Section 2.

[32] Onyenekenwa Cyprian Eneh, "Managing Nigeria's Environment: The Unresolved Issues," *Journal of Environmental Science and Technology* 4, no. 3 (2011): 250–263, 258.

[33] Ibid., p. 259

[34] Act no. 6 of 2000, Laws of the Federation of Nigeria.

[35] Ibid., Section 7(1) h and i.

[36] Irekpitan Okukpon, "Phasing Out Gas Flaring in Nigeria: A Critical Assessment of the Regulatory Regime" (LLM dissertation, University of Cape Town, 2000), 54.

Nigeria, the respondent state also said that it was in the process of establishing a Judicial Commission of Inquiry to investigate the issues of human rights infringement in the Niger Delta area (Ogoniland).[37] Without a doubt, there have been numerous human rights violations in the Niger Delta region, including but not limited to violations of the right to life, property, health and equal protection before the law.[38] The perpetrators are, however, rarely brought to book due to institutional corruption and as a result, there has been lack of confidence in the justice system.[39] There have been reports of extrajudicial killings of civilians in the Niger Delta region by some security guards at the oil installation points but the killers are not penalised.[40] The policemen invited by Shell to disperse crowds who were allegedly impeding environmental destruction, killed some civilians at Iko village. The government set up a Judicial Commission of inquiry to investigate the murders, but to date, none of the culprits has been held accountable.[41]

Concerning the admissibility and exhaustion of local remedies when the case was brought before the Commission, Article 56 of the African Charter governs the admissibility of communication submitted to the African Commission and provides that local remedies, if any, be exhausted, unless these are unduly prolonged. This requirement gives domestic courts an opportunity to decide upon cases before they are brought to an international forum and thus, prevent contradictory decisions of law at the national and international levels.[42] Another reason for the exhaustion of domestic remedies is to allow the government of the responding state to be notified of a human rights violation in order to have the chance of remedying such infringement before pushing it to an international court.[43] In declaring the communication admissible, the

---

[37] *SERAC case* (n. 15), para. 30.

[38] Ifeanyi I. Onwuazombe, "Human Rights Abuse and Violations in Nigeria: A Case Study of the Oil Producing Communities in the Niger Delta Region," *Annual Survey International and Comparative Survey* 22, no. 1 (2017): 115–160, 118, 119.

[39] Ibid., 119.

[40] Ibid., 123.

[41] Ibid., 124.

[42] Christof Heyns and Magnus Killander, eds., *Compendium of Key Human Rights Documents of the African Union* (Pretoria: Pretoria University Law Press, 2013), 340.

[43] Free Legal Assistance Group and Others v Zaire (2000) AHRLR 74 (ACHPR 1995) Communication 25/89, 47/90.

Commission reiterated its stance in the case of *Jawara v The Gambia*[44] where it held that 'only domestic remedies which are available, effective and adequate (sufficient) need to be exhausted'.[45] The Ogoniland case evidences that the government of Nigeria had ample notice and time to rectify the situation.[46] In this case, the communication does not contain any information on domestic court actions brought by the complainants to halt the violations alleged. However, on numerous occasions the Commission brought the complaint to the attention of the government at the time, but no response was given to the Commission's requests.[47]

The Commission further declared its awareness that at the time of submission of this communication, the then military government of Nigeria had enacted various decrees ousting the jurisdiction of the courts and thus, depriving the people in Nigeria of the right to seek redress in the courts for acts of government that violate their fundamental human rights. The Commission therefore took cognizance of the fact that Nigeria has incorporated the African Charter into its domestic law with the result that all the rights contained therein can be invoked in Nigerian courts including those violations alleged by the complainants. In such instances, the Commission held that no adequate domestic remedies are existent.[48] It should also be noted that the government in its *note verbale* submitted to the Commission admitted to the violation committed. The Commission therefore admitted the communication.

3   ACTIVISM OR ADVENTURISM: THE INTERPRETATION OF ARTICLE 24 OF THE AFRICAN CHARTER BY THE AFRICAN COMMISSION

One of the significant features of the decision of the Commission in the *SERAC and Another v Nigeria* case is the extensive interpretation of the provisions of the African Charter. Regarding the alleged violation of the Article 24 which guarantees the right to a general satisfactory

---

[44] (2000) AHRLR 107 (ACHPR 2000), para. 32.

[45] Ibid., para. 32.

[46] Heyns and Killander, *Compendium of Key Human Rights Documents of the African Union*, 340.

[47] Ibid., 338–339.

[48] *Civil Liberties Organisation v Nigeria* [(2000) AHRLR 188 (ACHPR 1995)].

environment, the Commission held that the Respondent State was responsible for the human rights violations committed by the non-state actor for failing to take appropriate measures to guarantee that non-state actors respect the peoples' rights.[49] In this regard, the Commission established that the Respondent State was in violation of this provision for its failure to protect the Ogoni people from acts of Shell, a non-state actor.[50] The right to a general satisfactory environment, as guaranteed under Article 24 of the African Charter on the right to a healthy environment, as it is widely known, therefore imposes clear obligations upon a government. It requires the state to take reasonable and other measures to prevent pollution and ecological degradation, to promote conservation and to secure an ecologically sustainable development and use of natural resources.[51] Article 12 of the International Covenant on Economic, Social and Cultural Rights (ICESCR), to which Nigeria is a party, requires governments to take necessary steps for the improvement of all aspects of environmental and industrial hygiene. The right to enjoy the best attainable state of physical and mental health enunciated in Article 16(1) of the African Charter obliges governments to desist from directly threatening the health and environment of their citizens. The Commission further tasked the state to:

> include ordering or at least permitting independent scientific monitoring of threatened environments, requiring and publicising environmental and social impact studies prior to any major industrial development, undertaking appropriate monitoring and providing information to those communities exposed to hazardous materials and activities and providing meaningful opportunities for individuals to be heard and to participate in the development decisions affecting their communities.[52]

This has been interpreted by Addaney and others to be equivalent to 'a positive obligation to protect and fulfil the right to satisfactory environment'.[53] The Commission further recognised that though Nigeria

---

[49] (2001) AHRLR 60 (ACHPR 2001), para. 69.

[50] Ibid., para. 70.

[51] Ibid., para. 52.

[52] Ibid., para. 53.

[53] Addaney, Boshoff, and Nyarko, "Protection of Environmental Assets in Urban Africa," 182.

had the right to extract oil, it nonetheless still has the duty to take care of the victims' rights.[54] The decision of the Commission deserves commendation for rightly positing Alexander Kiss' observation about environmental degradation that:

> An environment degraded by pollution and defaced by the destruction of all beauty and variety is as contrary to satisfactory living conditions and the development of personality as the breakdown of the fundamental ecologic equilibria is harmful to physical and moral health.[55]

The state is under an obligation to respect these rights and this largely entails non-interventionist conduct from the state; for example, to desist from carrying out, sponsoring or tolerating any practice, policy or legal measures violating the integrity of the individual or communities. Further, environmental protection has been recognized as a fundamental principle of environmental law.[56] It has been noted to be a fundamental element for the enjoyment of human rights including but not limited to the rights to health and life.[57] Procedural rights (access to information, public participation and access to justice) under international environmental law whose main purpose is to bring substantive human rights to realisation have also been recognised under international human rights.[58] This implies that whereas it is granted that states should exercise their right to development, they should not do so at the expense of a compromised environment.[59]

The Commission was progressive in interpreting the right to food to include food sources, which implicitly refers to the environment, and further holding that the right to food is inseparably linked to the dignity of human beings.[60] It argued that the African Charter and international law require and bind Nigeria to protect and improve existing

---

[54] SERAV v Nigeria case, para. 54.

[55] Ibid., para. 64.

[56] Addaney, Boshoff, and Nyarko, "Protection of Environmental Assets in Urban Africa," 182.

[57] Ibid., 6.

[58] Ibid.

[59] Ibid., 6.

[60] SERAC v Nigeria case, para. 65.

food sources and to ensure access to adequate food for all citizens.[61] Without touching on the duty to improve food production and guarantee access, the minimum core of the right to food requires that the government of Nigerian does not destroy or contaminate food sources and should not allow private parties to destroy or contaminate food sources, and prevent peoples' efforts to feed themselves.[62] On the other hand, the decision stands out for its bold admission that the government of Nigeria through NNPC has the right to produce oil to generate income for realising the economic and social rights of Nigerians.[63] Nonetheless, the Commission found the Federal Republic of Nigeria to have violated the right to general satisfactory environment of the Ogoni people. The Commission consequently appealed to the government of Nigeria to carry out the relevant social and environmental impact assessments for any future development projects.[64] It has been pointed out that the human rights obligations enumerated by the Commission are both procedural and substantive in nature.[65] Substantive aspects being the obligations that governments are mandated to fulfil and procedural being the means through which the substantive obligations are achieved. These obligations have been said to be a true reflection of international environmental law.[66]

Concerning the remedies, the Commission deserves commendation for the comprehensive legislative, administrative and socio-economic measures that it recommended for addressing such violations as well as their long-lasting impact on the welfare, survival and development of the Ogoni people.[67] For instance, the African Commission appealed to the government to guarantee the protection of the environment, livelihood and health of the people through remedial measures.[68] These measures included ensuring that suitable environmental and social impact studies are undertaken in any future oil development and that safe operation

---

[61] Ibid.

[62] Ibid.

[63] Ibid., para. 52.

[64] SERAV v Nigeria case.

[65] Addaney, Boshoff, and Nyarko, "Protection of Environmental Assets in Urban Africa," 190.

[66] Ibid., 9.

[67] SERAV v Nigeria case, para. 71.

[68] Ibid., para. 71.

of any development is promoted and ensured through effective and impartial supervisory bodies for the petroleum industry. It further implored the government to provide information on the health and environmental risks and meaningful access to regulatory and decision-making bodies to communities and aggrieved individuals who are likely to be affected by such operations.[69]

Despite the commendable approach taken by the African Commission, there are several gaps and deficiencies in its decision. For instance, the Commission fell below expectations when it did not, anywhere in its decision, condemn the nefarious acts of the Shell Company. While states are the principal subjects of international (human rights) law, it ought to have made allusion to the non-state actors who are parties to the violations of the African Charter. While its decision could not have been binding on Shell, mere mention in its judgment could have made little difference in terms of civil society engagement for the respect of rights guaranteed under the African Charter. This is important for future decisions because the Commission should have known that failure to condemn the act of non-state actors alongside that of the government may make any decision given illusory. This is based on the fact that some of these non-state actors are sometimes more powerful than some developing states and therefore make such states powerless against their excesses.[70] The lived realities of Africa show that unless international tribunals start making concrete and direct pronouncements (of blameworthiness) of the violations of rights by these non-state actors, their utter disregard for human rights will continue and their impunity in connivance with or without states in Africa will continue unabated. Most importantly, the Commission invoking the rights-based approach to adjudicating on matters that are connected to the degradation of the environment would certainly deliver much more results to victims whose environmental rights have been violated by either state or non-state actors.[71] Also, the Commission would have considered the rights-based

---

[69] Ibid.

[70] Chairman Okoloise, "Contextualizing the Corporate Human Rights Responsibility in Africa: A Social Expectation or Legal Obligation?" *African Human Rights Yearbook* 1 (2017): 191–220.

[71] Tinashe Madebwe, "A Rights-Based Approach to Environmental Protection: The Zimbabwean Experience." *African Human Rights Law Journal* 15 (2015): 110–128; John Knox. "Human Rights and the Environment: Carrying the Conversation Forward."

approach more closely in arriving at the decision if it had contemplated the fact that the right to clean and healthy environment as guaranteed under the African Charter is not a stand-alone right but started with the recognition of the right to life under the UDHR and the covenants.[72] This was especially necessary because a human rights-based approach has been advanced as a mechanism that enables governments to curb environmental nuisances caused by non-state actors.[73] This is achieved through the principle of rule of law.[74]

The Commission missed a fundamental point in the *SERAC v Nigeria* case on the right to development of the Ogoni people, which is expressly provided for under Article 22 of the African Charter.[75] The right to development would have been better advanced if the Commission had found a violation of it, as the Commission subsequently did in its latter decision.[76] It is trite knowledge that most African communities depend largely on natural resources and the environment for survival and development. Therefore, it would have been expected that the Commission would have established a violation of the right to development of the Ogoni people. The Commission further failed to invoke other relevant IEL treaties and conventions notably the Convention on Biological Diversity,[77] the Conservation of Migratory Species of Wild Animals,[78]

In *Human Rights and the Environment 13th Informal ASEM Seminar on Human Rights*, October 21–23, 2013, Copenhagen, Denmark, www.aseminfoboard.org.

[72] Ben Boer, "Environmental Principles and the Right to a Quality Environment" (Legal Studies Research Paper No. 17/05; January 2017).

[73] Addaney, Boshoff, and Nyarko, "Protection of Environmental Assets in Urban Africa," 190.

[74] Ibid.

[75] Justice C. Nwobike, "The African Commission on Human and Peoples' Rights and the Demystification of Second and Third Generation Rights Under the African Charter: Social and Economic Rights Action Center (SERAC) & The Centre for Economic Social Rights (CESR) v Nigeria," *African Journal of Legal Studies* 1, no. 2 (2005): 142–143.

[76] *Centre for Minority Rights Development (Kenya) and Minority Rights Group International on behalf of Endorois Welfare Council v Kenya* (2009) AHRLR 73.

[77] UN Convention on Biological Diversity 1760 UNTS 79 (1992).

[78] UN Conservation of Migratory Species of Wild Animals 1651 UNTS 333 (1979).

and the UN Convention to Combat Desertification.[79] The failure to invoke these conventions in the *SERAC v Nigeria* case certainly has effect on the application of these treaties on environmental protection in Africa.

The above drawbacks from the decision of the *SERAC case* are indicative of the impacts the decision might have arguably made in the lives of the people of Ogoniland and Africa on one hand, and the global community on the other hand. The Commission was metaphorically being looked upon for succour by victims of environmental degradation through the *SERAC case* because it was at that time, the only human rights tribunal that had the power to monitor treaty-based provision on the right to environment. No such right is explicitly provided for either under the UN human rights treaties or other regional treaties.[80] The absence of the right to environment in most international human rights treaties save for the African Charter has been said to be due to the fact that at the time most of these treaties were drafted, the issue of environmental protection was not a common concern.[81] However, in recent times, as has been earlier noted, environmental protection is not only a right but has been recognised as a principle of international law.[82] This section having analyse the approached adopted by the Commission in interpreting the right to general satisfactory environment in the context of oil extraction through a rights-based approach sets the stage for examining how the lessons are drawn have applied at the domestic level in Africa.

---

[79] See, for example, the Convention Concerning the Protection of the World Cultural and Natural Heritage 1037 UNTS 151, 27 UST 37 (1972) 11 ILM 1358 article 11(4); Convention on Wetlands of International Importance (the Ramsar Convention) (1972) 11 ILM 963 article 2; UN Convention on the Law of the Sea (1982) 21 ILM 1261 article 236; Alice Louise Bunker, "Protection of the Environment During Armed Conflict: One Gulf, Two Wars," *Review of European Community and International Environmental Law* 13, no. 2 (2003): 201–213.

[80] Dinah Shelton, "Legitimate and Necessary: Adjudicating Human Rights Violations Related to Activities Causing Environmental Harm or Risk," *Journal of Human Rights and the Environment* 6, no. 2 (2015): 139–155.

[81] Erika de Wet and Anél du Plessis, "The Meaning of Certain Substantive Obligations Distilled from International Human Rights Instruments for Constitutional Environmental Rights in South Africa," *African Human Rights Law Journal* 10, no. 2 (2010): 346–376.

[82] Addaney, Boshoff, and Nyarko, "Protection of Environmental Assets in Urban Africa," 185.

4   IMPLICATIONS OF THE DECISION ON THE DOMESTIC PROTECTION OF THE RIGHT TO ENVIRONMENT IN AFRICA

The government of Nigeria has taken some concrete steps towards the prevention of a repeat of the horrid incidences that lead to the *SERAC v Nigeria* case. Some of the steps are both legislative and institutional.[83] Another bold step to ensuring full compliance of the judgment was taken in 2011 when the Federal Government of Nigeria asked the United Nations Environment Programme (UNEP) to carry out an independent investigation of the level of environmental degradation and pollution of Ogoniland.[84] The report was released but never implemented. However, in 2016 the government set up a committee to implement the UNEP Report which recommends clean-up of the Ogoniland.[85] It was estimated that the clean-up exercise will cost US$1 billion and is to be carried out for 25 years cycle.[86] Beyond the clean-up of Ogoniland, the question that calls for enquiry is whether the *SERAC v Nigeria* decision is in consonance with the constitutional framework of Nigeria and whether the Ogoni people can get environmental justice in the current constitutional set up.

The 1999 Constitution of the Federal Republic of Nigeria (CFRN) is the highest law of the land. Chapter 4 of the CFRN provides for fundamental rights which are basically civil and political rights, while Chapter 2 entails the Fundamental Objectives and Directive Principles of State Policies (FODPSP).[87] The FODPSP contains objectives and policies largely economic, social and cultural rights.[88] Section 20 under the FODPSP does not provide for the right to environment but rather places

---

[83] Konne, "Inadequate Monitoring and Enforcement in the Nigeria Oil Industry," 190.

[84] Ibid., 184.

[85] "Buhari Sets to Launch Ogoni Land Clean-Up," *The Vanguard* (Lagos), March 5, 2016, https://www.vanguardngr.com/2016/03/buhari-sets-to-launch-ogoniland-cleanup-minister/.

[86] "Ogoni Clean-Up Will Cost $1b, Niger Delta Needs a New Vision Says Osinbajo," *The Vanguard* (Lagos), February 14, 2017, https://www.vanguardngr.com/2017/02/ogoni-clean-will-cost-1b-niger-delta-needs-new-vision-says-osinbajo/.

[87] Nathaniel A. Inegbedion, "Constitutional Implementation: The Nigerian Experience," In *The Implementation of Modern African Constitutions: Challenges and Prospects*, ed. Charles Manga Fombad (Pretoria: Pretoria University Law Press, 2016), 25–41.

[88] Kehinde Mowoe, *Constitutional Law in Nigeria* (Lagos: Malthouse Press Limited, 2008), 273.

an obligation on the state to 'protect and improve the environment' among other things.[89] This should ordinarily give rise to a challenge for citizens if the state fails but section 6(6)(c) forbids courts to exercise judicial powers over issues under the FODPSP except where the National Assembly has made laws on such matters as was held in the case of *Attorney General of Ondo State v Attorney General of the Federation and 35 others*.[90] It is unfortunate that just as the military government used decrees to shut citizens from litigating their rights under the African Charter, section 6(6)(c) of the CFRN could be arguably termed 'constitutional decree' despite the return to democracy.[91] The lack of a substantive provision on the right to environment could be argued to imply that it is a deliberate move by Nigeria to avoid being responsible for state actions under the 'rule of law' principle. Rule of law facilitates the holding of states accountable for violating their legal obligations/provisions. Although from different jurisdictions and geographical locales, examples from the European and American counterparts indicate that most disputes arise under the principle of rule of law. For instance, the case of *Okyay* and *Others v Turkey*[92] involved a thermal power plant which the applicants alleged had the potential to put the life and health of the population of Aegean region at risk and also damage the environment. It was further alleged that it would compromise the right to a clean and healthy environment. Although the applicants did not argue that they had suffered any loss or damage, they successfully challenged the operations of the thermo plant before their domestic courts. The Turkish authorities were found to have violated their obligations to enforce constitutional and environmental rights. The European Court of Human Rights (ECtHR) found that the applicants had a right to live in a healthy and balanced environment and that this right had been violated. Further, it was held that they had a right under Turkish Law and under Article 6(1) of the European Convention to protection against damage to the

---

[89] Olawale Ajai, "The Balancing of Interests in Environmental Law in Nigeria," In *The Balancing of Interests in Environmental Law in Africa*, ed. Michael Faure and Willemien du Plessis (Pretoria: Pretoria University Law Press, 2011), 379–411.

[90] (2002) 9 Nigerian Weekly Law Report (NWLR) (Pt. 772), 222.

[91] Ademola O. Jegede, "From Military Rule to Constitutional Government: The Case of Nigeria," in *Constitutionalism and Democratic Governance in Africa: Contemporary Perspective from Sub-Saharan Africa*, ed. M.K. Mbondenyi and T. Ojienda (Pretoria: Pretoria University Law Press, 2013), 352.

[92] App. No. 36220/97, ECtHR Reports of Judgments and Decisions.

environment and that Turkish authorities had violated this right by failure to comply with their law and to comply with the judgment of the domestic courts in time. Nigeria can learn from the experiences of the above cases and adopt a similar approach in addressing environmental human rights issues. As already pointed out, however promising this judgment may be, it does not appeal to the Nigerian position until it has made substantive provisions for the right to a clean and healthy environment. Further, it is important to note that the decisions of the African Commission, under whose jurisdiction Nigeria falls are non-binding. They are only persuasive and serve as a guide and a reminder to the state parties of their obligations.[93]

Another bottleneck that makes the decision of the *SERAC v Nigeria* incompatible with the CFRN is on the issue of natural resources, with item 39 of the Second Schedule to the CFRN vesting control and ownership of natural resources on the Federal Government.[94] This is in contradiction to Article 24 of the African Charter. However, it has been stated by the Nigerian Supreme Court (the apex court) in the case of *Abacha v Fawehinmi* that the African Charter is not superior to the CFRN.[95] Due to this glaring constitutional 'infirmities' in the light of Nigeria's international obligations,[96] realising environmental rights has been at the mercy of the government. These weaknesses have stunted the lofty goals which the Commission set to achieve through its decision in *SERAC v Nigeria*. Despite the existence of item 39 of the Second Schedule of the CFRN, Ajai contends that the CFRN does not explicitly confer on the federal government the legislative power to coordinate the conservation or management of all aspects of the environment and development.[97] The implication of this argument is that governments at the state level should be able to make significant impacts on environmental protection without any disturbance from the federal government.

Comparatively, Nigeria lags behind in terms of the constitutional protection of environmental rights in comparison with South Africa and

---

[93]De Wet and Du Plessis, "International Human Rights Instruments for Constitutional Environmental Rights in South Africa," 351.

[94]Known as the Exclusive Legislative list.

[95](2001) 51 Weekly Report of Nigeria (WRN) 1, paras. 83–85.

[96]Nwobike, "The African Commission on Human and Peoples' Rights and the Demystification of Second and Third Generation Rights Under the African Charter," 133.

[97]Olawale Ajai, "The Balancing of Interests in Environmental Law in Nigeria," In *The Balancing of Interests in Environmental Law in Africa*, ed. Michael Faure and Willemien du Plessis (Pretoria: Pretoria University Law Press, 2011), 379–411.

Kenya. Unlike the Nigerian Constitution, the 1996 Constitution of South Africa guarantees the right to a healthy environment. The South African Constitution is inclusive of an enforceable Bill of Rights, making it renowned globally.[98] Article 24 guarantees the right to healthy environment that is not harmful to health or well-being.[99] This right is not only justiciable but has been tested in the courts. For instance, in the *Fuel Retailer Association of Southern Africa v Director General Environmental Management, Department of Agriculture, Conservation and Environment, Mpumalanga Province,*[100] the Constitutional Court expressly stated that the Constitution envisages an integration of the protection of the environment and socio-economic development.[101] Such a decision is largely impracticable in Nigeria because of the lack of constitutional guarantee for environmental rights.

The 2010 Constitution of Kenya (KC) also guarantees environmental rights and promotes environmental justice. In the African context, this connotes 'rights to have access to, use and control of natural resources by communities'.[102] The Constitution of Kenya guarantees to everyone the right to a healthy environment.[103] It gives anyone the right to sue in cases where their right to the environment is threatened or violated. Also, Articles 67 and 70 mandate courts to jettison the issue of *locus standi* in such circumstance. The Kenya High Court in the case of *Friends of Lake Turkana Trust v Attorney General & 2 others*[104] held that an obligation is placed on the government by virtue of Article 69(1) (d) of the Kenyan Constitution to encourage public participation in the management, conservation and protection of the environment.[105] While the Kenyan Constitution environmental rights friendly, the CFRN is

[98] Linda Stewart, "Adjudicating Socio-economic Rights Under a Transformative Constitution," *Penn State International Law Review* 28, no. 3 (2010): 487–512.

[99] Michael Kidd, *Environment' in Iain Currie & Johan De Wall, The Bill of Rights Handbook* (Cape Town: Juta, 2013), 518.

[100] 2007 (6) SA 4 (CC).

[101] Ibid., para. 45.

[102] Kariuki Muigua and Francis Kariuki, "Towards Environmental Justice in Kenya," January 2015, http://www.kmco.co.ke/attachments/article/140/Towards%20Environmental%20 Justice%20in%20Kenya-January%202015.pdf.

[103] 2010 Constitution of Kenya, Art. 42.

[104] ELC Suit No. 825 of 2012.

[105] Muigua and Kariuki, "Towards Environmental Justice in Kenya," 23.

anti-environmental rights and makes a mockery of the recommendations of the *SERAC v Nigeria's* case.

The foregoing having been said, even without a constitutional provision on the right to a clean, healthy and sustainable environment, Nigerians are still victims of human rights violations arising out of environmental misuse or damage. This can be through common law or international law. The right to a clean and safe environment can hence be argued to have always existed in Nigeria through the Law of Torts and nuisance. Nigerian courts have awarded damages to plaintiffs (victims) and issued injunctions in cases where they have been affected and inconvenienced by excessive noise and bad smell arising out of activities of the defendants (their neighbours).[106] Tort law recognises the duty of care[107] which has been likened with the principle of good neighbourliness.[108] A person owes a duty of care to his neighbour whom he foresees as likely or expected to suffer damage or harm as a result of his actions.[109] Similarly, one's actions should not interfere with another's right to enjoy the environment of their property or land.[110] In other words, these common law provisions can rightly be regarded as forming part of Nigeria's environmental regulatory framework although it has been argued that this avenue is costly and not many citizens would afford it.[111]

International human rights law is another avenue through which the victims of human rights violations can directly pursue their claims. Nigeria ratified the African Charter and because it is a dualist state,[112] it went ahead to domesticate it through an Act of Parliament.[113] This means that in line with Article 24 and 25 of the Charter, all people have a right to a generally satisfactory environment and state parties are under obligation to promote and educate the public on this right.

---

[106]Tebite v Nigeria Marine and Trading Co. (NMTC) (1971) 1ULR.432; Abiola v Ijoma (1970) 2All NLR 268.

[107]*Donoghue v Stevenson* (1932) AC 562.

[108]Rio Declaration on Environment and Development (1992) A/CONF.151/26. Article 2, 18 and 19.

[109]*Donoghue v Stevenson.*

[110]Tebite V Nigeria NMTC and Abiola v Ijoma.

[111]Madebwe, "A Rights Based Approach to Environmental Protection," 116–117.

[112]Section 12 of the Constitution of the Federal Republic of Nigeria, 1999.

[113]African Charter on Human and Peoples' Right (Ratification and Enforcement) Act.

Domestication of the Charter therefore places Nigeria under duty and obligation to secure a satisfactory environment and to educate her people about it. In addition, it can be argued that the right to environment has acquired the status of international customary law.[114] This therefore gives victims of human rights violations an avenue through which to pursue their rights, even without a Constitutional provision. It has however been noted that these provisions have not been implemented by Nigeria. The environmental rights in the Charter have not been domesticated into the Nigerian law and hence no implementation of the same.[115] This implies that the people have not been educated on their rights either.

5   Conclusion

The Commission's decision in the *SERAC v Nigeria* case is very progressive and pragmatic as it applied the purposive principle of interpretation and expanded the threshold for economic, social and cultural rights especially on the right to environment and the right to development to reflect the peculiarity and vulnerability of local communities, while also reasserting the indivisibility of human rights in the African Charter. The Commission should be commended for its remarkable reference to relevant international human rights instruments in its interpretation of the African Charter as envisaged by Article 60.[116] However, for the giant strides made by the African Commission to be meaningful in the lived realities of all Nigerians and the Ogoni people, in particular, there is a need for constitutional amendments to incorporate the various recommendations of the Commission in the *SERAC v Nigeria's* case. Such amendment should also be people-driven as compared to the 1996 Constitution of South Africa and the 2010 Constitution of

---

[114]Ben Boer, "Environmental Principles and the Right to a Quality Environmental," in *Principles of Environmental Law*, ed. Ludwing Kramer and Emanuela Orlando (Cheltenham: Edward Elgar, 2018), 69–70.

[115]Onyeka Williams Igwe, "The Challenges of Domesticating the African Charter on Human and Peoples' Rights *Holus Bolus*: The Case of Nigeria," *Australian Journal of Management Policy and Law* 2 (2015): 19–27.

[116]Article 60 of the African Charter provides that, 'The Commission shall draw inspiration from international law on human and peoples' rights'.

Kenya. However, this is mindful of the fact that, though the African Charter is now part of the Nigerian legal corpus through the enactment of the African Charter on Human and Peoples' Rights (Ratification and Enforcement) Act,[117] the provision of Section 6(6)(c) of the 1999 Nigerian Constitution and the decision of the Nigerian Supreme Court in *Abacha v Fawehinmi* have continued to make courts[118] in Nigeria deny citizens their rights under the African Charter on the grounds that environmental rights are not fundamental rights under the Constitution (cannot be litigated upon), and that the provisions of the African Charter (that guarantee such rights) are not superior to the provisions of the Nigerian Constitution.[119] Certainly, until all these costly but necessary steps are taken by the Nigerian government, the *SERAC v Nigeria* case may only become meaningful to anyone else but those whose rights were directly violated. The foregoing notwithstanding, it is important to note that human rights tribunals are not without limitations. Human rights procedures, time and specifically litigation are lengthy and may not mitigate environmental harm in time to prevent irreversible damage to the environment. Further, important to note is the fact that human rights tribunals and procedures may not stop or halt environmental damage.

---

[117] Laws of the Federation of Nigeria (LFN), Chapter A9 (Chapter 10 LFN 1990) (No. 2 of 1983).

[118] This unwilling attitude is evidence from the fact that the Nigerian Superior Courts have so far only declared the violation of the right guaranteed under the African Charter in an isolated decision of *Gbemre v Shell Petroleum Development Company Nigeria Limited and Others* (2005) AHRLR 151 (NgHC 2005).

[119] Section 6(6)(c) places a bar on judicial powers thus: 'shall not except as otherwise provided by this Constitution, extend to any issue or question as to whether any act of omission by any authority or person or as to whether any law or any judicial decision is in conformity with the Fundamental Objectives and Directive Principles of State Policy set out in Chapter II of this Constitution'—and unfortunately so, Section 20 which guarantees to Nigerians right to the environments falls under Chapter II. The Supreme declared thus on the status of the African Charter in Nigeria: '...To this extent I agree with their Lordships of the Court below that the Charter possesses "a greater vigor and strength" than any other domestic statue. But that is not to say that the Charter is superior to the Constitution as erroneously, with respect, was submitted by Mr. Adegbrouwa, learned counsel for the respondent. Nor can its international flavor prevent the National Assembly or the Federal Military Government before it removing'.

Victims may instead be compensated for injuries arising out of the harm caused by environmental damage. In other words, the scope of matters which human rights tribunals can handle is limited to human rights rather than environmental issues.

REFERENCES

(2001) AHRLR 60 (ACHPR 2001).

(2002) 9 Nigerian Weekly Law Report (NWLR) (Pt. 772), 222.

(2001) 51 Weekly Report of Nigeria (WRN), 1, Paras. 83–85.

Addaney, Michael, Elsabé Boshoff, and Michael Gyan Nyarko. "Protection of Environmental Assets in Urban Africa: Regional and Sub-Regional Human Rights and Practical Environmental Protection Mechanisms." *Australian Journal of Human Rights* 24, no. 2 (2018): 182–200.

African Charter on Human and Peoples' Rights, June 27, 1981, OAU Doc. CAB/LEG/67/3 rev. 5, 1520 U.N.T.S. 217, 245 (1982).

African Charter on Human and Peoples' Right (Ratification and Enforcement) Act.

Ajai, Olawale. "The Balancing of Interests in Environmental Law in Nigeria." In *The Balancing of Interests in Environmental Law in Africa*, edited by Michael Faure and Willemien du Plessis, 379–411. Pretoria: Pretoria University Law Press, 2011.

Amnesty International (Amnesty). "Nigeria: Petroleum, Pollution and Poverty in the Niger Delta" (2009). http://www.amnesty.eu/static/documents/2009/Nigeria0609Report.pdf.

App. No. 36220/97, ECtHR Reports of Judgments and Decisions.

Boele, Richard, Heike Fabig, and David Wheeler. "Shell, Nigeria and the Ogoni: A Case Study in Unsustainable Development: I. The Story of Shell, Nigeria and the Ogoni People—Environment, Economy, Relationships: Conflict and Prospects for Resolution." *Sustainable Development* 9, no. 2 (2001): 74–86, 74, 76.

Boer, Ben. "Environmental Principles and the Right to a Quality Environmental." In *Principles of Environmental Law*, edited by Ludwig Kramer and Emanuela Orlando, 69–70. Cheltenham: Edward Elgar, 2018.

Boer, Ben. "Environmental Principles and the Right to a Quality Environment." Legal Studies Research Paper No. 17/05, January 2017.

"Buhari Sets to Launch Ogoni Land Clean-Up." *The Vanguard* (Lagos), March 5, 2016. https://www.vanguardngr.com/2016/03/buhari-sets-to-launch-ogoniland-cleanup-minister/.

Bunker, Alice Louise. "Protection of the Environment During Armed Conflict: One Gulf, Two Wars." *Review of European Community and International Environmental Law* 13, no. 2 (2003): 201–213.

Central Intelligence Agency (CIA). "The World Factbook: Nigeria" (2013). https://www.cia.gov/library/publications/the-world-factbook/geos/ni.html.

Centre for Minority Rights Development (Kenya) and Minority Rights Group International on behalf of Endorois Welfare Council v Kenya (2009) AHRLR 73.

Civil Liberties Organisation v Nigeria [(2000) AHRLR 188 (ACHPR 1995)].

Convention on Biological Diversity 1760 UNTS 79 (1992).

Convention Concerning the Protection of the World Cultural and Natural Heritage 1037 UNTS 151, 27 UST 37, (1972) 11 ILM 1358.

Conservation of Migratory Species of Wild Animals 1651 UNTS 333 (1979).

Convention on Wetlands of International Importance (the Ramsar Convention) (1972) 11 ILM 963.

Convention on the Law of the Sea (1982) 21 ILM 1261.

de Wet, Erika, and Anél du Plessis. "The Meaning of Certain Substantive Obligations Distilled from International Human Rights Instruments for Constitutional Environmental Rights in South Africa." African Human Rights Law Journal 10, no. 2 (2010): 346–376.

Donoghue v Stevenson (1932) AC 562.

ELC Suit No. 825 of 2012.

Eneh, Onyenekenwa Cyprian. "Managing Nigeria's Environment: The Unresolved Issues." Journal of Environmental Science and Technology 4, no. 3 (2011): 250–263, 258.

Free Legal Assistance Group and Others v Zaire (2000) AHRLR 74 (ACHPR 1995), Communication 25/89, 47/90.

Gbemre v Shell Petroleum Development Company Nigeria Limited and Others (2005) AHRLR 151 (NgHC 2005).

Government of the Federal Republic of Nigeria. Act no. 25 of 2007, Laws of the Federation of Nigeria.

Government of the Federal Republic of Nigeria. Act no. 6 of 2000, Laws of the Federation of Nigeria.

Government of the Federal Republic of Nigeria. Act no. 58 of 1988, Chapter 131, Laws of the Federation on Nigeria.

Government of the Federal Republic of Nigeria. Laws of the Federation of Nigeria (LFN), Chapter A9 (Chapter 10 LFN 1990) (No. 2 of 1983).

Government of the Republic of Kenya. "Constitution of Kenya" (2010).

Heyns, Christof, and Magnus Killander, eds. Compendium of Key Human Rights Documents of the African Union. Pretoria: Pretoria University Law Press, 2013.

Igwe, Onyeka Williams. "The Challenges of Domesticating the African Charter on Human and Peoples' Rights Holus Bolus: The Case of Nigeria." Australian Journal of Management Policy and Law 2 (2015): 19–27.

Inegbedion, Nathaniel A. "Constitutional Implementation: The Nigerian Experience." In *The Implementation of Modern African Constitutions: Challenges and Prospects*, edited by Charles Manga Fombad, 25–41. Pretoria: Pretoria University Law Press, 2016.

Jegede, Ademola O. "From Military Rule to Constitutional Government: The Case of Nigeria." In *Constitutionalism and Democratic Governance in Africa: Contemporary Perspective from Sub-Saharan Africa*, edited by M.K. Mbondenyi and T. Ojienda, 352. Pretoria: Pretoria University Law Press, 2013.

Kidd, Michael. "Environment." In *The Bill of Rights Handbook*, edited by Iain Currie and Johan De Wall, 518. Cape Town: Juta, 2013.

Knox, John Henry. "Human Rights and the Environment: Carrying the Conversation Forward." In *Human Rights and the Environment 13th Informal ASEM Seminar on Human Rights*, October 21–23, 2013, Copenhagen, Denmark. www.aseminfoboard.org.

Konne, Barisere Rachel. "Inadequate Monitoring and Enforcement in the Nigerian Oil Industry: The Case of Shell and Ogoniland." *Cornell International Law Journal* 47, no. 1 (2014): 181–204.

Madebwe, Tinashe. "A Rights-Based Approach to Environmental Protection: The Zimbabwean Experience." *African Human Rights Law Journal* 15 (2015): 110–128.

Mowoe, Kehinde. *Constitutional Law in Nigeria*. Lagos: Malthouse Press Limited, 2008.

Muigua, Kariuki, and Francis Kariuki. "Towards Environmental Justice in Kenya." January 2015. http://www.kmco.co.ke/attachments/article/140/Towards%20Environmental%20Justice%20in%20Kenya-January%202015.pdf.

Nigerian National Petroleum Corporation. "Oil Production." http://nnpcgroup.com/NNPCBusiness/UpstreamVentures/OilProduction.aspx.

Nwobike, Justice C. "The African Commission on Human and Peoples' Rights and the Demystification of Second and Third Generation Rights Under the African Charter: Social and Economic Rights Action Center (SERAC) & The Centre for Economic Social Rights (CESR) v Nigeria." *African Journal of Legal Studies* 1, no. 2 (2005): 142–143.

"Ogoni Clean-Up Will Cost $1b, Niger Delta Needs a New Vision Says Osinbajo." *The Vanguard* (Lagos), February 14, 2017. https://www.vanguardngr.com/2017/02/ogoni-clean-will-cost-1b-niger-delta-needs-new-vision-says-osinbajo/.

Okoloise, Chairman. "Contextualizing the Corporate Human Rights Responsibility in Africa: A Social Expectation or Legal Obligation?" *African Human Rights Yearbook* 1 (2017): 191–220.

Okukpon, Irekpitan. "Phasing Out Gas Flaring in Nigeria: A Critical Assessment of the Regulatory Regime." LLM dissertation, University of Cape Town, 2000.

Onwuazombe, Ifeanyi I. "Human Rights Abuse and Violations in Nigeria: A Case Study of the Oil Producing Communities in the Niger Delta Region." *Annual Survey International and Comparative Survey* 22, no. 1 (2017): 115–160.

"Report of an Independent Statistic and Analysis by the U.S. Energy Information Administration (EIA) on Nigeria, Country Analysis Brief." Last updated on May 6, 2016. https://www.eia.gov/beta/international/analysis_includes/countries_long/Nigeria/nigeria.pdf.

Rio Declaration on Environment and Development (1992). A/CONF.151/26. Article 2, 18 and 19.

Tebite V Nigeria NMTC and Abiola v Ijoma.

Shelton, Dinah. "Legitimate and Necessary: Adjudicating Human Rights Violations Related to Activities Causing Environmental Harm or Risk." *Journal of Human Rights and the Environment* 6, no. 2 (2015): 139–155.

Social and Economic Rights Action Centre (SERAC) and Another v Nigeria (SERAC case) (2001) AHRLR 60 (ACHPR 2001).

Stewart, Linda. "Adjudicating Socio-economic Rights Under a Transformative Constitution." *Penn State International Law Review* 28, no. 3 (2010): 487–512.

Tebite v Nigeria Marine and Trading Co. (NMTC) (1971) 1ULR.432; Abiola v Ijoma (1970) 2All NLR 268.

Viljoen, Frans. *International Human Rights Law in Africa*, 2nd ed. Oxford: Oxford University Press, 2012.

Voigt, Christina, and Evadne Grant. "The Legitimacy of Human Rights Courts in Environmental Disputes." *Journal of Human Rights and the Environment* 6, no. 2 (2015): 131–138.

INDEX

© The Editor(s) (if applicable) and The Author(s), under exclusive license   413
to Springer Nature Switzerland AG, part of Springer Nature 2020
M. Addaney et al. (eds.), *Governance, Human Rights,
and Political Transformation in Africa*,
https://doi.org/10.1007/978-3-030-27049-0